Social and Political Change in Revolutionary China

WORLD SOCIAL CHANGE
Series Editor: Mark Selden

Transforming Asian Socialism: China and Vietnam Compared
Edited by Anita Chan, Benedict J. Tria Kerkvliet, and Jonathan Unger

North China at War: The Social Ecology of Revolution, 1937–1945
Edited by Feng Chongyi and David S. G. Goodman

Istanbul: Between the Global and the Local
Edited by Caglar Keyder

FORTHCOMING TITLES

Toward a Social History of Bangkok: Gender, Class, and Popular Culture in the Siamese Capital, 1905–1940
Edited by Scot Barmé

Comparative Family Ethnographies: Thai and Vietnamese Researchers Study Families in Process
Edited by Myron Orleans

Vietnamese Society under Reform: Development and Conflict
Edited by Hy Van Luong

Social and Political Change in Revolutionary China

The Taihang Base Area in the War of Resistance to Japan, 1937–1945

David S. G. Goodman

ROWMAN & LITTLEFIELD PUBLISHERS, INC.
Lanham • Boulder • New York • Oxford

ROWMAN & LITTLEFIELD PUBLISHERS, INC.

Published in the United States of America
by Rowman & Littlefield Publishers, Inc.
4720 Boston Way, Lanham, Maryland 20706
http://www.rowmanlittlefield.com

12 Hid's Copse Road, Cumnor Hill, Oxford OX2 9JJ, England

British Library Cataloguing in Publication Information Available

Library of Congress Cataloging-in-Publication Data

Goodman, David S. G.
Social and political change in revolutionary China : the Taihang Base area in the War of Resistance to Japan, 1937–1945 / David S. G. Goodman.
p. cm.
Includes bibliographical references and index.
ISBN 0-7425-0864-1 (alk. paper) — ISBN 0-7425-0865-X (pbk. : alk. paper)
1. T'ai-hang Mountains Region (China)—Social conditions. 2. Social change—China—T'ai-hang Mountains Region. 3. T'ai-hang Mountains Region (China)—Politics and government. 4. Sino-Japanese Conflict, 1937–1945. I. Title: Taihang Base area in the war of resistance to Japan, 1937–1945. II. Title.

HN740.T34 G66 2000
303.4'0951—dc21 00–031109

Printed in the United States of America

∞™ The paper used in this publication meets the minimum requirements of American National Standard for Information Sciences—Permanence of Paper for Printed Library Materials, ANSI/NISO Z39.48-1992.

Contents

Tables

Preface

Intellectuals in Shanxi Province, North China have long liked to think of the province as central to the definition and history of the Chinese state. Whilst such views are always necessarily contested, they are perhaps less contestable with respect to the emergence of the People's Republic of China. Shanxi Province was on the front-line of conflict with Japan during the 1937–1945 War of Resistance that launched the Chinese Communist Party on its ascent to national government. In the Northeast, Northwest and Southeast of Shanxi, base areas and border regions were established that were the main bulwark of Chinese behind-the-lines resistance to Japanese invasion in North China. Though clearly under the leadership of headquarters in Yan'an—in the Northeast of Shaanxi Province just across the Yellow River to the west—these were the areas where the Chinese Communist Party developed substantial social roots and derived much of its organizational strength for its later attempted transformation of society.

The Taihang Base Area of Southeast Shanxi was one of the most important base areas established at this time. It was the source base area, established initially by the 129th Division of the Eighth Route Army, from which grew the Shanxi-Hebei-Shandong-Henan [JinJiLuYu] Border Region and all its constituent base areas. Though not the first border region of the North China battlefield, it became the largest, both in land area and population. It was also the long-term site of operations of the field headquarters of the Chinese Communist Party's Eight Route Army and of the North China Bureau of the Central Committee of the Chinese Communist Party during the War of Resistance. From January 1938 on, Deng

Xiaoping was stationed in the Border Region as the Political Commissar of the 129th Division and an increasingly important leading cadre of the Chinese Communist Party. Though not as important then as he was to become later, Deng's close relationship with Mao Zedong and his leadership of the Taihang Region were key determinants of both Chinese Communist leadership of local resistance, and later politics within the Chinese Communist Party.

The importance of the Taihang Base Area to the development of the Communist movement in China was acknowledged during the 1950s with the publication of two books. In China, one of the first studies of any base area or border region published after 1949 was Qi Wu's *Yige geming genjudi de chengzhang: KangRi zhanzheng he jiefang zhanzheng shiqi de JinJiLuYu Bianqu gaikuang* [The Transformation of a Revolutionary Base Area: An Outline of the Shanxi-Hebei-Shandong-Henan Border Region during the War of Resistance to Japan and the War of Liberation] which appeared in 1957. Qi Wu is the nom de plume of a now-retired cadre in the Ministry of Finance who became a historian at the Chinese Academy of Social Sciences after the Cultural Revolution. Like many of his colleagues in that ministry, he had served in the equivalent departments of the Taihang Base Area and the JinJiLuYu Border Region during the War of Resistance to Japan, and later during the Civil War. Outside China, Isabel and David Crook wrote and published *Revolution in a Chinese Village: Ten Mile Inn* which dealt with a village in Wu'an County of the Taihang Base Area, around the same time. An anthropologist and a teacher, they were interested in land reform after the War of Resistance and became 'foreign experts' teaching in Beijing.

However, during the era of Mao-dominated politics in China that started in the late 1950s, the history of the Taihang Base Area (and indeed other base areas in other parts of the country) was not so much suppressed as ignored. Chinese would be aware of its name and perhaps its location, but not much else. Indeed, they might even learn about events or people that were part of the experience of the Taihang Base Area or the JinJiLuYu Border Region without any explicit identification of place. For example, the heroine Liu Hulan, who was praised by Mao Zedong and who became a model for emulation by successive generations of young people, was a native and had been an activist for the Communist forces in the area before her precocious death. Scholars outside China would similarly have had little explicit recognition of the Taihang Base Area or knowledge of its activities. In consequence they were largely unable to recognize that the once model production brigade of Dazhai, the Red Flag Canal and Long Bow Village (made famous by William Hinton's *Fanshen*) were all situated in the former Taihang Base Area and that their later politics owed much to the earlier experience of the war years.

In 1987 I visited Taiyuan, the provincial capital of Shanxi Province, and a friendly cadre thrust a just published book into my hand literally as a parting gift: Taihang geming genjudishi zongbian weihui (ed) *Taihang geming genjudi shigao* [Outline History of the Taihang Revolutionary Base Area]. It was fascinating on two counts: the calligraphy for its title had been written by no less a person than Deng Xiaoping himself (then China's 'Paramount Leader') and I wondered why. Traditionally, calligraphy is provided in this way by an individual who either has a close relationship to the subject matter being described, or who wished to identify with the event, personality or idea. Yet, the lack of consciousness of the Taihang Base Area amongst scholars outside China was matched by an almost complete ignorance of Deng Xiaoping's involvement. Deng was regarded as Mao Zedong's loyal lieutenant, but often located in Yan'an with Mao rather than in the Taihang Base Area and its Border Region as the latter's eyes and ears during the War of Resistance.

In the event, the story of Deng's involvement in the Taihang Base Area and the Shanxi-Hebei-Shandong-Henan Border Region is as important to his political career, and to the development of post-Mao politics, as Deng's close relationship to Mao Zedong during the 1930s and 1940s. Deng's loyal service to Mao in the border region during the war years was the platform for his rise up the hierarchy of the Chinese Communist Party during the 1950s and early 1960s. His recruitment and leadership of a large number of cadres in the border region who later came to dominate the Chinese Communist Party during the decade of the Cultural Revolution provided him with considerable protection even when he was politically troubled. Moreover, this group played a central role in the emergence and implementation of the agenda for change in post-Mao China under Deng's leadership. The publication of a history of the Taihang Base Area in 1987 was then no simple academic exercise but part of the retrieval of the Chinese Communist Party's history that lay very much at the heart of the reform era. The intrigue of this relationship between Deng Xiaoping and the Taihang Base Area led to *Deng Xiaoping and the Chinese Revolution: A Political Biography*, published in 1994, which deals with these aspects of the base area's historical memory in greater detail.

At the same time, the detail of history that was now presented was inherently exciting. China has always been attractive to researchers because of the diversity of its social experience. Yet for a number of decades research on China had concentrated (and to some considerable extent had been forced to concentrate by lack of access to sources or indeed for long periods to China itself) on generalization and a description of homogeneity. During the late 1970s and early 1980s a number of scholars outside China working on the development of the War of Resistance to Japan had already developed approaches that emphasized the importance of different base areas and their experiences, and the need to differentiate amongst them. However, it was not until the late 1980s when a wider range of documentary sources became available and archives opened in China itself, that it became possible to adequately address the research demands of this paradigm shift in approach. The realization that at last it might be possible to research the dynamics of social and political change, and their interconnections, at a local level but during an earlier period than I had previously been engaged in (though one which encompassed the roots of support for the Communist movement) was both a revelation and irresistible. *Social and Political Change in Revolutionary China* is the result of that endeavor.

The focus of this study is the process of revolutionary change that occurred during the War of Resistance to Japan in three adjacent counties of the Taihang Base Area: Liaoxian (its name was changed to Zuoquan in September 1942, in memory of Zuo Quan, the Chinese Communist general killed there in May of that year), Wuxiang and Licheng. A narrow geographical focus has been chosen both because of the overwhelming amount of material generated through research, and because of a desire to understand local processes of change as far as possible. The three counties of Liaoxian, Wuxiang and Licheng were at the center of the Taihang Base Area, and are situated high in the southern part of the Taihang Mountains. They were not only the largest sources of recruitment to armed resistance and the Chinese Communist Party in the base area and its most secure counties, but also, together with Shexian (now in Hebei Province, but then in Henan) the site of organizational activities for both the base area and border region. It is based on published documents, archive material, and interviews with veterans of the Taihang Base Area. A discussion of documentation is provided in the Bibliography.

Some introductory explanation of essential technical terms is perhaps useful for those less familiar with the history of the Chinese Communist Party in North China during the War of Resistance to Japan.

In general, the standard *pinyin* transliteration system in use in the People's Republic of China for rendering Chinese characters into roman letters has been employed in this volume. The exception is Chiang Kai-shek, leader of the Nationalist Party, who is much better known in this rendering than as Jiang Jieshi. Before 1949 Beijing was known as Beiping, and that nomenclature has been adopted here.

Terms such as 'border region' [*bianqu*], 'guerilla area' [*youjiqu*] and 'base area' [*genjudi*] are almost inherently confused in the history of the War of Resistance. Border regions were usually larger than both guerilla areas and base areas, and usually contained a number of both guerilla areas and base areas. Base areas themselves would usually contain regions where the Chinese Communist Party was somewhat more secure; more contested guerilla areas where the Chinese Communist Party was engaged in regular conflict with the Japanese; and enemy-occupied districts [*dizhanqu*]. During the war, border regions had an institutional existence in the Border Region Governments (such as the Shanxi-Hebei-Shandong-Henan Border Region Government), which were units of state (or proto-state) administration. The conceptualization of base areas was much looser. Base areas had no formal institutional existence though they were primarily regions of military activity and resistance. As the war progressed the term was applied increasingly by participants to any area of CCP-led resistance and administration. In that process the superior organization was often a district or regional committee of the CCP, which then became identified as the leadership of the base area.

Under the conditions of guerilla war and particularly because of the Chinese Communist Party's rapid expansion during 1937–38, organizational growth was fluid and necessarily somewhat uncoordinated. The terms 'border region,' 'base area' and 'guerilla area' were used almost synonymously, and have been used interchangeably for the most part since within the People's Republic of China. Distinctions between the operation of Communist Party, local government and military organizations in a specific district and at a specific administrative level have also not been well maintained, as was also often the case in practice at the time, and these too provide little assistance in distinguishing the activities of border regions and base areas. Base areas were established, merged, became part of border regions, sometimes regressed into less secure guerilla areas, and fluctuated wildly in size during the course of the War of Resistance to Japan.

To try and maximize clarity of explanation as far as the Taihang region is concerned, the term 'border region' is used exclusively to refer to the administrative level of the Shanxi-Hebei-Shandong-Henan Border Region, first proposed in the middle of 1941; 'base area' to the smaller, constituent districts, of which there were four after June 1941—the Taihang, Taiyue, South Henan and Hebei-Shandong-Henan Base Areas. The Taihang Base Area grew out of the Southeast Shanxi Base Area, and came to have a central position in the Shanxi-Hebei-Shandong-Henan Border Region. It was the seat of the Border Region Government; the strongest base area; and the only district directly administered by the Border Region Government. Because of the Taihang Base Area's seminal role in the development of the Border Region, it is sometimes identified elsewhere (including contemporary documents) as the 'Taihang Region.' Confusingly too, the Taiyue Base Area is sometimes included as part of the 'Taihang Region': although a separate base area in much of its development, the Taiyue CCP committee was subordinated to that of the Taihang Base Area before mid-1939 and after September 1943.

To complicate matters further, the Chinese Communist Party organization leading the Taihang Base Area was variously known as the Hebei-Henan-Shanxi Provincial Committee (October 1937), the Shanxi-Hebei-Henan District Committee (August 1938), the Shanxi-Hebei-Henan Regional Committee (April 1939) and later still the Taihang Regional Sub-bureau of the Central Committee of the Chinese Communist Party (October 1943.) There are two possible levels of confusion here, one linguistic, the other organizational. In Chinese Communist administration much use is made of the term '*qu*,' which may refer to an area, district or region at any level from the quite local to the multiprovincial. To attempt to make position in the relevant administrative hierarchy at different stages of the war clearer, reference will be made to 'district' when a sub-base area unit of organization is intended, and to 'region' when an area at least equal to the base area is indicated. Thus the August 1938 Shanxi-Hebei-Henan Committee of the Chinese Communist Party will be referred to as a 'District Committee'; whilst that of April 1939 will be identified as a 'Regional Committee.' The *qu* that were subordinate to the county level will be referred to as 'subdistricts.' The full administrative hierarchy in descending order is therefore border region, region (base area), district, county, subdistrict and village.

Contemporaneously and in retrospect, the Chinese Communist Party has recognized organizational continuity throughout these various stages of the development of the Taihang Base Area. For example, the regular conferences organized by the Chinese Communist Party's Organization Department of each of those committees were numbered consecutively throughout the war despite formal changes in institutional leadership. *Zhandou* [Combat] was one of the more famous publications of the regional organization of the Chinese Communist Party throughout the war years. Its issues were numbered consecutively despite changes in the nomenclature and organization of the party committee technically responsible for its production. In consequence there is a tendency for all the organizations of the base area and Chinese Communist Party in Southeast Shanxi during the war to be equated with the Taihang district or region.

Border regions were so called because they were located on the borders of influence of the Chinese Communist Party and the Japanese. To add to the confusion many were also located on the borders of two or more provinces. Thus the Shanxi-Hebei-Shandong-Henan Border Region was located on the borders of those four provinces and did not cover all four provinces completely. In the names of the border regions it is customary to refer to the provinces by their classical single character descriptors. Thus the Shanxi-Hebei-Shandong-Henan Border region is often referred to as the Jin-Ji-Lu-Yu Border Region. Shanxi's single character descriptor is *Jin*, Hebei's is *Ji*, Shandong's is *Lu*, Henan's is *Yu*.

The Chinese Communist Party armed forces in North China during the War of Resistance to Japan were known as the Eighth Route Army because of the arrangements initially made under the Second United Front with the Nationalist Party. In that agreement the CCP's troops in North China were renamed and renumbered as three divisions—the 115th, the 120th and the 129th—of the Eighth Route Army of the national armed forces. The Nationalist Party High Command renumbered the armed forces before the end of 1937 but by that stage the Eighth Route Army had distributed itself so successfully throughout North China that the name stuck in the popular consciousness. The 129th Division was sent to establish itself in Southeast Shanxi and was the original main force in the emerging Shanxi-Hebei-Shandong-Henan Border Region.

The Chinese Communist Party's armed strength included several layers of military organization. There were the main force, regular soldiers, of which the 129th Division was the core in the Taihang Base Area. However, as the war progressed new regiments were raised locally to increase the size of the regular army. The regular troops were supplemented by various types of largely part-time guerillas and self-defense militia. Every able-bodied man was considered part of the local self-defense force. Within these local self-defense forces would be a core of permanent but part-time militia [*minbing*] who were usually chosen from the young, strong men in the locality. The militia forces would also be a recruiting ground for the mobile guerilla troops [*youjidui*] who operated usually under more local control.

In Southeast Shanxi, as throughout the province, troops of the New Army (originally known as Dare-to-Die Troops) also fought alongside the soldiers of the Eighth Route Army. The New Army had been established by the Sacrifice League, which itself worked closely with the Chinese Communist Party. The Sacrifice League was the Shanxi Sacrifice League for National Salvation (*Shanxi xisheng jiuguo tongmenghui*, more usually referred to in Chinese as the *Ximenghui*). The pre-war warlord of Shanxi had been Yan Xishan who initially was more wary of Chiang Kai-shek and the Nationalist Party than he was of the Chinese Communist Party despite a nominal commitment to the Nationalist Party regime. Yan encouraged Chinese Communist Party organizers to establish and develop the Sacrifice League in Shanxi during 1936 as preparation to Japanese invasion. From the Chinese Communist Party's point of view the Sacrifice League was an excellent example of the 'United Front' in operation: both as their long-proposed alliance of nationalistically inclined social forces, and as a vehicle for more covert operations. Eventually, when the alliance between Yan Xishan and the Chinese Communist Party broke down (at the end of 1939), the Sacrifice League and much of its organization and membership, including most of the New Army, was subsumed into the Chinese Communist Party and its activities.

In Shanxi under Yan Xishan the administrative hierarchy was slightly different to the rest of China. Subordinate to the province were districts, and then counties. Each county then had a number of village-regions, each of which had administrative villages and finally natural villages. The village-region was a peculiarly Shanxi creation, abolished by the CCP as it created its new political order throughout the province.

A chronology of the Taihang Base Area during the War of Resistance follows this Preface; together with maps of the Shanxi-Hebei-Shandong-Henan Border Region; and each of the counties of Liaoxian (Zuoquan), Wuxiang and Licheng. These are followed by a list of standard abbreviations to sources and collections of documents used in notes and references.

In general the use of Chinese terms has been avoided. However, measures of land, weight and grains have been left in their original. These include, together with their approximate metric equivalents:

1 *mu* of land = 0.06 hectare = 1/6 acre
1 *shang* of land = 3 *mu*
1 *jin* of weight = 0.5 kilo = 1.1 pounds
1 *sheng* (usually grain) = 3 *jin*
1 *dou* (usually grain) = 30 *jin*
1 *dan* (usually grain) = 10 *dou*

Social and Political Change in Revolutionary China has resulted from a project that has involved a large number of institutions and people over the years. Funds for research have been provided at various times by the Australian Research Council, through its Large Research Grants Scheme; the Pacific Cultural Foundation; and the University of Technology, Sydney, through its Research Incentive Program. The financial assistance provided by all those institutions is gratefully acknowledged. Research has taken me to a number of libraries and archives, but particularly to the libraries at Stanford University and Australian National University; and to the Taiyuan Archives of the Chinese Communist Party in Shanxi; as well as Nationalist Army and Ministry of Justice Archives in Taipei. I would like to thank the curators and staff of those institutions for all their invaluable assistance.

Many individuals have been both directly and indirectly involved in providing support to the project, and the production of this book. I would like to explicitly acknowledge their participation and my debt of gratitude.

First and foremost the entire project would have been impossible without the assistance and particularly the access to sources provided by Professor Tian Youru, Director of the Modern Shanxi History Institute. He has been the most able and astute guide around the archives, arranger of documentary sources to be made available, and persuader of individuals to permit themselves to be interviewed about their experiences. His encouragement and friendship have been equally as invaluable.

In China a number of former participants in and leading cadres of the Taihang Base Area agreed to be interviewed for this project, and encouraged others to be interviewed. In particular, I am grateful to the assistance rendered by Li Xuefeng, Rong Zihe and Chi Biqing in both those respects. Because of the understandable sensibilities involved, even at the distance of sixty years or more, interviewees have not been identified, nor are quotations from their interviews directly attributed. None of these individuals, none of those interviewed, nor indeed any others cited in this Preface or elsewhere, is directly responsible for the arguments, interpretations or views expressed in this book.

Over the years, a number of people have provided research assistance of various kinds. In particular, I would like to acknowledge the assistance of Li Xueqian, Shanxi University; Guo Pingjian, Shanxi Teacher's University; Sun Wanning, Curtin University; and Yang Erming, Shanxi University. It was a pleasure to work with you all.

I have been working in the Institute for International Studies at the University of Technology, Sydney since 1994. Both have been ideal intellectual environments for a practicing researcher, not least because they have made it possible for me to complete this project with a period of study leave. Moreover, both the research project and this book have gained immeasurably from seminars, conversations and discussions within the Institute on questions of social change, both generally and related to China.

Over the years since this project started, I have benefited greatly from the encouragement and intellectual stimulus provided by a number of colleagues, particularly Lucien Bianco, Chen Yung-fa, Feng Chongyi, John Fitzgerald, Mark Selden, Fred Teiwes, and Wei Hongyun. Moreover, Feng Chongyi, Mark Selden, and Fred Teiwes, as well as Agnes Stefanowska and Peter Zarrow read and provided much-needed critical assistance on earlier drafts. I also have the greatest luxury of being married to my best friend and closest intellectual colleague, Mabel Lee, whose support and insights have been invaluable.

Chronology: The Taihang Base Area, 1937–1945

1937

October	129th Division and 344th Brigade of 115th Division of Eighth Route Army led by Liu Bocheng arrive in Pingding County. Joined by CCP Beiping-Hankou Railway Provincial Committee. Establishment of CCP Hebei-Henan-Shanxi Provincial Committee.
November	Taiyuan taken by Japanese. 129th Division CCP Meeting, Shiguai Village, Heshun County. Decision to establish Hebei-Henan-Shanxi Base Area in Southeast Shanxi. Initial bases of activity: West Hebei (Zanhuang, Xingtai), Central Shanxi (Pingding, Xiyang), North Henan and Southwest Hebei (Cixian, Shexian). Bo Yibo leads First Column Dare-to-Die Troops to Qinxian.
December	Zhu Rui establishes North China Military and Administrative Cadre Institute in Jincheng.

1938

January	Deng Xiaoping replaces Zhang Hao as Political Commissar, 129th Division. CCP Hebei-Henan-Shanxi Provincial Committee holds 1st Activists Conference. District committees established for

	Central Shanxi (Pingding, Xiyang, Heshun, Liaoxian, Wuxiang); Hebei-Shanxi (Zanhuang, Xingtai); Hebei-Henan (Cixian, Shexian); South Taihang (Licheng, Pingshun); and Shanxi-Henan (Jincheng); as well as a Taiyue Branch Office (Qinxian).
March	Decision to establish Taihang Mountains Base Area. Qinyuan Incident.
April	Japanese withdrawal from Changzhi region. Eighth Route Army Headquarters moves into Taihang Base Area.
May	129th Division troops and 344th Brigade 689th Regiment into South Hebei. Zhu Rui establishes Eighth Route Army South Shanxi Cadre School in Qinxian. CCP Hebei-Henan-Shanxi Provincial Committee moves to Qinxian. *Zhongguoren bao* [Chinese Daily] started by CCP Hebei-Henan-Shanxi Provincial Committee.
June	Taiyue District Committee of CCP Hebei-Henan-Shanxi Provincial Committee established.
July	Rong Zihe leads Third Column Dare-to-Die Troops to Changzhi. Decision to establish South Hebei Base Area.
August	Establishment of CCP Shanxi-Hebei-Henan District Committee.
September	Shangdang Bank established.
October	Fall of Wuhan, Japanese attention refocuses on CCP. CCP Shanxi-Hebei-Henan District Committee relocates to Taihang Mountains.
November	344th Brigade 685th Regiment moves to Southwest Shandong. Establishment of Hebei-Shandong-Henan Base Area. Yang Shangkun appointed Secretary, North China Bureau CCP Central Committee. North China Bureau moves to co-locate with Eighth Route Army Headquarters in Taihang Base Area.

1939

January	CCP North China Bureau starts *Xinhua ribao* [New China Daily, North China Edition] replaces *Zhongguoren bao*.
March	Yan Xishan organizes Qiulin Meeting (Shaanxi) to reorganize New Army.

	Taihang Base Area 1st Organisational Work Conference.
April	Establishment of CCP Shanxi-Hebei-Henan Regional Committee.
July	Japanese re-take Changzhi.
	Japanese build railway from Baigui to Changzhi (completed in December) to physically divide Taihang and Taiyue Base Areas; and reinforce the Handan-Changzhi Road to further divide the Taihang Base Area into North and South Taihang Base Areas.
September	1st Congress of CCP in Shanxi-Hebei-Henan Region (under name of Civil Movement Working Conference).
October	South Hebei Bank established.
	Establishment of New China News Agency, North China Branch.
December	Establishment of North Taihang, South Taihang and Taiyue Base Areas. When the South Taihang Base Area was abandoned, the North Taihang Base Area simply reverted to its earlier name as the Taihang Base Area.
	Open conflict between CCP, Nationalist Party and Yan Xishan forces in West Shanxi, South Taihang Area and Zhongtiao Mountains (to early March).
	CCP forces capture mountain section of Handan-Changzhi Road.

1940

January	Lu Xun Arts School established in Wuxiang.
March	Truce between CCP and Nationalist Party forces. Eighth Route Army withdraws from South Taihang. CCP South Taihang District Committee merges with Shanxi-Henan District Committee and goes underground until 1943.
April	Taihang, Taiyue and South Hebei Base Areas Senior Cadres Meeting at Licheng. Decision to establish Shanxi-Hebei-Henan Border Region Government.
	Taihang Base Area 2nd Organizational Work Conference.
June	Taihang Branch of Japanese Awakening League established.
	Taihang Military District established.
	Eighth Route Army Headquarters Branch Office established in Shexian, Henan.
July	Shangdang Bank merged into South Hebei Bank.
August	Establishment of Joint Office for South Hebei, Taiyue and Taihang Base Areas to coordinate activities and to prepare

	for establishment of the Shanxi-Hebei-Henan Border Region Government.
	Start of Hundred Regiments Campaign.
December	End of Hundred Regiments Campaign.
	Taihang Base Area 3rd Organisational Work Conference.

1941

February	CCP Shanxi-Hebei-Henan Regional Committee decision to revive mass organizations for peasants, women, youth and workers.
March	Decision to establish Border Region Provisional Assembly.
April	Elections start for Border Region Provisional Assembly.
May	Second line of Japanese blockade built along PingHan Railway.
	Regeneration of Taihang Patriotic Peasants Association.
June	Decision to incorporate Hebei-Shandong-Henan Base Area in proposed Border Region.
	Taihang Base Area 4th Organizational Work Conference.
July	Shanxi-Hebei-Shandong-Henan Border Region Provisional Assembly meets in Liaoxian.
September	Shanxi-Hebei-Shandong-Henan Border Region Government starts operations.
October	Sixth Trigram Uprising in Licheng.

1942

January	Administrative restructuring starts throughout region.
March	Third line of Japanese blockade along line of PingHan Railway built from Yuanshi to Wu'an.
April	Insurrection in Shahe.
May	Japanese 'Mop-up': Zuo Quan killed in Liaoxian.
June	Critical drought.
August	Taihang Base Area 5th Organizational Work Conference.
September	2nd Session of Border Region Provisional Assembly.
	Start of rent and interest reduction campaign.
	CCP North China Bureau establishes Taihang Sub-bureau under Deng Xiaoping to coordinate party activities in Border Region.
October	Japanese 'Mop-up'centers on Pingding, Xiyang, Wuxiang, Zuoquan.
	Drought worsens.

November	Famine Relief emergency measures started by Border Region Government.

1943

January	CCP North China Bureau Taihang Sub-bureau Senior Cadres meeting in Wen Village, Shexian.
March	Rectification starts under Taihang Sub-bureau.
April	Border Region introduces Unified Progressive Tax.
May	Nationalist Party forces in South Taihang defect to Japanese.
June	Taihang Sub-bureau initiates program of economic redevelopment.
August	CCP forces victorious in Linxian Battle over remnant Nationalist Party forces and Japanese puppet troops.
September	South Taihang and parts of North Henan incorporated into Taihang Base Area (Linxian, Lingchuan, Jincheng). 3rd Session of Border Region Provisional Assembly.
October	Establishment of CCP Taihang Regional Committee. *New China Daily (North China edition)* becomes *New China Daily (Taihang edition).*

1944

January	Insurrection in Linxian.
February	Japanese withdrawal begins from forward positions.
March	Border Region initiates public industrial cooperatives.
April	Locust plague in North Henan and West Hebei.
May	Anti-locust preventative measures in Licheng, Lucheng and Pingshun.
June	Border Region decides to elect Border Region Assembly. Renewed locust attacks in West Hebei.
July	CCP forces break Japanese 2nd line of blockade along PingHan Railway.
August	Renewed locust attacks in North Henan and West Hebei.
September	CCP Taihang Region Committee convenes summary meeting on rectification and arranges close reexamination of cadres' personal histories.
November	Taihang Region Conference of Labor Heroes opens in Licheng.

1945

January	U.S. Army observers visit Taihang Military District Headquarters.

February	Taihang Base Area 6th Organizational Work Conference.
March	CCP forces break Japanese blockade along PingHan Railway.
	1st session of Border Region Assembly.
April	Liaoxian and Heshun County towns retaken by CCP.
	Rent and interest reduction campaign ceases.
June	CCP forces capture Anyang, Henan.
August	CCP forces reenter a number of county towns, including Zanhuang, Lucheng, Qinxian.
	CCP North China Bureau replaced by Shanxi-Hebei-Shandong-Henan Bureau under Deng Xiaoping.
	Yan Xishan's troops return to Southeast Shanxi.

Major Sources

TDZH 1989 (1937–38 and 1939 volumes) 1994 (1940 and 1941 volumes); Taihang geming genjudishi zongbian weihui (ed) *Taihang geming genjudi shigao* [Outline History of the Taihang Revolutionary Base Area] Taiyuan, Shanxi renmin chubanshe, 1987; Taihang geming genjudishi zongbian weihui (ed) *Dashijishu* [Chronology] Taihang geming genjudi shiliao congshu No.1, Taiyuan, Shanxi renmin chubanshe, 1991; Taihang geming genjudishi zongbian weihui (ed) *Yubei zhandou* [The Struggle for North Henan] Taihang geming genjudi shiliao congshu No.11, Taiyuan, Shanxi renmin chubanshe, 1988; Tian Youru 'Taihang kangRi genjudi shi yanjiu songshu' ['Research on the History of the Taihang Anti-Japanese Base Area'] in *Dangshi tongxun* [Newsletter on Party History] No 353 (No 7 1987) p.39; Zhonggong Changzhi shiwei dangshi yanjiushi (ed) *Zhongguo gongchandang Shanxisheng Changzhishi lishi dashijishu* [Historical Chronology of the CCP in Changzhi City, Shanxi] Beijing, Zhonggong dangshi chubanshe, 1994; Zhonggong Hebei Shengwei dangshi ziliao zhengji bianshen weiyuanhui and Taihang (Hebei bufen) shiliao lianhe zhengbian bangongshi (ed) *Jixi minxunchu yu Jixi Youjidui* [The West Hebei Training Regiment and the West Hebei Guerilla Troop] Taihang geming genjudi shiliao congshu No.10, Shijiazhuang, Hebei renmin chubanshe 1989; Zhonggong Shanxishengwei dangshi yanjiushi (ed) *Taiyue geming genjudi jishi* [A Chronology of the Taiyue Revolutionary Base Area] Taiyuan, Shanxi renmin chubanshe, 1989; Zhonggong Shanxi shengwei dangshi yanjiushi (ed) *Zhongguo gongchandang Shanxi lishi gangyao* [Outline History of the CCP in Shanxi] Beijing, Zhonggong dangshi chubanshe, 1991; Zhonggong Shanxi shengwei dangshi yanjiushi (ed) *Zhongguo gongchandang Shanxi lishi dashijishu* [Chronology of the CCP in Shanxi] Beijing, Zhonggong dangshi chubanshe, 1994; Zhonggong Shanxi shengwei zuzhibu, Zhonggong Shanxi shengwei dangshi yanjiushi, Shanxi sheng danganju (ed) *Zhongguo gongchandang Shanxi sheng zuzhishi ziliao 1924–1949* [Organizational History of the CCP in Shanxi, 1924–1949] Taiyuan, Shanxi renmin chubanshe, 1994.

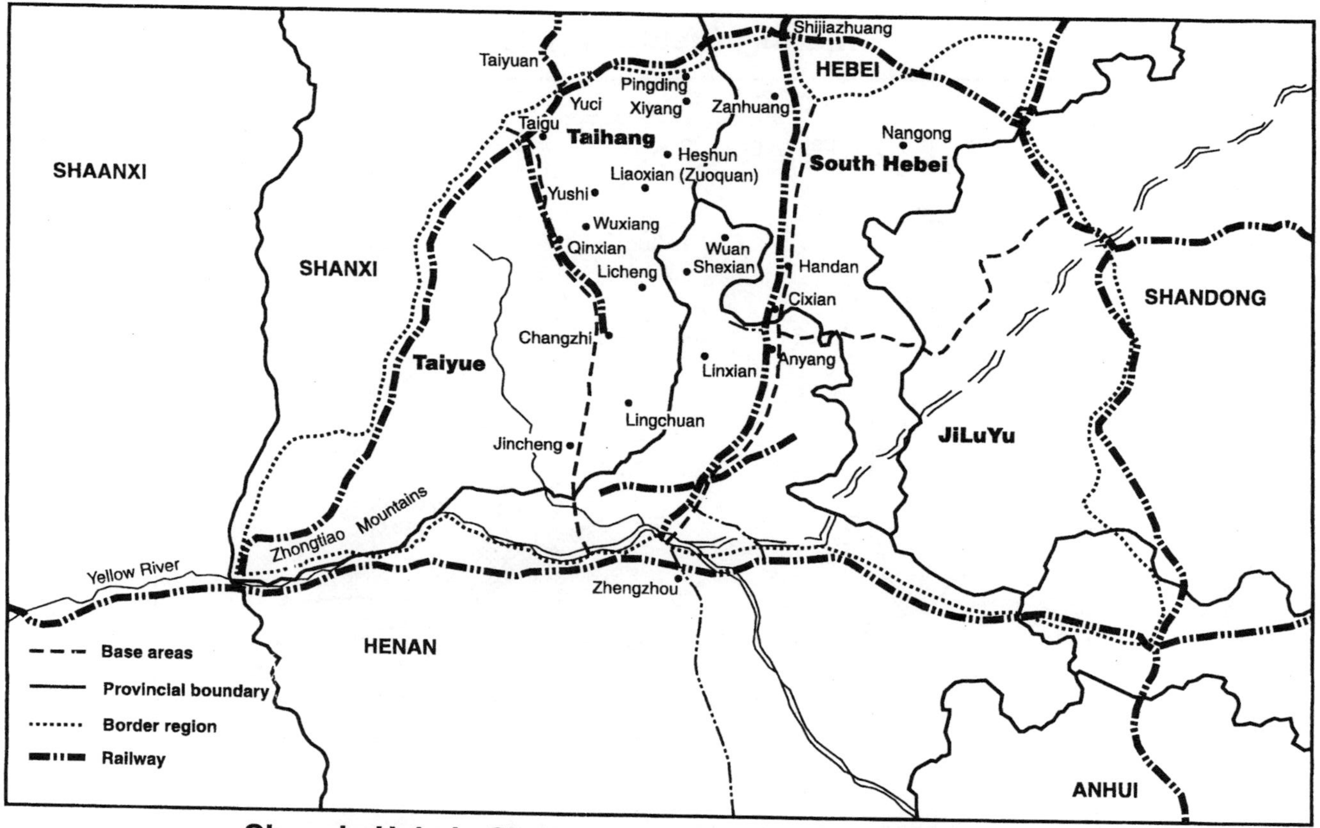

Shanxi - Hebei - Shandong - Henan Border Region, 1945

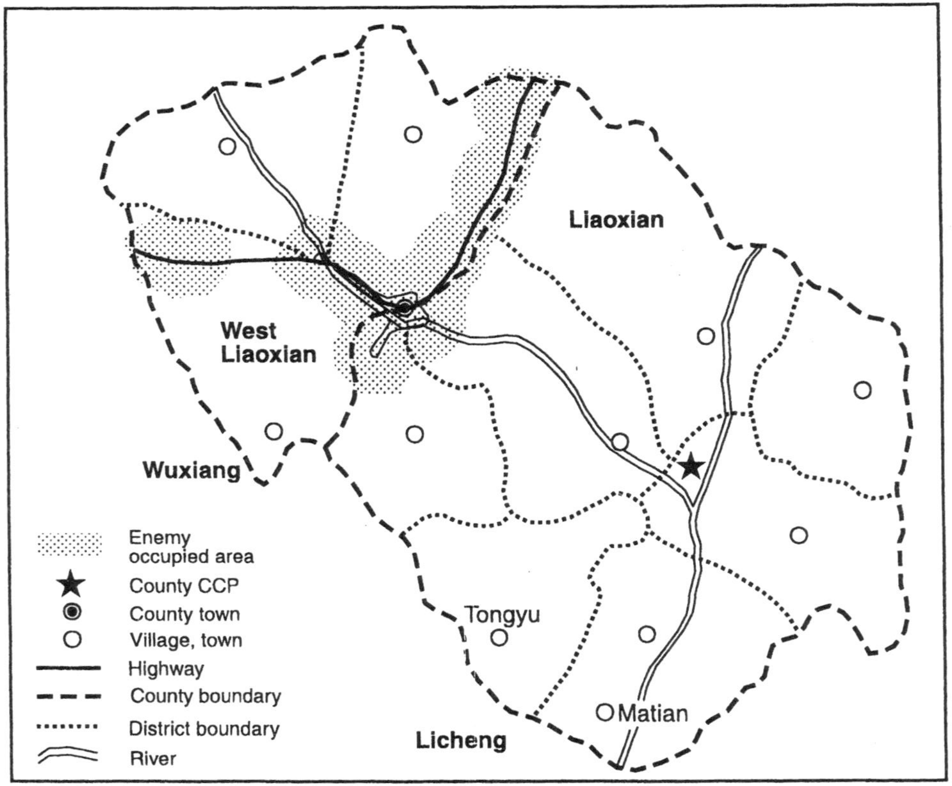

Liaoxian (Zuoquan) County

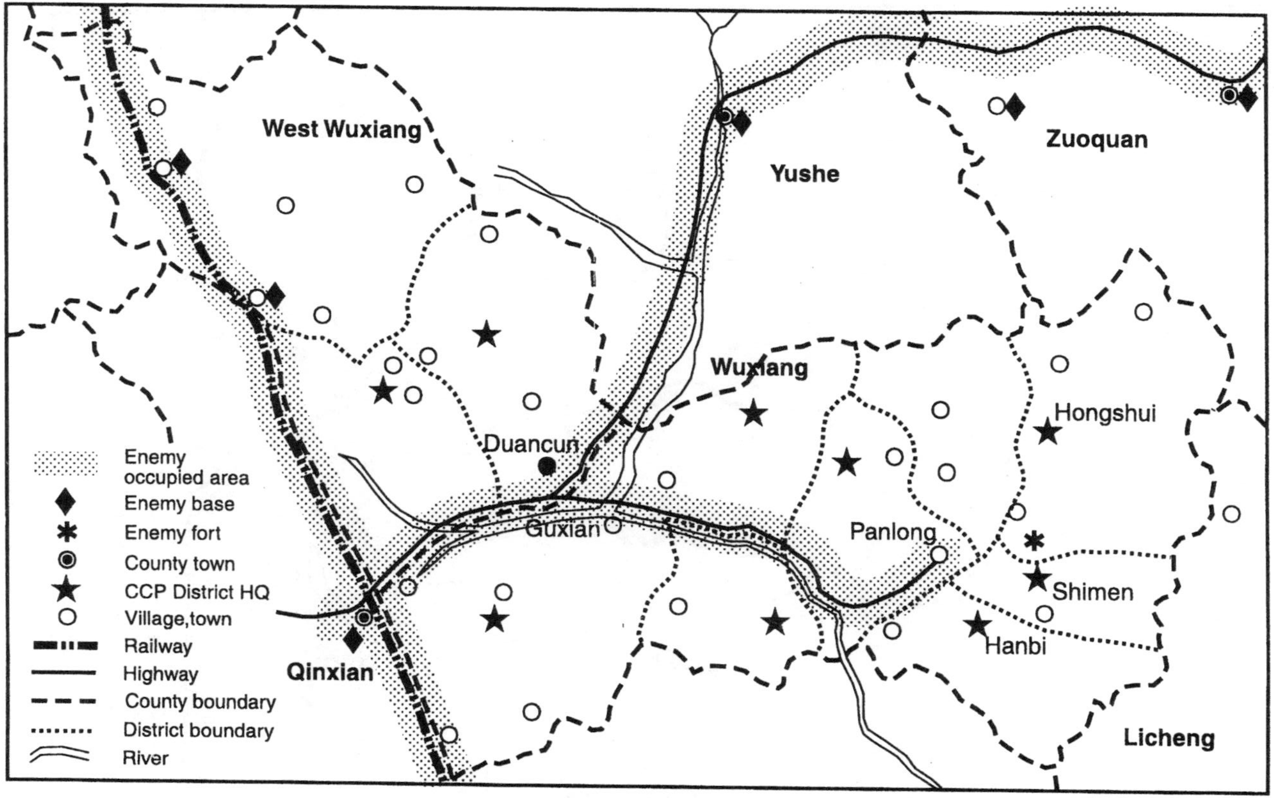

Wuxiang County

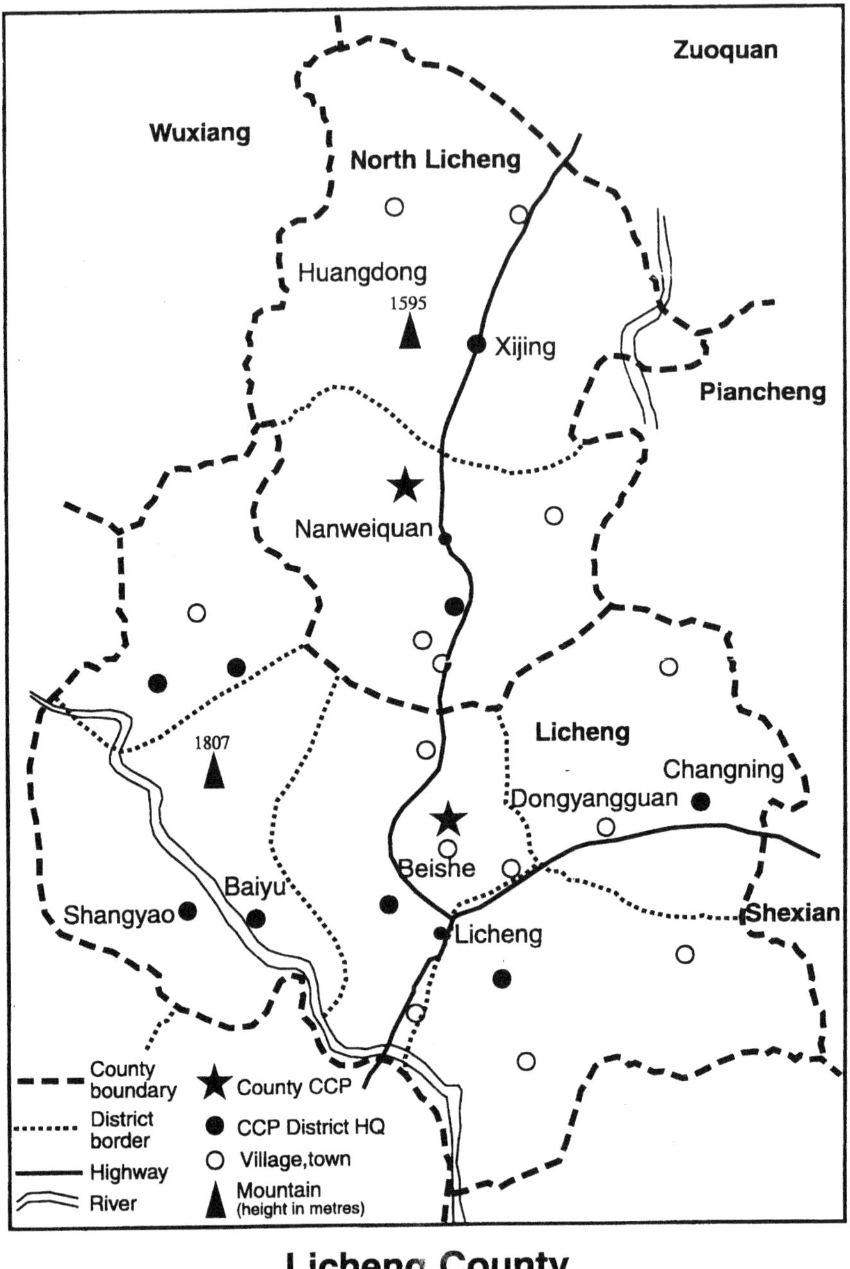

Licheng County

Abbreviations

FREQUENTLY USED SOURCES AND COLLECTIONS OF DOCUMENTS

BZYJ — Zhonggong JinJiYu quwei zuzhibu *Boruoqu zhibu yanjiuhui jilu* [Minutes of the Conference on Party Branches in Less-Developed Areas], July–August 1942.

BZZM — Zhonggong Zuoquan xianweiyuanhui and Zuoquan xian renmin zhengfu (ed) *Balujun zongbu zai Matian* [The Eighth Route Army's HQ in Matian] Taiyuan, Shanxi renmin chubanshe, 1990.

CJJ — Taihang geming genjudishi zongbian weihui (ed) *Caizheng jingji jianshe* [Financial and Economic Development] (2 vols) Taihang geming genjudi shiliao congshu No.6, Taiyuan, Shanxi renmin chubanshe, 1987.

CJZX — JinJiLuYu Bianqu caizheng jingji shi bianjizu and Shanxi, Hebei, Shandong, Henan sheng danganguan (ed) *KangRi zhanzheng shiqi JinJiLuYu Bianqu caizheng jingjishi ziliao xuanbian* [Collection of Materials on the Economic and Financial History of the Shanxi-Hebei-Shandong-Henan Border Region during the War of Resistance to Japan] (2 vols) Beijing, Caizheng jingji chubanshe, 1990.

CHL — Zhonggong Licheng xianwei dangshi yanjiushi *Zhongguo Gongchandang Licheng xian jianshi 1937–1949* [A Concise History of the CCP in Licheng County 1937–1949] Taihang geming genjudi shiliao congshu, Taiyuan, Xinhua chubanshe, 1991.

DJ — Taihang geming genjudishi zongbian weihui (ed) *Dang de jianshe* [Party Development] Taihang geming genjudi shiliao congshu No.2, Taiyuan, Shanxi renmin chubanshe, 1989.

DWD — Taihang geming genjudishi zongbian weihui (ed) *Difang wuzhuang douzheng* [Local Armed Struggle] Taihang geming genjudi shiliao congshu No.3, Taiyuan, Shanxi renmin chubanshe, 1990.

FOC — Zhonggong JinJiYu quwei *JinJiYu quwei disici zuzhihui jilu* [Minutes of the Fourth Organizational Conference of the Shanxi-Hebei-Henan Regional Committee], June 1941.

GBG — Taihang geming genjudishi zongbian weihui (ed) *Gongan baowei gongzuo* [Security and Protection] Taihang geming genjudi shiliao congshu No.9, Taiyuan, Shanxi renmin chubanshe, 1989.

GSX — JinJiLuYu genjudi shiliao xuanbianzhe (ed) *JinJiLuYu genjudi shiliaoxuan* [Selected Materials on the History of the Shanxi-Hebei-Shandong-Henan Base Area] Taiyuan, Shanxi shengwei, 1989, 4 vols (1937–40, 1941–42, 1943–45, 1945–47).

HCZ — Zhonggong Shanxisheng Zuoquanxian dangshi yanjiushi (ed) *Zhonggong Zuoquanxian lishi dashijishu 1937.7–1949.9* [Historical Chronology of the CCP in Zuoquan County 1937–1949] Taiyuan, Shanxi renmin chubanshe, 1993.

HZ — Zhongguo gongchandang Zuoquan xianwei dangshi yanjiushi *Zhongguo gongchandang Zuoquan xian jianshi 1937–1949* [A Brief History of the CCP in Zuoquan County 1937–1949] Taihang geming genjudi shiliao congshu, Taiyuan, Shanxi renmin chubanshe, 1995.

IHW — Zhonggong Shanxisheng Wuxiang xianwei dangshi yanjiushi *Zhonggong Wuxiang jianshi* [An Introductory History to the CCP in Wuxiang] Wuxiang, Zhonggong Shanxisheng Wuxiang xianwei dangshi yanjiushi, 1990.

KZW — Zhonggong Wuxiang xianwei xuanchuanbu and Zhonggong Wuxiang xianwei dangshi yanjiushi (ed) *KangRi zhanzheng zhongde Wuxiang* [Wuxiang in the Anti-Japanese War] Zhonggong Wuxiang, 1995.

LDB — Zhonggong JinJiYu qudangwei *Liaoxian diaocha baogao* [Report of an Investigation into Liaoxian], May 1942.

LGD — Zhonggong JinJiYu qudangwei Licheng kaochatuan *Li Gua Dao shijian diaocha baogao* [Report of the Investigation into the Sixth Trigram Movement Incident], April 1942.

LOH — Zhonggong Shanxisheng Licheng xianwei zuzhibu, Zhonggong Shanxisheng Licheng xianwei dangshi yanjiushi, Shanxisheng Licheng xian danganju (ed) *Zhongguo gongchandang Shanxi sheng Licheng xian zuzhishi ziliao 1937–1987* [Organizational History of Licheng County, Shanxi Province CCP, 1937–1987] Taiyuan, Shanxi renmin chubanshe, 1993.

LX Licheng xianzhi bianxi weiyuanhui (ed) *Licheng xianzhi* [The Record of Licheng County] Beijing, Zhonghua shuju, 1994.

LXH Li Xuefeng *Li Xuefeng huiyilu: Taihang shinian* [The Memoirs of Li Xuefeng: Ten Years in the Taihang Mountains] Beijing, Zhonggong dangshi chubanshe, 1998.

LZ Li Bu'an (ed) *Licheng zhilue* [Licheng Chronicle] Beijing, Renwen chubanshe, 1993.

QY Taihang geming genjudishi zongbian weihui (ed) *Qunzhong yundong* [The Mass Movement] Taihang geming genjudi shiliao congshu No.7, Taiyuan, Shanxi renmin chubanshe, 1989.

SOC Zhonggong Taihang qudangwei *Taihang quwei diliuci zuzhihui jilu* [Minutes of the Sixth Organizational Conference of the Taihang Region Party Committee], February–March 1945.

SOH Zhonggong Shanxi shengwei zuzhibu, Zhonggong Shanxi shengwei dangshi yanjiushi, Shanxi sheng danganju (ed) *Zhongguo gongchandang Shanxi sheng zuzhishi ziliao 1924–1949* [Organizational History of the CCP in Shanxi, 1924–1949] Taiyuan, Shanxi renmin chubanshe, 1994.

TDZH Shanxisheng danganguan (ed) *Taihang dangshi ziliao huibian* [Collection of Materials on the History of the Party in the Taihang Base Area] Taiyuan, Shanxi renmin chubanshe, 1989 (1937–38 and 1939 volumes); 1994 (1940 and 1941 volumes).

TGCG *Taihangqu guomin caifu gaikuang* [Outline of National Wealth in the Taihang Region], 1944.

TRSX *Taihangqu renmin shenghuode xiaohao* [Everyday consumption in the Taihang Region], 1944.

TSJD1 *Taihangqu shehui jingji diaocha (diyiji)* [Social and Economic Survey of the Taihang Region—First Collection], August 1944.

TSJD2 *Taihangqu shehui jingji diaocha (dierji)* [Social and Economic Survey of the Taihang Region—Second Collection], 1945.

TW Taihang geming genjudishi zongbian weihui (ed) *Tudi wenti* [The Land Question] Taihang geming genjudi shiliao congshu No.5, Taiyuan, Shanxi renmin chubanshe, 1987.

TYG Taihang qu yinhang gongshang gongzuo cankao ziliao bianzhe weiyuanhui (ed) *Taihangqu yinhang gongshang gongzuo cankao ziliao* [Reference Materials on Bank and Commercial Work in the Taihang Base Area] Shexian, 1945.

WF Zhonggong Wuxiang xianwei xuanchuanbu and Zhonggong Wuxiang xianwei dangshi bangongshi (ed) *Wuxiang fenghuo*

[The Flames of War in Wuxiang] (2 vols) Licheng, Licheng CCP Committee, 1985.

WOH Zhonggong Shanxisheng Wuxiang xianwei zuzhibu, Zhonggong Shanxisheng Wuxiang xianwei dangshi yanjiushi, Shanxisheng Wuxiangxian danganju (ed) *Zhongguo gongchandang Shanxisheng Wuxiangxian zuzhi shi ziliao 1933.8–1993.12* [Organizational History of the CCP in Wuxiang County, Shanxi, 1933–1993] Taiyuan, Shanxi renmin chubanshe, 1994.

WS Taihang geming genjudishi zongbian weihui (ed) *Wenhua shiye* [Cultural Affairs] Taihang geming genjudi shiliao congshu No.8, Taiyuan, Shanxi renmin chubanshe, 1989.

WX Wuxiangxian xianzhi bianji weiyuanhui bangongshi (ed) *Wuxiang xianzhi* [The Record of Wuxiang County] Taiyuan, Shanxi renmin chubanshe, 1986.

XZYJ Zhonggong JinJiYu quwei zuzhibu *Xianjinqu zhibu yanjiuhui jilu* [Minutes of the Conference on Party Branches in Advanced Areas], July 1942.

YZ Taihang geming genjudishi zongbian weihui (ed) *Yubei zhandou* [The Struggle for North Henan] Taihang geming genjudi shiliao congshu No.11, Taiyuan, Shanxi renmin chubanshe, 1988.

ZJ Taihang geming genjudishi zongbian weihui (ed) *Zhengquan jianshe* [Political Development] Taihang geming genjudi shiliao congshu No.4, Taiyuan, Shanxi renmin chubanshe, 1990.

ZJY Zhonggong JinJiYu qudangwei *Guanyu zhibu jianshe yanjiu de jige wenti* [Several Questions from Research into Development of Party Branches] 30 September 1943, Minutes of the CCP Shanxi-Hebei-Henan Regional Committee, 5 September 1943.

ZOH Zhonggong Shanxisheng Zuoquan xianwei zuzhibu, Zhonggong Shanxisheng Zuoquan xianwei dangshi yanjiushi, Shanxisheng Zuoquan xian danganju (ed) *Zhongguo gongchandang Shanxisheng Zuoquan xian zuzhishi ziliao 1937.10–1987.10* [Organizational History of the CCP in Zuoquan County, Shanxi, 1937–1987] Taiyuan, Shanxi renmin chubanshe, 1992.

Introduction

The Revolutionary Process

The People's Republic of China has its origins in arguably the greatest peasant revolution in the history of the world. During the War of Resistance to Japan from 1937 to 1945 the Chinese Communist Party was transformed from a marginalized force on the periphery of Chinese society, politically as well as geographically, into the major contender for national power. This was duly accomplished in 1949 with the establishment of the People's Republic. The war enabled the Chinese Communist Party to develop a base of support, in terms of both numbers and legitimacy for the future, in large part but by no means exclusively in the base areas and border regions of rural North China. Not without considerable justice the Chinese Communist Party, and Chinese historians more generally, have subsequently emphasized not simply its positive social impact during those years, but also the extent of that party's popular mobilization and the support which resulted.

Until recently it had not been possible to examine this transformation in any great detail, largely because the sources were not available. The history of the War of Resistance tended to be somewhat one-dimensional, whether told by the Chinese Communist Party [CCP], historians in the People's Republic of China [PRC] or researchers in the rest of the world. There was little sense of the intense regional variation that characterized the experience of the CCP at that time, or of the processes of social and political change involved. In particular, the social and political interactions that lay at the heart of the revolutionary process in the behind-the-lines base areas of North China were barely visible, and certainly not without a heavy filter provided by the CCP itself.

During the War of Resistance, Mao Zedong and the CCP had its headquarters in Yan'an, the center of the Shaanxi-Gansu-Ningxia Border Region. Yan'an, in the northeast of Shaanxi Province, was somewhat isolated and fairly secure, not least because it was not on the front line of conflict with the invading Japanese Army. The two most important CCP-led border regions behind the line of Japanese incursion were based in and around the Taihang Mountains that separate Hebei and Shanxi Provinces, north to south. The Taihang Mountain Range was itself bifurcated east to west by the ZhengTai Railway that linked the capitals of those two provinces—Shijiazhuang and Taiyuan, respectively. To the north was the Shanxi-Chahar-Hebei Border Region, and to the south was the Shanxi-Hebei-Shandong-Henan Border Region. The Taihang Base Area was at the core of the Shanxi-Hebei-Shandong-Henan Border Region, and at its center in turn were three mountain counties: Liaoxian, Wuxiang and Licheng.

An interpretation of three counties of Southeast Shanxi cannot present a comprehensive or definitive view of the revolutionary process in North China during the War of Resistance, though it may deepen understanding of the dynamics of change. It contributes to an understanding of the social and political origins of the Chinese revolution by considering how both the rural population and the CCP adapted and changed within that process. In particular, it examines the roles and interactions of a variety of social and political groups, highlighting the activities of urban intellectuals, teachers and peasant small-holders as agents of social and political change.

THE WAR OF RESISTANCE IN HISTORY

One wider consequence of CCP success in first the War of Resistance and then later in the establishment of the PRC is to have drawn attention to the concept of peasant revolution more generally. The CCP's own view of its strategy and tactics during the war—especially the notion of popular mobilization based on social reform[1]—were a beacon to agrarian revolutionaries throughout the less-industrialized parts of the world, but particularly in East and Southeast Asia, during the second half of the twentieth century.[2] At the same time, China during the late 1930s and 1940s became a focus of investigation for academics outside the PRC interested in theorizing about the dynamics of social and political change, and particularly peasant revolution.[3] In part this may explain why the earliest and most well-known, as well as often the most controversial, interpretations of the CCP's experience during the War of Resistance were all concerned with the articulation of 'grand theory.'[4]

The first of these interpretations was Chalmers Johnson's articulation of the theory of peasant nationalism, which argued that the Chinese peasantry had been politicized by Japanese aggression.[5] Although not as opposed as it appeared at the time of its publication, Mark Selden's study of 'The Yenan Way' adopted a form of argument based on a theory of social exchange—peasants supported the revolution because their standard of living improved. Selden emphasized the importance of the CCP's appeal to social and economic reform, rather than to nationalism.[6] Tetsuya Kataoka highlighted the role of the CCP's organizational capacity and abilities as the crucial element in bringing about change, and discounted the impact of appeals to either nationalism or social reform.[7] Ralph Thaxton also discounted any vestige of an argument based on social exchange, preferring instead to view the War of Resistance from the perspective of the peasantry's moral economy. As a result, unlike Kataoka he discounted the organizational presence of the CCP and saw the War of Resistance as a peasant-led revolution that resulted from the latter's moral outrage at the injustices and collapse of traditional society.[8]

The essential problem with each of these approaches is the extent to which they were intended to be, or have subsequently been taken by others to be used as monocausal explanations of social and political change in China. Each clearly highlights different aspects of the CCP's experience and social and political change during the War of Resistance. Equally as clearly, each is deficient in providing a comprehensive explanation of social and political change at that time, not least because they need not be mutually exclusive. Change is necessarily complex, and the danger of the search for 'grand theory' is that it encourages the development of false dichotomies. At a fairly early stage in the development of Western studies of the War of Resistance, Lucien Bianco pointed out that appeals to both nationalism and social reform could and did coexist. Indeed the very success of the CCP at the time was based on the commitment to both nationalism and social reform together.[9] Moreover, as Bianco has frequently argued since, for all that the Chinese revolution is 'often considered . . . the very archetype of peasant revolution' both the CCP and the peasants were necessary ingredients and neither on its own was sufficient for success, despite the unequal nature of the alliance.[10] It is the various and changing interpenetration of these and other factors which becomes important in attempting an interpretation of social and political change during the War of Resistance.

Although the search for 'grand theory' may have had limited explanatory powers, this phase of research nonetheless highlighted a series of practical and methodological issues that in turn have indicated the way forward for further inquiry. The practical problem has been one of information; the more methodological issues center on an increasing awareness of the need to dissaggregate the processes of social and political change.

Until the 1980s the most significant impediment to more broadly based, detailed research was a lack of sources. The evidentiary base for further research was extremely limited, even in Taiwan or Japan, in respectively, Chinese Nationalist Party-controlled government and military archives, or remnant Japanese military and corporate documentation. Within the PRC most of the documents from the war years were not accessible, even to Chinese historians. There was almost no access to archives, and very few of the original documents were republished. Those that were, like the only slightly less limited analysis that accompanied them, tended to concentrate on the 'Yan'an Experience,' particularly after the late-1950s. One result was that each of the four major explanations in search of their particular 'grand theory' of CCP success during the War of Resistance had necessarily been bound to a narrow range of sources: Johnson to Japanese survey data from the war years; Selden to CCP internal documents from the Shaanxi-Gansu-Ningxia Border Region that dealt mainly with the development of mass line policies; Kataoka similarly to CCP internal documents, but in this case almost all of which dealt with organizational development; and Thaxton to secondary accounts of what had happened in North China during the War of Resistance produced as part of a specific political movement within China during the 1960s.

This impediment to further analysis began to change with political events in the PRC after 1978, particularly as the CCP sought to rediscover the diversity of its own wartime history. By the second half of the 1980s, collections of documents from the War of Resistance (often transcribed and typeset for the first time) were being published in large numbers, and local histories of border regions, base areas, counties and even villages started to appear.[11] Greater domestic political openness led to increased access to other sources of information. By the mid-1990s it had become possible for both Chinese researchers and those from other countries to access archives for unpublished material, and to conduct interviews with veterans of the CCP's base areas.

Even before the political changes of the post-Mao era made more detailed research as possible as it has become, a number of scholars (mainly in North America) had started to question the overgeneralization of CCP experience inherent in previous explanations of the War of Resistance. In particular there was a concern that China's regional variation might have led to significant differences in the experiences of revolutionary change. There was a drive both to concentrate research on specific base areas, and to set these studies in wider historical perspective. At Stanford University, Lyman Van Slyke encouraged a group of researchers to concentrate on different base areas during the War of Resistance.[12] At about the same time, Elizabeth Perry was working on a more long-term study of North Anhui that sought to relate the local environment to the emergence of rebellion in the second half of the nineteenth and the first half of the twentieth century.[13] By the middle of the 1980s this more disaggregated approach to the explanation of social and political change had made such headway that it was possible to organize a project to examine a range of CCP base areas over time, and not even exclusively those in North China or only during the War of Resistance.[14] The essential strategy that lies behind these developments has not been to abandon theory, but rather to develop sounder theorizing by building explanation from the bottom up, particularly by acknowledging the differential factors and approaches that were significant in different localities and base areas.

UNDERSTANDING REVOLUTION

The emergence of a history of the War of Resistance through essentially a series of case studies of base areas and border regions is bound to be a slow process, especially as an increasing amount of data is made available.[15] All the same, this strategy has already proved productive and has extended the understanding of the CCP's revolution to a greater range of base areas and a more complex series of social and political interactions.[16] Moreover, increased access to sources of new information, especially in archives and through interviews, has made it possible to combat continuing concerns about overgeneralization by permitting a series of even more local studies than might have been conceived during the 1980s. This focus is essentially a further stage in the development of studies of the War of Resistance, as attention moves not only from the national level of analysis to that of border region and base area, but also from base area to locality: to village and district,[17] or as in the case of this study, to county.

This greater concentration on locality contributes to the history of the War of Resistance in two significant ways. In the first place, it highlights the processes of social and political change. The identification and explanation of regional variation during the war is particularly useful for highlighting the wider political dimensions of change, but does not of itself reveal anything about the social and political interaction that brought together the CCP and local populations with such dramatic political consequences. There is a further need to disaggregate time and agency, and to focus on the relationship between them. In the second place, these local studies highlight not only the variability and contingency of revolution, but also different understandings of the CCP's revolutionary process. In particular it becomes possible to examine the extent to which there was a revolution during, rather than as a result of, the war.

In the various attempts to find a 'grand theory' for the War of Resistance there was a tendency to concentrate more on the motivation for change and on outcomes, rather than on social and political change as process. This is of course another form of overgeneralization, though one whose avoidance could only be assayed once a much greater number and range of sources had, as more recently, become available.[18] It is also a perspective on social and political change shared with much of the literature that defines and analyzes revolution more generally.[19]

The starting point for the identification of a revolution is usually the specifics of its resulting fundamental social and political transformation, rather than its forms of political behavior or types of political process. To match the search for 'grand theory' the study of revolutions usually proceeds from examination of the 'great revolutions,' and even when it extends beyond that square tends to be more concerned with set-piece events and ultimately successful revolutions. John Dunn's analysis of revolutions as 'very complex series of actions initiated in highly particular circumstances and at particular points of time' is most specific and quite typical in that sense.[20] Considerably less attention has been paid to the inner workings of revolutions, and revolution as process.[21] Jack Goldstone has recently drawn attention more centrally to the revolutionary process, but still deals with revolution defined by outcome, highlighting the process to, rather than of, revolution.[22] Though questions of agency have not been ignored, they have not in general been greatly emphasized.[23] In large part the concern with outcomes rather than process in the definition of revolution follows the strong imperative for structural perspectives on social and political change that still dominates the literature.[24]

In complete contrast, recent research on the War of Resistance has been more concerned to examine the processes of social and political change, and has contributed to the development of more dynamic and differentiated interpretations. In particular, research has highlighted the extent and the ways in which the process of political change was contested. CCP success is now no longer taken for granted, or at least not everywhere all the time. Resistance to the CCP was rarely absent, and not only from organized political interests and military forces but also from within local communities, even when the CCP might have seemed to be acting in the interests of those targeted for change. To meet these repeated uncertainties the CCP was frequently forced to adopt flexible and adaptive approaches to mobilization, whilst at the same time being prepared to act more coercively: to pay close attention not only to the military and political security of its position in a locality, but also the party's organizational control of its own lower levels.

Military and political control was the primary concern for the CCP as it started to establish itself in each locality. Base areas were established from the top down, with military and political support, or at least presence, taking precedence over concerns about social revolution. Programs of social change were not unimportant, especially in ensuring the maintenance of long-term support for the CCP-led base areas, and local movements for social reform often contributed to the initial support for local communist activities. However, for the most part in each locality there is an observable pattern in which the CCP's first concern was with the establishment of political order and institutions. Wei Hongyun, in a recent study of the Shanxi-Chahar-Hebei Border Region, has even suggested that these were two distinct and independent phases of CCP strategy, with the goals of social reform being pursued somewhat as an afterthought.[25] At least for the Shanxi-Chahar-Hebei Border Region these remarks accord totally with Hartford's earlier observations about the lack of a causal relationship between CCP success and its appeal to social reform during the war years,[26] as well as Esherick's concern to emphasize the potential impermanence of social reform at that time (though with respect to another part of North China).[27]

Recent research has also modified the role of the CCP as the sole agent of change during the War of Resistance. There were other actors who played more than just supporting roles, and in any case there may have been social changes at that time that did not contribute directly to the immediate or longer-term success of the CCP. The political environment included a range of other political parties, organized groups, and even other armies, from the Chinese Nationalist Party through the political and military forces of specific warlords, to secret societies, religious groups and bandits. Even the Japanese side of the conflict needs to be disaggregated: it not only included invading troops and colonial administrators but also local Chinese supporters in both civilian and military activities.

In Shanxi a major role in the development of resistance was played by the Sacrifice League (for National Salvation) during the first few years of the war. Established by Yan Xishan, the warlord of Shanxi, in 1936 through alliance with the CCP the Sacrifice League brought together a broad coalition of resistance to Japanese aggression—including Yan Xishan's followers, supporters of the Nationalist Party in the province, local elites, intellectuals and urban workers—and played a central role in both provincial politics and the activities of base areas in the province until 1940.[28] Also in Shanxi, the General Mobilization Committees were another part of the CCP's united front strategy: designed to rally broad support behind resistance, they were active for about the first year of the war.[29]

At the same time, the social environment included more than just an undifferentiated peasantry oppressed by a local ruling elite. For example, war caused large-scale migration, and many to be found in base areas of resistance were (temporarily) displaced urban young people and intellectuals, including many teachers and students who left the larger cities at Japanese invasion and in many cases returned to their home towns and counties. Commerce was fundamental to the operation of a successful, long-term base area and required local merchants and traders of various kinds to become involved. Recent research has particularly focused attention on greater sophistication in the analysis of the peasantry, as well as on the emergence of middle peasants—a social category used by the CCP to identify owner-cultivators of the land—as both a consequence of, and a major driver for social and political change during the war.[30]

As the following account of the Taihang Base Area indicates, though the political was far from absent in the determination of land redistribution during the war, explicit political campaigns of land reform appear to have been confined to the end of 1939 and beginning of 1940. Nor were they otherwise usual in the behind-the-lines base areas of North China. Instead, rent and interest controls were increasingly imposed on the leasing of land, with land redistribution following from sales and purchases for the most part, rather than outright confiscation and administrative allocation. The result was a rise in the numbers of those identified as middle peasants with, in general, landlords and rich peasants selling, and poorer peasants buying. A recent study of one village in the Shanxi-Chahar-Hebei Border Region describes the increased equality within villages that emerged without an increase in open class conflict between landlords and peasants as a 'silent revolution.'[31] However, it would be misleading to regard those identified as middle peasants as an undifferentiated sociopolitical category or new local ruling elite. Some were 'old' middle peasants who had already been owner-cultivators at the outbreak of the war; others 'new' middle peasants, who had bought land as landlords and rich peasants sold now uneconomic or unrealizable assets during the war; and others still became middle peasants (if in lesser numbers) because they were former landlords or rich peasants who had been persuaded or decided to sell.[32]

The CCP was certainly central to the processes of social and political change, but this does not mean that change can be explained exclusively in terms of the CCP's organizational or policy development: always a danger given that CCP internal documents are a necessary major source for research. While identifying CCP policy and organizational development must be part of any explanation, it is far from the whole story. Certainly, both can be seen to have changed quite regularly and often in response to the immediate environment, including local reactions to various initiatives and programs. Moreover, CCP policy and organization need to be distinguished from CCP political behavior in other ways (including the implementation of policy, and the internal and external operation of formal organization) as well as from popular or local reactions.

Base area as local government and base area as CCP organization were never identical, though interrelated and interdependent, not least by the CCP's own design as it attempted to build and maintain support through united front activities. In the Taihang case, the party's attempt to expand its own organization did not even occur until 1945 as victory beckoned. CCP membership in the Taihang Base Area, and presumably in other front-line base areas, remained relatively restricted throughout the war. There were sizeable numbers of CCP members in the various locally based units of the Eighth Route Army, and to a lesser extent under the North China Bureau and the border region government. However, CCP membership under the direction of the Taihang Base Area reached a maximum of 36,111 in November 1939; for the rest of the war years its more usual figure was just under 24,000 people.[33] There were party cadres who led the CCP's local organizations at village, subdistrict and county level, but there were many more cadres in local government and the mass organizations which supported it (for the mobilization of peasants, workers, young people and women) who were not members of the CCP.

For its part, the CCP was no more of a single, homogenous, political actor than the society it had emerged from and was very much part of. At the level of grand design the CCP may have been a revolutionary organization and it may have been trying to lay the foundations of a later party-state. However, during the war it was forced to expand and recruit, often at breakneck speed. The result was often much less than a Leninist model of organizational efficiency and ideological purity. Indeed, it could hardly have been otherwise given the imperatives of guerilla warfare and decentralized administration. Whilst there were clear chains of command that linked Yan'an and the CCP's headquarters, through base areas to county CCP committees and village branches, it would also be more surprising if the various units at the different levels of the CCP's organization and its associated networks within base areas did not act with a high degree of autonomy. One almost necessary consequence was the potential for political conflict, particularly between levels within the CCP organization at base area and county levels, and in the villages. Another was the high degree of parochialism that characterized CCP organization within a base area. As Joseph Esherick notes in his studies of the revolutionary process in the Shaanxi-Gansu-Ningxia Border Region, this parochialism was particularly acute at village level where political and social leadership were often indistinguishable (itself a major source of potential conflict with superior levels within the base area) but also extended to higher administrative levels where particularistic ties had led to recruitment.[34]

These observations about the CCP's policy and organizational environment highlight the complex series of interactions encompassing the CCP and local society that were at the heart of the processes of social and political change during the war. Nor for that matter is it necessary to regard the various social actors outside the CCP and its circle of influences—including not only peasants, but also local elites, workers, displaced urban youth and traders—as always only passive participants in the processes of social and political change. Change resulted from the interaction of different levels within the CCP and its networks, on the one hand, and different actors in society, on the other.

In short, a concern with process rather than outcome provides a different perspective on social and political change, and one which emphasizes agency and behavior rather than structure and inevitability. Change becomes less certain, more attenuated, nonlinear and almost certainly incremental. Although in retrospect the CCP has sometimes wanted to be seen as more omniscient and single-minded during the war, at the time it was frequently able to rejoice in its own ability to learn, both from its mistakes as well as its successes. For example, toward the end of the war, a Deputy Director of the Organizational Department of the Taihang Regional Party Committee of the CCP summed up his department's work since 1937 at the annual Organizational Work Conference. He detailed the department's successes and failings in some detail, with the latter receiving considerably more attention, and ended as he had begun by describing the 'cadre development history of the Taihang Region' as 'one immense and protracted learning process.'[35] It is a metaphor which can be extended further. Social and political change during the War of Resistance appears as a complex learning and unlearning process for everyone involved, in which the participants—the revolutionaries and the society around them alike—were affected by the dynamics of their social and political interactions and often underwent individual transformations themselves.

The process of social and political change necessarily often seems somewhat uncertain and paradoxical in retrospect, and certainly appeared no less ironic at the time. Odoric Wou has mischievously, but not without some justice, pointed out that there is rather too much emphasis on the peasantry in contemporary explanations of 'peasant revolutions.' He highlights the roles of intellectuals, urban workers and displaced students in the development of the CCP, as well as the centrality of the rural elite to the process of social and political change.[36] The pre-war experience of Li Xuefeng, the first Director of the CCP's Organization Department for the Taihang Base Area, and its leading cadre from February 1938 to the end of the war is a good individual example of Wou's argument. Li was the son of a gentry family and a graduate from Shanxi University who by the mid-1930s was an underground CCP organizer, first in Beiping and then later with the railway union on the Beiping-Wuhan Railway in southwest Hebei. As he freely admitted, at the end of 1937 when he first went to the Taihang Mountains 'We were city boys. What did we know? . . . Here I was, supposed to be developing base areas and I had no idea what they were, let alone how to set one up.'[37]

The CCP developed dramatically during the War of Resistance, but it often developed in apparently very contradictory ways. It was after all a secret organization throughout the war, as Deng Xiaoping (who was also based physically but not organizationally in the Taihang Base Area at this time, as Political Commissar of the 129th Division of the Eighth Route Army) was wont to stress at the time, when encouraging the development of the CCP's organizational strength.[38] Even when it was able to be more openly active, as in the Taihang Base Area after 1939, it still maintained some covert operations. That the process of change appeared equally as full of ironies and paradoxes to those who considered themselves revolutionaries at the time is also clear. Indeed, they often complained in a somewhat frustrated way about the contradictory directions they were supposed to take, as, for example, this cry from the heart delivered by a cadre at a conference convened to discuss the development of CCP branches during July 1942: 'Under these kinds of situation, it is impossible to build the party without changing class relations and destroying the feudal forces. But the problem is that today's party-building has to be carried out on the basis of developing the united front.'[39]

Equally paradoxically, whilst the War of Resistance is usually held to be an essential part of China's revolutionary process, the revolutionary aspects of social and political change at that time have often been minimized rather than highlighted by historians and commentators outside as well as inside China. In large part that emphasis reflects the CCP's practice during the war. Within China for most of the war years, and immediately after, the CCP was generally anxious to build a broad base of support and in consequence either temporarily abjured or downplayed its revolutionary intent. For example, by way of preparation for the coming war with Japan and an alliance with the Nationalist Party, the CCP had ostentatiously withdrawn its commitment to land reform. Similarly, after Japan's defeat and particularly before the outbreak of the Civil War the CCP often presented themselves as 'agrarian reformers.' Necessarily the CCP's perspectives of those times carried over into the Cold War. Outside China, later research has also tended implicitly to minimize the revolutionary nature of social and political change at that time particularly when comparison is made to the violence and cataclysm of the land reform movement of 1946 and after, as well as the even later developments of the post-1949 regime, all of which took place on a much larger scale across the whole country.

To the extent that the question is raised, there is thus a tendency for the War of Resistance to be regarded as revolutionary because the CCP's expansion and development in the base areas at that time led to the later assumption of national power in 1949. The social revolution brought by land reform in and after 1946, and the political revolution of the civil war and 1949, are seen to have resulted from the CCP's development of its base of support during the war. However, it is also possible that the events of the war years were themselves inherently revolutionary, and in many ways that is a more intriguing line of enquiry, not least because of what came later.

Creating a standard of revolutionary, as opposed to other forms of directed social change, such as reform, is generally not easy, and the difficulties are compounded in this context. As already noted, revolution is usually defined, albeit somewhat circularly, by the agenda of its revolutionaries and its outcomes. These goals are also usually system-wide rather than partial, as is the case where change is to be explained in a base area or locality. A more general problem is that from many perspectives revolution and reform exist along a continuum, rather than being clearly differentiated. Indeed, the differences are sometimes rhetorical rather than substantive. In the description of CCP politics, the terms are often used interchangeably (following the practice of the CCP itself) as, for example, is the case here in the description of the base area's program of social reform, which included the decidedly radical policy of land reform.

Along a continuum of social change, revolution might reasonably be located toward the extreme at which discontinuities with the past are greatest, where new political institutions are created and existing social structures overthrown. For this reason it is likely that revolution will appeal to new legitimacies. Revolution is also usually identified with sudden, dramatic change and coercion, though as recent research has shown it is not necessarily characterized by violence.[40] Reform, or at least some nonrevolutionary form of social change, might be more centrally located on the continuum, with the suggestion of more incremental change based on compromise with, and adjustment to, the status quo. For those reasons, reform is more likely to draw its legitimacy from the past or current society, however these might be imagined.

In disaggregating revolution as process rather than in terms of a 'particular point in time' some of these differences become even more finely balanced. Revolutionaries, over time, may be faced by the dilemma of needing to be both visionary and practical: incrementalism and compromise can just as easily become their stock in trade as political leaders. Revolution implies an acceleration in the speed of change but this too can be achieved incrementally. The element of compromise is crucial, but difficult to operationalize. Context is everything, with revolutionary change occurring relatively quickly, and with compromise where it does occur, occurring within the revolutionary agenda.

To a large extent the defining characteristics of revolution as process are then the ways in which the revolutionaries manage and respond to the dynamics of social change. In particular, revolutionaries seek not only to maintain but also to monopolize the agenda of change. Given that revolutionary rhetoric is more likely to be extreme and that it can lead to rising expectations amongst those mobilized, this can also lead to a potential conflict within the revolutionary process. The revolutionary imperative is both to create new social and political structures, and to homogenize and unify under the leadership of the revolutionary organization. In the case of the Taihang Base Area the CCP's difficulties in dealing with issues of female emancipation was a clear example of such a divided revolutionary imperative; but such tensions also manifested themselves within the CCP, between upper and lower levels of the organization.

Understanding the processes of social and political change in China during the War of Resistance is itself a long and complex process, that did not start and does not end with a study of the Taihang Base Area. The analysis of social and political change requires a series of studies that concentrate on interactions not only at the level of the base area, but also in a number of localities across all the various base areas, placing their development in the context of each base area as well as the entire war. This study of the Taihang Base Area concentrates on change in three adjacent counties—Liaoxian (Zuoquan), Wuxiang and Licheng—in addition to considering the development of the base area as a whole.

The county is a particularly convenient focus for analysis given the limits to information about specific villages, but it is rather more than that. The county is both the longest-lived level in China's administrative hierarchy[41] and the lowest administrative level within the state. It is the political forum where state and society have their most fundamental interactions in China. Even in wartime the county retained this function regardless of political and military control, whether by the Japanese, the resistance, or Chinese collaborators and control of county-level government remained an important determinant of village life. As a result those interactions are reflected to a large extent in county histories and county archives.

THE TAIHANG BASE AREA

The centrality of the Taihang Base Area to the CCP's development during the War of Resistance has been masked to a large extent by the subsequent politics of the PRC. In 1937, when the CCP sent only a couple of hundred of its regular soldiers eastward across the Yellow River to establish base areas in each of what later became the Shanxi-Chahar-Hebei and Shanxi-Suiyuan Border Regions, it sent some 6,000 under the command of Liu Bocheng into the later to become Taihang Base Area. This base area gave birth to the Shanxi-Hebei-Shandong-Henan Border Region, the largest and most complex of the border regions of the War of Resistance, and extended CCP influence out of the Taihang Mountains into South Hebei, North Henan and Shandong.

Of perhaps even greater significance, the mountain heart of the Taihang Base Area became the operational base for the CCP's front-line activities in North China against the Japanese. The field headquarters of the Eighth Route Army (the Communist forces in North China) under Peng Dehuai were located here; and various larger-scale operations, most notably the Hundred Regiments Campaign of 1940, were directed from here. Close by were the offices of the North China Bureau of the CCP's Central Committee under Yang Shangkun (from November 1938); as well as Deng Xiaoping, at this time Mao Zedong's loyal lieutenant and essentially his operational executive at the front-line, who was nominally (from January 1938) the Political Commissar of the Eighth Route Army's 129th Division, the main CCP military force in the base area and border region.

Many of those who were to hold senior leadership positions in the CCP after the establishment of the PRC served here during the War of Resistance. Indeed, a larger number of those who became members of the CCP Central Committee's Political Bureau after 1949 spent the war years in either the organizations of the Shanxi-Hebei-Shandong-Henan Border Region or its constituent parts, than in other border regions or base areas, including Yan'an.[42] The reputation of all base areas outside Yan'an was depressed during the era of Mao-dominated politics. However, the profile of the Taihang Base Area and the Shanxi-Hebei-Shandong-Henan Border Region was undoubtedly doubly disadvantaged by the association with many who came to be regarded as Mao's opponents, including among former members of the Political Bureau not only Deng, but also Peng Dehuai, Yang Shangkun, Bo Yibo, and Li Xuefeng.[43]

That history undoubtedly explains why the Shanxi-Hebei-Shandong-Henan Border Region has by no means been as well known as the other two more famous border regions of the War of Resistance: Shaanxi-Gansu-Ningxia, with Yan'an at its heart; and Shanxi-Chahar-Hebei, the first of the formal border regions, and the only one formally sanctioned by the national government. It also helps explain why interest in both the Taihang Base Area and the border region should grow again after 1978 under the leadership of Deng Xiaoping. As a result of his experience in the Taihang

Base Area he had become the central figure in a series of interconnected networks of power and influence, which became particularly crucial in the development of CCP politics during the 1970s and 1980s, including Deng Xiaoping's return from disgrace and the launch of the reform era.[44]

The origins of the Taihang Base Area and the Shanxi-Hebei-Shandong-Henan Border Region are often attributed to the activities of the troops led by Liu Bocheng, the 129th Division of the Eighth Route Army, which first established itself in Pingding County, just south of the Shijiazhuang-Taiyuan (ZhengTai) Railway, in October 1937.[45] Whilst the relationship between the 129th Division and the Border Region was clearly very close,[46] even at an early stage there were also other actors involved. These included the 344th Brigade of the 115th Division of the Eighth Route Army, which had accompanied the 129th Division on its entry to the area and which was to be associated with it ever after. Although the areas of Southwest Hebei, North Henan and Southeast Shanxi had not been major areas of CCP activity before the war, there were pockets of activists that could be built on. These included both railway workers and coal miners, especially in Southwest Hebei and North Henan, as well as one or two Anti-Japanese Resistance local governments formed as political order broke down with the invasion.

On the Shanxi side of the border region an even more crucial role was taken by the Sacrifice League, which under Bo Yibo and Rong Zihe[47] had political and military authority in Southeast Shanxi courtesy of Yan Xishan as Directors, respectively, of the 3rd and 5th Administrative Districts of the province: the former based on Qinxian (at the center of the Taiyue Base Area) and the latter at Changzhi, the major city of the region of the Taihang Base Area. Indeed, during 1937–1939 there were effectively two separate base areas that shared institutions: the Southeast Shanxi Base Area that was part of Yan Xishan's provincial administration; and the activities organized by the CCP's Hebei-Henan-Shanxi Provincial Committee and its successor bodies.

The CCP's Taihang Base Area grew out of a series of smaller base areas established at the end of 1937 in what is now Southeast Shanxi and Southwest Hebei, but which was then also included North Henan.[48] In the early months its main centers of activity were Pingding County; Zanhuang and Xingtai in Southwest Hebei; Shexian, in North Henan, and next door Cixian in Southwest Hebei; as well as Jincheng, in the southernmost part of Southeast Shanxi. There was also a branch office for the Hebei-Henan-Shanxi Provincial Committee in Qinxian, which was the genesis of the Taiyue Base Area. During 1938 and 1939 the Taihang Base Area's activities first expanded and then became more concentrated on the area north of a line between Handan and Changzhi, along the spine of the Taihang

Mountains in the counties of Pingding, Xiyang, Xingtai, Zanhuang, Heshun, Yushe, Wuxiang, Liaoxian, Licheng and Shexian, and these were to be its major areas of activity to the end of the war.

By 1944 the Taihang Base Area had grown to have an estimated population of 2.8 million people in its core areas and another 1.8 million in its guerilla districts, across 58 counties. This was by far the largest component of the Shanxi-Hebei-Shandong-Henan Border Region, which when formally established on 7 July 1941 (the deliberately chosen fourth anniversary of Japanese invasion) had claimed jurisdiction over some seven million people in 148 counties, organized into four regions: the Taihang, Taiyue, South Hebei and Hebei-Shandong-Henan Base Areas.[49] The area of operation for the border region was that bound on the south by the Yellow River, in the east by the Tianjin-Dezhou-Xuzhou Railway, in the north by the ZhengTai Railway and in the west by the Datong-Yuncheng (TongPu) Railway. Although at various times the border region was active in counties in Southeast Shanxi, North Henan and Southwest Hebei, as well as the western parts of Shandong, its major center of activities was in the Taihang Base Area. The Border Region Government was located here; and the centrality of the base area to the operation of the border region was recognized in its direct administration by both the Border Region Government and the Taihang Region CCP Committee.

Liaoxian, Wuxiang and Licheng Counties were at the heart of the Taihang Base Area both physically and organizationally. The area where the three counties meet in the north of Licheng, the east of Wuxiang and the south of Liaoxian was one of the most secure parts of any base area during the war. High in the Taihang Mountains, there were no Japanese or allied forces based here, and it was difficult for them to operate so far from their usual lines of communication and supply. Japanese troops only passed through this particular mountain area to any serious effect a few times during the war, though on one occasion in May 1942 a significant part of the base area's civil organization was destroyed in Liaoxian along with a large number of guerilla activists, including the Deputy Chief-of-staff of the Eighth Route Army, Zuo Quan.[50]

One result of this relative security was that the offices and headquarters of the Taihang Base Area and the Border Region Government, as well as of the 129th Division and the Eighth Route Army were all located in the mountain area where Liaoxian, Wuxiang and Licheng meet for most of the war. The headquarters of the Eighth Route Army, having spent just over a month elsewhere in Wuxiang during April and May 1938, and a few days in Licheng during July 1939, settled in first Zhuanbi Village and then Wangjiayu Village, Wuxiang, from July 1939 to mid-October 1940; and in Wujunsi Village and Matian, both in Liaoxian, from November 1940 to August 1945 save for twenty days back in Zhuanbi Village.[51] To take another couple of examples, the center of banking activity for the whole of the Shanxi-Hebei-Shandong-Henan Border Region was also located here with the offices of the South Hebei Bank in Xijing Village, Licheng, in the northern part of the county not far from where Deng Xiaoping later established an experimental agricultural village.

The extent to which the CCP successfully mobilized the local population of these three counties to fight in the war, for participation in various campaigns, as well as to join the CCP itself was quite remarkable. For example, in his speech toward the end of the war at the 1st Taihang Conference of Heroes in Killing the Enemy, Li Da specifically singled out all three as the base area's major sources of recruitment to guerilla and militia troops.[52] In agricultural production and peasant organization matters, these three counties were again the most active during 1940 and 1941 in persuading peasants to join the Patriotic Peasants Association, to join the armed forces and to engage in production.[53] By August 1941, the 39 counties in the Taihang Base Area had a total of 24,512 CCP members under the regional party committee.[54] These three counties had the largest memberships: almost a third of the regional total was to be found in Wuxiang (16 percent), Licheng (8.2 percent) and Liaoxian (7.2 percent).[55] During 1939–42, Liaoxian and Licheng were not subject to district-level administration but were directly administered by the regional CCP committee. Unsurprisingly, all three were experimental counties at various times for the testing and improving of policies.

Liaoxian, Wuxiang and Licheng Counties are the center of attention not simply because they were core areas in the base area (though that is clearly useful from the point of view of ensuring an adequate evidentiary base) but also because the experience of each was somewhat different throughout the war. Liaoxian was the administrative center of the entire base area; Wuxiang was the radical heart of the base area in its pursuit of social reform; and Licheng provided resistance to reform. All three were mountain counties, ranging in elevation from about 650 to 2200 meters, with most habitation normally at or about an elevation of 1000 meters. All three were overwhelmingly rural, with the majority of the population engaged in agriculture. However, in the two decades before the War of Resistance all three had been touched by modernization in various ways. Liaoxian had become a considerable commercial center for both coal and mountain goods, especially wool; Wuxiang had seen the concentration and corporatization of agriculture, and was a developing center of rural industries, notably textiles and iron. Licheng had next to no industry and remarkably for Shanxi no coal, but was somewhat wealthier. In additional contrast to Liaoxian and Wuxiang, it had a particularly small proportion of poor peasants and low land concentration, with high levels of education having developed an extensive system of modern schools.

Table 0.1 provides an indication of the relative size and wealth of each of these counties during the War of Resistance. Reliable comparative data are not available on the size of the population in each of the three counties at that time. However, there are separately reported data on the population of each county for different pre-war years, and these are presented in Table 0.1, together with the number of natural villages[56] in each county. Data to indicate the relative wealth of each county are even less reliable, both because of the war and because the local economy in this part of the Taihang Mountains had been in a severe depression since 1931. Some indication of the relative wealth of each locality may be gained from income per capita, and arable land productivity per *mu* for each of the three counties at the end of 1943, when the local economy was becoming somewhat stabilized.

Although Liaoxian, Wuxiang and Licheng were three counties on the eve of the War of Resistance, during the war they were further subdivided so that they became seven counties. A process of subdivision was common practice under the exigencies of guerilla war.[57] Liaoxian was divided into two in September 1941: Liaoxian and West Liaoxian (Liaoxi).[58] West Liaoxian was the northwesternmost part of the county around the county town, occupied by Japanese forces. The CCP-led regime in Liaoxian was centered on Tongyu Village and Matian township—the latter the site of Eighth Route Army headquarters for most of 1940–45—and the highest part of the Taihang Mountains south of the ZhengTai Railway. In September 1942 Liaoxian was renamed Zuoquan in memory of the CCP commander (Zuo Quan) killed there earlier that year.

Wuxiang was also separated into two, but earlier in July 1940: East Wuxiang (Wudong) and West Wuxiang (Wuxi).[59] East Wuxiang was the

Table 0.1 Relative Size and Wealth of Liaoxian, Wuxiang and Licheng Counties, 1943

County	Population (year as indicated)	Number of natural villages	Income per capita (*yuan*)	Land productivity (*dan* per *mu*)
Liaoxian	71,936 (1935)	451	7.09	1.23
Wuxiang	141,200 (1936)	875	6.48	1.02
Licheng	77,955 (1935)	301	7.83	1.43

Sources: Population—HZ p.2; WX p.39; LX p.642. Villages—ZOH p.1; WOH p.7; LOH p.1. Income and land productivity data for 1943—TGCG p.1335.

larger center of CCP activity in the county, concentrated in the mountains above a river valley. West Wuxiang was the smaller geographical part of the county away from the highest regions of the Taihang range and beyond the occupied central part of the county occupied after 1940 by Japanese forces. Because of its centrality to the Taihang Base Area, East Wuxiang is sometimes referred to as Wuxiang without a geographic descriptor and that practice will be followed here.

Licheng became three wartime counties: North Licheng (Libei), Licheng and Piancheng. Piancheng separated in March 1940,[60] North Licheng in November 1943.[61] North Licheng was the area of highest military security on the whole, though meetings were often held and organizations often operated out of the more accessible southern part of the county, around the county seat of Licheng itself. For example, the Conference of Senior Cadres from the Taihang, Taiyue and South Hebei Base Areas, which decided to establish a border region government was held in Licheng in April 1940. Licheng, Libei and Piancheng were the only counties in the Taihang Base Area without regular Japanese occupying forces during 1940–43.

SOCIAL AND POLITICAL CHANGE IN SOUTHEAST SHANXI

This study of the Taihang Base Area is concerned with the complex interrelationships of social and political change during the War of Resistance, particularly as these led to the foundations of CCP rule both locally and on a wider scale. It is based largely on newly available primary sources of information (discussed in the Bibliography) but those sources remain neither comprehensive nor ideal: errors of fact and interpretation necessarily remain. Nonetheless, the attempt has been made to retrieve a reliable narrative which focuses not only on events in Liaoxian (Zuoquan), Wuxiang and Licheng in some detail, but also on the development of the base area as a whole, not least to provide a wider context to the processes of change of which they were part.

As previously noted, Wei Hongyun and others have highlighted a range of relationships between the establishment of the base area's political order and the drive for social reform. This study is divided into two parts, each of which concentrates on one of those main aspects of change. The first part (Chapters 1–4) deals with the three stages that can be identified in the development of the base area's political order: the establishment of military presence and control by local forces; the maintenance of social stability and political order; and the development of the institutions and structures of CCP rule, including the control of lower levels by administratively higher levels within the CCP itself. Chapter 1 outlines the development of the Taihang Base Area generally during the War of Resistance. The following three chapters then each examines the specific experiences of Liaoxian, Wuxiang and Licheng in turn. Together these chapters chart how the base area was shaped by a series of relationships: between the resistance and the Japanese; encompassing Yan Xishan, the CCP and the Nationalist Party; within the CCP; within the local elite; and between the local CCP and various local elites. They also emphasize the importance of the county-level of government in local development.

As already indicated, the base area emerged from a number of different activities, and in Southeast Shanxi largely through cooperation with Yan Xishan. Even so in Liaoxian, Wuxiang and Licheng, local establishments opposed the Sacrifice League's activities and were reluctant to support resistance governments. The initial Japanese assault on Southeast Shanxi was halted in April 1938, and for a while led to the rapid expansion of resistance activities. However, local cooperation between Yan Xishan and the CCP failed increasingly after March 1939, and virtually came to a halt by October 1939. In the meantime, the Japanese return to the region, and particular the recapture of Changzhi in July 1939, enhanced a sense of crisis for all sides within the resistance. The end of 1939 and first three months of 1940 saw civil war and the CCP's seizure of power locally, with the exception of Wuxiang, where it was already in control. During 1940–43 the CCP was able to emphasize the institutional development of the base area, though beset not only by the Japanese military threat, but also by domestic problems of stability and occasionally resistance. As the Japanese presence in Southeast Shanxi decreased in intensity during and after 1943, so the CCP was more able not only to carry out its programs of social reform, but also to strengthen its own organizational capacities.

Chapter 2 details Liaoxian's political development, emphasizing the close relationship with the base area's leadership, particularly during the 1940s. The CCP had been a junior partner in the county's resistance coalition before the end of 1939, and accompanied the resistance government when it retreated to the south of the county, the area around Tongyu and Matian, in the middle of 1939 as the Japanese occupied the county town. After the CCP seized power in February 1940, this area became known as 'Little Yan'an' because of its concentration of leadership personnel and offices for the Eighth Route Army as well as the Taihang Base Area.

Chapter 3 considers Wuxiang, one of the few counties in the Taihang Base Area where the CCP had an organizational existence before 1937. An earlier peasant mobilization movement had met with some success and was an extremely useful basis on which to build the development of the CCP during the war. One consequence was that the CCP became the dominant partner in the local Sacrifice League, and came to control the county government at a relatively early stage for the Taihang Base Area. Another consequence was that the Wuxiang CCP was always in the lead of movements for social reform, and able to establish and maintain a degree of independence from the base area leadership.

Where both Liaoxian and Wuxiang had significant Japanese garrison forces to deal with, Licheng never had a permanent occupying Japanese force. All the same, as Chapter 4 describes, there was greater resistance to political institutionalization here than elsewhere, and the CCP even experienced difficulties in controlling its own organization. A major explanation of these problems lies in the relationship between the Licheng Returned Students Federation and the CCP. The Returned Students Federation had been formed by progressive members of the local elite, and had been instrumental in shaping the local resistance movement, the Sacrifice League and the county CCP. As the CCP in Southeast Shanxi reached for political power at the end of 1939 and beginning of 1940, in Licheng it turned against those of its members who were considered from privileged backgrounds—notably, intellectuals and local elite families—especially those who had cooperated through the Returned Students Federation and the Sacrifice League. These actions bequeathed serious organizational problems to the Licheng CCP for the rest of the war. Native leaders of the county CCP were regarded with suspicion by the base area organization, and outsiders were excluded from the informal networks of information.

The second part of this study of the Taihang Base Area (Chapter 5–8) deals with the CCP's attempts to introduce a program of social reform, in particular, the replacement of the old rural elite by new structures of wealth, status and power. It too identifies three stages in the development of the drive for social reform, which started with ideologically determined programs for change; led to several repetitions of peasant and local community resistance, followed by CCP adaptation; and then finally resulted in the development and maintenance of a social base of support for the Communist movement. Chapter 5 outlines the course of social reform in the base area as a whole. In particular it highlights the discussions within the CCP on the nature of class and revolution that came to focus on the role and revolutionary potential of the middle peasant. The following chapters describe in turn the drive for social reform in each of Liaoxian, Wuxiang and Licheng.

The pace and direction of social reform was very much determined by the wider political environment. During 1937–39 when the CCP was not in most places in direct control of local politics, and was in any case attempting to maintain a broad social coalition of resistance, exemplified by its relationship with Yan Xishan, social reform was far from high on the agenda. This changed dramatically with the civil war of 1939–40 and its associated tensions. The CCP concentrated its efforts on those social categories it considered more reliable—the poor and the landless—and turned its back on those from more privileged backgrounds—especially intellectuals and those who owned land—even where individuals had rallied to the Communist cause. In many places, county CCP leaderships initiated programs of radical land reform that physically attacked the wealthy and redistributed their land to the landless. Although there remains inadequate information on the scale of confiscation and reallocation, there is little doubt that land reform of this kind was widespread, not only in the Taihang Base Area, but also in the other Shanxi base areas.[62]

The local CCP did not readily abandon its championing of the poor and landless after March 1940 and the end of the civil war. Indeed, in some counties local leaders continued policies based on rural class conflict regardless. However, during 1940 the base area leadership of the CCP came to realize that such policies had been counterproductive as it needed the support of richer social categories in order to ensure supply for itself and the local population. Much confiscated land was returned, and for the remainder of the war years the CCP relied on campaigns of rent and interest reduction to achieve wealth redistribution (through encouraging landowners to sell land) rather than attempting direct land reform.

Even more reluctantly, as Chapter 5 details, the CCP came to rely on owner-cultivators rather than the landless and poor peasants to provide village leadership of social reform. The change of strategy was not achieved easily or quickly and was the subject of considerable inner-party debate on 'the middle peasant question' during 1942–44. It also led to tensions in villages amongst the more established owner-cultivators, upwardly mobile peasants, and poorer and landless peasants. Quite apart from their commitment to the underprivileged, many CCP members were ambivalent about privileging a form of land-owner, particularly those who, in some cases, they regarded as having become 'war profiteers' through their earlier land purchases. These discussions were complicated by the particularities of land-holding in the Taihang Mountains where land ownership was generally more widely distributed even than elsewhere in North China. Whilst there certainly were landlords and tenants, there was also a much higher than average proportion of owner-cultivators.

Chapter 6 considers the course of social reform in Liaoxian. It highlights the dramatic and long-term impact of rural class conflict during 1939–40; its advocacy of the middle peasant strategy; and the strength of the local women's movement. From December 1939 to March 1940 Liaoxian experienced the most violent and severe land reform in the Taihang Base Area for which the local CCP leadership was censured by Deng Xiaoping and Yang Xiufeng (for the nascent Border Region) and which resulted in almost equally as severe counterreactions. One of these was that the Liaoxian CCP's support for poor and landless peasants was replaced by an emphasis on owner-cultivators; a move which became a considerable source of resentment at village level. One explanation for the relatively high profile achieved by women's issues and organizations in Liaoxian would seem to have been the role played by the Patriotic Women's Association in the formation of the local county CCP.

In Wuxiang, as Chapter 7 details, the commercialization of agriculture before the war meant that land ownership had become highly concentrated, with remarkably few owner-cultivators by the standard of the Taihang region. Peasant poverty and dislocation as a result of that commercialization had been the fertile ground that had supported the CCP before 1937 and was to provide it with significant support locally. As a result social reform started even before a more dramatic period of violent land reform at the end of 1939 and beginning of 1940. Though more extreme solutions were set aside after 1940, social reform proceeded apace in Wuxiang though with somewhat less emphasis on the role of owner-cultivators than elsewhere in the base area. Indeed, the leadership of the Wuxiang CCP was generally in the forefront of opposition to the middle peasant strategy in the inner-party debate of that time.

In complete contrast, social reform in Licheng was to prove highly problematic and became inextricably bound up in the political conflicts within the CCP, and between the CCP and the local elite described in Chapter 4. As Chapter 8 outlines, social change in Licheng not only proceeded slower than in the base area as a whole, but also resulted in considerable resistance. An attempted armed uprising in October 1941 by the Sixth Trigram Movement was followed by a number of other insurrections, as well as more subtle subversion of the Licheng CCP's program for social reform.

At the center of this account of Liaoxian (Zuoquan), Wuxiang and Licheng, as well as the Taihang Base Area more generally, are concerns with the social basis of political change—the interactions of structures of wealth, status and political power. In particular, it is concerned with the extent to which local, landlord ruling elites were replaced by new social forces. Understanding and operationalizing concepts of wealth, status and political power in the North China of the late 1930s and early 1940s is not easy. The sources for study, though much improved, remain imperfect. A major concern is that most sources of information, as is indicated in the Bibliography at the end of this volume, emanate from the CCP. As a result, the history of those years is still dominated by the eventually victorious CCP and an account of the changing social structure based on its interpretation of class analysis. There is the danger of employing the

CCP's sociopolitical categorizations of the time as if they were a rigorous and precise articulation of class that reliably and predictably linked wealth, status and power. Equally, it would be misleading to equate the CCP's system of class analysis during the war years with that which came later.

The CCP's sociopolitical categorizations resulted from the operationalization of Marxist-Leninist notions of class. Though they often were (and still are to some extent) construed as a measure of wealth, the distinctions between categories are fundamentally political rather than economic. In most cases, the CCP's categories referred to positions in a generalized division of labor for the economy as a whole, with imputed political behavior for each category. Indeed, categories were created to highlight political rather than socioeconomic distinctions. There was little room for socioeconomic variation; and assumed attitude to the CCP was often the lodestone of political assessment.

During the war, individuals were allocated to a specific 'class status' that reflected their current sociopolitical position. Although the term used in Chinese for class status—*chengfen*—is often translated as 'class origin,' it has been rendered here as class status to differentiate the war-time usage from that applied after 1949. Under the PRC, individuals were classified according to both a 'class origin' (their current class position) and a 'class background' (their family background). Though the intention was that class origin should be mutable, the political reality was that these identifications came to categorize the individual for life (or at least until the early 1990s).[63] In contrast during the war, it was at least at first entirely possible for an individual to change their own class status as their position in the economic division of labor changed. Indeed, such differences were promoted as, for example, those with large landholdings were encouraged to surrender or sell property, and to become peasant small-holders, while the landless obtained land.

Even so, the designation of class status was inherently imprecise for both political and practical reasons. The changing, and sometimes rapidly changing, political situation meant there was a tendency for the CCP's categorization to be unsystematic and very much of the moment. In the Taihang region this tendency was reinforced by the CCP's previous low profile: those who were familiar with CCP procedures for the most part had little local knowledge, and vice versa. Moreover, there was pressure at any point in a given campaign for local cadres to identify some individuals as belonging to those social categories which were the subject of the campaign. For example, Philip Huang has highlighted the extent to which landlords were often few and far between and had consequently to be constructed.[64]

Practically, the definition of social categories required local cadres to exercise their judgment. The definition of middle peasant and poor peasant—two of the more important social categories in the CCP's operationalization of its wartime class analysis—both included an assessment of need. Judgment was also required in deciding how much land a peasant had to rent to be classified as a tenant or poor peasant, given that the practice was fairly universal. At least partly in consequence, assignation to class status was necessarily variable, not consistent, and usually determined by local factors; tendencies reinforced by spatial differences and decentralized command structures.[65] One consequence of these environmental influences is a constant need to inquire behind the rhetoric. For example, landlords were not always wealthier than peasants, even before the war started, even when assets as well as income were taken into account.[66]

Inconstancies in the operationalization of the CCP's sociopolitical categorization are also observable as the war proceeded, once again driven by political imperatives. As the 1940s progressed and the CCP's reform programs started to have an impact on social structures, many cadres preferred for various reasons to identify individuals by their previous rather than their current class status. In the Taihang Base Area, not all those designated as landlords at the beginning of the war were later permitted to change their class status even when they had surrendered most of their land, become in socioeconomic terms a peasant small-holder, and thrown their support behind the CCP cause.

On the other hand, the CCP's sociopolitical categories were those employed at the time, however imperfectly. They do not just chart the revolutionary process: in a very real sense they were the drivers of social and political change. Class analysis and class conflict were fundamental to the CCP's organizational and political behavior, which was why, in Philip Huang's words 'The Party maintained the fiction that class divides ran through each and every village.'[67] It determined how the CCP recruited as well as how it conceived and implemented social reform. Changes in its class analysis went together with the development of its program of social reform and reflected the adaptive process of policy implementation entailed in that attempt to create revolution.

At the start of the War of Resistance, the CCP's class analysis derived from its experience in developing the Jiangxi Soviet during 1931–34, and later refined in North Shaanxi during 1935–36.[68] This sociopolitical classification usually extended to about six broad land-related categories, and a range of almost infinitely adaptable occupational categories, some of which overlapped with each other as well as with the land-related categories.

The land-related categories played the central role in the CCP's drive for social reform and included landlords, rich peasants, middle peasants, poor peasants, and tenants. There were also the various categories of the landless, which included not only farm hands but also (though variably) tenants and different kinds of workers. The two fundamental dimensions for assessing land-related class status were whether an individual rented land or was a rentier, whether an individual hired labor or sold their labor for wages.

There were a number of different categories of landlord, though distinctions were not always sustained either politically or analytically. Generally, a landlord was defined as someone who lived entirely on rents and other income, and did not personally engage in labor. Distinctions were often made between local and absentee landlords. Further elaborations were also made at various times on political grounds to identify 'enlightened' landlords, who had supported the CCP cause in some way or who had surrendered or sold land; and landowning 'traitors,' who had either fled or sided with the Japanese, and so placed themselves in a position where the CCP felt justified in confiscating and redistributing their land.

Particularly as the 1940s progressed, the category of landlord was identified alongside and combined with that of managerial landlord. The category of managerial landlord essentially covered a number of possibilities, all of which depended similarly on the work of others for their living. A managerial landlord might be someone who enagaged in the management of their own estate, or have other commercial and industrial interests; or it might be someone who managed the estate of someone else.

A rich peasant was defined as someone who engaged in agriculture or other labor, but had excess land to rent out. A middle peasant was a self-sufficient owner-operator, who did not either rent land out or work the land of others. At times this category was reconfigured in terms of a need to rent land, rather than the activity itself. By the end of the war in the Taihang Base Area many of those who were described as middle peasants were not only renting out land but also engaged to work on the land of others.

A poor peasant usually owned some land, but not enough to support a family, and in consequence rented land to make up the difference. A tenant was someone who owned no land, but had recognized rights of cultivation on an annual, long-term or permanent basis to land owned by others. Tenants paid rent on all land cultivated. A farm laborer also owned no land, but hired out their labor, either as a regular hired hand or for a contracted period.

To these land-related categories were added several that were more self-explanatory and described occupations, though even these categories were often flexibly operationalized. The category of 'worker,' for example, which had a certain political mission within the communist movement, was not only applied to industrial workers, but also to artisans, handicraft workers, shepherds and farm laborers, though sometimes those individual social categories were also used. Occupational categories also included traders and peddlers; vagrants (often a euphemism for bandits); cadres and officials; and soldiers.

There was also a class status of intellectual, which usually referred to teachers, but was sometimes extended to include anyone with more than rudimentary schooling. To confuse matters further, the category of 'intellectual' was also used sometimes to refer to members of the former landlord-gentry (because they were previously the only members of society to be educated), especially when they were supportive of either the resistance or the CCP. And to confuse even further, the social category of intellectuals was also sometimes subdivided according to the class background of their original family.

The CCP assigned political roles to each of these categories at different stages during the War of Resistance, depending on its assessment of the situation, and planned its responses and interactions accordingly. Landlords and rich peasants, for example, were not always completely discriminated against, despite in some sense being the most obvious targets for the CCP's social mobilization. Peng Tao, director of the Taihang Base Area's Propaganda Department, described the evolution of CCP policy toward landlords and rich peasants in February 1943.[69] Before mid-1939 the CCP had only opposed 'power-holding' landlords, that is, not those prepared to support resistance government. From October 1939 to May 1940 it had openly attacked landlords and rich peasants generally as tensions with Yan Xishan worsened and eventually led to civil war. After the end of this conflict the CCP tried to establish a new modus vivendi with landlords and rich peasants, largely because of the military and economic pressures it faced. Landlords could not join the CCP but could support the national cause, though this became increasingly conditional as the war progressed. From May 1942 the CCP moved again against landlords and overexploitative rich peasants, though this time its pressure came in a less open and violent form through more mediated rent and interest reduction campaigns.

The middle peasant emerged as the most important of the CCP's sociopolitical categories during the War of Resistance, and is in many ways also the most interesting. The Taihang Base Area's social structure changed dramatically during the war. On the eve of war, landlords and rich peasants dominated the Taihang region, if not as overwhelmingly as elsewhere in North China. By 1945, peasant small-holders predominated. In terms of the CCP's social categories, almost two-thirds of landholding households in the Taihang Base Area were now designated as middle peasants who owned almost two-thirds of all farmland. The proportion of the base area's landholders who were designated as middle peasants had roughly doubled, as had their proportion of owned farmland. Moreover, almost all those who had previously been poor and landless peasants had now become landowners (albeit mostly on a small scale) and labor-for-hire was in extremely short supply.

The turning point in this transformation was the CCP's decision during 1942 to build social reform around a middle peasant rather than a poor peasant standard; and to encourage middle peasant village leadership, rather than as previously, relying on newly recruited poor and landless peasants. During 1940–42 poor peasants and workers had proved politically ineffectual in leadership roles. Unlike their middle peasant successors, many could not afford time away from production; were illiterate and so presented difficulties to and for the CCP's organization; and clashed too easily with local landlords and rich peasants. Both collectively and as individuals the base area CCP had found poor peasants difficult to control.[70]

The middle peasant strategy allowed the CCP to achieve its goals of mobilizing support for resistance government at the same time as the party organization itself developed a social base of support. By concentrating its social reform program on the middle peasant, the CCP was able to meet the social and economic aspirations of those who were long-term owner-cultivators; and to encourage poor peasants, tenants and landless laborers with the prospect of becoming peasant small-holders themselves. It was also able to some considerable extent to reassure those who had previously been landlords and rich peasants that they too had an economic and even political future because of their shared interests in landownership with the middle peasant. Moreover, the concept of the middle peasant played no small role in uniting party cadres anxious, and sometimes overanxious, for social change. Though a middle peasant strategy may not have delivered the maximum some CCP cadres were advocating, at least it maintained the momentum of social reform without jeopardizing the war effort.

The success of the middle peasant strategy is also interesting because of its consequences for the development of the CCP's class analysis. The middle peasant was always a particularly imprecise category, and its application was frequently contested particularly on whether and to what extent a middle peasant could be a rentier or hirer of labor. Moreover, during the war the notion of middle peasant came to include a number of significant subgroups, with different backgrounds, expectations, observed behaviors and assumed political outlooks. Increasingly the CCP found itself wanting to differentiate social categories according to previous as well as current class status. As Chapter 5 details, this led to a variety of social categories of middle peasant according to whether an individual had previously come from an owner cultivator, landlord or rich peasant, or landless or poor peasant background. There is a direct line of practice here that stretches through the Land Reform campaign of 1946, which also built on the middle peasant strategy in a similar manner,[71] to the post-1949 system of class analysis based on class origin and class background.

Tables 0.2–0.4 provide an overview of the impact of the CCP's drive for social reform in the Taihang region during the war based on CCP survey data (and using the CCP's social categories) at every date for which information is available. The data for each year are not strictly comparable: they are based on different samples; moreover, the base area was contracting to the end of 1942 and expanded again from the middle of 1943. However, the figures presented are based on large to extremely large samples

Table 0.2 Landowning Households in the Taihang Region, 1936–1945 (percentage of all households owning land, by social category)

Social Category	Date 1936	1941	1942	1943	1944	1945
Landlord	2.8	2.7	2.4	2.4	2.2	1.8
Rich peasant	7.4	8.1	6.9	6.8	6.5	6.3
Middle peasant	34.8	43.5	46.8	48.0	57.4	64.4
Poor peasant	50.3	40.4	42.1	38.8	31.8	26.0
Tenant	1.3	1.5	1.0	1.1	0.5	0.4
Artisan	0.7	2.4		0.7		
Trader	1.0	1.4		0.7		0.2
Vagrant	0.3	0.1		0.2		
Other	1.0		0.8	1.3	1.6	0.8

Sources: Figures for 1936 are from a survey of 24,768 households in 159 villages across 22 counties; for 1941, from a survey of 9,055 households in 53 villages; for 1942 from a survey of 2,177 households in 15 villages across 12 counties; for 1943, from a survey of 18,671 households in 148 villages across 16 counties; for 1944 are recalculated combining two identical surveys—one of 44 villages, the other of 15 villages, differentiated according to when villages had commenced campaigns of rent and interest reduction—of 11,405 households in 59 villages across 39 counties; and for 1945, from a survey of 5,880 households in 29 villages across 16 counties. Those for 1936, 1941, and 1943 may be found in TJSD1; those for 1942, 1944 and 1945 may be found in TJSD2: p.1349 (1936), pp.1374–75 (1941), p.1408 (1942), p.1381 (1943), p.1429 (1944), and pp.1436–37 (1945).

drawn from all districts of the base area, including those parts which were both secure and not so secure. Figures for 1936 are based on a survey undertaken in 1943 when interviewees were asked to recall their class status seven years earlier. Because the distinction between landlord and managerial landlord was rarely maintained in practice at the time, and is only partly reflected in available data, categories have been combined.

Table 0.2 provides data on social change in terms of households. It is based on those households owning land and does not include households not owning land, or indeed the total population involved. These are particularly important distinctions given that it is estimated that wages accounted for a third of rural gross income in the Taihang region at the beginning of the war, and that it can therefore be assumed that a substantial proportion of both households and the population were wage-earning, nonlandowners.[72]

Table 0.3 provides an overview of changes in landownership by CCP social category for the Taihang region during the war, again for every year that data are available.

In general, 1937–45 saw a decline in the numbers of those designated as landlord and poor peasant households, and a dramatic increase in the number of those designated as middle peasants. The pattern of land-hold-

Table 0.3 Landownership in the Taihang Region, 1936–1944 (percentage of farmland, by social category)

Social Category	Date 1936	1941	1943	1944
Landlord	26.3	16.8	12.9	5.3
Rich peasant	23.4	19.4	16.6	13.4
Middle peasant	31.4	43.1	47.0	65.0
Poor peasant	17.6	19.7	21.3	15.4
Tenant	0.8	0.4	0.7	0.1
Artisan	0.1	0.3	0.5	
Trader	0.2	0.4	0.6	
Others			0.4	0.8

Sources: Figures for 1936 are from a survey of 24,768 households in 159 villages across 22 counties; for 1941, from a survey of 9,055 households in 53 villages; for 1943, from a survey of 18,671 households in 148 villages across 16 counties; for 1944 are recalculated combining two identical surveys—one of 44 villages, the other of 15 villages, differentiated according to when villages had commenced campaigns of rent and interest reduction—of 11,405 households in 59 villages across 39 counties. Those for 1936, 1941, and 1943 may be found in TJSD1; that for 1944 may be found in TJSD2: p.1349 (1936), pp.1374–75 (1941), p.1381 (1943), and p.1429 (1944).

ing also changed with middle peasants coming to replace landlords as the social category owning the most land. However, leaving aside problems of categorization, there are a number of features of change that are somewhat masked by these statistics. One is that though they suggest a fairly even set of trends there were quite severe variations over time, in different parts of the base area, and even in the same part of the base area as between militarily secure and contested villages.

Over time one of the most significant variations was in the size of the middle peasantry, which grew in landholdings during 1938–39, decreased somewhat during 1940–41, grew a little again in both landholdings and numbers during 1942 and then expanded dramatically during 1944–45. The size and distribution of landholdings and hence class status depended largely on land quality, and the extent of pre-war commercialization of agriculture. The CCP's programs of social reform were necessarily confined to the secure parts of the base area, where their impact was more acutely felt. The figures in these tables are averaged for the whole base area: a series of distributions that almost certainly never occurred anywhere specifically.

Another and probably even more important aspect of social change masked by the figures is the extent to which the average land-holdings for each of the CCP's social categories during the war did not remain constant. Table 0.4 uses CCP survey data for 1936, 1941, early 1943, and 1944 to calculate the average landholding for each of the party's social categories at those times.

Even allowing that land is of variable agricultural quality and value, Table 0.4 clearly indicates a general equalization of landholdings during the war. At the same time, by far its most remarkable conclusion is that there was an overall decrease in average landholdings for each of the CCP's social category. This decrease seems somewhat paradoxical given the CCP's discussion and adoption of its middle peasant strategy. However, more peasants benefited from these changes even though the size of average landholdings for each social category decreased, because the total number of those owning land increased so dramatically.

Table 0.4 refers to aggregate data for households owning land, and not to the total population of the base area. The aggregate data for all categories except that of landlords reflects the significant upward social mobility that resulted from the CCP's program of social reform. In particular, in terms of the CCP's categories, some middle peasants became rich peasants; poor peasants and tenants became middle peasants. Even more dramatically, landless peasants and laborers became poor peasants, and some even became middle peasants. Overall, there was a huge influx of those who had previously been landless into the ranks of landownership.

The aggregate data that show decreased average landholdings for the categories of landlord and rich peasant also reflect household division.

Table 0.4 Average Landholding by Social Category in the Taihang Region, 1936 and 1944 (*mu* per household)

Social Category	Date 1936	1941	1943	1944
Landlord	185.1	135.3	56.8	25.9
Rich peasant	62.9	30.1	15.1	24.9
Middle peasant	17.9	12.5	10.9	12.8
Poor peasant	6.9	6.2	6.1	5.6
Tenant peasant	9.1	3.3	7.1	2.5

Source: Calculated from information in TJSD1, and TJSD2: p.1349 (1936), pp.1374–75 (1941), p.1381 (1943), and p.1429 (1944).

Whilst it was certainly the case that many of those designated as landlords and rich peasants sold some off their land, either voluntarily or under the pressure of rent and interest reduction campaigns, they also took other evasive action. In particular, many divided their landholdings and households within the same family.

The aggregate data that show decreasing average landholdings for tenants reflect both the transformation of the landless into peasant smallholders, and well as that as social categories, tenant peasants and landless laborers usually did not own land.

More precise analysis of the impact of these changes is unfortunately not available. There are inadequate data on the exact numbers involved. In particular, the precise numbers of those previously landless who became landowners during the war is not known. However, at the time it was estimated that in the secure parts of the Taihang Base Area about two-thirds of all farm laborers became landholding peasants during 1940–42 alone.[73] Significantly, too, there is insufficient information about the transfers between various social categories.

The account that follows suggest that the experience of the Taihang Base Area, and Liaoxian, Wuxiang and Licheng in particular, during the War of Resistance was inherently revolutionary. A process of revolutionary political change had started in late 1937 and 1938, before even the CCP was the ruling authority in each locality. At that time the CCP in each county had been part of a coalition that opposed the former local elite and established a form of resistance government after removing the local establishment. The years 1939–40 saw not only a civil war but a political revolution that established CCP rule at county level throughout the base area. Thereafter, new political institutions were created, including a system of elected village and county congresses and governments, under the supervision of the CCP and through its organization. Moreover, as the war progressed, in contrast to the pre-war years, mass mobilization and the rhetoric of mass politics came to dominate public life.

Socially, in each of these three counties there was a significant redistribution of landownership during the war from those who were considered to have had a surplus to those who had little or none. Although circumstances were different in all three counties, in each the social and political structures that had sustained the previous local elites had been replaced: peasant small-holders now dominated villages, and the CCP controlled county governments. In general, where compromise occurred—as in the emergence of policy on landownership—it was within the revolutionary agenda, rather than representing adjustments to the pre-war status quo. Often much to their surprise, landlords and rich peasants who cooperated with the CCP were not exempt from the consequences of the new policy.

The process of change to 1945 certainly did not achieve all that later came about, but it nonetheless represented revolutionary social and political change compared to the pre-war years. For the CCP as the PRC enters its second fifty years this may not be an unimportant consideration. The history of the War of Resistance presents the CCP with a source of revolutionary traditions on which to draw, should it so desire.

NOTES

1. For early contemporary accounts that a program of social and economic reform would be the best possible vehicle for popular mobilization, see comments attributed to Mao Zedong (p.159) and Peng Dehuai (p.186) in Gao Kefu *Dibalujun zaiShanxi* [The Eighth Route Army in Shanxi] Shanghai, Xinhua shudian, 1938. Ren Bishi in early 1938 argued that economic reform would be 'the surest way of encouraging the masses to organize for resistance (against the Japanese)' in 'Shanxi kangzhande huiyi' ['A Memoir of the Resistance in Shanxi'] in *Ren Bishi xuanji* [Selected Works of Ren Bishi] Beijing, Renmin chubanshe, 1987, p.136. Originally published in *Xinhua ribao* [New China Daily] 13 January 1938. Recent confirmations of this view by later CCP and Chinese historians include: Gong Yuzhi 'Guanyu KangRi zhanzheng shi yanjiu' ['Research on the History of the War of Resistance'] in *Zhonggong dangshi yanjiu* [Research on CCP History] No.6 1995, p.7; and Wei Hongyun *KangRi zhanzheng yu Zhongguo shehui* [The War of Resistance to Japan and Chinese Society] Shenyang, Liaoning renmin chubanshe, 1997.

2. John W Lewis (ed) *Peasant Rebellion and Communist Revolution in Asia* Stanford, Stanford University Press, 1974; Joel Migdal *Peasants, Politics and Revolution: Pressures toward Political and Social Change in the Third World* Princeton, New Jersey, Princeton University Press, 1974; and Jeffrey Paige *Agrarian Revolution* New York, Free Press, 1975.

3. The most comprehensive account in English of the War of Resistance to Japan is Lyman Van Slyke 'The Chinese Communist Movement during the Sino-Japanese War, 1937–45' in *The Cambridge History of China* Vol. 13, Republican China, 1912–1949, Part II, Cambridge, Cambridge University Press, 1986, Chapter 12, p.609. On China's peasant movements more generally, see: Lucien Bianco 'Peasant Movements' in *The Cambridge History of China* Vol. 13, Republican China, 1912–1949, Part II, Cambridge, Cambridge University Press, 1986, Chapter 6, p.270.

4. Excellent overviews of the literature on the CCP's experience in the War of Resistance and China's twentieth-century revolutions may be found in: Kathleen Hartford and Steven M Goldstein 'Introduction: Perspectives on the Chinese Communist Revolution' in Kathleen Hartford and Steven M Goldstein (eds) *Single Sparks: China's Rural Revolutions* New York, M E Sharpe, 1989, p.3; Odoric Y K Wou *Mobilizing the Masses: Building Revolution in Henan* Stanford, Stanford University Press, 1994, 'Introduction'; and Joseph W Esherick 'Ten Theses on the Chinese Revolution' in *Modern China* Vol. 21 No. 1, January 1995, p.45.

5. Chalmers Johnson *Peasant Nationalism and Communist Power: The Emergence of Revolutionary China 1937–1945* Stanford, Stanford University Press, 1962. A counter-critique may be found in Donald G Gillin '"Peasant Nationalism" in the History of Chinese Communism' in *Journal of Asian Studies* Vol. 23 No. 2, 1964, p.269.

6. Mark Selden *The Yenan Way in Revolutionary China* Cambridge, Massachusetts, Harvard University Press, 1971. Later revised as Mark Selden *China in Revolution: The Yenan Way Revisited* New York, M E Sharpe, 1995. A partial counter-critique may be found in Chen Yung-fa: *Yan'an de yinying* [Yan'an's Shadows] Taipei, Academica Sinica, Institute of Modern History, 1990. The later reflections of both Johnson and Selden on their 'debate' may be found in: Chalmers Johnson 'Peasant Nationalism Revisited: The biography of a book' in *The China Quarterly* no.72, 1977, p.766; and Mark Selden 'Yan'an Communism Reconsidered' in *Modern China* Vol.21 No.1, January 1995.

7. Tetsuya Kataoka *Resistance and Revolution in China: The Communists and the Second United Front* Berkeley, University of California Press, 1974. A critique may be found in: Chen Yung-fa *Making Revolution: The Communist Revolution in Eastern and Central China 1937–1945* Berkeley, University of California Press, 1986, p.6 ff.

8. Ralph Thaxton *China Turned Rightside Up: Revolutionary Legitimacy in the Peasant World* New Haven, Connecticut, Yale University Press, 1983. For a counter-critique, see: Chen Yung-fa and Gregor Benton *Moral Economy and the Chinese Revolution* Centre for Anthropology and Sociology, University of Amsterdam, 1986.

9. Lucien Bianco *Origins of the Chinese Revolution, 1915–1949* Stanford, Stanford University Press, 1971, especially pp.148–159. Originally published as *Les Origines de la révolution chinoise, 1915–1949* Paris, Editions Gallimard, 1967.

10. Most notably: 'The Chinese revolution is often considered the greatest peasant revolution in history, even the archetype of peasant revolution. Certainly the Chinese Communists could not have won power without the peasant armies and the support of so many villagers. Yet without the Communists the peasants

would, quite simply, never have conceived the idea of a revolution' in Lucien Bianco 'Peasant Movements' in *The Cambridge History of China* Vol. 13, Part II, Cambridge, Cambridge University Press, 1986, Chapter 6, p.270. See also: Lucien Bianco 'Peasant Responses to CCP Mobilization Policies, 1937–1945' in Tony Saich and Hans van de Ven (ed) *New Perspectives on the Chinese Communist Revolution* New York, M E Sharpe, 1995, p.175.

11. In North China these have included a number of multivolume collections, most notably: Jin Ji Lu Yu bianqu caizheng jingjishi bianjizu and Shanxi, Hebei, Shandong, Henan sheng danganguan (ed) *KangRi zhanzheng shiqi JinJiLuYu bianqu caizheng jingjisji cailiao xuanbian* [Selected Documents on Economy and Finance in the JinJiLuYu Border Region during the War of Resistance against Japan] Beijing, Zhonggong caizheng jingji chubanshe, 1990 [CJZX]; Shanxisheng danganguan (ed) *Taihang dangshi ziliao huibian* [Collection of Materials on the History of the Party in the Taihang Base Area] Taiyuan, Shanxi renmin chubanshe, 1989 and continuing [TDZH]; ShaanGanNing bianqu caizheng jingjishi bianxiezu, Shaanxisheng dang'anguan [The Editorial and Writing Group of the History of the Finances and Economy of the ShaanGanNing Border Region and the Shaanxi Provincial Archives] *KangRi zhanzheng shiqi Shaanganning bianqu caizheng jingji shiliao zhaibian* [A collection of historical materials on the finances and economy of the ShaanGanNing Border Region during the resistance war period] Xi'an, Shaanxi Renmin Chubanshe, 1982; Gansusheng shehui kexueyuan lishi yanjiushi [Gansu Social Science Academy, History Research Department] (ed) *Shaanganning geming genjudi shiliao xuan* [A collection of historical materials on the ShaanGanNing revolutionary base area] Lanzhou, Gansu Renmin Chubanshe, 1982 and continuing; Zhongyang dang'anguan [Central Party archives] *ShaanGanNing bianqu kangri minzhu genjudi: wenxian juan* [The ShaanGanNing Border Region—an Anti-Japanese democratic base area: collected documents] Beijing, Zhonggong Dang'an Chubanshe, 1990 and continuing; Party History Research Center, CCP Shanxi Provincial Committee *JinSui Geming Genjudi Dashiji* [A Chronicle of the JinSui Revolutionary Base Area] Shanxi Renmin Chubanshe, 1989; Shandong sheng dang'an guan [Shandong Provincial Archives] (ed) *Shandong geming lishi dang'an ziliao xuanbian* [Selections from the Shandong revolutionary history archival materials] Jinan, Shandong renmin chubanshe, 1986 and continuing; Zhonggong Shandong shengwei dangshi ziliao zhengji yanjiu weiyuanhui [Shandong Communist Party history materials Compilation and Research Committee] *Shandong dangshi ziliao* [Shandong Party history materials] Jinan, 1983 and continuing; JinChaJi Bianqu caizheng jingji shi bianxiezu, Hebei sheng danganguan, Shanxi sheng danganguan *JinChaJi bianqu caizheng jingjishi ziliao xuanbian* [Selected Materials on the Financial and Economic History of the JinChaJi Border Region] Tianjian, Nankai daxuechubanshe, 1984; Taihang geming genjudishi zongbian weihui (ed) *Taihang geming genjudi shiliao congshu* Taiyuan, Shanxi renmin chubanshe, 1991 and continuing.

12. The group at Stanford included Chen Yung-fa, Eastern and Central China; Kathleen Hartford, the Shanxi-Chahar-Hebei Border Region; and David Paulson, the Shandong Base Area. See: Chen Yung-fa *Making Revolution: The Communist Revolution in Eastern and Central China 1937–1945* Berkeley, University of Califor-

nia Press, 1986; Kathleen Hartford *Step-by-Step: Reform, Resistance and Revolution in the Chin-Ch'a-Chi Border Region* Stanford, Stanford University, PhD diss., 1980; and David Paulson *War and Revolution in North China: The Shandong Base Area, 1937–1945* Stanford, Stanford University, PhD diss., 1982.

13. Elizabeth J Perry *Rebels and Revolutionaries in North China, 1845–1945* Stanford, Stanford University Press, 1980. Another early study that adopted a similar disaggregated perspective was: Carl E Dorris 'Peasant Mobilization in North China and the Origins of Yenan Communism' in *The China Quarterly* No. 68, December 1976, p.697. While such approaches were generally not visible within the PRC, there were a few researchers experimenting in this direction. See, for example: Huang Xuanwen *Xiaohe fengyun: Henansheng Neihuangxian Qiankoucun* [Storm on the River: Qiankou Village, Neihuang County, Henan Province] Henan renmin chubanshe, 1976; and Dong Qian *Meiyou renmin de shijie—weikun Qinyuan tongxun* [A world without people—the story of the seige of Qinyuan] Beijing, Renmin chubanshe, 1979.

14. Kathleen Hartford and Steven M Goldstein (eds) *Single Sparks: China's Rural Revolutions* New York, M E Sharpe, 1989.

15. An overview of this general approach, and a summary of research to date may be found in Feng Chongyi & David S G Goodman (ed) *North China at War: the Social Ecology of Revolution, 1937–1945* Lanham, Maryland, Rowman & Littlefield, 2000, especially Feng and Goodman 'Explaining Revolution,' and Gregor Benton 'Comparative Perspectives: North and Central China in the Anti-Japanese Resistance.'

16. Notably: Chen Yung-fa *Making Revolution: The Communist Movement in Eastern and Central China, 1937–1945* Berkeley, University of California Press, 1986; Odoric Y K Wou *Mobilizing the Masses: Building Revolution in Henan* Stanford, Stanford University Press, 1994; and Li Xiangqian 'KangRi zhanzheng yu Zhongguo xibei nongcun shehuide biandong' ['The Transformation of Village Society in Northwest China during the War of Resistance to Japan'] in Feng Chongyi and Gu Deman (ed) *Huabei Kang Ri genjudi yu shehui shengtai* [The Social Ecology of Base Areas in North China during the War of Resistance to Japan] Beijing, Dangdai Zhongguo chubanshe, 1998, p.25.

17. Most notably: Edward Friedman, Paul Pickowicz and Mark Selden *Chinese Village, Socialist State* New Haven, Connecticut, Yale University Press, 1991; Joseph W Esherick 'Deconstructing the Construction of the Party-State: Gulin County in the Shaan-Gan-Ning Border Region' in *The China Quarterly* No.140, December 1994, p.1052; Joseph W Esherick 'Revolution in a Feudal Fortress: Yangjiagou, Mizhi County, Shaanxi, 1937–1948' in *Modern China* vol.24 no.4, October 1998; and Pauline B Keating *Two Revolutions: Village Reconstruction and the Cooperative Movement in Northern Shaanxi 1934–1945* Stanford, Stanford University Press, 1997.

18. Tony Saich 'The Chinese Communist Party and the Anti-Japanese War Base Areas' in *The China Quarterly* No.140, December 1994, p.1000.

19. A comprehensive overview of revolutionary theory may be found in Farrokh Moshiri 'Revolutionary Conflict Theory in an Evolutionary Perspective' (p.4) and Ted Gurr and Jack A Goldstone 'Comparisons and Policy Implications'

(p.324) both in Jack A Goldstone, Ted Robert Gurr, and Farrokh Moshiri (ed) *Revolutions of the Late Twentieth Century* Boulder, Colorado, Westview Press, 1991.

20. John Dunn *Modern Revolutions: an introduction to the analysis of a political phenomenon* Cambridge, Cambridge University Press, 1972, p.232.

21. For comment on this, see, particularly: Krishan Kumar *Revolution* London, Weidenfeld and Nicholson, 1971, p.75.

22. Jack A Goldstone *Revolution and Rebellion in the Early Modern World* Berkeley, University of California Press, 1991. Goldstone highlights the coincidence and interaction of a state crisis, a disunited elite, and mass mobilization in leading to revolution.

23. Most notably, Ted Gurr *Why Men Rebel* Princeton, New Jersey, Princeton University Press, 1970, is concerned with agency in a socio-psychological explanation of revolution; as is James C Davies 'Towards a Theory of Revolution' in the *American Sociological Review* vol.28, no.1, February 1962, p.5, which provides an explanation based on relative deprivation.

24. Exemplified by Chalmers Johnson *Revolutionary Change* London, University of London Press, 1968; Charles Tilly *From Mobilization to Revolution* Reading, Mass., Addison-Wesley, 1978; and Theda Skocpol *States and Social Revolutions: A Comparative Analysis of France, Russia and China* Cambridge, Cambridge University Press, 1979. The start of a poststructuralist analysis may be found in W F Wertheim *Evolution and Revolution* Harmondsworth, Penguin, 1974, especially p.89 ff.

25. Wei Hongyun 'Social Reform and Value Change in the Jin Cha Ji Anti-Japanese Border Region' in Feng and Goodman *North China at War: The Social Ecology of Revolution, 1937–1945* Lanham, Maryland, Rowman & Littlefield, 2000.

26. Kathleen Hartford 'Repression and Communist Success: the Case of Jin-Cha-Ji, 1938–1943' in Kathleen Hartford and Steven M Goldstein (eds) *Single Sparks: China's Rural Revolutions* New York, M E Sharpe, 1989, p.92.

27. Joseph W Esherick 'Deconstructing the Construction of the Party-State: Gulin County in the Shaan-Gan-Ning Border Region' in *The China Quarterly* No.140, December 1994, p.1052

28. Wang Shengbo *Ximenghui shi* [History of the Sacrifice League] Taiyuan, Shanxi renmin chubanshe, 1987; and Donald G Gillin *Warlord Yen Hsi-shan in Shansi Province, 1911–1949* Princeton, New Jersey, Princeton University Press, 1967, p.231 ff. Feng Chongyi 'The Making of the Jin Sui Base Area: Peasants, Intellectuals and Democratization' in Feng and Goodman *North China at War: the social ecology of revolution, 1937–1945* Lanham, Maryland, Rowman & Littlefield, 2000; and David S G Goodman 'JinJiLuYu in the Sino-Japanese War: The Border Region and the Border Region Government' in *The China Quarterly* No.140, December 1994, p.1007, both detail the impact of the Sacrifice League on base area activities.

29. *Zhandi zongdongyuan* [Battlefield General Mobilization] Taiyuan, Shanxi renmin chubanshe, 1986, 2 vols.

30. See, for example: Odoric Y K Wou *Mobilizing the Masses: Building Revolution in Henan*, Stanford, Stanford University Press, 1994, p. 313 ff; as well as Pauline B Keating 'Getting Peasants Organized: Village Organizations and the

Party-State in the Shaan Gan Ning Border Region,' Wei Hongyun 'Social Reform and Value Change in the Jin Cha Ji Anti-Japanese Border Region,' and Tian Youru 'Social and Political Change in the Villages of the Taihang Anti-Japanese Base Area,' all in Feng and Goodman *North China at War: The Social Ecology of Revolution, 1937–1945* Lanham, Maryland, Rowman & Littlefield, 2000.

31. Edward Friedman, Paul Pickowicz and Mark Selden *Chinese Village, Socialist State* New Haven, Connecticut, Yale University Press, 1991, p.84ff.

32. Isabel and David Crook *Revolution in a Chinese Village: Ten Mile Inn* London, Routledge, 1959; and Victor Nee 'Towards a social anthropology of the Chinese revolution' in *Bulletin of Concerned Asian Scholars* vol.11, no.3, 1972, p.40.

33. Zhonggong JinJiYu qudangwei 'Zuzhi gongzuo baogao' ['Report on Organization Work'] 1 August 1941, in TDZH vol.4: 1941, p.553.

34. Joseph W Esherick 'Deconstructing the Construction of the Party-State: Gulin County in the Shaan-Gan-Ning Border Region' in *The China Quarterly* No. 140, December 1994, especially p.1077 ff; Joseph W Esherick 'Revolution in a Feudal Fortress: Yangjiagou, Mizhi County, Shaanxi, 1937–1948' in *Modern China* vol.24, no.4, October 1998, p.370 ff.

35. Liu Jianxun 'Speech at the 6th Organizational Work Conference of Taihang Region' 25 February 1945, in SOC p.14.

36. Odoric Y K Wou *Mobilizing the Masses: Building Revolution in Henan* Stanford, Stanford University Press, 1994, especially p.12 ff.

37. LXH p.21. According to Li, he only found out when provided with an explanation (in some detail) by Deng Xiaoping in December 1937 (p.31 ff.) He was not alone in his relative ignorance, which presumably explains the Hebei-Henan-Shanxi CCP Provincial Committee's development of a set of guidelines in March 1938. These may be found in Zhonggong JiYuJin shengwei 'Jianli Taihang genjudi huiyi baogao' ['Report of Meeting of the Establishment of the Taihang Base Area'] 20 March 1938, in TDZH vol.1, p.133.

38. See, for example: Deng Xiaoping 'Dang yu KangRi minzhu zhengquan' ['The party and the anti-Japanese democratic government'] 15 April 1941, in Deng Xiaoping *Deng Xiaoping Wenxuan, 1938–1965* [Selected Works of Deng Xiaoping 1938–1965] Beijing, Renmin chubanshe, 1989, p.20; and in 'Wunianlai duidi douzheng de gailue zongjie yu jinhou duidi douzheng de fangzhen: Deng Xiaoping tongzhi zai Taihang fenju gaogan huiyishang de baogao' ['Summary of conflict with the enemy during the last five years and the consequent policy for struggle: Comrade Deng Xiaoping's report at Taihang Sub-bureau meeting of senior cadres'] 26 January 1943, in GSX vol.3, p.27.

39. BZYJ 29 July 1942, p.11.

40. Ted Gurr and Jack A Goldstone 'Comparisons and Policy Implications,' p.338 ff.

41. Joseph B R Whitney *China: Area, Administration and Nation Building* The University of Chicago, Department of Geography, Research Paper No.123, 1970, p.141.

42. David S G Goodman 'JinJiLuYu in the Sino-Japanese War: The Border Region and the Border Region Government' in *The China Quarterly* No.140, December 1994, p.1009.

43. Peng Dehuai and Yang Shangkun were both physically located in the Taihang Base Area during the war though not organizationally part of the base area or border region. Peng Dehuai was the Minister of Defense who spoke out against the strategy of the Great Leap Forward in 1959. Yang Shangkun was a member of the CCP's Secretariat, accused of having 'bugged' Mao Zedong's bedroom he was dismissed during the Cultural Revolution. Bo Yibo had been the senior CCP member of the Sacrifice League and became the leader of the Taiyue Base Area during the war. After the establishment of the PRC he became Minister of Finance but clashed with Mao over economic affairs at an early stage. Li Xuefeng was the long-term CCP secretary of the Taihang Base Area who became Secretary of the CCP's North China Bureau only to be dismissed for 'fundamentalism' during May 1970.

44. David S G Goodman *Deng Xiaoping and the Chinese Revolution: A Political Biography* London, Routledge, 1994, especially Chapters 6 and 7.

45. Accounts of the Taihang Base Area include: Isabel and David Crook *Revolution in a Chinese Village: Ten Mile Inn* London, Routledge, 1959; Taihang geming genjudishi zongbian weihui (ed) *Taihang geming genjudi shigao* [Outline History of the Taihang Revolutionary Base Area] Taiyuan, Shanxi renmin chubanshe, 1987; Taihang geming genjudishi zongbian weihui (ed) *Dashijishu* [Chronology] Taihang geming genjudi shiliao congshu No.1, Taiyuan, Shanxi renmin chubanshe, 1991. The standard published accounts of the Shanxi-Hebei-Shandong-Henan Border Region are: Qi Wu *Yige geming genjudi de chengzhang: KangRi zhanzheng he jiefang zhanzheng shiqi de JinJiLuYu Bianqu gaikuang* [The Transformation of a Revolutionary Base Area: An Outline of the Shanxi-Hebei-Shandong-Henan Border Region during the War of Resistance and the War of Liberation] Beijing, Renmin chubanshe, 1957; and Qi Wu *JinJiLuYu bianqu shi* [A History of the Shanxi-Hebei-Shandong-Henan Border Region] Beijing, Dangdai Zhongguo chubanshe, 1995.

46. Ding Ling *Yierjiushi yu JinJiLuYu Bianqu* [The 129th Division and the Shanxi-Hebei-Shandong-Henan Border Region] Beijing, Xinhuashe, 1950 (originally *Jiefang ribao* [Liberation Daily] 14–19 August 1944).

47. Rong Zihe was originally and during the War known as Rong Wusheng. He became more usually known as Rong Zihe during 1948. For the sake of clarity this form of his name will be used throughout.

48. Shexian was part of Henan until after the War. At that later stage part of Licheng County was also removed from Shanxi's jurisdiction and placed under Shexian; and the Zhinan area was removed from Hebei's jurisdiction and became part of Shandong.

49. Deng Xiaoping tongzhi yu JinJiLuYu bianqu jianshe: fang Rong Zihe tongzhi' ['Comrade Deng Xiaoping and the Development of the Shanxi-Hebei-Shandong-Henan Border Region: an interview with Comrade Rong Zihe'] in Yang Guoyu et al (ed) *Ershiba nian jian: xubian* [During Twenty-eight Years: Sequel] Shanghai wenyi chubanshe, 1990, p.23.

50. Taihang geming genjudishi zongbian weihui (ed) *Taihang geming genjudi shigao* [Outline History of the Taihang Revolutionary Base Area] Taiyuan, Shanxi renmin chubanshe, 1987 p.134–36.

51. BZZM p.452.
52. Li Da 'Kaizhan qunzhongxingde shadi yingxiong yundong' ['Start a Mass-style Kill the Enemy Movement'] November 1944, in DWD p.435.
53. 'JinJiYuqu nongjiu zhouhui liangnianlai gongzuo cailiao' ['Materials on the work of the Shanxi-Hebei-Henan district peasant's association during the last two years'] June 1941, in TDZH vol.4: 1941, p.377.
54. This figure excludes CCP members serving in the Eighth Route Army or offices of the North China Bureau of the CCP based in the Taihang Base Area.
55. Zhonggong JinJiYu qudangwei 'Zuzhi gongzuo baogao' ['Report on Organization Work'] 1 August 1941, in TDZH vol.4: 1941, p.544–46.
56. A distinction is made between 'administrative' and 'natural' villages. Administrative villages usually contain several natural villages, which are usually the communities of habitation.
57. Wei Hongyun and Zou Zhiyuan in *Huabei KangRi genjudi shi* Beijing, Dangan chubanshe, 1990, p.342.
58. ZOH p.97.
59. WOH p.27.
60. LOH p.23. Piancheng had been part of Licheng County but not contiguous with the rest of the county for some four hundred years. It was to the northeast of the rest of Licheng County, but separated by the river valley of the Zhang that was part of Shexian. Piancheng had originally been a contiguous part of Licheng County from 598 until the middle of the Ming Dynasty. A mountain area, as is Licheng, the movement of population and such trade as existed, was along the mountain ranges. However, the valley dwellers along the Zhang River in Shexian had long complained that upstream and downstream should be under the same jurisdictions. Not only were there intervening county boundaries, but at that time Shexian was in the north of Henan Province. A change was granted, and the Piancheng district became noncontiguous with the rest of its county. Although a county throughout the War of Resistance, afterwards it was absorbed into Shexian, which itself changed jurisdiction to come under Hebei Province. See: Zhang Jizhong *Shanxi Lishi zhengqu dili* [A Political and Administrative Geography of Shanxi] Taiyuan, Shanxi renmin chubanshe, 1992, p.221.
61. LOH p.50.
62. Documentary sources remain limited. Reference to rural class conflict in the Shanxi-Hebei-Chahar Border Region may be found in 'JinChaJi Bianqu gegong juti zhengce ji dangde jianshe jingyan' ['The Experience of Specific Policies and Party Development in the Shanxi-Hebei-Chahar Border Region'] 4 June-21 August 1941, in *Peng Zhen wenxuan* [Selected Works of Peng Zhen] Beijing, Renmin chubanshe, 1991, p.2; and in the Shanxi-Suiyuan Border Region in: Liang Zhixiang *JinSui geming genjudi shi* [History of the Shanxi-Suiyuan Revolutionary Base Area] Taiyuan, Shanxi guji chubanshe, 1999, p.180.
63. For further discussion on this point, see most usefully: Gordon White *The Politics of Class and Class Origin* Contemporary China Paper No.9, Australian National University, 1976.
64. Philip C C Huang 'Rural Class Struggle in the Chinese Revolution: Representational and Objective Realities from the Land Reform to the Cultural Revolution' in *Modern China* Vol.21, no.1, January 1995, p.114.

65. Jerome Ch'en 'The Development and Logic of Mao Tse-tung's Thought, 1928–49' in Chalmers Johnson (ed) *Ideology and Politics in Contemporary China* Seattle, University of Washington Press, 1973, p.74 ff.

66. Odoric Wou describes the distinctive nature of landlordism in the Taihang area of North Henan as 'the poor exploiting the rich,' because of the obligations that accompanied landownership, in Odoric Y K Wou *Mobilizing the Masses: Building Revolution in Henan* Stanford, Stanford University Press, 1994, p.314. For further confirmation from surveys in the Taihang Region, see, for example: TRSX p.1341 ff.

67. Philip C C Huang 'Rural Class Struggle in the Chinese Revolution: Representational and Objective Realities from the Land Reform to the Cultural Revolution' in *Modern China* Vol.21, no.1, January 1995, p.137.

68. Ilpyong J Kim 'Mass Mobilization Policies and Techniques Developed in the Period of the Chinese Soviet Republic' in A Doak Barnett (ed) *Chinese Communist Politics in Action* University of Washington Press, 1969, especially p.80 ff; and Mark Selden *China in Revolution: The Yenan Way Revisited* New York, M E Sharpe, 1995, especially p.55 ff, and p.66 ff.

69. Peng Tao 'Qunzhong yundong de fazhan yu jieji guanxi de bianhua' ['The development of mass movements and the transformation of class relations'] February 1943, in TW p.227.

70. See the comments of Li Dazhang in 'Guoqu qunzhong gongzuode jiandan huigu yu jinhoude gonzuo fangzhen' ['Review of Masses Work in the Past and Policy for the Future'] February 1943, in QY p.183.

71. Zhonggong Taihang qudangwei (ed) *Tudi gaige baogao* [Report on Land Reform] Taihang qudangwei, 1947; Zhonggong Taihangqu sandiwei *Sanfenqu tudi gaige yu qunzhong yundong cailiao jicun* [Collection of Materials on Land Reform and Mass Mobilization in the 3rd District] Taihang sandiwei, 1947.

72. TW p.72.

73. TJSD1 p.1383.

Part I

Political Order

1

Base Area and Border Region

As was the case throughout the base areas of North China during the War of Resistance, the development of the Taihang Base Area was heavily influenced by the circumstances of Japanese presence and the geopolitics of the local situation.[1] The Japanese North China Army attempted to conquer Shanxi quickly during the second half of 1937 and the first part of 1938, coming from the northeast and moving on toward Wuhan. Both in the early stages of the war and later when they returned to Shanxi in larger numbers at the end of 1938 after the fall of Wuhan, Japanese influence remained strongest closer to the lines of supply and communication, especially railway lines and main roads. In Southeast Shanxi this not only involved the Japanese in re-laying the rail lines originally laid by Yan Xishan to a nonstandard gauge,[2] but also constructing a new line from Baigui (just south of Taigu on the Taiyuan to Yuncheng line) to Changzhi, and attempting to improve and fortify the Handan-Changzhi Highway both during the second half of 1939 in order to combat guerilla activity in the Taihang Base Area.[3] For its part, the base area developed its core in the high mountain counties along the spine of the Taihang Mountains north of the Handan-Changzhi Highway and south of the ZhengTai Railway. The mountain valleys and ravines provided readily defensible positions, and were maximally distant from areas of Japanese concentration over fairly impenetrable terrain.

In addition, the development of the Taihang Base Area was also particularly shaped by the operation and consequences of the united front in Shanxi; the extent of involvement by central CCP organizations; and the attempt to introduce radical change, which involved an ongoing discussion about class and revolution within the base area CCP that came to center on the status and role of the middle peasant. The inner-party debate and its interactions with the social and political conflict that developed within rural society are detailed in Chapter 5.

All united front activities were important but the alliance between the CCP and Yan Xishan that resulted in the Sacrifice League is central for understanding the emergence of the Taihang Base Area. It not only presented the opportunity for military and political security at a formative stage, but also complicated the structures and operations of local resistance activities. Outside of the CCP, its involvement in local government was downplayed for the most part to the middle of 1939. For local party organizations, handling relations amongst the different elements within the Sacrifice League was often to prove very stressful, even after relations with Yan Xishan were severed.

The co-location of the field headquarters of the Eighth Route Army, the CCP Central Committee's North China Bureau and the 129th Division command, as well as Deng Xiaoping,[4] necessarily meant that the Taihang Base Area was likely to receive close attention from these organizations, as well as from the party's leadership in general. This relationship allowed the leaders of the Taihang Base Area a certain amount of protection within the CCP's internal politics, but it also to some extent limited their room for maneuver, and certainly meant that unapproved developments were liable to be rapidly censured.

While the social story of the War of Resistance is often told in terms of class conflict between landlords and peasant, equally as important in the development of the Taihang Base Area were tension and conflict surrounding the social and political roles of various different kinds of peasants. The problems the CCP faced as it struggled to implement programs of social reform led to a series of contested solutions about the correct balance to be struck between revolutionary theory and revolutionary practice. In particular the rise in the number and wealth of middle peasants during the war was not only challenged within the CCP in terms of the appropriateness of their mobilization and leadership roles—the 'middle peasant question'[5]—but it also became a source of wider social tension.

The political order of the Taihang Base Area emerged from the combined attempts to ensure military and political security; to develop a system of government and administration; and to ensure CCP control and direction of that system of government and the base area. The major turning point in that process came during the second half of 1939. In the earlier part of the war, the activities of the various constituent base areas were both protected and constrained by their operation within a united front strategy, particularly and overwhelmingly by the alliance between Yan Xishan and the CCP. The return of Japanese troops to Southeast Shanxi in force during the middle of 1939 coincided with a deterioration in the resistance alliance. The CCP's initial areas of activity were both more threatened militarily, and became more unified and organized as a base area.

MILITARY AND POLITICAL SECURITY

The development of the Taihang Base Area's military and political security environment is best understood in terms of four broad periods. The first from October 1937 to the end of 1938 was the period of the rapid physical expansion of the several base areas that eventually came together to form the Taihang Base Area. The second from the beginning of 1939 to March 1940 was marked by a determined Japanese return to the area, as well as increasing tensions between the CCP and Yan Xishan that eventually resulted in civil war. The third period from March 1940 to mid-1943 was the most intense period of Japanese aggression; and the fourth from mid-1943 to the end of the war, was characterized by the decreasing Japanese presence in Southeast Shanxi, and the base area's reexpansion both politically and economically.

United Fronts

The idea of a base area in Southeast Shanxi started with Mao Zedong in late 1935, as preparations were being made for the CCP's 'Eastern Expedition.'[6] During the first half of 1936 a substantial CCP force, including Mao, crossed the Yellow River from North Shaanxi in order to investigate additional sites for potential CCP bases. Based in the Liuliang Mountains in West Shanxi it came into open conflict with Yan Xishan, and possibly convinced him of the need to cooperate.[7] A side expedition led by Nie Rongzhen moved into Southeast Shanxi during April and May where potential future sites were identified in Changzhi, Jincheng and Qinxian.[8]

The need to ensure the security of the base area militarily was uppermost at the time of the Eastern Expedition, as it was throughout the War of Resistance, even though between March and August 1938 at the height of the base area's expansion many local party branches may have begun to act otherwise, much to the dismay of the more senior CCP leadership. At the start of the war the political environment for the coming conflict was somewhat different on either side of the Taihang Mountains, but in all cases political alliances were wrought in the face of Japanese invasion designed to first maximize the emergence of organized resistance, and then later to permit the base area's growth.

On the east side of the mountains in Southwest Hebei and North Henan, anti-Japanese Resistance governments of various kinds had been formed as the national governmental system broke down. In both Cixian and Shexian, new county governments were formed with both CCP and Nationalist Party involvement. Elsewhere in Southwest Hebei, one of the more famous of these operations was led by Yang Xiufeng, later to become Chairman of the Shanxi-Hebei-Shandong-Henan-Border Region Government. Yang was a CCP organizer and had been a history professor in Beiping, at the Normal University. When war broke out he fled south together with a number of students. They became involved in local resistance activities, and Yang was appointed Director of the South Hebei Administrative District with Nationalist Party support.[9]

On the west side of the Taihang Mountains in Shanxi, organized resistance was initially largely in the hands of the Sacrifice League, the most tangible result of the alliance between Yan Xishan and the CCP. The Sacrifice League not only ensured that resistance activities were largely unified in Shanxi, but also presented the CCP with tremendous opportunities to establish itself and develop organizational capacity. From the CCP's perspective this was to prove particularly important in those many counties where they had no previous organization and few, if any, members.

The CCP could not compete openly against Yan Xishan and indeed for some time there were two CCP provincial committees. One was open and led by Bo Yibo, the organizer of the Sacrifice League, and its sole activity was to manage the CCP's alliance with Yan Xishan. The other was covert, included An Ziwen (the later Head of the CCP's Organization Department after 1949) amongst others, and was concerned with the wider range of political activities and organization.[10] Although one result of these arrangements was that CCP membership in the province was not large, it did not need immediately to be: in many parts of Shanxi, CCP members wielded considerable influence, and were often the effective government at the start of the war. According to a Nationalist Party source, 66 of the 105 county heads, for example, were nominally Sacrifice League officers though also members of the CCP.[11] Through the Sacrifice League the CCP was particularly strong in Southeast Shanxi. Yan Xishan had restructured his administration of the province at the outbreak of war, appointing Bo Yibo and Rong Zihe to leadership of the two Southeastern Shanxi districts centered on Qinxian and Changzhi, respectively. An Ziwen had left Taiyuan for Qinxian at the start of the war; Bo Yibo followed in November at the head of the 1st Column of the Sacrifice League's 'Dare to Die' Troops.[12]

CCP activities centered on Pingding and Xiyang in east Shanxi; Zanhuang, Xingtai and the railway towns of the PingHan Railway in west Hebei; Shexian in north Henan; and Jincheng and Qinxian in southeast Shanxi,[13] and began to grow rapidly in the last three months of 1937. There had been some, but little CCP activity in these areas beforehand.[14] In particular, there had been fairly strong CCP branches in Qinxian and Wuxiang until forced to flee after fairly aggressive opposition from Yan Xishan. The CCP Provincial Committee for the PingHan Railway had about 100 members at the outbreak of war, but operations generally in Hebei Province had stopped and started with some regularity.[15]

In October, Liu Bocheng led the 6,000 troops of the 129th Division, together with the 344th Brigade of the 115th Division into Pingding across the ZhengTai Railway from the north. They were soon joined there by thirty members of the CCP PingHan Railway Committee, all of whom were to become active in the leadership of the Taihang Base Area[16] and its first party committee—the CCP Provincial Committee for Hebei-Henan-Shanxi—was established. At the same time, the West Hebei Militia Training Office, established by Yang Xiufeng in South Hebei to recruit soldiers for the resistance, had marched east from Hebei to meet up with the 129th Division in Pingding.[17] Both party headquarters and the military command moved south to Liaoxian, which became the center of the base area, establishing a branch office in Qinxian with Bo Yibo and the forces of the Sacrifice League. In the meantime, Zhu Rui, who had been sent on ahead of the main force by Liu Bocheng, established the North China Military and Administrative Cadre Institute in Jincheng, and by January 1938 it had already graduated some 3,000 cadres.[18]

The Japanese presence in Southeast Shanxi increased dramatically in the first three months of 1938, as they moved into the Jincheng and Changzhi areas as part of a pincer movement on Linfen in Southwest Shanxi to where Yan Xishan had withdrawn, and where their progress had been slowed. CCP activities in Jincheng ceased and Zhu Rui withdrew his cadre training institute to Qinxian where it became the Eighth Route Army South Shanxi Cadre School, later to move to Yan'an. The Qinxian area also marked the extent of Japanese advance at this stage, heralded by one of the most famous mass mobilizations of the war. Led by the Sacrifice League, the entire county town of Qinyuan was evacuated, so that when the Japanese troops arrived to lay seige there was not only a ghost town with no people, but there was also (probably of greater importance) no food.[19]

As the Japanese withdrew, the Southeast Shanxi Base Area was able to expand first into Qinxian, Dunliu and Huguan counties, to the west of Changzhi, as well as into Wuxiang, Yushe, Liaoxian, Heshun and Licheng in the Taihang Mountains.[20] In July the rapidly expanding base area gained its biggest prize when Rong Zihe led the 3rd Column of 'Dare-to-Die' Troops from Qinxian into Changzhi, the largest city of Southeast Shanxi with a population of some 150,000 people. Success led the leaders of the base area to approach Yan Xishan with a request to establish a border region government, following the example of the Shanxi-Chahar-Hebei Border Region recently established to the north.[21]

However, success also led the CCP national leadership to urge caution, particularly on the issue of open party activity. They did not want to give Yan Xishan cause to reconsider his alliance, and instructed the base area CCP leadership in no uncertain terms to stay politically hidden and only to take actions in the Yan Xishan-sanctioned name of the 'Southeast Shanxi Base Area,' definitely not that of the CCP. The issue had become particularly acute with respect to the activities of the Central Shanxi district CCP committee (centered on Pingding and Heshun), which was reprimanded by Liu Shaoqi and the CCP Central Committee,[22] and restructured by the base area CCP committee in consequence. The Central Shanxi leadership had enthusiastically expanded their operations during the first half of 1938, and had particular success in recruiting landless laborers and industrial workers. However, it had also come out in public opposition to the united front with Yan Xishan, criticizing what it described as the 'Yibo Line' (after Bo Yibo, leader of the Sacrifice League) as a form of defeatism.[23]

War and Civil War

The CCP national leadership's concerns were to prove well-founded during 1939, as deteriorating relationships within most united front activities exacerbated the direct challenge to the military security of the base area caused by the return of Japanese forces. After their withdrawal from Southeast Shanxi in the first part of 1938, the Japanese forces were prepared to commit more resources this time. The structural projects of railway building, road improving, blockade and fort construction were part of a grander design that saw many more troops moved into the region and the establishment of a new civilian authority, the Shandang Administration for the Qinxian and Changzhi districts of Shanxi.[24] However, in contrast to the *blitzkrieg* tactics attempted in early 1938, from the beginning of 1939 more steady progress was attempted and more successfully. In Hebei and Henan the base area was pushed back from the PingHan Railway toward the Taihang Mountains. In Southeast Shanxi the base area was forced out of Changzhi in July 1939, ensuring that the Taihang Base Area stayed north of the Handan-Changzhi Road for some time.

Within the base area there were increasing tensions between the CCP and its domestic allies as the former grew in strength, despite attempts to stay out of sight. In Hebei there were armed clashes between local Chinese militias in Zanhuang and Qinbo; and the Wu'an County Government turned explicitly against the CCP.[25] The appointment of a new Nationalist Party governor for Hebei led to the attempted dismissal of Yang Xiufeng in November 1938 as Director of the South Hebei Administrative

District. However, Yang stood his ground and from then until mid-August 1939 when the issue was resolved by open conflict in favor of the CCP, there were actually two separate governments for the district in competition.[26]

In Shanxi, the essential incompatibilities in the relationship between Yan Xishan and the CCP manifested themselves increasingly during 1939. Yan Xishan moved to counter the CCP's influence and to remove its cadres from the leadership of both the Sacrifice League and the New Army. The CCP national leadership changed tactics and attempted to ensure the party maintained control of those county governments and units of the New Army under its influence.[27] While the CCP was largely successful in Southeast Shanxi, its actions made the civil war that eventually broke out in December 1939 the more likely.

The change in tactics and deteriorating relations with Yan Xishan also presented political challenges to the CCP's base area leadership, both in planning its next steps and in explaining change to its members and party branches. At some point open conflict in Southeast Shanxi was inevitable, but the situation was far from totally under the control of the base area leadership. Moreover, each local situation was different: in some places, such as Wuxiang, the CCP already openly ran government well before December 1939; but in others, such as Licheng, and even more Liaoxian, CCP activities were more muted and its organization less developed.

Maintaining the CCP's organizational discipline and a sense of political direction under these circumstances was also no easy matter. The censure of the Central Shanxi party organization during 1938 had already highlighted the uncertainties within the CCP over political direction, and these were exacerbated by the wider conflicts within its united front strategy toward the end of 1939. As the military and political pressures on the base area mounted there were clearly those who thought that desperate times required desperate measures: perhaps even, from a CCP perspective, that faced by the failure of the alliance with the bourgeoisie, the only way forward would be to rely exclusively on the proletariat. Certainly some party branches do appear to have regarded the onset of change during late 1939 and early 1940 as a signal for more radical politics, including not only the overthrow of the landlord and rich peasant class but also various interpretations of proletarian uprisings. There is evidence of this kind of behavior in both Liaoxian and Wuxiang, for example, as discussed in Chapters 6 and 7, respectively. One necessary result was considerable social dislocation that magnified the impacts of the worsening economic and military situations.

The civil war that started in December 1939 and lasted until March 1940 was actually two sets of conflict between the CCP and separately Yan Xishan, and the troops of the Nationalist Party forces led by Wei Lihuang.

The conflict between the CCP and Yan Xishan was essentially over control of Southeast Shanxi, politically as well as for the disposition of units of the New Army. The CCP moved rapidly to ensure its control of local government, as well as of military forces. Where the CCP encountered resistance, or thought it might, as for example, in Liaoxian, revolutionary action was taken with the opposition being arrested and executed. In other places, other tactics were adopted to ensure control. These seizures of power certainly led to excess, and perhaps help explain why some members of the CCP interpreted these events as portending a still more revolutionary future.

The conflict with Nationalist Party forces was more over space, and there was no apparent coordination between Yan Xishan and the Nationalist Party forces in their opposition to the CCP. Nationalist Party troops had begun to crowd into the southern parts of the Taihang and Taiyue Ranges during 1939, particularly to the south of the Handan-Changzhi Road. As the Japanese reinvaded Southeast Shanxi they pushed in front of them Nationalist Party central government troops led by Wei Lihuang who had been based in Henan.[28] Ironically, Wei's military successes to that time had come to some considerable extent from his explicit adoption of CCP guerilla strategy.[29] However, his forces were now being herded against those of the Eighth Route Army, which also responded aggressively.

The fighting was severe and costly to base area resources. In the area south of the Handan-Changzhi Highway during January and February alone it is estimated that some 10,000 CCP troops were killed during the fighting, with a similar number on the Nationalist side.[30] Peace came with a negotiated settlement at the beginning of March 1940. Although the fighting and its outcomes centered on Southeast Shanxi, in the CCP's eyes the discussions were considered so important they were led by Zhu De (as Commander-in-Chief of the Eighth Route Army) assisted by Deng Xiaoping. Zhu and Wei Lihuang reached agreement that the Eighth Route Army would withdraw from the area south of the Handan-Changzhi Highway, centered on Linxian and Lingchuan.[31] This became an area settled by Nationalist Party forces administratively outside the Taihang Base Area, with only some underground CCP activities and no further military conflict until September 1943.[32]

Japanese Encirclement

The consequences of this short civil war were significant for the base area. Some aspects of the political and military situation were relatively clear-cut. The CCP had taken political power at county level throughout the region and Yan Xishan was essentially sidelined for the remainder of the war and confined to his mountain base area in Jixian, Southwest Shanxi.[33] Relations stayed strained between Yan and Chiang Kai-shek (Yan even entered into negotiations with Japan) and the Nationalist Party started organising again throughout the province, including in the Taihang Base Area.[34] Units of the New Army were brought directly under the direction of the Eighth Route Army, with whom they had in any case been working very closely.

Less immediately obvious was the new strategy to be adopted by the CCP, which was now operating openly. Whilst the local and even more the national leadership, particularly in the form of the North China Bureau, were slow to dampen the domestic social and political violence that had accompanied the civil war, both were not moving to abandon the concept of a broad united front. Eventually, the Sacrifice League was gradually brought to an end and closed in 1942.[35] However, the two Southeast Shanxi base areas (Taihang and Taiyue) were now brought together with the neighboring CCP base area in South Hebei to establish a border region government that would extend beyond the province and attempt to maintain a broad coalition of nationalist support.[36]

The end of effective cooperation between the CCP, the Nationalist Party and Yan Xishan generally weakened the base area's security, especially as the Japanese attack on Southeast Shanxi intensified. Yan's failure to support Wei Lihuang's forces in the south of Shanxi when they came under Japanese attack during early 1941, for example, led to Wei's forced evacuation from the area. Somewhat surprisingly therefore, the base area, or rather the Eighth Route Army, decided to go on the offensive against the Japanese Army. The 'Hundred Regiments Campaign,' which ran from August to December 1940, was a series of battles fought to remove Japanese positions in the north of the Taihang Base Area, largely along the ZhengTai Railway.[37] The CCP at first mobilized 22 and then eventually 104 regiments to attack the Japanese units, with the majority coming from the Taihang Base Area.[38] Particularly because of the large numbers of troops that were involved and the change in tactics, the Hundred Regiments Campaign has often been an issue of debate, academically and politically.[39] Moreover, whilst in the immediate term it was extremely successful in disrupting Japanese military and civilan activities, in the longer term it led to heavy Japanese retaliation.

The Japanese advanced slowly, building fortifications as they encroached on the base area, section by section, and sending waves of shock troops through the CCP occupied areas in a series of 'mop-up' operations. There were some 263 separate attacks on CCP forces in the Taihang Base Area during the 'mop-up's of 1941; and a further 410 in 1942. Although the impact of Japanese advance was locally variable, in general the territory of the base area was reduced by a third, and according to a more recent history 'only 50 *li* in the whole base area' did not experience some Japanese incursion.[40] Moreover, the reduction in the land area of the base area was matched by a decrease in the numbers it could mobilize to its defense. Throughout the war, the village-based emergency defence forces have been estimated at about 300,000 to 400,000 people; with estimates for the better armed part-time militia rising from a low of 10,000 at the end of 1940, to 56,000 in May 1942, but decreasing again afterwards during the rest of that year and 1943.[41] As an emergency defensive strategy, base area organizers created self-defense networks of four to five villages, protected by a common militia.[42]

During 1941 the Central Shanxi district—including Pingding, Heshun, Xiyang, Yushe, North Liaoxian, and West Wuxiang, some of the earliest settled parts of the base area—fell to the Japanese onslaught. In Hebei and Henan a second line of fortifications was built parallel to the PingHan Railway but closer still to the Taihang Mountains, driving resistance quite literally underground in these counties.[43] The core of the base area was essentially confined to Liaoxian, (East) Wuxiang, Licheng, Piancheng and Shexian, with almost only guerilla activities in other counties. In both 1942 and 1943, the Japanese forces penetrated right to the heart of the base area; killing Zuo Quan, Deputy Chief of Staff of the Eighth Route Army in Liaoxian in May 1942, and severely disrupting civilian activities.

In a sense, the occupation of the area south of the Handan-Changzhi Highway by non-CCP troops during the period of blockade and mop-up was an advantage to the Taihang Base Area, providing a buffer between it and any Japanese attack in that direction. From the base area's perspective this arrangement was acceptable whilst the Nationalist Party and remnant troops who occupied the area held their ground. However, in the first part of 1943 these troops defected to the Japanese, and became a direct threat to the Taihang Base Area. The base area's military responded directly, attacking and defeating the now opposition troops in Linxian (North Henan) during August. Linxian and another eighteen counties were then added to the base area, and formed its 7th and 8th districts.[44]

The Japanese were unable to increase the intensity of their attack still further during 1944, and indeed because of needs elsewhere both in China and the wider world were forced to withdraw resources from Southeast Shanxi. All the same, the external security of the base area remained under threat until well into 1945 despite the relative positional stalemate that had been achieved. Particularly during 1943 and 1944 environmental factors—drought and locust plagues—weakened the ability of the base area to expand further and became equally as urgent matters for attention and mobilization.

SOCIAL AND ECONOMIC CONTROL

Although the notions of guerilla operations and local government may seem antithetical, the maintenance and development of government was an important function of the base area, not least for extractive and mobilizatory purposes. Whatever else it did the base area needed to be able to recruit volunteers for the armed forces and to find resources to support its own operations, and to sustain those activities for a long, possibly indefinite period. The base area's ability to govern was necessarily related to its external military and political security, but throughout the war there were also other environmental, economic and social challenges to internal stability.

Social Stability

Environmental concerns often posed the most serious threat to internal stability. These were nothing new for the Taihang region. During 1876–79 the area had experienced drought, locust storms, famine and then bubonic plague, all of which resulted in a 35 percent population decrease within six years.[45] In the early 1930s another drought resulted in famine and land emiseration as even landlords and rich peasants were forced to sell landholdings. During the War of Resistance, there was a severe flood in 1939, and droughts every year from 1940 to 1943. There was a major famine in Liaoxian, Wuxiang, Licheng, Yushe, Xiangyuan, and Lucheng in 1940. Plagues of locusts hit the Taihang region, largely in Southwest Hebei and North Henan in 1943 and 1944, and were followed by famine.

One result was severe population loss from disease as well as war and starvation. For example, several counties reported sizeable drops in population from bubonic plague between 1939 and 1943.[46] The pressures on social order were often great, especially when there was famine, with peasants resorting to practices, which had become the norm at such times to find food, including stripping and eating the bark off trees; selling wives and children; and eating those who had died.[47] Populations were displaced within the base area as people moved looking for both food and work, and refugees came into the base area from surrounding areas where there was no government-provided relief, especially during 1943. In that year it was estimated that the base area was supporting 250,000 refugees to add to the 100,000 victims of natural disater already receiving relief.[48]

The economic challenges to the base area's stability included the need to resource its activities and the consequences of trade and interaction with the wider economy in North China. The need to support additional administrative and military personnel, including the families of those who left their homes to serve elsewhere, dramatically increased the tax burden, which had been a contentious social issue even before the war, particularly as the rural economy declined after 1931. Tax was usually charged by household or unit of land with no consideration of assets or income, and there is evidence even from outside the CCP that this was one reason the party was welcomed by the poorer peasantry in West Shanxi during the first half of 1936; and why the Sacrifice League, which had a similar program of tax reform, was welcomed in Southeast Shanxi during 1938.[49]

The lack of economic institutions across the different parts of the region before May 1940 meant both that this tax burden was unevenly distributed, and that the local economy was particularly vulnerable to movements in its wider economic environment. The result was substantial inflation and an inability to trade in those goods, particularly manufactured items, the base areas needed to import. Inflation became a critical problem for the base area in 1940 with a dramatic fall in the base area's currency (the South Hebei Bank dollar) against those of both the Nationalist Government and the local Japanese administration.[50] As its currency declined in value it became even easier for Japanese buyers to purchase the base area's much needed grain output, thereby depriving the base area of both food and export income. By 1941 currency problems almost undermined the base area's room for any action as it developed an unfavorable balance of trade with the Japanese-controlled area in Southeast Shanxi that was equivalent to half the value of the grain it had raised in taxation.[51]

The social challenges to stability all resulted from the actions of the base area itself and so had the potential to be politically more destructive. The CCP's attempt to implement a program of social reform led to a substantial increase in rural class conflict, which was itself an essential part of the revolutionary process in action. The series of political campaigns that started haltingly in 1939 created both disruption and a revolution of rising expectations. Attacks on landlords were destabilizing enough and had serious intended and unintended consequences for respectively local power structures and economic production as the local social elites reacted by fleeing their villages.[52] However, this was followed for the rest of the war by a series of running disputes within the CCP as well as at village level within the peasantry over the distribution of economic wealth and control of the emerging structures of political power, as various parts of the newly empowered peasantry sought increasingly to maximize their gains. Although not every village became involved, and there were different degrees of intensity, this conflict was to prove extremely corrosive both socially and within the CCP.

Alongside rural class conflict, but not necessarily associated with the introduction of a program of social reform was the sometime heavy-handedness of local government. Though many cadres acted perfectly appropriately, there were also occasions when cadres at village, subdistrict, and even county level acted otherwise. Various reviews of cadre misbehavior highlighted an apparent overreadiness to arrest and even kill people; the practice of forced recruitment for military service; as well as the development of village protection schemes, where cadres left villagers alone in return for payment. Such inappropriate behaviour might have been for narrow personal or political reasons on occasion, but some was just as likely to have occurred out of frustration, especially at the height of Japanese attacks when resources were in short supply and desperate action seemed required. Deng Xiaoping, amongst other leaders in the Taihang region, repeatedly emphasized the danger from that kind of behavior, which in his view ran the risk of alienating people and support. For example, he urged restraint in March 1941:

> The Public Security Bureau is not a terrorist organisation and should be part of the democratic system. It has a duty to protect any anti-Japanese organisations and individuals. Those landlords who are not anti-government enjoy rights and freedom of speech, as well as religion and thought, just the same as workers and peasants.[53]

Occasionally, however, increased social conflict and the inability of local cadres to manage difficult situations did result in open and armed rebellion. During the 1940s there were three serious uprisings of this kind: in Licheng during October 1941; Shahe, in April 1942; and Linxian, in January 1944.[54]

Base Areas

The institutional development of the Taihang Base Area can be divided into two radically different periods. In the first, from the outbreak of war to the end of 1939, the structure of local government depended on the situation in each county and village. On the whole, there was considerable village-level stability, alongside uncertainty in the shape and form of the emerging CCP base area, dependent on the course of the military and political situation. The second period, from March 1940 to the end of the war saw the emergence of a unified Taihang Base Area and the development of the structures and institutions of the border region that accompanied it. In contrast to the earlier period, there was greater social change and conflict at village level.

One usual explanation of the CCP's ability to gain a foothold in North China at the start of the war is in terms of the power vacuum created when Chiang Kai-shek's Nationalist Party government withdrew to the south and west of China. From the local perspective of county and village there was rather less of a power vacuum than existed at the national level, and indeed whilst local authorities and ruling elites might have been weak in their capacity to either tax or mobilize the local populations,[55] to a remarkable extent the social and political structures remained at least temporarily in place. There were certainly examples of the ruling elite bolting in the face of Japanese invasion, as, for example, in the case of the Qiao family of Qixian. Where this happened then necessarily the local political and social system they left behind started to collapse.[56] However, this was far from a general phenomenon throughout the (later to become) Taihang Base Area, and was largely confined to the surrounding plains and towns (such as Qixian) along the railways where Japanese presence was greatest. Even in those parts of the region where neither Sacrifice League, CCP nor any other form of resistance government made any particular attempt to maintain political order, village life did not change simply because the war had started somewhere else. Wu'an may have been an extreme example, but very little changed in the villages in the north of the county until Japanese troops arrived in 1940[57]; whilst in the south, the old patterns of village life were still reported as being in place in the middle of 1942.[58]

Similarly at county level there was no real power vacuum. Indeed the Sacrifice League often encountered considerable difficulties in even having the authority of its newly appointed county heads accepted by the local establishment, as the cases of Liaoxian and Licheng demonstrate. Part of the hostility of local establishments to the Sacrifice League was precisely because of the involvement of the CCP. As a result, where it was able, the CCP tended to work within the Sacrifice League, and this was undoubtedly a considerable advantage to the development of its local organization. For the most part local participants, and particularly members of the local social elite who were prepared to join the Sacrifice League, or similar activities, were usually more concerned to create a resistance movement in general, without thought of wider politics. In the words of one veteran cadre (who had originally been a member of the Nationalist Party) 'Yan Xishan might have differentiated between Communist and Nationalists, but it's not clear that those guys themselves did!' Even in the longer term, when as in Licheng those who had joined the Sacrifice League unwittingly later became disillusioned, their subsequent challenges to established authority were always likely in consequence to prove somewhat ineffectual.

Until 1939 and the start of the break between the CCP and Yan Xishan very little changed at the local level. As Lai Ruoyu indicated (later in 1945 when reviewing the base area's development) village cadres were simply appointed through the Sacrifice League and 'left to get on with it' without much if any direction, and no organizational attention.[59] In the early months of the war it almost certainly seemed like an appropriate strategy. Social stability was generally maintained, and the CCP was generally able to achieve its immediate goals through the existing structures of power. For example, it was claimed that by April 1939 county governments had managed to organize 31 percent of the inhabitants in the then Southeast Shanxi Base Area (2.5 million of an estimated 8 million) for either war service or in various support activities. Those organized were said to have included '170,000 workers; 823,000 peasants; 112,00 youth; and 100,000 women.'[60]

All the same not everything was plain sailing for the new cadres, and the base areas's rapid expansion and large base of support brought their own problems, not least with the expectations coming from those being mobilized. The growth of the militia was a good case in point. Peasants often apparently did not understand the principles of self-defense and expected payment, regarding their mobilization as a form of employment. Some rich and middle peasants were apparently more concerned with status, having joined to be upwardly mobile within their own villages. For their part, members of the local rural elite who joined local militias were reported as sometimes expecting the base area to provide them with an office or command post.[61]

More fundamental institutional change and regional innovation came as a result of the military and political insecurities of 1939 that culminated in civil war and the CCP's assumption of political power. This process had started with the introduction of village, subdistrict and county elections that started at the end of 1938 in Cixian and proceeded fitfully during 1939.[62] Banking institutions had been formed in September 1938 (the Shangdang Bank) and October 1939 (the South Hebei Bank) but typically for this phase of the base area's development, there was little attempt at coordination across the region. The unevenness of the tax burden across the base areas, and the vulnerability of its economy to external influences could only be tackled by coordinated efforts over a larger area than was possible whilst the Southeast Shanxi Base Area was nominally subject to Yan Xishan.

Border Region

The outbreak of civil war at the end of 1939 led to more fundamental institutional change, first as the CCP moved to ensure its control of county-level government, and then with the truce of March 1940, as the base area moved to coordinate activities within the Taihang region and to develop a border region government. In April the CCP's North China Bureau organized a senior cadres meeting in Licheng that addressed the issues of building new institutions and the development of a Shanxi-Hebei-Henan Border Region.[63] It restructured the New Army, bringing it directly under the command of the 129th Division; as well as proposing the creation of a Taihang Military Region coterminous with the base area. It decided to establish a Joint Office for the South Hebei, Taiyue and Taihang Base Areas to coordinate activities and to prepare for the establishment of the Shanxi-Hebei-Henan Border Region Government the following year.[64]

Dealing with the economic environment was a major motivation in the development of a border region and the establishment of the Joint Office,[65] and some of its first acts included introducing trade and currency regulations, and amalgamating the various financial institutions into one note-issuing bank for the whole border region—the South Hebei Bank.[66] The relationship between the base area and the border region was particularly close, to such an extent that they are often though incorrectly equated. The Taihang Base Area was established as a directly administered region of the border region, first under the Joint Office and then later the Border Region Government, with six districts, in a move that paralleled the CCP organization under the Shanxi-Hebei-Henan Regional Committee. Liaoxian and Wuxiang were in the base area's Second District (renamed the Third District the following year) and Licheng was in the Third District (which became the Fourth District.)

The border region government proposed at the Licheng meeting of April 1940 was established and started operation in September 1941. However, in the intervening period its design had become somewhat more elaborate. In April 1941 Deng Xiaoping had suggested that the border region have an elected assembly in addition to a border region government.[67] Then shortly before the first provisional assembly met, its regional focus was enlarged to include the Hebei-Shandong-Henan Base Area, resulting in the establishment of the Shanxi-Hebei-Shandong-Henan Border Region.

In general, the introduction of direct elections for local governments at all levels—village, subdistrict and county—was a central institutional reform of the post-March 1940 era.[68] Elections were part of the base area's appeal to popular participation and support, though unlike the campaigns designed to ensure social reform, these were targetted more at the local elite. Indeed, in a sense there was a balance intended between an appeal to the peasantry on the question of social reform through mass mobilization campaigns and mass organizations (the Patriotic Peasants, Workers, Women's, and Youth Associations, also overhauled as part of base area reform[69]) and an appeal to the local elite on the issue of political participation and nationalist resistance through the organization of local government elections.

Elections were governed by the 'Three-thirds System' that established equal quotas for three categories of candidates: CCP members, 'advanced elements' (of 'leftists and progressives') and 'neutrals.' In practice these proportions were often varied slightly, though not usually by as much as the 1941 elections to village, subdistrict and county level governments in the Taihang Base Area would seem to suggest. Table 1.1 summarizes information on those candidates elected in terms of their 'Three-thirds System' categorization. Members of the Nationalist Party were willingly recruited, but as individuals, as were non-party members of the local gentry.[70] In addition to the 'Three-thirds System,' there was a requirement for each local government in the Taihang Base Area to ensure the election of at least one woman.[71]

Deng Xiaoping's proposal for a Border Region Assembly was an extension of the program to encourage political participation through elections. His original proposal was for a directly elected assembly and because this was not possible under wartime conditions, the assembly became the Provisional Assembly when elected in 1941. Direct elections were postponed until the second half of 1944, with the Border Region Assembly eventually meeting in March 1945. In proposing the establishment of a Border Region Assembly Deng had heavily emphasized its democratic aspects:

> We Communists always oppose a one-party dictatorship, and don't approve of the Nationalists having a one-party dictatorship. The CCP certainly doesn't have a program to monopolise government because one party can only rule in its own interests and won't act according to the Will of the People. Moreover, it goes against democratic politics.[72]

Table 1.1 1941 Election Results in the Taihang Base Area

Three-thirds Category	Election Village Elections December 1941	Subdistrict Election August 1941	County Election August 1941
CCP members	36	51	43
Advanced elements	46	30	32
Neutrals	18	19	25

Source: Statistics calculated from figures by county presented in Zhonggong JinJiYu qudangwei 'Qu xian cun "sansanzhi" qingkuang tongjibiao' ['Table of the "Three-thirds system" in Counties, Subdistricts and Villages'] 1941 in TDZH vol.4: 1941, p.990.

Deng may have been defining 'government' narrowly as local government and administration, and certainly was not talking about open competition in politics more generally,[73] but nonetheless the principle of open and competitive elections in that context was observed in practice as well as in principle. In Liaoxian, Li Xuefeng, the CCP secretary of the regional party committee stood for election against a 'democratic personage' Yan Lianpu. Both addressed their constitutents at an election meeting on 22 June 1941 in Tongyu Township. Li was elected with a fairly large majority. In Licheng, another contested election between a 'democratic personage,' Xie Haoli, and a leading CCP member resulted in Xie Haoli being elected.[74]

The most important functions of the Shanxi-Hebei-Shandong-Henan Border Region Government were concerned with economic management, taxation and famine relief. Though most of these activities were administratively managed at county-level and below, the Border Region Government played a crucial coordinating, planning and legitimating role. It reorganized the tax system, established a system of regional economic management (which permitted economic revival, especially within the Taihang Base Area) and organized the provision of famine relief across the border region. It also played a supportive role in the maintenance of social and political stability at village level through its frequently maintained defense of the individual right to freedom from arrest and arbitrary execution.[75] This became particularly important as rural class conflict increased, for particularly under the conditions of guerilla war, experience elsewhere (including in other base areas) suggests differences of perceived privilege can all too readily become characteristics of 'enemy agents, spies and collaborators,' capable only of violent resolution.[76]

Two tax systems were introduced by the Border Region Government. The first in 1941 was based on the 'equitable burden' previously introduced in Shanxi by Yan Xishan[77] and was essentially a very low property tax, with a low rate of payment and a fairly high threshold. The following year a revised version of the 'equitable burden'—the 'universal progressive tax'—was drafted and local legislation passed in 1943. This too was a wealth tax where income and production were largely exempt, though it differed in the calculation of wealth and tax. In particular it based its calculation of wealth on the productive capacity of property over an average number of years, and taxed individuals on a rising parabolic curve.[78]

The Border Region Government also responded quickly to develop some form of regional economic management system. Part of this related to the administration of economic warfare with the enemy occupied areas. This involved stabilising the value of money within the border region, essentially by administrative means, particularly the creation of a single currency-zone based on the South Hebei Bank Dollar, and moving to control trade. Whilst it was generally successful in this endeavor, there was a miscalculation by the South Hebei Bank at the end of 1942 and the money supply was increased by an excess of 35 percent, with inflationary results.[79]

The other side of its management activities was to put in place a program of regional economic reconstruction, which it was able to do increasingly after the middle of 1943.[80] In addition to its necessary focus on agricultural development, through a scheme of agricultural loans, this concentrated on the development of industry, in particular the production of woven cotton cloth. Experiments during 1940 with local government owned and run economic enterprises had poor results and were abandoned the following year. Thereafter, private enterprises and cooperatives were encouraged, with government confining itself to a more supportive role in terms of market management and the provision of financial institutions.[81]

Economic warfare and economic recovery allowed the Border Region Government to take a leading role in disaster relief, especially during 1943 and 1944 as environmental conditions deteriorated. The Border Region Committee established a Famine Relief Committee which exempted victims from taxation, resettled them (30,000 in 1943) and provided grain relief (to 336,000 people in 1943). The numbers of people (largely administrative and military personnel) who had to be supported from the resources of the base area was always a matter of concern to its leadership. This was a major reason for the introduction of the system of 'dual work' for almost all local cadres: they were expected to engage in production for themselves as well as any political or administrative responsibilities they had.

In 1941 generally throughout North China the CCP national leadership initiated a policy of 'Better Troops, Simpler Administration' that aimed to reduce the numbers of publicly funded personnel to no more than 3 percent of the population. By early 1943 the total number of supported administrative staff in the Taihang Base Area had been reduced to 4 percent of the population (a decrease of 51 percent in staff, and 46 percent in public expenditure).[82] Moreover, in similar vein to encourage production and limit waste, the number of independent households was restricted: divorce was banned in July 1943,[83] and in some places widows were permitted to remarry.[84] However, the environmental disasters of 1943 and 1944 meant further substantial shortages in the available public grain. The Border Region Government met the demand through trading in the unregulated market outside the base area. It bought and sold its own South Hebei Bank currency to such good effect that it was then able to buy grain (and often border region grain) at inflated prices.[85]

CCP DEVELOPMENT

The development of the CCP's organization in the Taihang Base Area and its control of the region appears deceptively straightforward. Whatever complications the united front brought otherwise, right from the beginning in October 1937 the CCP had established a single party committee—the Hebei-Henan-Shanxi Provincial Committee—that led its activities on both sides of the Taihang Mountains, and which was responsible for all the component areas that later emerged as the Taihang Base Area of the Shanxi-Hebei-Shandong-Henan Border Region. Indeed, to some considerable extent, as already noted, there was a high degree of coordinated development of those original politically and geographically disparate activities.

There was precise organizational continuity between the Hebei-Henan-Shanxi Provincial Committee, and its successor bodies: the Shanxi-Hebei-Henan District Committee, from August 1938 to April 1939; the Shanxi-Hebei-Henan Regional Committee from April 1939 to October 1943 (though for a short time during 1940 it was known as the North Taihang Regional Committee); and the Taihang Regional Committee, for the rest of the war. This continuity is emphasized by the continuity of its individual leading cadres, almost all of whom served in the Taihang Base Area from late 1937 through most of the war[86]; and further highlighted by the continuity in the base area party committee's organizationally superior body within the CCP organization. The CCP Central Committee's Taihang Region Military and Political Committee under Deng Xiaoping directed the base area from January 1938 through to September 1942, when its functions were taken over by a newly established Taihang Sub-bureau of the CCP Central Committee.

However, this view of the CCP in the Taihang Base Area as a single, homogeneous organization that simply exercised its control over the region from within is fundamentally misleading. There were political relations that developed and control mechanisms that had to be worked at, within the CCP, as well as between the CCP and local government, throughout the base area over the period of the war. Most cadres in local government, the mass organizations, and the different parts of the base area's military organization were not members of the CCP. The CCP preferred to exercise its influence less publicy, even after March 1940: through party groups in the more important government bodies, such as the Border Region Government; or through the quiet word to local governments and mass organizations from the local party secretary. CCP membership was always fairly small, with usually no more than 25,000 members for the whole base area. Although its leadership and senior cadres were fairly constant, its cadre force and general membership were considerably less so, with major reorganizations in 1940 and at the end of 1944: that of 1940 was initially designed to ensure political reliability after the breakdown of the united front with Yan Xishan; that of 1944 as part of the CCP's national rectification movement that was attempting to homogenize and centralize the party.

Party Rule

The key feature of party rule was that its institutions were established and operated from the top down. The structures of power and influence that surrounded each CCP committeee within the Taihang Base Area extended in three dimensions: with its superior organizations in the CCP's hierarchy; with its subordinate organizations; and with the institutions of local government and the mass organizations.

The relationship between the CCP committee for the base area and the party's national leadership was always close. Like any other base area, it was subject to direction, especially when, as in November 1941, the national leadership was critical of its activities. On that occasion, the Central Committee criticized Li Xuefeng and the CCP in the base area for its implementation of policy on peasant landholding earlier in the year, specifically that they had been overzealous in their attack on landlords, rich peasants and middle peasants.[87] However, the location of the field headquarters of the Eighth Route Army and the CCP North China Bureau necessarily meant that these bodies effectively played a directing role in the affairs of the base area. The most notable occasions included the change of direction in the relationship with Yan Xishan signalled by Yang Shangkun (on behalf of the North China Bureau) in July 1939; Zhu De's leadership of negotiations with Wei Lihuang in February 1940; Peng Dehuai's launch of the Hundred Regiments Campaign during the second half of 1940; and Deng Xiaoping's involvement in establishing first the border region, and then later its assembly.

The CCP's national leadership became involved in the base area's affairs on those occasions for the most part because the issues at stake were deemed to be of wider significance. In similar vein, as the Taihang Base Area developed, its CCP leadership was also concerned to ensure that every level of organization within the party—that paralleled the government hierarchy at district, county and subdistrict levels—was similarly fully integrated, and not liable to independent policymaking, or overly autonomous policy implementation. Maverick behavior was always a danger in a situation of rapid organizational expansion, where, as in most parts of the base area, there had been little previous experience of CCP operations.

In general, whilst a complete restructuring of a party organization by the CCP base area committee was fairly rare, it was also not an unknown procedure. As already noted the Central Shanxi CCP committee was restructured in the middle of 1938; and a number of county level CCP committees, including those in Wuxiang and Licheng (twice) were politically reorganized.[88] All the same, the CCP's internal command structure did not always work perfectly, and there were other failures that resulted in much less draconian action. One of its more spectacular breakdowns in communication between levels within the CCP organization was the already noted mishandling of elections at village, subdistrict, county, and even border region-level in 1941. (See Table 1.1.) Even before the full results had become known, the secretary of the CCP base area committee was criticising lower level party organizations for not having treated the elections seriously enough, and having ended up with inappropriate results.[89]

The development of relations between different levels of the CCP and their respective levels of local government was more complex. Before 1941 the operation of the united front left many cadres and party members uncertain about political direction and allegiances. As many cadres have subsequently confirmed, there was an overreaction to the emphasized confirmation of the united front in the middle of 1938 that surrounded the restructuring of the Central Shanxi CCP organization. As a result, sole allegiances to Yan Xishan were reinforced rather than more nuanced understandings of the role of a CCP member in such a situation. When the political parting of the ways came, many CCP members were more than a little confused, and 'Many cadres did not want to struggle against Yan and the Nationalist Party.'[90] This pattern of oscillation between extremes was one that was to be repeated in the development of the base area, particularly as the CCP attempted social reform in the 1940s.

After March 1940 the organizational lines of responsibility for the CCP appeared much clearer, at least in theory. The principle of CCP direction was that it was responsible for policymaking but left administration to local governments and the mass organizations. Organizational practice and individual behavior frequently ignored such distinctions, suggesting both a lack of understanding by cadres and party members and a lack of training. There was a tendency for CCP organizations to interfere in the work of local governments, to assume government functions, and for CCP cadres and sometimes even ordinary party members to act in a high-handed manner toward local government and mass organization officials. Local governments sometimes tried to take their revenge by acting to delay the implementation of CCP directives.[91] However, in general, the problem, as leaders such as Deng Xiaoping repeatedly pointed out throughout the 1940s was that CCP interference was doubly inefficient: it overburdened CCP cadres and led other officials to be inactive, reluctant to do anything knowing that all decisions and actions would be taken by the CCP anyhow.[92]

The problems of inappropriate CCP-government relations were a principal focus of Xu Zirong's report to the Fourth Organizational Work Conference in June 1941. In particular, he was concerned that most government work at county level was not being routed through the county government at all but rather through the CCP county committee. In early 1941 apparently this had even led to the Joint Office (for the Taihang, Taiyue and South Hebei Base Areas, the forerunner of the Border Region Government) remaining uninformed for several months about a whole series of appointments at the level of county head. Xu Zirong also told of a branch secretary in Shexian who had fixed a board over his door which read 'I am in charge of the head of the village.'[93] Ironically, the Organizational Work Conference at which Xu spoke was a series of six through the war years organized by the CCP base area committee's Organization Department (of which Xu was Director at the time) that always dealt not only with party affairs, but also leadership issues in local government and mass organizations.[94]

Members and Cadres

In September 1937 a young educated teacher of 19 who had returned to his native place with the outbreak of war attended a public meeting of about a hundred people in the temple square at Yangxuan Village, Pingding County, called to encourage resistance to Japan. The meeting had been organized by Peng Tao of the CCP PingHan Railway Provincial Committee, and Zhang Hao (from the 129th Division) also spoke. 'They looked really swell in their uniforms with red tabs on their collars. We wondered who they were' recalled the veteran cadre who had been that young teacher about the day he joined the revolution. The meeting was targeted at intellectuals and urban workers, urging them in fairly radical terms to 'emancipate their thinking' and 'overthrow the ossified politics that had led to war.'

Similar meetings were held throughout this part of the base area and in West Hebei in the next few months, and resulted in an early membership for the base area CCP that was predominantly comprised of urban intellectuals (basically anyone with a formal education, but mainly teachers, with a few bank workers, clerks, bookkeepers) and to a lesser extent industrial workers.[95] The extent of this urban bias should be no surprise and its influence on the leadership of the base area should also not be underestimated. The original core of civilian CCP activists came as did Peng Tao from the CCP PingHan Provincial Committee, and they were soon joined by former teachers and students from the North China universities and colleges closed by the war, such as Yang Xiufeng in West Hebei. Many of those recruited in the early few months of the CCP Hebei-Henan-Shanxi Provincial Committee's activities proved to be long-term members of the CCP and eventually became senior cadres, both in the base area and after the establishment of the PRC.

There were altogether several hundred urban intellectuals who joined the local CCP organization at that time. By August 1940 those classified as 'intellectuals' occupied 72 percent of appointments as county level CCP cadres in the base area, 14 percent of appointments as subdistrict CCP cadres, 74 percent of position as county-level government officials, and 33 percent of appointments to leadership positions in the various mass organizations.[96] Though some of these (no more than 5 percent of county-level CCP cadres, and perhaps 10 percent of county-level government officials) were undoubtedly rural intellectuals—peasant children who had gained an education in an urban center—it would seem likely that the overwhelming majority were drawn from the early urban recruits to the base area CCP.

Party recruitment in the Taihang Base Area always proceeded fitfully, though sometimes spectacularly, as in the early stages of the war. By the end of June 1938 party membership under the CCP Hebei-Henan-Shanxi Provincial Committee exceeded 10,000.[97] At first the national CCP leadership responded encouragingly simply reminding the local organization of the problems that might result from such rapid expansion.[98] However, in August after the CCP Central Committee had received a fuller report, Liu Shaoqi simply instructed the base area to stop further expansion for the moment, criticizing the 'press-gang mentality' which in his view the party committee had either adopted or allowed to emerge unchecked.[99]

As it happened, the organizational difficulties of rapid expansion had also started to become more apparent to the local CCP themselves. On reflection, many of them were highly critical of the rapid expansion they had been part of. They were probably being over critical of themselves (possibly even to good political effect at the time) for this had been an expansion they had been relatively powerless to check, and indeed to do so might well have hindered the development of the Southeast Shanxi Base Area and Sacrifice League activities, though perhaps not necessarily the growth of the local CCP organization.[100]

Nonetheless the problems encountered had been real enough. One set of problems concerned the cadre force, many of whom had, as already noted, been 'white area' cadres working underground in the cities of North China and had little experience for dealing with the rural, and sometimes extremely poor environments where they found themselves working. In particular, one series of criticisms often heard was that cadres had 'lacked patience, understanding and subtlety' in dealing with peasants who were 'traumatized by the Japanese invaders killing and looting, and who were only too willing to join the guerillas.'[101]

CCP membership had grown to over 20,000 by the end of 1938, and despite concerns kept growing in 1939. By the time of the 1st Taihang Base Area CCP Congress, held in September 1939 in Wuxiang, membership had reached 30,150 people and was to increase still further to reach 36,111 in November 1939. The party congress (convened as the local CCP's Civilian Mobilization Work Conference so as not to alarm Yan Xishan) proved to be the only representative conference of the CCP during the war, and met to elect representatives to the 7th CCP National Congress. The composition of the 272 representatives who attended indicated the early recruitment and organization patterns of the base area. The overwhelming majority were active in Central Shanxi and West Hebei; had joined the CCP only in the last two years (that is since the CCP base area committee had been formed); and were males under 25 years old (though 6 percent were women). Just under half had completed tertiary education, but some 38 percent were illiterate.[102]

This time the consequences of CCP growth led to action, not least because of the changes in the wider political environment that resulted in the assumption of local political control. A 'consolidation' campaign and re-registration of party memberships was implemented during the first few months of 1940 that reduced CCP membership in the base area to 24,978 by August 1940.[103] Although initially targeted against sympathetic attitudes to Yan Xishan, as the campaign developed it changed its focus, as a debate developed within the base area CCP about the relationship between class and revolution.[104] New party members were sought amongst industrial workers and landless laborers; members of the rural social elite, rich peasants, middle peasants, and intellectuals were discriminated against. The report on the consolidation campaign presented its results by demonstrating the increase in the ratio between party members who were workers and poor peasants as against those who were middle peasants or higher in status, district by district.[105]

Although the CCP in the base area was still to undergo further change in its composition to the end of the war, the size of its membership and organization stayed relatively static (allowing for the reintegration of the counties in the southern area of the Taihang Mountains during the second half of 1943.) Table 1.2 provides an indication of the size and distribution of CCP strength by county and district within the base area, based on the situation as at August 1941. Figures for Liaoxian and Licheng are shown separately because although physically located in other districts, for CCP affairs they were at this time base area-level experimental counties for the development of policies and procedures, and so directly subordinated to the base area party committee.[106]

Some attempt was made during 1941 to remedy the more extreme effects of the earlier party consolidation campaign, but with little imme-

Table 1.2 CCP Branches and Membership in the Taihang Base Area, August 1941 (by county)

District/County	Sub-districts	Branches	Members	*District*/County	Sub-districts	Branches	Members
1st District (West Hebei)				*4th District (South Tainan)*			
Zanhuang	8	88	1021	Huguan	1	8	58
Yuanshi	5	40	363	S Pingshun	5	74	575
Lincheng	7	79	918	N Pingshun	4	14	262
Neiqiu			345	Changzhi			
Shahe	5	44	355	Ludong	4	48	378
East Xingtai		55	463				
West Xingtai	8	110	1148				
Gaoyi							
Jingjing							
Huolu							
2nd District (Central Shanxi)				*5th District (North Zhang River)*			
East Pingding	6	38	541	N Wu'an	8	59	780
East Xiyang	5	60	1015	S Wu'an	4	28	188
East Heshun	5	50	876	Cixian	22	131	1564
West Heshun	6	47	919	Shexian	7	55	900
West Pingding	3	51	400	Piancheng	3	18	252
West Xiyang	5	47	567	N Linxian	3	13	150
Taigu	3	19	243	Anyang			16
Yuci	4	29	318				
Shouyang	4	21	208				
3rd District (East Shanxi)				*Directly subordinated counties*			
Wuxiang	7	132	3156	Liaoxian	11	126	1763
East Wuxiang	5	50	756	Licheng	8	115	1764
Yushe	6	85	1527				
Xiangyuan	7	64	635				
Qixian	2	7	86				
Total						1,805	24,512

Source: Zhonggong JinJiYu qudangwei 'Zuzhi gongzuo baogao' ['Report on Organization Work'] 1 August 1941, in TDZH vol.4: 1941, p.540.

diate success. Moreover, the critique of perceived privilege which lay at its heart developed into a further attack on village cadres during 1942 as the CCP campaigned to introduce rent and interest reduction, and more generally on middle peasants. As Chapter 5 details, the role of the middle peasants and their revolutionary potential (or otherwise) was to be a constant issue for the party and indeed the course of rural social reform during 1940–45. The issue was only resolved once the region's cadres had participated in the rectification movement at the end of 1944, which ensured greater CCP centralized control of cadres in the Taihang Base Area.[107]

These political uncertainties would have been sufficient to discourage people from wanting to become cadres without the added problems of a hard-pressed guerilla war. The result was that for most of the 1940s the base area CCP committee had problems persuading people to become cadres. On one occasion, at a 1942 conference on party branch development, Xu Zirong pointed out dejectedly 'Half of the cadres in Heshun have gone. Cadre vacancies in Yuanshi are being filled all the time, but it doesn't work. Most of the local cadres just give up and go home.'[108] Cadre shortages were widespread, particularly during 1943–44, even in those counties, notably Pingding, Heshun, Wuxiang and Liaoxian (Zuoquan) where a tradition had rapidly established itself of villages producing their own cadres.[109] Quite apart from the problems that resulted from political uncertainty, the transferability of cadres was limited. Few were able or prepared to leave their family or land to go and work in another village, let alone another county or district. Usually such moves were only possible where personal circumstances intervened, such as divorce or marriage.[110] Despite these shortages, the cadre force under the CCP committee of the base area was estimated to be 4,990 people by 1945.[111]

NOTES

1. See Lyman Van Slyke 'The Chinese Communist Movement during the Sino-Japanese War, 1937–45' in *The Cambridge History of China* Vol. 13, Republican China, 1912–1949, Part II, Cambridge, Cambridge University Press, 1986, Chapter 12, p.646 ff, especially p.652—'In short, geography (one might even say military geography) might be more important to the success of a base area than its social and economic structure.'

2. Yan's relationship with Chiang Kai-shek and the Nationalist Party government before the War was only ever strained at best, and indeed led to open conflict in 1930. One goal in building narrower gauge railways had been to restrict the intrusion of central government into the province. See Donald G Gillin *Warlord Yen Hsi-shan in Shansi Province, 1911–1949* Princeton, New Jersey, Princeton University Press, 1967, p.89; and Jiang Shunxing and Li Liangyu (ed) *Shanxi wang Yan Xishan* [Yan Xishan, King of Shanxi] Henan renmin chubanshe, 1990, p.95.

3. Whilst the new railway line successfully split the Taiyue and Taihang Base Areas, the development of the Handan-Changzhi Highway was only temporarily successful. Control of the mountain section of this road between and including Shexian (in Henan) and Licheng was retaken by the base area at the end of 1939 and never relinquished. See Li Daqing and Dong Weifa 'Balujun yierjiushi Licheng gongzuotuan yu Zhanhe youjiduide chuangjian' ['The Licheng Work Team of the Eighth Route Army's 129th Division and the Establishment of the Zhan River Guerilla Unit'] in *Shanxi dangshi tongxun* [Newsletter of Shanxi Party History] no.3, 1987, p.33; and Taihang geming genjudishi zongbian weihui (ed) *Taihang geming genjudi shigao* [Outline History of the Taihang Revolutionary Base Area] Taiyuan, Shanxi renmin chubanshe, 1987, p.65.

4. Deng had a close relationship with Mao Zedong at this time, despite their physical separation. See David S G Goodman *Deng Xiaoping and the Chinese Revolution: A Political Biography* London, Routledge, 1994, p.39 ff; and Benjamin Yang *Deng: A Political Biography* New York, M E Sharpe, 1998, p.87 ff.

5. Li Xuefeng provided a detailed history of the 'middle peasant question' in his summary report to the Taihang Base Area's Sixth Organizational Meeting on 8 March 1945, in SOC p.62. For an earlier and detailed discussion of the middle peasant question, see session led by Lai Ruoyu at the meeting of the regional party committee on 5 September 1943, in ZJY p.21.

6. Li Ji *Dongzheng jishu* [Record of the Eastern Expedition] Taiyuan, Shanxi renmin chubanshe, 1986, p.6.

7. Donald G Gillin *Warlord Yen Hsi-shan in Shansi Province, 1911–1949* Princeton, New Jersey, Princeton University Press, 1967, p.220 ff.

8. Nie Rongzhen *Nie Rongzhen huiyilu* [Nie Rongzhen's Reminiscences] Hong Kong, Mingbao chubanshe, 1991, p.277.

9. According to Jack Belden, who interviewed Yang later in 1947, he had been a 'democratic personage' recruited to the United Front cause by Japanese invasion and Nationalist intransigeance. This would have to have been a major propaganda coup. Yang had been a member of the CCP since being recruited as a student in Paris during 1929. He went on to study as revolutionary activist in Moscow and to work initially in Germany, later returning to Beiping. See Jack Belden *China Shakes the World* Penguin, 1973, p.110. More recent descriptions of Yang's life and work may be found in: Bo Yibo 'Gongchandangyuande kaimo Yang Xiufeng tongzhi' ['Comrade Yang Xiufeng—a Model Communist Party Member'] in *Renmin ribao* [People's Daily] 9 January 1984; and Yang Xiufeng 'Guanyu wo zai Jixi minshunchu he Jixi youjiduide gongzuo qingkuang' ['Work Conditions when I was in the West Hebei Training Office and West Hebei Guerilla Troupe'] 1983, in DWD p.105.

10. One was the CCP Shanxi (Open) Work Committee, and the other was the CCP Shanxi Province Work Committee. See Zhonggong Shanxi shengwei dangshi yanjiushi (ed) *Zhongguo gongchandang Shanxi lishi gangyao* [Outline History of the CCP in Shanxi] Beijing, Zhonggong dangshi chubanshe, 1991, p.15.

11. Warren Kuo *Analytical History of the Chinese Communist Party* Taipei, Institute of International Relations, 1970, vol.4, p.9.

12. Bo Yibo 'Wodang zai Shanxi tongyizhanxian chenggongde yizhao' ['The Success of the Party in the Shanxi United Front'] in *Dangshi wenhui* [Selections from Party History] no.2, 1985.

13. Names and particularly geographic descriptors are inherently confusingly in this context. Quite apart from post-War administrative changes, the counties of east Shanxi were designated as Central Shanxi; the designated West Hebei Militia Training Office was a formal body established by the South Hebei Administrative Office; and the later West Hebei District of the Taihang Base Area included part of the east Shanxi counties.

14. Liu Bocheng 'Women zai Taihangshanshang' ['Going Up the Taihang Mountains'] in *Renmin ribao* [People's Daily] 21 June 1962.

15. Qi Wu *Yige geming genjudi de chengzhang: KangRi zhanzheng he jiefang zhanzheng shiqi de JinJiLuYu Bianqu gaikuang* [The Transformation of a Revolutionary Base Area: An Outline of the Shanxi-Hebei-Shandong-Henan Border Region during the War of Resistance and the War of Liberation] Beijing, Renmin chubanshe, 1957, p.198.

16. LXH p.25.

17. Zhonggong Hebei Shengwei dangshi ziliao zhengji bianshen weiyuanhui and Taihang (Hebei bufen) shiliao lianhe zhengbian bangongshi (ed) *Jixi minxunchu yu Jixi Youjidui* [The West Hebei Training Regiment and the West Hebei Guerilla Troop] Taihang geming genjudi shiliao congshu No.10, Shijiazhuang, Hebei renmin chubanshe 1989, p 10.

18. Zhu Rui 'Shiqigeyuelaide JinJiYu quwei gongzuo' ['The Last Seventeen Months' Work under the Shanxi-Hebei-Henan Party Committee'] March 1939, in *Shanxi geming genjudi* [Shanxi Revolutionary Base Areas] no.1 1986, p.3; DJ p.9.

19. Bo Yibo 'Taiyue genjudi shi zenyang jianchi kangzhande' ['How the Taiyue Base Area was Established in the War of Resistance to Japan'] in *Jiefang ribao* [Liberation Daily] 3 July 1943; Dong Qian *Meiyou renmin de shijie—weikun Qinyuan tongxun* [A world without people—the story of the seige of Qinyuan] Beijing, Renmin chubanshe, 1979.

20. Bo Yibo *Qishinian fendou yu sikao* [Seventy Years of Struggle and Reflections] Zhongong dangshi chubanshe, Beijing, 1996, vol.1, p.261.

21. LXH p.38.

22. Liu Shaoqi (Hu Fu) 'Gei JinJiYu shengweide zhishixin' ['Letter of Guidance to the Shanxi-Hebei-Henan Provincial Committee'] 18 August 1938, in DJ p.106.

23. LXH p.46. Li Xuefeng and Zhu Rui visited Heshun in June 1938.

24. The province had previously been subdivided by the Japanese into a North Shanxi Autonomous Region and three administrative areas centered on Yuci, Linfen and Yuncheng. See Shanxisheng shizhi yanjiuyuan (ed) *Shanxi tongzhi* [Encyclopedia of Shanxi] vol.7 *Tudi zhi* [Land] Beijing, Zhonghua shuju, 1998, p.69.

25. Report of speeches to the 1st CCP base area congress by Yu Lin (Zanhuang) and Wang Jijun (Qinbo) as well as comments on Wu'an, in LXH p.77.

26. Bo Yibo and Song Renqiong 'Gongchandangyuande mofan Yang Xiuifeng tongzhi' ['The Model CCP Member Yang Xiufeng'] in *Renmin ribao* [People's Daily] 9 January 1984.

27. Yang Shangkun 'Gei JinJiYu quweide zhishixin' ['Letter of Instruction to the Shanxi-Hebei-Henan District Committee'] July 1939, in TDZH vol.2: 1939, p.420.

28. Zhao Rongsheng *Huiyilu Wei Lihuang* [Remembering Wei Lihuang] Beijing, Wenshiziliao chubanshe, 1985.

29. Edgar Snow *Scorched Earth* London, Victor Gollancz, 1941, vol.2, p.245; Zhao Rongsheng 'Wei Lihuang xiangyao canjia gongchandang' ['Wei Lihuang wanted to join the CCP'] in *Chuanji wenxue* [Biographical Notes] vol.59, no.3.

30. Taihang geming genjudishi zongbian weihui (ed) *Taihang geming genjudi shigao* [Outline History of the Taihang Revolutionary Base Area] Taiyuan, Shanxi renmin chubanshe, 1987 p.68.

31. Li Yong and Zhang Zhongtian (ed) *KangRi minzu tongyi zhanxian dashiji* [Chronology of the United Front in the War of Resistance to Japan] Beijing, Zhongguo jingji chubanshe, 1988, p.260.

32. YZ, especially p.4. Even Warren Kuo, who provides a list of infringements of the United Front, only cites one minor skirmish between Nationalist Party troops and the CCP in this area at this time: in *Analytical History of the Chinese Communist Party* Taipei, Institute of International Relations, 1970, vol.4, p.81.

33. Donald G Gillin *Warlord Yen Hsi-shan in Shansi Province, 1911–1949* Princeton, New Jersey, Princeton University Press, 1967, p.282 ff.

34. Shanxisheng difangzhi bianzuan weiyuanhui (ed) *Minguo shiqi Shanxisheng gezhong zuzhi jigou jianlu* [Record of Organizations in Shanxi during the Republican Era] Taiyuan, 1983, p.3.

35. SOH p.781–82.

36. David S G Goodman 'JinJiLuYu in the Sino-Japanese War: The Border Region and the Border Region Government' in *The China Quarterly* No.140, December 1994, p.1007.

37. Lyman Van Slyke 'The Chinese Communist Movement during the Sino-Japanese War, 1937–45' in *The Cambridge History of China* Vol. 13, Republican China, 1912–1949, Part II, Cambridge, Cambridge University Press, 1986, Chapter 12, p.676 ff.

38. Tian Youru 'Baituan dazhan de weida yiyi ji bu zu' ['The Significance of the Hundred Regiments Campaign'] in *Dangshi tongxun* [Newsletter on Party History] no. 517, October 1987, p.47.

39. Shortly after, Deng Xiaoping was extremely critical of the change in tactics, in 'Shiju he jige zhengce wenti: zai beiju taolun Jinan gongzuo shi de fayan' ['The current situation and questions of policy: talks at the symposium organized by the North China Bureau (of the CCP Central Committee)'] March 1941 (p.21) and even more pointedly in 'Fandui mamu dakai Taihangqu de yanzhong jumian' ['Oppose carelessly opening up the Taihang district'] 28 April 1941 (p.24) in GSX vol.2. Criticism of the Hundred Regiments Campaign was also voiced at the 4th Organization Work Conference, held in June 1941, as for example, by Xu Zirong who complained bitterly about the tendency 'not to mobilize the masses to fight a guerilla war . . . but rather to depend on the army' in his 'Zuzhi gongzuo zongjie' ['Summary Report on Organizational Work'] in FOC 27 June 1941, p.23. See also: Tian Youru 'Baituan dazhan de weida yiyi ji bu zu' ['The Significance of the Hundred Regiments Campaign'] in *Dangshi tongxun* [Newsletter on Party History] no.517, October 1987, p.47.

40. Taihang geming genjudishi zongbian weihui (ed) *Taihang geming genjudi*

shigao [Outline History of the Taihang Revolutionary Base Area] Taiyuan, Shanxi renmin chubanshe, 1987 p.118.

41. Yang Yikui 'Ji Taihangqu renmin wuzhuangde jianshe' ['A Record of the Development of People's Armed Forces in the Taihang Region'] in *Junshi ziliao* [Materials on Military Affairs] no.3, 1986, in DWD p.122. Militia numbers only started to increase dramatically in late 1944. By the end of the War they are estimated to have reached 100,000.

42. Zhang Keqian, in comments on 30 June 1941 at the 4th CCP Organization Work Conference: FOC June 1941, p.60.

43. Deng Xiaoping described these developments in some detail in 'Genjudi jianshe yu qunzhong yundong' ['The establishment of base areas and the mass movement'] 20 February 1943, in *Deng Xiaoping Wenxuan, 1938–1965* [Selected Works of Deng Xiaoping 1938–1965] Beijing, Renmin chubanshe, 1989, p.65–77.

44. Wei Houyan 'Linxian renmin canjun canzhan qingkuang' ['Linxian People Join the Army and the Fight'] p.163, and Ming Hailong 'Wodang zai xiuhuowu jinxing tongzhan gongzuo de qingkuang' ['The Ways in which the CCP Carried out the Work and Fight of Re-unification'] p.242, both in YZ. For a description of CCP activities on moving back into this area, see: Taihang geming genjudishi zongbian weihui (ed) *Taihang geming genjudi shigao* [Outline History of the Taihang Revolutionary Base Area] Taiyuan, Shanxi renmin chubanshe, 1987 p.189.

45. An account of the Nineteenth Century Great Famine may be found in Paul Richard Bohr *Famine in China and the Missionary: Timothy Richard as Relief Administrator and Advocate of National Reform 1876–1884* East Asia Monograph, Cambridge, Massachusetts, Harvard University Press, 1972. Population details from Bi Shilin (ed) *Zhongguo renkou—Shanxi fence* [China's Population—Shanxi volume] Beijing, Zhongguo caizheng jingji chubanshe, 1989, p.51.

46. For example, Bo'ai County's population dropped 28.6 percent between 1939 and 1943, Lingchuan's by 19.4 percent over the same period: *Banianlai Riben faxisi cuihui Taihangqu renminde gaishu* [General Description of The People of The Taihang Region after Eight Years of Japan's Fascist Destruction] 1945, in CJZX vol.1 p.557.

47. JinJiLuYu Bianqu zhengfu 'Taihangqu yijiusi'er, sisan liangniande jiuzai zongjie' ['Summary of Famine Relief in the Taihang District during 1942 and 1943'] 1 August 1944, in CJJ vol.1, p.233. Information on previous famines is provided in Walter H Mallory *China: Land of Famine* New York, American Geographical Society, 1926.

48. Qi Wu 'Fazhan jingji, baozhang gonggei' ['Develop the Economy, Ensure Supply'] Introduction to CJJ vol.1, 1987, p.27ff.

49. Donald G Gillin *Warlord Yen Hsi-shan in Shansi Province, 1911–1949* Princeton, New Jersey, Princeton University Press, 1967, p.220. Gillin quotes the views of Fukada Yuzo, published in 1939, and a contemporary unamed correspondent for *The North China Herald*.

50. 'KangRi zhanzheng shiqi Jichao faxing yilai yu Jiangbi bizhi tongjibiao' ['Table of Values for South Hebei Bank and Jiang Kai-shek's Currencies issued during the Period of the War of Resistance'] November 1947 (p.989) and 'Jichao

faxing yilai yu weilianyinquan cizhi tongjibiao'['Table of Values for South Hebei Bank Currency and (the Japanese backed) Federal Reserve Bank Bonds'] November 1947, in CJZX vol.2: p.990.

51. Qi Wu 'Fazhan jingji, baozhang gonggei' ['Develop the Economy, Ensure Supply'] Introduction to CJJ vol.1, 1987, p.16.

52. As the Patriotic Peasant Association later reported 'Left-wing behaviour, including the random arrest and killing of hostile elements scared people, and caused panic among the social elites who fled to the enemy occupied areas,' in JinJiYuqu nongjiu zonghui 'JinJiYuqu nongjiu zonghui liangnianlai gongzuo cailiao' ['Materials on the work of the Shanxi-Hebei-Henan region peasant's association during the last two years'] June 1941, in TDZH vol.4: 1941, p.377.

53. Deng Xiaoping 'Shiju he jige zhengce wenti: zai beiju taolun Jinan gongzuo shi de fayan' ['The current situation and questions of policy: talks at the symposium organized by the North China Bureau (of the CCP Central Committee)'] March 1941, in GSX vol.2, p.23. See also: 'Deng Xiaoping tongzhi zai Taibei junzheng weiyuanhui kuodahui shang de baogao' ['Report by Comrade Deng Xiaoping at enlarged meeting of the North Taihang Military and Administrative Committee'] 3 November 1939 in Taihang gefenqu dang de wenjian xuanji bianzhe *Taihang gefenqu dang de wenjian xuanji* [Selection of Documents on the Party in Each District of the Taihang Region (4 vols)] 1944, vol.1, 1939, p.114–120; and Zhonggong zhongyang beifangju 'Licheng huiyi guanyu zhengquan jianzheng wentide jielun' ['The Licheng Meeting's Conclusions on Political Development'] April 1940, in TDZH vol.3: 1940, p.253.

54. The Licheng uprising is discussed in Chapter 8. There is little information as yet available on the Shahe and Linxian rebellions. The rebellion in Shahe was followed by a 'large-scale purge' of its CCP leadership and a halt to recruitment of new members for some time, which suggests an additional dimension. The purge is described by Xu Zirong in his remarks to the Conference on Party Branches in Less-Developed Areas on 23 August 1942, in BZYJ p.9.

55. Prasenjit Duara *Culture, Power and the State: Rural North China, 1900–1942* Stanford, Stanford University Press, 1988.

56. The Qiao family lived at Qiaojia dayuan, more recently made famous as the site for filming *Raise the red lantern*. For a history of the Qiao family, see Wu Yiji *Zai zhongtang—Qiaojia dayuan* [In the Great Hall: Qiaojia dayuan] Taiyuan, Shanxi renmin chubanshe, 1993.

57. Isabel and David Crook *Revolution in a Chinese Village: Ten Mile Inn* London, Routledge, 1959, especially p.31 ff.

58. Comments by Xu Zirong, in BZYJ, 23 August 1942, p.2.

59. Summary Report to Taihang Base Area's Sixth Organizational Meeting on 1 March 1945, in SOC p.37.

60. Peng Tao 'JinJiYu shiqigeyuede qunzhong gongzuo' ['17 Months of Mass Work in Shanxi-Hebei-Henan'] April 1939, in *Jinzhong shizhi ziliao* [Central Shanxi Historical Materials] no.1, 1988, p.41. The figures are considerably larger than later in the War: at this time the base area included large areas of the Changzhi Plain, and the less mountainous areas around Qinxian.

61. Zhonggong JinJiYu qudang wuweihui (Peng Tao) 'Guanyu fan "saodang" zhong wuweihui gongzuode zongjie' ['Summary of the Work of the Armed

Forces Committee against the enemy's "Mopping-up" operations'] December 1941, in TDZH vol.4: 1941, 1994, p.954.

62. Li Xuefeng 'Zhonggong JinJiYu di'yici daibiao dahui shangde gongzuo baogao' ['Report to the 1st Representative Assembly of the CCP in Shanxi-Hebei-Henan'] September 1939, in TDZH vol.2: 1939 p.485.

63. The major direction was provided by Deng Xiaoping and Yang Shangkun. See: Deng Xiaoping 'Deng Xiaoping zai Zhonggong zhongyang beifangju Licheng huiyi shangde fayan' ['Deng Xiaoping's opening speech at the Licheng Meeting of the CCP Central Committee's North China Bureau'] 11 April 1940 (p.248); and Yang Shangkun 'Zai Zhonggong zhongyang beifangju Licheng huiyishangde baogao' ['Report to the Licheng Conference of the CCP Central Committee Northern Bureau'] 16 April 1940, p.195, in TDZH vol.3: 1940. Dong Kuisheng 'Licheng gaogan huiyi jiankuang' ['An Introduction to the Licheng Senior Cadre's Meeting'] in *Weiwei Taihang* [The Towering Taihang Mountains] no.2: 1986, p.56.

64. Tian Youru 'JiTai lianbande lishi zuoyong' ['The historical function of the Joint Office for the South Hebei, Taihang and Taiyue Base Areas'] in *Shanxi dangshi tongxun* [Newsletter of Shanxi Party History] no.1: 1986, p.49.

65. Yang Xiufeng 'Zai Licheng huiyishangde baogao' ['Report to Licheng Meeting'] 16 April 1940, in CJZX vol.1, p.69.

66. JiTai lianban 'Banfa maoyi zanxing tiaoli' ['Provisional Trade Regulations'] 7 June 1941, in CJJ vol.1, p.859.

67. Deng Xiaoping 'Guanyu chengli JinJiYu bianqu linshi canyihui de tiyi' ['Proposal to Establish the Shanxi-Hebei-Henan Border Region Provisional Assembly'] 16 March 1941, in BZZM p.27; 'Deng Xiaoping tongzhi yu Jin Ji Lu Yu bianqu jianshe: fang Rong Zihe tongzhi' ['Comrade Deng Xiaoping and the Development of the Shanxi-Hebei-Shandong-Henan Border Region: an interview with Comrade Rong Zihe'] in Yang Guoyu et al (ed) *Ershiba nian jian: xubian* [During Twenty-eight Years: Sequel] Shanghai wenyi chubanshe, 1990, p.19.

68. Li Xuefeng 'JinJiLuYu Bianqu zhengfu chengli yu minzhu yundong' ['The Establishment of the Shanxi-Hebei-Shandong-Henan Border Region and the Democracy Movement'] 2 September 1941 report to Taihang CCP Committee Cadre's Conference, in *Weiwei Taihang* [The Towering Taihang Mountains] no.2 1986, p.15.

69. Zhonggong JinJiYu qudangwei 'Guanyu jiaqiang qunzhong gongzuode jueding' ['CCP Shanxi-Hebei-Henan regional committee decision concerning strengthening mass work'] 15 February 1941, in TDZH vol.4, 1941, p.151.

70. Lyman van Slyke 'The Chinese Communist Movement during the Sino-Japanese War, 1937–45' in *The Cambridge History of China* Vol.13, Republican China, 1912–1949, Part II, Cambridge, Cambridge University Press, 1986, Chapter 12, p.702.

71. LXH p.113.

72. Deng Xiaoping 'Guanyu chengli JinJiYu bianqu linshi canyihui de tiyi' ['Proposal to Establish the Shanxi-Hebei-Henan Border Region Provisional Assembly'] 16 March 1941, in BZZM p.29.

73. On another occasion he made it clear that 'The principle in elections is that those nominated by the CCP will be elected,' in 'Deng Xiaoping tongzhi zai Taibei junzheng weiyuanhui kuodahui shang de baogao' ['Report by Comrade

Deng Xiaoping at enlarged meeting of the North Taihang Military and Administrative Committee'] 3 November 1939, in Taihang gefenqu dang de wenjian xuanji bianzhe *Taihang gefenqu dang de wenjian xuanji* [Selection of Documents on the Party in Each District of the Taihang Region] 1944, vol.1: 1939, p.114.

74. LXH p.121–122.

75. Rong Zihe 'Taihangqu sannian laide jianshe he fazhan—sanshisinian sanyue bari Rong fuzhuxi zai JinJiLuYu Bianqu diyijie canhuiyi Taihangqu huiyi baogao' ['Reconstruction and Development in the Taihang Base Area during the Last Three Years—Vice Chairman Rong's Report to the Taihang Session of the 1st meeting of the JinJiLuYu Border Region Assembly'] 8 March 1945, in ZJ p.299.

76. See, for example, Fred R von der Mehden *Comparative Political Violence* Englewood Cliffs, New Jersey, Prentice-Hall, 1973, p.56 ff.

77. 'Shanxi wuzhuanshu guiding xin heli fudan banfa' ['Shanxi No.5 Administrative District Regulation on the Method of the New Equitable Burden'], p.539; and 'JinJiLuYu bianqu heli fudan zhengshou zanxing banfa caoan' ['Shanxi-Hebei-Shandong-Henan Border Region Draft Regulations for the Administration of the Equitable Burden'] August 1941, in CJJ, vol.2: p.543.

78. 'JinJiLuYu bianqu tongyilei jinshui zanxing shuice' ['Shanxi-Hebei-Shandong-Henan Border Region Regulations on the Universal Progressive Tax'] May 1943, in CJJ vol.2, p.578; and 'JinJiLuYu bianqu zhengfu zhuxi gei zhuanyuan, xianzhang de zhishixin' ['Letter of Instruction from Chair of the Shanxi-Hebei-Shandong-Henan Border Region to District and County Heads'] 26 June 1943, in CJZX vol.1, p.1051.

79. Qi Wu 'Fazhan jingji, baozhang gonggei' ['Develop the economy, ensure supply'] Introduction to CJJ vol.1, 1987, p.14.

80. Deng Xiaoping 'Taihangqude jingji jianshe' ['Economic development in the Taihang Area'] 2 July 1943, in Deng Xiaoping *Deng Xiaoping Wenxuan, 1938–1965* [Selected Works of Deng Xiaoping 1938–1965] Beijing, Renmin chubanshe, 1989, p.78.

81. Qi Wu 'Fazhan jingji, baozhang gonggei' ['Develop the economy, ensure supply'] Introduction to CJJ vol.1, 1987, p.45 ff. Detailed statistics may be found in 'Linianlai Taihangqu jinrong huobi tongji ziliao' ['Historical Statistics on Banking and Currency in the Taihang Region'] 18 February 1946, in CJZX vol.2, p.970.

82. Chen Dong 'Deng Xiaoping tongzhi yu Jin Ji Lu Yu bianqu jianshe: fang Rong Zihe tongzhi' ['Comrade Deng Xiaoping and the Development of the Shanxi-Hebei-Shandong-Henan Border Region: An Interview with Comrade Rong Zihe'] in Yang Guoyu et al (ed) *Ershiba nian jian: xubian* [During Twenty-eight Years: Sequel] Shanghai wenyi chubanshe, 1990, p.19.

83. ZJ p.58.

84. TW p.30.

85. Rong Zihe 'Taihangqu yijiusier, sisan liangniande jiuzai zongjie' ['Summary of Disaster Relief during 1942 and 1943 in the Taihang Region'] 1 August 1944 (p.235); and 'Taihangqu sannian laide jianshe he fazhan—sanshisinian sanyue bari Rong fuzhuxi zai JinJiLuYu Bianqu diyijie canhuiyi Taihangqu huiyi baogao' ['Reconstruction and Development in the Taihang Base Area during the last three years—Vice Chairman Rong's Report to the Taihang Session of the 1st

meeting of the JinJiLuYu Border Region Assembly'] 8 March 1945, in CJJ vol.1, p.282.

86. Li Xuefeng, the long-time party secretary for the Hebei-Henan-Shanxi Provincial Committee was only originally a member of the Provincial Committee, becoming party secretary in February 1938 and serving to the end of the War. On that original committee, he was joined by Xu Zirong (Director, Propaganda Department), An Ziwen (Qinshui, and later Director, United Front Department), Yang Xiufeng (West Hebei), Peng Tao (organizer, and later Director, Mobilization Department), and He Yingcai (Director, Organization Department). Details on the evolution of the Taihang Base Area's CCP organization may be found in SOH p.501 ff.

87. Zhonggong zhongyang 'Zhonggong zhongyang guanyu nongmin tudi wenti gei Li Xuefeng de zhishi' ['Instruction to Li Xuefeng on the question of peasants and land from the CCP's Central Committee'] November 1941, in TDZH vol.4: 1941, p.919.

88. For example, the Licheng CCP Committee was reorganized in early 1943. See, Minutes of the CCP Shanxi-Hebei-Henan Regional Committee, 5 September 1943, in ZJY p.1. Lai Ruoyu discusses the general issue in his account of the base area's organizational development in his summary report to the Taihang Base Area's Sixth Organizational Meeting, 1 March 1945, in SOC p.36. At that time Lai Ruoyu was Director of the Organization Department. The minutes of the summary session of the Conference on Party Branches in Less-developed Areas during August 1942 held that: 'In a corrupt branch or committee some comrades will have made mistakes. The problems should be separated from the people. Deal with the key problems and carry on ideological education. Those who are most corrupt should be punished. (It's shameful not to distinguish the enemy from ourselves.) The most corrupt branches and committees will have to be dismissed and rebuilt,' in BZYJ 24 August 1942, p.16.

89. Li Xuefeng, opening remarks to Fourth Organizational Work Conference, 27 June 1941, in FOC.

90. LXH p.104.

91. For example, Xu Zirong in his remarks to the Conference on Party Branches in Less-developed Areas criticized local governments for having 'poured cold water' on attempts to introduce a more radical land policy, in BZYJ 24 August 1942, p.4.

92. Deng Xiaoping 'Dang yu KangRi minzhu zhengquan' ['The party and the anti-Japanese democratic government'] 15 April 1941, in Deng Xiaoping *Deng Xiaoping Wenxuan, 1938–1965* [Selected Works of Deng Xiaoping 1938–1965] Beijing, Renmin chubanshe, 1989, p.8.

93. Xu Zirong, Summary Report 28 June 1941, in FOC 27 June 1941, p.30.

94. See the discussion of county government and mass organization officials (also somewhat confusingly called 'cadres') in Zhonggong JinJiYu qudangwei 'Zuzhi gongzuo baogao' ['Report on Organization Work'] 1 August 1941, in TDZH vol.4: 1941, p.540.

95. Details on the early involvement of industrial workers are provided in Yang Jue 'JinJiYuqude gongren yundong' ['The Worker's Movement in the Shanxi-Hebei-Henan District'] April 1941, in QY p.283.

96. Zhonggong JinJiYu qudangwei 'Zuzhibu gei Beifangjude gongzuo baogao' ['Organization Department Report to North China Bureau'] August 1940, in TDZH vol.3: 1940, p.536. After 1940 the presence of intellectuals' as a separate category was not noted separately in organizational work reports. This change in practice was presumably related to the debates on class and revolution that emerged within the CCP. See Chapter 5.

97. Zhonggong JiYuJin shengwei 'Gei beifangju bing zhongyangde zong baogao' ['General Report to North China Bureau'] 22 June 1938, in TDZH vol.1, p.239. As with all party membership figures for the base area throughout the War, these include only CCP members organized under the base area's CCP leading committee. They exclude party members serving in the 129th Division Command, the offices of the North China Bureau, or the Eighth Route Army Headquarters Command, but serving in the territory of the base area.

98. Zhang Wentian (Luo Fu) and Liu Shaoqi (Hu Fu) 'Guanyu zai fensui diren jiulu jingonghou jindongnan gongzuo wentide zhishi' ['Instruction on Problems of Work in Southeast Shanxi after Smashing the Enemy's Nine Army Attack'] 4 May 1938, in TDZH vol.1, p.209.

99. Liu Shaoqi (Hu Fu) 'Gei JinJiYu shengweide zhishixin' ['Letter of Guidance to the Shanxi-Hebei-Henan Provincial Committee'] 18 August 1938, in DJ p.106.

100. Throughout the War the CCP in the Taihang Base Area remained at under 1 percent of the population, in keeping with its vanguard strategy. It made no attempt to become the larger membership-based kind of party that emerged after the establishment of the PRC where membership of the CCP has usually been about 4–6 percent of the population. Indeed, during the War there was a CCP rule that party membership should not exceed 3 percent of the population.

101. JinJiYuqu nonjiu zonghui 'JinJiYuqu nongjiu zonghui liangnianlai gongzuo cailiao' ['Materials on the Work of the Shanxi-Hebei-Henan region Peasant's Association during the Last Two Years'] June 1941, in TDZH Vol.4: 1941, p.377.

102. Li Xuefeng 'Zhonggong JinJiYu di'yici daibiao dahui shangde gongzuo baogao' ['Report to the 1st Representative Assembly of the CCP in Shanxi-Hebei-Henan'] September 1939, in TDZH vol.2: 1939, p.485.

103. Zhonggong JinJiYu qudangwei 'Zuzhibu gei Beifangjude gongzuo baogao' ['Organization Department Report to North China Bureau'] August 1940, in TDZH vol.3: 1940, p.536.

104. See Chapter 5.

105. Zhonggong JinJiYu qudangwei 'Zuzhibu gei Beifangjude gongzuo baogao' ['Organization Department Report to North China Bureau'] August 1940, in TDZH vol.3: 1940, p.557.

106. On the development of experimental counties, see Li Xuefeng 'Gonggu Taibei genjudi yu Taibei dangde zhandou renwu' ['Crucial Tasks in Consolidating the Taibei (Taihang) Base Area and the Taibei (Taihang) Party'] 17 March 1940, in TDZH vol.3: 1940, p.95.

107. Li Xuefeng, in his report to the Taihang Base Area's Sixth Organizational Meeting on 8 March 1945, in SOC 20 February 1945, p.64 ff.

108. Xu Zirong, in comments to the Conference on Party Branches in Less-developed Areas on 23 August 1942, in BZYJ p.1.

109. Lai Ruoyu, summary comments to the Taihang Base Area's Sixth Organizational Meeting on 1 March 1945, in SOC p.29 ff.

110. Men sometimes volunteered to act as cadres on condition that the party organization found them a wife; others volunteered to move so that they could get divorced. In his opening speech to the Taihang Base Area Fourth Organizational Work Conference on 27 June 1941 Li Xuefeng encouraged districts and counties to attract new young cadres by helping them to find wives and establish familes; in FOC, June 1941, p.20.

111. Lai Ruoyu, summary report to the Taihang Base Area's Sixth Organizational Meeting, 1 March 1945, in SOC p.29. 2,864 of these were district-level cadres; 2,126 were county-level cadres.

2

Liaoxian: The Administrative Center

Liaoxian, or Zuoquan as it became in September 1942, occupies a special place in the official memory of the CCP. Almost sixty years later, Li Xuefeng, the former secretary of the CCP committee for the Taihang Base Area referred to Liaoxian as 'the centre of the Taihang Region, even the centre of the North China base areas in politics, economics, military affairs and culture.'[1] Even allowing for some enthusiasm from someone who lived there from 1940 to 1945, in an organizational sense his claim is far from specious. After the establishment of the Hebei-Henan-Shanxi Provincial CCP Committee in Pingding, the 129th Division and the base area party committee (which was at that time still designated as the editorial department of the 129th Division in any case) moved south through Xiyang and Heshun to Liaoxian. It was to become the first, and later, after November 1940, the long-term administrative center of the base area.

When Deng Xiaoping joined the 129th Division as its Political Commissar in late January 1938, he came to Xihetou Village, in Liaoxian, where the base area's first activists conference was about to be held. Later toward the end of 1940, the regional party committee returned to the south of the county, and established and developed many key base area institutions here, including cadre training schools and cultural institutes. When the Shanxi-Hebei-Shandong-Henan Border Region was established, its first assembly met in Liaoxian, and the Border Region Government was also located here at that time. From a wider perspective, it was, as already noted, the long-term location of the field headquarters of the Eighth Route Army, its 129th Division, and the North China Bureau of the CCP which were all based in Matian, in the far south of the county, during 1940–45.

Small wonder that to its inhabitants at the time it became known as 'Little Yan'an.'

However, Liaoxian as the center of the Taihang Base Area, and indeed other resistance organizations too, is only the major part of the county's story during the War of Resistance. Despite the early presence of the CCP in Liaoxian, its local organization was largely undeveloped until 1940. Before the end of the united front in Shanxi, Liaoxian was under the control of the Sacrifice League, which though led locally by members of the CCP, was based on a broad coalition including the Nationalist Party and less party-affiliated local leaders. It established a regime that amongst other things pioneered programs for encouraging women's participation in politics and the workforce, and developed a countywide system of primary education.

After 1939 the very south of Liaoxian was a heavily protected and almost self-contained redoubt for the CCP. However, the rest of the county was either occupied by the Japanese and their supporters, or was heavily contested. Topography is a key to understanding Liaoxian's divided experience during the war. The county town is in the northwestern part of the county, which was more accessible and a major trade route between Hebei and the rest of Shanxi, although its surrounding agricultural land was traditionally not very productive. The more fertile southern part of the county is high in the Taihang Mountains and extremely inaccessible, even today. The Japanese first took the county town and its surrounding area, and then attempted to pacify the rest of Liaoxian from there. The CCP divided the county into two wartime administrative counties: West Liaoxian, around the county town, and Liaoxian County in the mountains. West Liaoxian was about half the size of Liaoxian County, in both land area and population, and was regarded as a guerilla county throughout the war. In Liaoxian as the Japanese extended their area of influence in the county during 1940–43, the base area retreated further into the mountains and their natural defense.

EXTERNAL SECURITY CONCERNS

Liaoxian's strategic importance during the War of Resistance originally came from its location as a border county. The road from Handan in Hebei followed the Zhang River back along its river valley back to Liaoxian and then on to Yushe and both Changzhi, the regional capital of Southeast Shanxi, and Taiyuan, the provincial capital. Occupying Liaoxian meant immediately controlling the neighboring counties to the east: Yushe and Qixian. Indeed, for some time in the middle of 1938 the base area also followed this pattern, establishing a CCP Centre for all three counties[2] ; and an administrative subdivision of the Sacrifice League based in Liaoxian that also took in Wuxiang, Licheng and Xiangyuan to the south.[3] Certainly in both the development of resistance and in the early stages of Japanese aggression this strategic significance was reinforced. However, as the Japanese grip on the county tightened and the high mountain area of the county, where it meets Wuxiang and Licheng, became increasingly developed as the heart of the base area, it was this southern area of the county that came to be of greater concern to both the Japanese and the CCP.

The groundwork that eventually permitted the development of the base area's administrative center in Liaoxian was originally laid entirely through united front activities. Well before the outbreak of war the Sacrifice League had developed a county organization; whilst at the outbreak of war a branch committee of the General Mobilization Committee was established in Liaoxian. The local Sacrifice League was particularly successful. Established the previous December by Shi Huaibi, a CCP organizer from Wuxiang, by February 1937 it had enrolled about 3,500 people; and recruited 480 educated young people for the National Army's Official Education Regiment. Education and educational activities were central to its development. Shi Huaibi was a former teacher and he recruited heavily from the staff and students of the county's primary schools, as well as amongst graduates. In May after a visit from Li Baolin of the Sacrifice League's leadership committee (and a CCP member) the county organization established the Liaoxian Patriotic Women's Association. The first meeting attracted a hundred people, many of whom were primary school teachers. The Patriotic Women's Association grew steadily throughout the war, even after the Sacrifice League closed. By the beginning of 1943 it had some 5,179 members, many of whom lived in West Liaoxian and whose activities were necessarily underground.[4]

The early months of the Sacrifice League's operations in Liaoxian were impossible for the CCP. The leaders of the Liaoxian County government were virulently anti-Communist, and tried to persuade people not to have anything to do with the Sacrifice League on the grounds that the county should 'Oppose Communism, Defend against Communism and Limit Communism.' Ironically the recently reestablished local branch of the Nationalist Party was supportive and participated fully in the organization and development of the county Sacrifice League. Yan Xishan had approved the appointment of Ouyang Jingrong (a member of the CCP) as head of the county administration and of the local Sacrifice League.[5] However, he was unable to take up office until the county head, Li Yueting, decided to pack up his family and leave, presumably as news of the Japanese invasion from the northeast filtered through. More open CCP organization was now possible, but even then remained restrained.

Until the end of 1939 the Sacrifice League county government ran Liaoxian, with increasing CCP involvement, but also with the support of the local organization of the Nationalist Party, local notables and other organizations. However, it was always an extremely uncertain environment. The Japanese attacked twice before eventually successfully occupying the county in July 1939. They took, but were unable to hold, Liaoxian from 13–22 April 1938, and were again in occupation for three days at the end of January 1939. When more permanent invasion came in July 1939 the county government moved south to Tongyu.

Even before July 1939 the constant threat of Japanese occupation created a stressful atmosphere, that was sometimes corrosive of resistance efforts. In April 1938, for example, as the organizations of the county government were evacuating the county town under threat of Japanese invasion, a section of the county public security defense force defected and opened fire on the county government. Though the *putsch* was defeated, the action led Yan Xishan to authorize and resource the establishment of a larger and better equipped Liaoxian Public Security Corps.[6]

The successes in fending off Japanese incursions helped to ensure the formation of self-defense units and to recruit guerillas during the second half of 1938 and the first half of 1939.[7] However, the final Japanese invasion of July 1939 was to prove a major setback. The county authorities withdrew south to Tongyu, and reestablished themselves in the southeast of the county. Many of the commercial interests in the county town also followed. A branch office of the government office was maintained in the former county town, and the CCP county committee set up a West Liaoxian Work Committee to supervise those now underground activities.[8]

The base area CCP's longer term response was more strategic. Troops from the 115th Division of the Eighth Route Army moved in and ensured the establishment of a CCP-led government during the first part of 1940.[9] The Eighth Route Army, the 129th Division and the North China Bureau were concentrating their administrative activities in military and civilian affairs in the mountain hinterland where Liaoxian met Wuxiang and Licheng Counties, though they did not move to the south of Liaoxian until November 1940. At least partly in order to protect these activities, starting in November 1939 Liaoxian was developed as an 'experimental county' in which the CCP's policies and procedures for supporting the activities of the base area could be tested and refined. These activities included not only mobilizing the local population for armed resistance, but also ensuring food supplies and developing the CCP's own organization.[10]

The base area's organizations in Liaoxian were centrally involved in the Hundred Regiments Campaign, part of which centered on the county, though the campaign was directed for the most part from Eighth Route

Army headquarters located in Wuxiang. The efforts put in by the local population were little short of heroic. Quite apart from the various militia units that were formed in the county specifically for this purpose, such as the Ertang Combat Group and the Chuankou Guerilla Troop, some 2,000 additional locals were recruited to the Eighth Route Army's forces; whilst 4,130 draught animals and 6,139 people were mobilized to ensure supplies to the CCP forces in the campaign.[11] In Liaoxian the military campaign may have kept the Japanese forces at bay, but it was expensive of resources and severely weakened the ability to resist further attacks, as local leaders acknowledged in retrospect.[12]

The Japanese response was immediate, sustained and sophisticated. Alongside concerted military expeditions, the Japanese local command developed a more long-term strategy that included the establishment of sympathetic local government run by residents, with some success.[13] At the same time it also attempted to obtain intelligence from and plant saboteurs and agents behind the CCP's lines. As might be expected given the fairly close proximity of Japanese and CCP forces, the intelligence battle was acute, and security of information was a major concern for the base area's leadership.[14]

During 1940–43 the Japanese advance pushed the base area back increasingly further into the south of the county. In particular, the 1940 and 1942 Japanese 'mop-up' campaigns took a heavy toll. For reasons of greater safety, during November 1940 the Eighth Route Army headquarters (together with the headquarters of the 129th Division, the North China Bureau of the CCP and the party committee for the base area) decided to retreat from the east of Wuxiang into the south of Liaoxian, to where the county government had retreated in the middle of 1939. Matian and Tongyu were chosen because of their perceived ability to physically support a headquarters operation, and their defensive position. They are located in a fairly well-watered and relatively fertile valley, high in the mountains, surrounded by even higher mountains that generally restrict access and that could afford considerable military protection.[15] By September 1941 any thought in the base area that the division of West Liaoxian and Liaoxian might be a temporary arrangement was abandoned, and separate county-level CCP and government organizations were established.

For West Liaoxian alone the war was to exact a heavy price. Out of a population of perhaps 20,000 in 1942, one in four was lost.[16] From September to the end of the war, 2,930 people died fighting for the base area; 430 were wounded and disabled; and another 2,200 died from hunger and disease.[17] Although the Japanese could not station troops in the far south of the county, they did begin to make incursions even there. The most famous occasion was at the end of May 1942 when a Japanese force of

25,000 attacked Matian, the site of the headquarters of the Eighth Route Army, killing the Deputy Chief-of-staff, Zuo Quan, and in the process taking a heavy toll of some of the base area's civilian activities: more than fifty bank workers and over a hundred workers at the base area's branch of the *New China News Agency* were killed.[18]

In addition to direct military operations, the local Japanese command also engaged in more socially and politically subversive activities. As elsewhere in North China, it introduced a 'peace preservation' program to isolate the CCP forces, and established its own local government and militia. Villages were brought over to the Japanese side in a variety of ways, including promises of protection from further Japanese depredations. In West Liaoxian there were altogether 143 villages, and even the CCP itself acknowledged unhindered Japanese control in 32 of them. In Liaoxian, despite the proximity of CCP forces Japanese political tactics proved fairly successful. In 1941 the county was supplying more recruits to the Japanese side than to the base area guerillas.[19] By 1942, 168 peace preservation villages had been established in Liaoxian and a stranglehold was developing on the southern part of the county.

The CCP's response was a campaign to discourage any Chinese cooperation with the enemy: an 'Anti-Spies and Anti-Traitors' Campaign launched by the North China Bureau in August 1943. Quite apart from a concern with intelligence operations, the tactic was clear—anyone found consorting with or operating for the Japanese in any way would be executed.[20] Li Xuefeng indicated that in his opinion up to that point, the local CCP organization had been too tolerant of opposition to the base area that came from within the local community.[21] Examples were made of local village leaders and the CCP publicized its actions, not least when these were accompanied by the redistribution of confiscated land and property. To the end of 1943 it was claimed that 59 spy rings had been uncovered and 300 spies executed.[22]

For its part the local CCP organization aided and abetted by both the North China Bureau and the Eighth Route Army headquarters also engaged in its own intelligence activities against the Japanese and their supporting troops. The base area attempted to place its agents in key positions in the Japanese-supporting militias and local governments, and to persuade both Japanese and Chinese who were supporting the Japanese to defect.[23] During 1942 and 1943 as the tide of war flowed with Japan, this strategy was only marginally successful. However, as Japanese pressure eased because of activities elsewhere in the war, defections increased.[24] All the peace preservation villages were recovered by the base area at the end of 1944. In April 1945 the county town was reoccupied by CCP forces, with the defection of its occupying Chinese troops who had been cooperating with the Japanese.

INTERNAL STABILITY AND GOVERNMENT

The constant encroachment on base area activities in Liaoxian during 1940–43 dramatically highlighted the problems local government faced in the county at that time. However, the uncertainties of control and allegiance were not new during the second part of the war, nor were they the only threats to social stability in Liaoxian. CCP members may have led the Sacrifice League in Liaoxian during the early part of the war, but they did not dominate it or the county's politics before the second half of 1939. The CCP's attempts to position itself both socially and politically at the end of 1939 and beginning of 1940 were fraught with difficulties, and led to open conflict with its former allies. Moreover, serious fluctuations in economic and environmental conditions in Liaoxian were major sources of instability throughout the war.

During the era of the Sacrifice League-led county government in Liaoxian, the CCP had always had to cooperate politically with other far larger organizations, including various associations of local notables and a branch of the Nationalist Party, which had several thousand members, compared to the CCP's much smaller seven hundred or so during 1938. After 1921 Liaoxian had experienced an economic boom with the county town becoming a considerable commercial center, and migrants being attracted in great numbers from Hebei and Henan.[25] There was also a regiment of the central government's army based in Tongyu, in the south of the county, which had come to Liaoxian from Hebei after the Japanese invasion.[26]

Three large groups led by local notables had competed for both economic influence and political control of the county through the Liaoxian Chamber of Commerce on the eve of the War of Resistance. One was led by Wang Jiayan, who was a large landlord and commercial trader from Xingtai. A second was led by Wen Zimo, who had been a student leader at Shanxi University and on returning home had become head of the county's education department, and was either sympathetic to the CCP or a member. Wen's followers included many of the county's teachers. The third group of local notables was that of 'The Three Zhaos': Zhao Xiyi, head of the Propaganda Department of the Liaoxian Nationalist Party organization; Zhao Ze'an, a graduate of Shanxi University; and Zhao Qing'an, another leader of the Liaoxian Nationalist Party.[27]

The CCP's path to power in Liaoxian was by no means smooth, and a CCP-led government was not established until April 1940. Relations with the various different power-brokers in Liaoxian and within the alliances that supported the Sacrifice League deteriorated through 1939. From the CCP's perspective, an important but not decisive move was control of the local defense forces. In March 1939 the county party committee stepped up the political pressure on the central government's forces in the south to leave. It organized a series of demonstrations and a petition against its continued presence. The soldiers were encouraged to move somewhere else 'to more actively fight the Japanese,' and eventually they left.[28] The CCP then ensured that the Liaoxian Public Security Corps was enlarged still further and reorganized as the Liaoxian Guerilla Group.[29]

Further political activity was severely restricted in the short term by the Japanese invasion. The county government retreated to Tongyu, as did the county CCP committee. Then in late 1939, as Chapter 6 details, the county party committee launched a campaign for land reform, which would certainly not have sat well with some of its allies in the Sacrifice League, let alone the wider landowning society. The local branch of the Nationalist Party was vocal in its opposition, and Yan Xishan sent troops to the south of Liaoxian to intervene. The Liaoxian CCP organized local demonstrations in Tongyu (one of which was reported to have had 3,000 participants) and as tension mounted eventually turned to the Eighth Route Army for assistance.[30] In February 1940, with the assistance of a small army of several thousand troops from the 115th Division led by Nie Rongzhen (who had come from the Shanxi-Chahar-Hebei Border Region)[31] the CCP took peremptory control of the resistance government in a move which Li Xuefeng was later to admit had been more than somewhat extreme.[32] The Three Zhaos were executed, as were a number of their followers who did not manage to escape. Wen Zimo was arrested, accused of having been 'a Trotskyist agent' and later also executed.[33]

The county government was completely overhauled in April 1940. New appointments were made as head of the county government (Ouyang Jingrong left and was replaced by Wang Yaoling, a twenty-year-old political education officer from the Eighth Route Army) and to almost all its departments.[34] Moreover, the regional administration under the county government was restructured with seventy-one administrative villages replacing the previous thirty-three village-regions, and new appointments being made to each in preparation for elections.[35]

The CCP's attempt to ensure its political control at this time extended well beyond the immediate circles of the local elite. It tried unsuccessfully to eradicate the local organization of the Nationalist Party, but only succeeded in driving it underground: it continued to have some success in recruiting members to its youth league during the 1940s, especially in West Liaoxian. The Nationalist Party was also active in the south of the county, ironically in Tongyu, the seat of the resistance government and the heart of CCP-controlled territory. There the Nationalist Party organized candidates in village elections, at least until 1942.[36]

The CCP also tried with varying degrees of success to suppress the various secret societies that had been active in the county. It was successful in closing down the 'Long Hairs'—a fairly recent import from Wu'an County in Hebei—but could not stop the operations of the 'Glorious Village' and the 'Village Restorationists'—two closely related secret societies concerned with self-defense that had well-developed local roots amongst landlords and rich peasants.[37] There are few recorded instances of open resistance to the local CCP after 1939. However, it would not be unreasonable to assume that some of the reported cases of spy and sabotage activity might have resulted from actions driven by resentment at the CCP's tightening of control in those parts of the county it still directed after Japanese occupation, and indeed it is even possible that the CCP's behavior at that time led some locals to prefer to participate in peace preservation activities and side with the Japanese. Certainly the five large-scale business concerns that had followed the resistance county government to Tongyu in July 1939, returned north to the county town after the CCP's takeover.[38]

Liaoxian's economic problems were only partly related to the changes at the end of 1939 and beginning of 1940. The county's economy had declined dramatically during the decade before the outbreak of war. This rate of decline seems to have been temporarily slowed, but not reversed, during the period of the Sacrifice League-led county government from October 1937 to September 1939. Thereafter economic fluctuations and weakness bedevilled the local economy until the end of 1944. In the two decades before the War of Resistance the county's economy had come to be based on two major industries: coal and sheep. However, both these industries had been badly affected by lack of the investment in infrastructure needed to reach their wider markets that had come with economic decline.[39] The coal industry in Liaoxian slowed down; and the number of sheep dropped considerably, from several hundred thousands in the mid-1930s to only 70,000 by 1940.[40]

From mid-1937 to the end of 1939 the county's economy declined but slowly. The number of industrial and commercial enterprises increased from 490 to 579, and their total capital decreased from 80,240 *yuan* to 79,300 *yuan*. However, the changed military and political situation in Liaoxian resulted in serious economic problems. In 1937 Liaoxian's agricultural output had been about 270,000 *dan* of grain: the main crops being corn and millet. By 1940 this output had fallen to 130,000 *dan*.[41] The number of commercial and industrial enterprises dropped dramatically (to 469) and the value of their capital was almost halved (to 42,000 *yuan*) within three months.[42] Inflationary pressures were great both immediately after December 1939 and in the longer term. Table 2.1 provides information on the rising prices of a number of staple products from before September 1939, through the end of 1939 and the beginning of 1940, to late

Table 2.1 Inflation in Liaoxian, 1937–1940 (price in South Hebei dollars)

Product	Price Pre-War to September 1939	September 1939 to June 1940	June 1940 to September 1940
Millet (per *dou*)	0.40	8.00	10.00
Cotton (per *jin*)	0.50	3.00	6.00
Salt (per *jin*)	0.28	0.70	0.80
Kerosene (per *jin*)	0.30	1.80	2.40

Source: JinJiYuqu nongjiu zonghui 'JinJiYuqu nongjiu zonghui liangnianlai gongzuo cailiao' ['Materials on the work of the Shanxi-Hebei-Henan region peasants' association during the last two years'] June 1941, in TDZH vol.4: 1941, p.406.

1940. Table 2.2 provides figures on the range of exchange rates for the South Hebei Dollar against a silver dollar in Liaoxian during 1940–42.

Disease was a major challenge to Liaoxian during the war. In particular, there were serious problems with malaria, typhus and scabies. According to the secretary of the CCP county committee in 1942, 2.1 percent of the population were sick in 1939, 21 percent in 1940 and 22.3 percent in 1941.[43] Altogether 7,394 people are reported to have died from disease and starvation in Liaoxian during the war: twice as many people as died as a direct result of combat.[44] In particular, almost 4,000 are reported to have starved to death during 1940 alone when there was a particularly severe drought, followed by famine. On this occasion the county government was active in famine relief work, providing grain to 8,732 famine victims as well as 3,092 in the families of those away fighting on active service.[45] Liaoxian did not experience as severe a drought again during the war.

Table 2.2 Exchange Rates, Liaoxian, 1940–1942 (South Hebei dollars)

Year	Cost of 1 silver dollar in South Hebei Dollars Low	High
1940	4.6	5.3
1941	6.0	8.5
1942	8.0	16.0

Source: 'Linianlai Taihangqu jinrong huobi tongji ziliao' ['Historical Statistics on Banking and Currency in the Taihang Region'] 18 February 1946, in TYG vol.1, Section 4, p.32.

However, production was severely disrupted again in August 1944 by a locust storm that moved into the county from the east. On that occasion, a mass mobilization of several thousand people attempted to beat the locusts off the crops.[46]

As already noted, the Liaoxian Sacrifice League had strong support from teachers and intellectuals at its inception, and as a result placed great emphasis on both training in general and improving literacy. The Sacrifice League-led government in the early part of the war overhauled the educational system. The goal of universal primary education was taken seriously. New primary schools were established all over the county, with the explicit intention of teaching the children of laborers and peasants. In particular, considerable efforts went into encouraging girls to attend.[47] By 1939 there were 171 junior primary schools with a total enrolment of 7,054; and 6 senior primary schools with 330 pupils.

These early attempts at social engineering were sustained in both West Liaoxian and Liaoxian after 1939. Certainly their continuation was made possible by the number of teachers who had joined the resistance movement through the Sacrifice League. By the end of the war every village had its own junior primary school with a total enrolment of 11,000. In addition, the governments encouraged part-time winter study and mass education programs in which 31,825 people were participating by the start of 1945. The mass education programs were particularly targeted at women. According to one participant, they responded not only by cutting their hair (a sure sign of rebellion before marriage) but also by 'demanding freedom of choice in marriage.'[48] Already by the end of 1941 there was some evidence that these various programs were having some influence: of the 2,211 village representatives elected in that year, 21 percent were women, as were just over 9 percent of the village leaders.[49]

Resistance government work in both West Liaoxian and Liaoxian was frequently disrupted, and largely restricted to the southern part of the county, particularly around Tongyu and Matian. Many of the activities were directly related to the guerilla war effort: ensuring grain supplies, recruiting and training troops and staff, and the development of medical services. Partly because of the location of the Eighth Route Army headquarters, Liaoxian developed a medical network. There was a small hospital, and by the end of 1943, 41 doctors and 24 pharmacies in the county.[50]

Village elections had been possible in CCP-controlled areas of the county during the middle of 1940 with about 60 percent of the county participating. Voting was in public, with beans as ballots that were placed in bowls in front of the candidates. More regularized elections at village, subdistrict and county level were held in 1941 in line with new CCP national policy on implementing the 'Three-thirds System.' Although there was some attempt to follow the approximate ratios intended in the CCP's national policy, there were clearly difficulties encountered. In Liaoxian at the subdistrict level some 60 percent of those elected were CCP members. In West Liaoxian the guerilla situation left it hard to find enough CCP members to take up places and very few 'progressive' representatives: half of all those elected in all the county's elections were from the 'neutral' category.[51] By the next round of elections, in April 1945, the CCP's directives were more strictly followed, and the elected county government had equal numbers of CCP members, progressives and neutrals. Liaoxian was renamed Zuoquan on 18 September 1942 at a ceremony in Matian, following a petition signed by over 10,000 people and proposed by the representative associations 'of the county's primary school teachers and gentry.'[52]

As elsewhere in North China, one immediate response in the early 1940s to the economic difficulties was the attempt to reduce the number of cadres and officials that had to be publicly supported. In Liaoxian's case, however, the target set by the local party committee was stricter than elsewhere. Where generally the limit set by the CCP's national leadership was no more than 3 percent of the population to be engaged in nonproduction work, in Liaoxian the target was one percent.[53] This difference was presumably because of the co-location of so many base area, 129th Division, Eighth Route Army and North China Bureau units and organization in the county that had also to be fed and supplied from local resources, even if their staff numbers were not counted for administrative purposes together with those of the county committee of the CCP and the local government.

As the pressure from the Japanese side eased, governments in both West Liaoxian and Zuoquan were able to engage increasingly more proactively and with greater effect in the promotion of production activities after December 1943. Labor was particularly in short supply because of the numbers of men who had joined military units.[54] One solution was the encouragement of mutual aid teams, another was the mobilization of women into the work force outside the home. One woman, Liu Ailian, even made her fame and fortune by organizing an all-women's mutual aid team.[55] Three-quarters of households in Liaoxian joined mutual aid teams for the spring ploughing of 1944; and cooperatives were started for the rudimentary textile industry, based on cotton cloth manufacture which employed 2,467 people, of whom 432 were women.[56]

THE CCP IN LIAOXIAN

Liaoxian in the War of Resistance is an excellent example of a CCP organization being created with no previous experience in the area. Unlike some other counties in the Taihang region (such as Wuxiang) the CCP had not been active here before; and there were few members of the party who had come from Liaoxian and had joined up when they travelled elsewhere for work or study. Indeed, a number of the earliest CCP members in Liaoxian came from neighboring counties. Even in the first few years of the war the local CCP's development was somewhat restricted, and did not really start in earnest until the end of 1939 with the changing military and political environment and the retreat of CCP activities into the mountains where Liaoxian meets with Wuxiang and Licheng. Table 2.3 provides data on the organizational development of the CCP in Liaoxian, and later also in West Liaoxian, during 1937 to 1945.

The starting point for the CCP in Liaoxian was the Sacrifice League. Its original local organizer was Shi Huaibi, a teacher and CCP member from Wuxiang. In September 1937 he was joined in the local organization of the Sacrifice League by two other CCP members. One was Hou Zhenya, who was also a teacher, though from Shahe. Hou had worked with Bo Yibo in the lead organizations of the Sacrifice League, and had been secretary to the members of the 'Open' CCP Shanxi Committee before being sent to Liaoxian. The other was Ouyang Jingrong (from Henan) who had been appointed to lead the county government.

In October, Shi Huaibi persuaded several teachers whom he knew from either Wuxiang or Liaoxian to join the CCP. These included Feng Ruiru, the headmaster of the Liaoxian First High School and Wang Shanling, its senior mistress; Yang Shangyu, another teacher from Liaoxian; and Wu Guangyang, a teacher from Wuxiang, whom Shi Huaibi had worked for when Wu had established the *Wuxiang Weekly* a few years earlier. Together under the auspices of the local Sacrifice League they formally established the Liaoxian County CCP Committee at a meeting held in a school in the county town. There was a sizeable group of women members involved in the establishment of the local CCP, and as Table 2.3 indicates this remained a characteristic throughout the war. About 10 to 12 percent of the Liaoxian CCP were women where a more usual proportion was less than five percent elsewhere in the Taihang Base Area.

When the new Hebei-Henan-Shanxi CCP Provincial Committee, still under the shelter of the 129th Division, arrived in Xihetou from the north on 15 November, local CCP organization was still rudimentary and party membership remained limited.[57] In early 1938, the 129th Division realized the organizational problems it faced in Liaoxian and drafted in a number of CCP cadres to assist, many of whom were southerners or southeasterners. They included two women, Chen Shunying and Jia Tingxiu, who were from Fujian. Chen was first the head of the county party committee's Organization Department, and then later secretary of the county CCP committee; Jia was the first head of the county party

Table 2.3 CCP Organizational Development in Liaoxian (Zuoquan), 1937–1945

Date	Party members Total	Male	Female	Number of branches
Liaoxian (Zuoquan)				
December 1937	240			
June 1938	469			27
November 1938	1,082			66
November 1939	2,138	1,906	232	136
August 1940	1,769	1,551	218	138
August 1941	1,806	1,598	208	138
November 1943	1,675	1,490	185	132
October 1944	2,156	1,967	189	171
April 1945	1,735	1,543	192	171
West Liaoxian				
August 1942	494	463	31	54
December 1943	390	363	27	54
March 1944	495	454	41	48
August 1945	552	523	29	35

Source: ZOH after p.95 and p.122.

committee's Propaganda Department. Because of the local CCP's obvious affinities with educational affairs, the large number of teachers and educated youth involved in the county's resistance activities, and the large number of graduates from colleges and universities elsewhere in North China who had returned home to Liaoxian with the start of the war, the county CCP committee was directed by the Hebei-Henan-Shanxi CCP Provincial Committee to develop a Peasant Training Institute, to prepare cadres for mobilization activities. By the end of the year the program had managed to organize a CCP network across the county and had recruited 240 CCP members.[58]

The pattern of a large body of home-grown but basically inexperienced talent led by a few more experienced CCP cadres from outside the county was also a regular feature of the Liaoxian CCP's evolution. Throughout the war, the majority of cadres, and even on most occasions the majority of the CCP County Committee's members were locals who had been recruited to the party at the end of 1937 and the beginning of 1938. All were educated and young.[59] However, as in early 1938 they were joined in the leadership of the Liaoxian CCP on a number of occasions by cadres appointed into the county by the base area's CCP committee.

With Japanese occupation on 5 July 1939 the Liaoxian CCP Committee withdrew to Tongyu, and at the end of August held its first county CCP congress.[60] Attended by thirty representatives it was essentially preparatory for the base area regional congress, though it did also discuss the need to expand and enlarge the local CCP organization, which was correctly regarded as undeveloped.[61] However, at this point, strategic considerations at a level within the CCP well above that of the county clearly became paramount in the local party's evolution. The withdrawal of the Eighth Route Army and associated headquarters to the eastern part of Wuxiang after the Japanese occupation of Changzhi was part of a trend in which CCP activities were coming to concentrate on the area where the three counties of Liaoxian, Wuxiang and Licheng meet. Li Xuefeng proposed that Liaoxian be established as an 'Experimental County,' under the direct leadership of the base area CCP committee, and specifically under himself (its secretary) and Peng Tao (Director of the Mobilization Department). The aim was not so much to implement policies and practices on a trial basis in Liaoxian before their wider application as to ensure the rapid mobilization of a base of support for the CCP in the county.[62] Its agenda targeted ensuring economic production in general and grain production in particular; as well as the development of democratic institutions, local armed forces, mass organizations and the local branches of the CCP.[63] To aid in this process Li Xuefeng and the base area CCP committee drafted in several more experienced cadres from elsewhere—including Yang Daifu, Chen Ping, and Zhai Ying (Li Xuefeng's wife)—to lead the local cadres.

In effect the local county organization had come under the direct control not simply of the base area but of the CCP's national leaders in the region. Separate institutions existed at national, base area and county level but the extent to which they operated closely together was as might be expected given their co-location, particularly later during late 1940 to 1943 as CCP activities were pushed back toward Matian and Tongyu, effectively company towns by that time. This new equation at the beginning of 1940 helps explain the accusation that Wen Zimo had been a 'Trotskyist': a description often used for attempts to resist organizational centralization within the CCP. In 1942 the relationship between on the one hand, Liaoxian and West Liaoxian, and on the other, the base area as a whole was formalized when both counties were placed under the direct leadership of the base area CCP committee.[64]

County-level party organization within Liaoxian during 1940–45 remained relatively weak, not least because of the war situation. A 2nd CCP Congress for the county was held in August 1941, but its major agenda item was discussion of the arrangements for the two new county-level organizations in West Liaoxian and Liaoxian, and the congress effectively marked the end of Liaoxian's special status as an 'Experimental County.'[65] As Japanese encroachments increased party members and cadres became discouraged, there were constant battles for dwindling resources, and concerns about the lack of training programs for cadres and party members increased.

At the Taihang Organizational Work Conference in 1941, the Director of the Liaoxian Organization Department voiced her concerns in no uncertain measure. She pointed out that cadres were opting out for economic reasons, and party members were leaving through lack of understanding of CCP policies. Cadres were expected to engage at least part-time in production, and with the increased difficulties many were no longer prepared to sacrifice their working time. Instead they were just giving up and walking away, sometimes without even telling people. The problem of time was indeed not inconsequential. One study (of Xiaozhuang Village) revealed that cadres were spending 50 percent of their time in meetings; another (of Matian) indicated that cadres were in meetings for 30 to 40 percent of their working time. For their part, ordinary CCP members were becoming disillusioned and had a growing belief (to be countered) that 'the old system was going to be restored.' In particular she blamed a misunderstanding of the recently introduced 'Three-thirds System' in elections, which many saw as 'the surrender of the party.'[66]

The overall result was a loss of organizational capacity not only in the guerilla areas of the county, but also in the core districts. There were squabbles over resources within the county party organization, and the workload for the remaining cadres worsened, and with it the frustrations they faced and the greater likelihood that they too would quit. During 1943, in Liaoxian cadres responsible for assisting with recruiting for the militia quarrelled over where each could recruit in the county, and over whether there should be separate county and subunit levels.[67] In West Liaoxian, the Director of that county CCP committee's Organization Department frankly admitted that the pressure of workload had led cadres to stop managing the politics of their positions, preferring instead just to give orders, which they demanded others follow without question.[68]

The proposed solutions throughout the early 1940s emphasized cadre education and training. However, as circumstances changed new problems became articulated. There were repeated complaints in both West Liaoxian and Liaoxian that cadres were more interested in ensuring their own economic and political positions and less about working to the common good. In part these criticisms were related to the wider debate about class and social change that was engulfing the CCP in the base area. However, it also related to tensions between long-serving and more recently appointed cadres, and wider perceptions that cadres were privileged in various ways. Whilst not accepting the total corruption of the cadre force the Director of the Liaoxian CCP committee Organization Department freely admitted that

> Cadres do enjoy more privileges. They can raise bank-loans, borrow grain from the army, and beat their wives. Cadres who engage in these kinds of behaviour are mostly capable and experienced cadres but they act this way because of social influences, poor class status, and through their own weaknesses.[69]

Her West Liaoxian colleague, in addition to accepting that cadres were interested in the pursuit of wealth and privilege, also noted that this was only one part of the problem. There were also cadres who were scared into inactivity lest they be accused of using their position to their own advantage.[70]

When in 1943 Li Xuefeng provided a summary of Zuoquan's work during the previous four years, he proposed a solution to the problem of ensuring cadre quality that emphasized ideological education and rectification.[71] This was motivated as much by national CCP policy as by the local situation in Zuoquan. The CCP's 1942 Rectification Campaign was a major turning point for the party nationally, and was a key stage in ensuring Mao Zedong's control of the party. It was also at the lower levels of the CCP's hierarchy a way of ensuring some greater political education, training and assessment of all those cadres who had only been recruited to the CCP during the War of Resistance.[72]

The Rectification Campaign was somewhat delayed everywhere else in the Taihang Base Area. However, as might be expected from a county-level organization that was not only close to the Taihang Base Area CCP Committee but also to locally based headquarters units of the CCP's national leadership, in Zuoquan it was completed by the end of 1944. By March 1945, Zuoquan was still the only county party committee to have completed the process. All cadres—CCP and non-CCP—had to register, go through a process of appraisal, political education and formal assessment, and then reapply for the positions they had previously held.[73] To much fanfare a special study class was even opened for primary school teachers in the county during 1944.[74]

As much as rectification was concerned with ideological remolding, there was also an organizational dimension. Local organizers were charged with making more strategic assessments about cadre placements, in contrast to the system that had basically just grown with the course of the war. In Zuoquan they came to the conclusion that there were perhaps after all too many cadres in the county, and estimated that it would perhaps be possible to reduce the number by about a hundred. At the same time, they also completely accepted that this was unlikely to happen: cadres were for the most part tied to their own land and families, and were in any case not culturally disposed to move somewhere else where food and language might well be different.[75]

POLITICAL CHANGE IN LIAOXIAN

The political revolution in Liaoxian followed a pattern that was fairly common throughout the Taihang Base Area. However, the institutionalization of CCP rule in Liaoxian was necessarily markedly different because of the co-location of Eighth Route Army and base area offices in and after 1940. The first stage in political change was the removal of the former local ruling elite, and the establishment of a resistance government based on a new social coalition. The CCP had no previous organization in the county and was almost completely dependent for its foundation on its own organizers from elsewhere, as well as its relationship with the Sacrifice League.

The return of Japanese troops in force during the middle of 1939 created a crisis for the county government, exacerbated by tensions within the resistance government. The CCP seized control of the county government in February 1940, but this action together with its relatively weak local organization bequeathed both economic and political problems that were only partly offset by the influx of large numbers of party officials and military personnel. From 1940 the Liaoxian CCP's activities were largely directly determined by the base area's leadership. Security and protection of the CCP's enclave in the south of the county were uppermost until Japanese pressure eased, permitting further expansion.

NOTES

1. LXH p. 106.
2. LDB p.21.
3. Wang Shengbo *Ximenghui shi* [History of the Sacrifice League] Taiyuan, Shanxi renmin chubanshe, 1987, p.132.
4. ZOH p.89.
5. The local branch of the Nationalist Party had imploded along with its provincial organization in 1930. It reformed with the onset of war and the opportunities presented by the Sacrifice League.

6. HZ p.23.

7. Xu Zirong 'Guanyu bage xiande zhibu gongzuo' ['Work on Party Branches in Eight Counties'] 30 August 1942 in DJ, p.237.

8. ZOH p.95; Ju Yuxiu, Wang Zhiming, Hao Jinrui 'KangRi zhanzheng shiqi Liaoxixiande duidi douzheng' ['West Liaoxian's Struggle against the Enemy during the War of Resistance'] in *Shanxi Dangshi Tongxun* [Shanxi Party History Newsletter] 1988, no.3, p.27.

9. Li Xiuren 'Wo liaojiede Liaoxian (Zuoquan) Heshun dangde jianshe he fazhan' ['Comments on the Establishment and Development of the Party in Liaoxian (Zuoquan) and Heshun'] in DJ p.572.

10. Li Xuefeng 'Gonggu Taibei genjudi yu Taibei dangde zhandou renwu' ['Crucial Tasks in Consolidating the Taibei (Taihang) Base Area and the Taibei (Taihang) Party'] 17 March 1940, in TDZH vol.3: 1940, p.95. Also, LXH p. 95.

11. HZ p.98 ff.

12. Peng Tao 'JinJiYu qude xinxingshi yu xinrenwu' ['New circumstances and new tasks in the Shanxi-Hebei-Henan area'] 27 June 1941, in TDZH vol.4: 1941, p.479.

13. These moves were part of the general Japanese strategy at this time, but seem to have been somewhat more successful here than elsewhere. See Lyman Van Slyke 'The Chinese Communist Movement during the Sino-Japanese War, 1937–45' in *The Cambridge History of China* Vol. 13, Republican China, 1912–1949, Part II, Cambridge, Cambridge University Press, 1986, Chapter 12, p.674 ff.

14. Li Xuefeng 'Guanyu Liaoxian gongzuode fayan' ['Speech about Liaoxian's Work'] 1 June 1941, in TDZH vol.4: 1941, p.351.

15. Chen Xilian 'Wo zai Liaoxiande yixie huiyi' ['Some Recollections of My Time in Liaoxian'] 1990, in BZZM p.54.

16. A 1942 report stated that the whole county had a population of 75,000, and that (East) Liaoxian had a population of 56,000: LDB p.22.

17. ZOH p.96.

18. On the May 1942 'mop-up' campaign, see Taihang geming genjudishi zongbian weihui (ed) *Taihang geming genjudi shigao* [Outline History of the Taihang Revolutionary Base Area] Taiyuan, Shanxi renmin chubanshe, 1987 p.134 ff; and Taihang geming genjudishi zongbian weihui (ed) *Dashijishu* [Chronology] Taihang geming genjudi shiliao congshu No.1, Taiyuan, Shanxi renmin chubanshe, 1991, p.113. Further information on the number and occupation of civilian deaths may be found in 'KangRi zhanzheng shiqi Jinan yinhang xisheng lieshi minglu' ['Name List of South Hebei Bank Martyrs during the Period of the War of Resistance'] November 1947, in CJZX vol.2, p.993. Various eyewitness accounts of the attack on Matian may be found in BZZM pp.97–146.

19. Peng Tao's comments to Taihang Base Area Fourth Organizational Conference, in FOC June 1941, p.16.

20. 'Matian shuqian junmin jihui lianhe gongshen panguo hanjian' ['Several Thousand Soldiers and Civilians in Matian Collectively Try the Traitors'] 28 September 1943, in GBG p.151.

21. Li Xuefeng 'Zuoquan sinian gongzuo jianjie ji jinhou gongzuo yijian' ['Overview of Work in Zuoquan during the last Four Years and Ideas for the Future'] 1943, in DJ p.309.

22. Liu Jiuxian 'Liaoxiande gongan baowei gongzuo' ['Liaoxian's Public Security Work'] September 1986, in GBG, p.370.
23. Deng Xiaoping 'Zhengzhi gongshi yu dizhanqu tongbao de guanxi' ['The relationship between the political offensive and followers in enemy-occupied regions'] 20 August 1942, in GSX vol.2, p.215.
24. Li Zhikuan 'Riren fanzhan tongmeng zai Taihang' ['Members of the Japanese Anti-War League in the Taihang Region'] in *Weiwei Taihang* [The Towering Taihang Mountains] no.1, 1987, p.52.
25. 'Zuoquan xian' ['Zuoquan County'] in Xu Guosheng and Chen Ninghua (ed) *Shanxi xian qu jingji fazhan shilue* [Historical outline of the economic development of counties and regions in Shanxi] Taiyuan, Shanxi jingji chubanshe, 1992, p.557.
26. LDB p.127.
27. LDB pp.15–18.
28. HZ p.76.
29. HCZ p.36.
30. HCZ p.38.
31. Yu Yongbo (ed) *Nie Rongzhen zhuan* [Biography of Nie Rongzhen] Beijing, Dangdai Zhongguo chubanshe, 1994, p.264.
32. Li Xuefeng 'Zuoquan sinian gongzuo jianjie ji jinhou gongzuo yijian' ['Overview of Work in Zuoquan during the last Four Years and Ideas for the Future'] 1943, in DJ p.310.
33. LDB pp.5–8.
34. ZOH p.41.
35. Yang Daifu 'Liaoxian shiyanxian gongzuo zongjie' ['Summary of Work in Liaoxian Experimental County'] October 1940, in TDZH Vol.3: 1940, p.717.
36. LDB p.150.
37. LDB pp.9–10.
38. LDB pp.140–41.
39. 'Zuoquan xian' ['Zuoquan County'] in Xu Guosheng and Chen Ninghua (ed) *Shanxi xian qu jingji fazhan shilue* [Historical outline of the economic development of counties and regions in Shanxi] Taiyuan, Shanxi jingji chubanshe, 1992, p.556–57.
40. LDB p.13.
41. Qi Wu 'Fazhan jingji, baozhang gonggei' ['Develop the economy, ensure supply'] Introduction to CJJ vol.1, 1987, p.41.
42. LDB pp.14–15.
43. Quoted in Taihang geming genjudishi zongbian weihui (ed) *Taihang geming genjudi shigao* [Outline History of the Taihang Revolutionary Base Area] Taiyuan, Shanxi renmin chubanshe, 1987, p.242.
44. HZ p.275.
45. LDB p.23.
46. HZ p.247.
47. It seems likely that this followed on from the work of the women's literacy class started by a North American missionary in 1920. This had been attended by a number of those who were later active in the Sacrifice League and the CCP.

The development of the women's literacy class as church activity is described in LDB pp.19–20.

48. Li Zikang 'Taihang lao jiefangqu jiaoyu gongzuo huiyi' ['Remembering Education Work in the Early-Liberated Parts of the Taihang Region'] in WS p.475.

49. ZOH p.40.

50. HZ p.267.

51. Zhonggong JinJiYu qudangwei 'Qu xian cun "sansanzhi" qingkuang tongjibiao' ['Table of the "Three-thirds system" in Counties, Subdistricts and Villages'] 1941, in TDZH vol.4: 1941, 1994, p.991–92.

52. HZ p.136.

53. HZ p.139.

54. Zuoquanxian gongshangke 'Yijiusisinian shangbannian gongye yu shougongye zongjie' ['Summary of Heavy and Handicraft Industry in Zuoquan during the First Half of 1944'] 2 July 1944, in CJZX vol.2, p.268.

55. Taihang Fuwei 'Funu gongzuo chubu yanjiu' ['Preliminary Research on Women's Work'] 4 October 1945, in QY p.434.

56. HZ p.243.

57. Shi Wenhua 'Dangde youlianhe youdouzhengde zhengce zai Shanxi Ximenghuide juti yingyong' ['The Sacrifice League in Shanxi as the Concrete Application of the Party's Policy of Unity and Struggle'] in *Dangshi yanjiu* [Research on Party History] no.4, 1984, p.72.

58. ZOH p.13.

59. Indeed in the middle of 1940, 4 out of 7 of the Liaoxian CCP Committee members were university or college graduates. See Zhonggong JinJiYu qudangwei 'Zuzhibu gei Beifangjude gongzuo baogao' ['Organization Department Report to North China Bureau'] August 1940, in *Shanxi geming genjudi* [Shanxi Revolutionary Base Areas] no.1, 1989, p.3; and in TDZH vol.3, 1940, p.569.

60. ZOH p.18.

61. HCZ pp.29–30.

62. LXH p.95; and Li Xuefeng 'Gonggu Taibei genjudi yu Taibei dangde zhandou renwu' ['Crucial Tasks in Consolidating the Taibei (Taihang) Base Area and the Taibei (Taihang) Party'] 17 March 1940, in TDZH vol.3: 1940, p.95.

63. Yang Daifu (Dai Fu) 'Liaoxian shiyanxian juti lingdaode jidian jingyan' ['Aspects of Concrete Leadership in Liaoxian Experimental County'] April 1940, in TDZH vol.3: 1940, p.274.

64. ZOH p.11.

65. HCZ p.61.

66. Zhai Ying's comments at Taihang Fourth Organizational Work Conference, 29 June 1941, in FOC p.48 ff.

67. Xu Zirong's comments at Taihang Fourth Organizational Work Conference, 28 June 1941, in FOC p.34.

68. Xu Tiangui's comments at CCP Shanxi-Hebei-Henan Regional Committee, 5 September 1943, in ZJY p.62.

69. Zhai Ying's comments at CCP Shanxi-Hebei-Henan Regional Committee, 5 September 1943, in ZJY p.54.

70. Xu Tiangui's comments at CCP Shanxi-Hebei-Henan Regional Committee, 5 September 1943, in ZJY p.56.

71. Li Xuefeng 'Zuoquan sinian gongzuo jianjie ji jinhou gongzuo yijian' ['Overview of Work in Zuoquan during the last Four Years and Ideas for the Future'] 1943, in DJ p.309.

72. Boyd Compton *Mao's China: Party Reform Documents, 1942–44* University of Washington Press, 1966.

73. Wang Yilun's report to Taihang Sixth Organizational Work Conference, March 1945, in SOC p.6.

74. HZ p.239.

75. Wang Yilun's report to Taihang Sixth Organizational Work Conference, March 1945, in SOC p.4.

3

Wuxiang: Military Affairs and Mobilization

Wuxiang was, and remains, one of the largest counties in the Taihang Mountains in terms of both population and land area. During the War of Resistance its population was approximately the same size as that of Changzhi, the regional capital of Southeast Shanxi. However, by the 1930s it was probably more of a heavy industrial center, though it certainly had less commerce. Coal and iron are found in Wuxiang in sizeable quantities, and even before the war coal was being mined and iron produced.[1] The county is long and narrow: 123 kilometers west to east, but only 20 kilometers south to north. The most accessible part of the county is in the centre, which is where the county town is located.[2] A river valley (of the Beiyuan, a tributary of the Zhang River system) permits fairly easy communications roughly south-north between the county's two less accessible mountain areas: to the north is Yushe and the road to Liaoxian and Hebei; to the south, Qinxian and the road to Changzhi.

Industry and communications explain the strategic importance of Wuxiang to both the Japanese forces and the Taihang Base Area. Iron and coal were necessary ingredients for industrialization: Shanxi's vast mineral resources had been a major point of attraction for the Japanese throughout the 1930s[3]; and on a less grand scale, Wuxiang was the birthplace of the Taihang Base Area's munitions industry. Controlling Wuxiang was crucial for Japanese access into and out of the Southeast Shanxi Plain around Changzhi, as well as the pacification of the rest of the Taihang region. For the CCP-led resistance Wuxiang was not only a crucial buffer area protecting the rest of its activities in the high mountain country to the east, it was also a key link between the Taihang and Taiyue Base Areas.

Indeed, the field headquarters of the Eighth Route Army was here from the fall of Changzhi in July 1939 until moving to Liaoxian in November 1940, first at Zhuanbi Village and then Wangjiayu Village.[4] The Hundred Regiments Campaign of 1940 was for the most part planned and directed from here.[5]

Just as Liaoxian is regarded as the Taihang Base Area's administrative centre, Wuxiang rests in the CCP's memory as the 'Mother of the Eighth Route Army.'[6] This is much less because the Eighth Route Army's first long-term headquarters was in the easternmost part of the county during 1939–40 than because of the extent of its military experience and involvement throughout the war. Wuxiang was the site of intense combat between the Japanese forces and the Chinese resistance: county histories record 6,368 individual actions.[7] In addition, Wuxiang was a major source of recruitment into the Eighth Route Army: 14,600 soldiers for its main line forces, of whom 3,200 were killed in combat.[8] The relationship between Wuxiang and the CCP forces of the War of Resistance has been enshrined in the establishment of the Eighth Route Army's Museum in the county town.

Alongside its involvement in military affairs, Wuxiang is also remarkable because of its radical politics during 1937–1945. As will be discussed in greater detail in Chapter 7, the county was not only the site of considerable social change and political ferment, but also at the forefront of attempts in the Taihang Base Area to implement programs of social reform. Its CCP committee seemed not only able to mobilize a large number of people for a wide variety of activities, but also always eager to attempt to push the limits in implementing new policies quite clearly toward ideologically defined goals. The county CCP was repeatedly criticized for its 'leftism'—that is in CCP terms, an excess of enthusiasm—on a number of occasions after 1939.[9] Indeed, it seems to have worn its 'leftist' tag with some pride, both at the time and in retrospect. Local cadres writing memoirs of their revolutionary activities in Wuxiang, always seem to refer at some stage to the county's 'leftism.'[10]

Wuxiang's radicalism (or at least that of its local CCP leadership) appears to have resulted from the strength of the CCP organization in the county; the dominant social structure, which made united front activities both less possible and also less necessary; and initially the absence of a sustained Japanese presence until the second half of 1940. Unlike in Liaoxian, in Wuxiang the CCP dominated the Sacrifice League and indeed assisted in its development, rather than the other way around. The local CCP was quickly able to establish new structures of political power, and to do this to some extent from the bottom up. Wuxiang was administered territorially through five districts and forty-eight village regions, under which were grouped administrative and natural villages. The CCP came to control districts, village-regions and villages at fairly early stages in the war, cementing their control of the county through the county government. The result of all these changes was that the CCP was running local government throughout Wuxiang well before both the end of the united front with Yan Xishan and the Japanese occupation of the county.

ACHIEVING GOVERNMENT

Unlike many of the counties in Southeast Shanxi, Wuxiang had a history of CCP organization from well before the outbreak of the War of Resistance. This not only influenced its own development in and after 1937, but also influenced in the shorter term the relationships within the united front and the development of local government in Wuxiang. Unlike Liaoxian where the county CCP had relied on the Sacrifice League for its initial organizational platform, in Wuxiang an independent and stronger CCP directed much of resistance politics from a relatively early stage.

The major cause of this difference was the earlier establishment of both a CCP organization, and perhaps of equal importance, of a mass movement that had at least temporarily been fairly successful, or at least threatened to be so. The origins of the communist movement in Wuxiang are to be found in the activities of Li Yisan, an early CCP organizer. A native of Wuxiang, he went to study at Taiyuan Teacher's College. On graduation in 1926 he went to Wuhan, and enrolled in studies of politics and revolution at the Wuhan branch of the Central China Military and Political Academy. In Wuhan Li Yusan joined the CCP, and later participated in both the Nanchang and Guangzhou Uprisings. He returned to Wuxiang in 1932 as a CCP organizer.

Li Yisan's first attempt to establish the CCP in Wuxiang was more successful in attracting long-term activists than in the development of organization. The Wuxiang party committee remained a covert operation from August 1933 to February 1934. Its principal activity seems to have been the publication of several issues of a journal devoted to ideological education—*The Shangdang Safflower*. However, the CCP branch was closed by Yan Xishan in one of his periodic repressions of organized political opposition.[11] All the same, during those few months Li had managed to recruit a number of teachers and one poor peasant who were to play a central role in the later evolution of the CCP in Wuxiang. The poor peasant was Wu Sanyou; and the teachers included Shi Huaibi (who later was the first organizer of the Sacrifice League in Liaoxian) as well as Gao Muhong and Wang Yutang. One who did not join the CCP at this time, but who worked closely with Shi Huaibi was Wu Guangtang, the later founding member of the CCP organization in Liaoxian, and CCP secretary of

Wuxiang. Wu had established a politically progressive newspaper at that time in Wuxiang, and Shi Huaibi worked on the newspaper as an editor.[12]

The second attempt to establish a Wuxiang CCP organization started a few months later in September 1934, and was considerably more successful. This time as an open exercise, its organizing members—peasants brought in by Wu Sanyou, and primary school teachers led by Li Yisan and Gao Muhong—took the path of mass mobilization. The county party committee established a Peasants Refusal League in May 1935. The League organized peasants to oppose 'landlords, rich peasants and bureaucratic capitalists' and to refuse to pay their debts, rents, grain taxes, and other taxes, as well as to resist conscription. As the movement picked up speed, the Refusal League soon established branches across a large number of the forty-eight village-regions into which Wuxiang was administratively organized. In the process the CCP was also able to establish twenty branches in those village-regions.[13] In the east of the county, 70 percent of the peasants were mobilized and they were withholding about 270,000 *jin* of grain.[14] However, by early 1936 the county CCP was in danger once again. The CCP's Eastern Expedition had crossed the Yellow River into Shanxi, and Yan Xishan not only moved against them but also against all other communist activities in the province. Yan Xishan's advisers had identified 'four red counties' of intense CCP activity, including Wuxiang, as potential sources of trouble. In consequence, the Wuxiang CCP Committee was one of the first to be forcibly closed down (again) and its members scattered.[15]

Despite closure, these early attempts at CCP organization in the county proved invaluable with the start of war. They bequeathed not only a core of fairly experienced, local cadres, but also a rural network of political mobilization that could probably be revived without too much difficulty. This was precisely the main task of a group of three CCP members who travelled to Wuxiang from Taiyuan in September 1937 at the direction of the Shanxi Provincial Committee: Xu Zirong, Gao Muhong and Wang Yutang. Xu Zirong had been secretary to the Shanxi CCP Provincial Committee and was later to become the Director of the Propaganda Department for the Taihang Base Area; Gao and Wang were (as already noted) former Wuxiang CCP activists returning home. Their collective task was to revive the county party committee; reactivate the nascent peasant association; assist with the development of the local Sacrifice League, and through it recruit to the CCP.[16] They were soon to be joined by other former Wuxiang CCP members who had been driven away in early 1936, and a group of about 30 students and teachers who were to become the backbone of the county party committee's cadre force during the war.

An initial attempt had been made at the end of 1936 and the beginning of 1937 to establish a local Sacrifice League organization in Wuxiang. Han

Hongbin and Yao Honggong, both Sacrifice League organizers and CCP members, had come from Taiyuan at the head of a ten-person group to organize activities in Wuxiang's village-regions. However, their success had been more than a little muted and for the time being the development of the Sacrifice League in Wuxiang was placed under the leadership of Liaoxian and Shi Huaibi, who was now working in that county. The establishment of a county level organization for the Sacrifice League was delayed until the arrival of the work team led by Xu Zirong.

Once started in Wuxiang, the Sacrifice League achieved almost instant success, particularly in developing its Youth League. Because of its size, local government in Wuxiang was organized with five districts under the county government, 48 village-regions subordinated to the districts, and about 200 administrative villages subordinated to them. Organizers were sent out to each of Wuxiang's forty-eight village-regions, and branches of the Sacrifice League were established by the end of November. By the end of the year, 15,000 people had joined, and a county General Mobilization Committee was established to solicit donations of all kinds to support the war effort, as elsewhere, under the rallying cry of 'Let those with money, give money; those with labour, give their labour; those with food, give food.'[17]

Equally as spectacular, for what was still in principle a covert operation, was the development of the CCP under the work team. In October a Temporary Work Committee (to establish a CCP organization) was established under the leadership of Wang Yutang, Gao Muhong and Han Hongbin, and by the end of 1937 there were already close on two thousand members. By the time the Wuxiang CCP Committee was formally established, in February 1938 in liaison with the CCP Hebei-Henan-Shanxi Provincial Committee, located at that time in Liaoxian, the local party had recruited close on 2,500 members.[18] The early strength of the local party had been amongst urban intellectuals (largely teachers and students) but the dramatic expansion was largely the result of work through the peasant association, and particularly the reestablishment of its earlier branches and the recovery of their support.

At first there was considerable resistance to both the Sacrifice League and the CCP from the existing county government. It had been alarmed by CCP activity during the mid-1930s—particularly the activities of the Peasants Refusal League—and was no more enamored now, particularly given the rapid public growth of the Sacrifice League. The county head, Zhu Li, was even more alarmed then, when at the Sacrifice League's suggestion Yan Xishan approved the appointment of new administrators to each of the forty-eight village-regions. By the middle of 1938, four-fifths of the village-regions were led by either members of the CCP or their supporters, as were half of the offices within the county government. CCP strategy talked of two kinds of officials in addition to the CCP members: landlords and their connections, and a much smaller group of 'neutrals.' The intention was to isolate the landlords, largely through the work of the branches of the peasant association, and to persuade the neutrals to join forces. It proved largely successful, though there was one official (in Hanbi) who would neither resign nor attend his office. He apparently just stayed at home in protest.[19]

In July 1938 Zhu Li was transferred out by the provincial government and replaced by an internal appointment, Guo Tengjiao, whose period in office was but short-lived. Guo managed to successfully annoy all his subordinates, not least by refusing to pay their salaries on the grounds that there was a war on. They then retaliated by refusing cooperation; collectively demanding and obtaining his resignation. At the beginning of 1939 he in turn was replaced (again internally) as county head by Tan Yonghua, who was director of one of the county districts, and already a member of the CCP. At an early stage in 1939 the county government decided to revolutionize local government in Wuxiang by holding direct elections for villages under the village-regions. The elections were organized for May 1939, later usually referred to in Wuxiang as 'Red May,' even sixty years on. The CCP campaigned through and with the local branches of the peasant association, and was generally successful, having its candidates elected in 85 percent of the contests. As a result the political leadership of the villages changed quite dramatically. The CCP's candidates had included a few landlords and some rich peasants, but it also included much larger numbers of factory workers, shepherds and farm laborers.[20]

The essence of the CCP's Red May campaign was that local peasants were organized simultaneously to amend the system for raising public taxes. To that time, government land taxes had been portioned out to villages, with each village, or more likely the largest landowner or landowners, determining the amount each family should pay, and the manner of payment. The land tax was a form of poll-tax based on the household, and took no account of the number of people in a household, the household's income or its assets. The village-region collected from the village, the district from the village-region, and the county from the district. Local branches of the peasant association and the CCP organized that mass and open tax apportionment meetings should be held in each village, and that the peasants attend in large numbers to question and argue about the particular burdens being proposed, with the aim of encouraging a new distribution where the tax burden was paid according to either wealth or the ability to pay. In some cases landlords and rich peasants agreed to the changes without further ado, but there were about thirty-five cases of fairly open, if mediated, public conflict.[21]

In addition to the election result, there was then also a significant social change in the distribution of the tax burden. Table 3.1 provides statistics

Table 3.1 Land Taxation Rates in Wuxiang, 1939 (percentage of individual annual income by social category)

Period	Social category Landlord	Rich peasant	Middle peasant	Poor peasant
Before Campaign	12.3	13.2	12.0	12.7
After Campaign	23.3	21.8	11.8	0.8

Source: TJSD1 p.1391.

about the changes in the proportions of average individual annual income that different social categories of landowner were estimated to pay in taxation both before and after the 1939 campaign in Wuxiang.

As Table 3.1 indicates, whilst middle peasants were required to pay roughly the same in tax before and after the 1939 campaign, landlords paid almost twice as much. As elsewhere, as for example in the Shanxi-Hebei-Chahar Border Region, poor peasants were largely exempt, only required to pay income tax if ownership or income were over stipulated levels.[22]

SOCIETY AND GOVERNMENT

One of the reasons for early CCP success in Wuxiang was clearly its prewar organization and the knowledge of the locality that came with an experienced group of cadres. However, another was just as clearly the social environment. Coal miners and factory workers in iron works had been one attraction for Li Yisan when he had returned to Wuxiang from Wuhan in 1932.[23] More important, there were many fewer landlords and rich peasants here than elsewhere in the Taihang Region. Moreover, Wuxiang's landlords were far wealthier than their equivalents in other Taihang counties. One consequence was that targeting landlords as a social category in their mobilization campaigns of 1938 and 1939 was likely to have less repercussions for the local CCP organization in Wuxiang than in many other neighboring counties. Another, was that in any case on the whole large-scale land-owners were less likely to be prepared to enter into any kind of united front activity with the CCP.

Not all landlords are as portrayed in the woodcuts and comic books the CCP produced during the war years or even later in the land-reform campaign.[24] The definition of a landlord, as discussed in the Introduction, is essentially someone who makes their living by owning land which is rented out. In general, there were plenty of landlords in the Taihang region who rented out land and remained poor, both absolutely and relatively. There were also those who accepted the need for social responsibility and did not overexploit, and there were certainly those who joined the CCP, and even went on to become cadres under the PRC. There were even some landlords of these kinds amongst the 5,980 landlords and rich peasants in Wuxiang.[25] However, the situation in Wuxiang was that forty-four landlords owned half of all the agricultural land in the county.[26]

Typically in the Taihang Region on the eve of war there was a relatively low level of concentration in landownership: usually there were few landlords and many middle peasants, with just under half the population classified as poor peasants.[27] In the region as a whole, landlord households were 2.8 percent of the total, and they owned 26.3 percent of the land.[28] Wuxiang in contrast, not only had a greater concentration of landholdings in the hands of very few landlords, it also had relatively few middle peasants (about one-fifth of households) and a larger proportion of poor peasants (about three-quarters of households.) As a result in each natural village there was often only a single landowner, and frequently the largest landholdings belonged to absentee landlords.[29]

By the start of the war the concentration of landownership had certainly become an issue in Wuxiang, as the activities of the earlier Peasant Refusal League indicated. There was a popular saying at the time that Wuxiang's establishment contained 'Four very important gentry families, eight who are just a bit less important, and seventy-two who have to keep up appearances.'[30] The concentration of land in the county was largely a consequence of commercialization over several decades, followed by the economic crisis of the 1930s. Most of the families of the largest landowners in Wuxiang had all invested heavily in other capitalist and financial activities around the end of the Qing Dynasty. Through increasing wealth they had all become some form of money lender, if only of necessity as their tenants defaulted, though some had actually also established banks and financial institutions. For most of these families, farming and landowning had become minority interests well before 1937. As the economy declined during the 1930s, they bought the land as it came on the market, as a cheap investment.

Zhao Taihe headed one of the 'four very important gentry families.' His father had been both a large-scale landowner and a tax farmer. By the start of the war the family holdings included coal mines, grain stores, and a series of pawnshops, as well as land. Another of the 'big four' was Hao Quanxiang, whose family had originally become traders during the late Qing. By 1937 he was running a merchant bank, commercial outlets in both Wuxiang and neighboring counties, and employed 150 workers in a construction company. Both they and the other two members of Wuxiang's 'big four' also owned land in south Liaoxian where the administrative center of the Taihang Base Area came to be established.[31]

Yan Xishan's relationship with Wuxiang's 'four very important gentry families' was itself sometimes very tense, and there was little question that they or indeed any of the remaining forty largest landlord families would cooperate with the Sacrifice League, let alone the CCP.[32] Many had left the county by the start of 1938, and almost all by the middle of 1939, though Hao Quanxiang was to become the Japanese-supported head of their version of the county government. During 1940–42 much of the land belonging to these large-scale landowning families was confiscated and redistributed to peasants and landless laborers.[33]

By early 1940 when the contradictions and difficulties resulting from the end of the united front with Yan Xishan were confronting other parts of Southeast Shanxi, the issues had long since been decided in Wuxiang. However, this did not mean that the county government had no further problems from the landlords with smaller landholdings who had stayed in the county. As Chapter 7 details, the success of Red May in 1939 led the Wuxiang CCP to be extremely proactive in promoting social and economic reform at the end of 1939 and beginning of 1940, particularly through its implementation of land policy. The CCP Central Committee may not have had Wuxiang specifically in mind when it issued its 6 March 1940 'Instruction for Solving the Problems of Political Power in Base Areas' that essentially emphasized the need for local organizations of the CCP to maintain a broad base of social support for their activities, but the reminder was certainly apposite.

Even by its own admission, the Wuxiang CCP had overstepped the mark in the extent to which it had promoted communism and the role of the proletariat. It had to relax the urgency and politicization of its drive for reform, not least to reassure those rich peasants and even middle peasants who had taken fright at the turn of events.[34] A pattern was established that occurred annually during 1940–43 in Wuxiang. Policies on social and economic reform were first implemented very enthusiastically, and then when problems were encountered, resulted in the local party leadership either apologizing for the excess, or being criticized by a superior body. This oscillatory attitude to policy implementation was not only likely to bring social conflict when an initiative was first pursued, but also afterwards when rehabilitative action was being taken. In 1941, for example, Xu Zirong admitted that there had been problems with a recalcitrant landlord. The earlier land policy which had attacked landlords and rich peasants had already been reversed

> in Wuxiang as we improved our work, we concentrated on correcting the left deviation. Someone called Guo took advantage of the situation to fight back, even attacking the ordinary people who had supported us. We were forced to punish him.[35]

Self-inflicted uncertainties were worsened after 1940 by both the military situation and by environmental difficulties. The military situation worsened considerably after June 1940 when the Japanese occupied the county town, splitting Wuxiang into two. Separate wartime counties were established in July 1940 for West Wuxiang and (East) Wuxiang. Quite apart from the difficulties this created for the CCP-led civilian administrations, the social impact of the war in Wuxiang was considerable. Between June 1940 and August 1945 more than 20,000 people were killed in Wuxiang (just over 15 percent of its then population); approximately 80,000 buildings were destroyed and over 40,000 animals (mainly sheep) were lost.[36]

In 1942 and 1943 Wuxiang experienced its worst drought for a hundred years. There had been no snow on the surrounding mountains in 1941, and in 1942 there was no rain all spring, resulting in no millet harvest, as would be usual. (Millet is the local staple.) The drought continued for ten months in a row, and in 1943 the millet harvest remained sparse. Troops from the Eighth Route Army were seconded to the two county governments to assist with irrigation work, in particular the drilling of deep wells, which became known as 'Anti-Japanese Wells' that helped alleviate some of the worst problems. At the same time, the pressure on resources was increasing as a result of the influx of refugees from Hebei and Henan who were escaping from still worse environmental disasters to the east of the Taihang region.[37]

Local government continued to function under these various pressures, though a number of adjustments followed. The decision had already been taken in early 1940 and before the Japanese occupation of the county town to reorganize local government within Wuxiang. The village-regions were abolished and replaced by 30 subdistricts, with 198 administrative villages subordinated to them. A contributory factor to the local administrative restructuring was a realization that the various factory workers, shepherds and farm laborers elected to leadership positions in the various villages during Red May were not immediately competent. Whilst they might have been regarded as politically reliable, few of them could read or write, and this became an essential prerequisite for cadre work, particularly as the base area developed.[38]

Later, in July 1940, when West Wuxiang was created as a separate wartime county the numbers of subdistricts in each of the two counties was reduced further to twelve in West Wuxiang and eight in Wuxiang.[39] Economic restrictions meant that the number of full-time cadres in both county administrations was always small. Before March 1942 there were only 56 cadres employed in county offices, and afterwards the number was reduced to 25; at the subdistrict level the reduction in full-time staff was from 162 to 85. Elections were held for villages, subdistricts, and county councils and governments in 1941, and again in 1943; and in the summer of 1944 it proved possible to convene the 1st People's Congress of Wuxiang County.[40]

MILITARY ENVIRONMENT

The third element in ensuring the CCP's rapid achievement of political order in Wuxiang was the lack of Japanese occupying forces in the county until June 1940. With the exception of a highly destructive foray in April 1938, Japanese troops only engaged in minor skirmishes in the first phase of the war. At the same time there can be little doubt that the threat of Japanese aggression was as important for the county before 1940 as after, not least in encouraging the mobilization of the local population for both military resistance and political activities. After June 1940 military concerns became crucial for the resistance as it tried to maintain its positions in the county.

Although the headquarters of the Eighth Route Army did not settle in Wuxiang until the second half of 1939, it had realized the importance of the county to the resistance at a fairly early stage. One of Yan Xishan's major industrial developments at an early stage in his development of Shanxi had been the Taiyuan Arsenal.[41] With the fall of Taiyuan to Japanese forces in November 1937 the workforce of about 8,000 in the Taiyuan Arsenal scattered. A number of them were natives of Wuxiang and on returning home established the Wuxiang Workers' Patriotic Union, which also included coal miners, iron workers, and artisans. The CCP organizers who arrived in September were not slow to see the possibilities beyond union action and encouraged the former Arsenal employees under Wang Hua'nan to establish a small munitions factory—the Wuxiang Resistance Armed Self-defense Iron Works. The initial site had about fifty workers, most of whom were from the former Arsenal, and they were supplemented by a few local people with technical expertise that was otherwise missing. In early 1938, Eighth Route Army headquarters expanded the Wuxiang operation to more than a hundred people, and its expertise and personnel were used to establish a number of other similar fairly low-technology munitions factories elsewhere in the base area, notably in Licheng and in the south of Liaoxian. One of the largest was in the east of Wuxiang, at Liugou, which was estimated to be able to produce about 7,000 guns and 6,500 land mines a day.[42]

At the same time that the Wuxiang Workers' Patriotic Union was being established, the county was also seeing its first large scale recruitment exercise. In October 1937 a recruitment team from the Eighth Route Army moved through the eastern part of the county (Panlong, Hanbi, Hongshui) and raised two guerilla groups of approximately 300 soldiers each and a smaller women's guerilla battalion.[43] These later grew to regiments under the Eighth Route Army, and their formation was the start of a pattern that altogether saw fourteen main line regiments have their origins in Wuxiang, in addition to a large number of recruits to other parts of the CCP forces.[44]

Japanese forces invaded Wuxiang during April 1938 as part of their attempt to take by Southeast Shanxi by storm. From the CCP side the action in Wuxiang has become known as the Changle Campaign, after the town in the center-east of the county where their advance was stopped by the resistance forces. The Japanese advance had been rapid but the retreat was highly destructive. On the way out of Wuxiang the Japanese troops massacred the inhabitants of Gujiazhuang and then burnt the village to the ground. They also laid waste to Guxian, the then county town, finally setting it on fire, and destroyed it so completely that the county seat was subsequently moved to Duancun. For the resistance, this one campaign had the heaviest casualties of the whole war, with more than 1,500 militia and soldiers being killed in action.[45]

When the Japanese returned to Southeast Shanxi in the middle of 1939 they concentrated at first on establishing themselves in the Changzhi and Qinxian areas. Although the Wuxiang county town is actually quite close to the Qinxian county town there is a difference in elevation of several hundred meters and the returning Japanese forces took as their first task the securing of the plain and particularly the communications line from Taiyuan to Changzhi. For the Taihang Base Area this was a crucial development as it effectively disrupted their communications and interaction between the Taihang and Taiyue Base Areas. As part of ensuring their lines of supply and communications the Japanese built a railway line from just south of Taigu (on the Taiyuan-Yuncheng railway line) to Changzhi, which was started in July and completed in December 1939. Part of the immediate CCP-led response to this second invasion was to try to destroy Taiyuan-Changzhi communications for the Japanese, and particularly this new railway line during May 1940.

In June 1940 the Japanese forces decided to advance north, away from the Taiyuan-Changzhi line of communications, into Wuxiang. The occupation of the county that started in June 1940 was altogether more gradual and politically sophisticated than the earlier attempt at conquest in 1938. Japanese troops occupied the new county town at Duancun. Alongside their military organization they established a civilian government. As already noted, this county government was led by the head of one of Wuxiang's largest landlord families, Hao Quanxiang. In addition, Chinese troops—some press-ganged, others volunteered—supporting the Japanese occupied a number of towns in the center of the county. One of the most famous to cooperate with the Japanese was Zhao Rui, a native of Wuxiang and a former officer under Yan Xishan, who defected in 1942.[46]

It was a gruelling war of attrition with the Japanese occupying the lower ground of the river valleys, and the main line of communication across the county south to north, and the CCP in the surrounding mountains, heavily dependent on militia and self-defense forces. The resistance engaged in sixteen major campaigns against the Japanese forces between June 1940 and August 1945.[47] The political dimensions were important to these operations, as they were from the Japanese side, especially during 1943 and 1944. Where Japanese established Peace Preservation Villages, the resistance sent in armed work teams to operate within Japanese lines. They acted to eliminate those who were, and to dissuade those who might otherwise think of being collaborators, through direct action followed by propaganda. The presence of Chinese recruits fighting alongside the Japanese, especially in the police and intelligence services, provided the opportunity to organize covertly, but also for the possibility of double agents. The local militia was able to establish fairly sophisticated intelligence networks both within the Japanese forces and in the wider community, to assist its military operations and in the attempt to secure and maintain its immediate environment.[48]

The longest campaign waged by the resistance was the Siege of Panlong, from June 1943 to February 1944. Zhao Rui, Yan Xishan's former officer who had defected, had led his troops along the valley of the Beiyuan River towards the eastern part of the county, and an area of particular CCP strength. The two earlier locations of the headquarters of the Eighth Route Army in Wuxiang had been in the mountains above the river valley in precisely this part of the county. The local CCP militia responded by pinning Zhao Rui's troops into Panlong and surrounding the town for eight months.[49] Zhao and his troops eventually raised the siege and escaped from the more hostile part of the county toward the center and the county town at Duancun. Zhao and his troops stayed in Duancun even after the withdrawal of Japanese troops, until 27 August 1945 when the War of Resistance in Wuxiang came to an end with the capture of the county town by the CCP forces.

DEVELOPMENT OF THE CCP

Although a Shanxi CCP Provincial Committee work team for the establishment of a party committee in Wuxiang under the leadership of Xu

Zirong had come to the county in September 1937, and indeed been relatively successful in establishing a Sacrifice League organization and recruiting members to the CCP, no county party committee had been formally established by the end of the year. In a formal sense this was because no superior CCP organization had approved the move. In practice, the CCP's organization in Southeast Shanxi was still evolving, and events were certainly running ahead of any possible planning. Moreover, there had been no work team from the Eighth Route Army involved in establishing activities in Wuxiang at an early stage, as there was elsewhere in the Taihang Region; and the attention of the region's CCP leadership was definitely focussed elsewhere, on Central Shanxi and West Hebei.[50]

The local CCP organization had continued expanding regardless, establishing 43 party branches with just under 2,500 CCP members by the time the party's base area organized a meeting of activists at Liaoxian in February 1938. Though this was a small matter at the time, and of no apparent political consequence, it was both typical of the future behavior of the Wuxiang CCP and highlighted a tension with its superior party committee that was to characterize its development throughout almost all the war years. There is no evidence that the county party organization ever opposed direction from the party committee for the base area. Indeed on many occasions it clearly accepted the party discipline that was imposed when the base area felt that Wuxiang had stepped out of line. However, it was often at odds with the Taihang leadership of the CCP on issues related to both the determination of organization and policy, as well as to how agreed policies should be implemented. These disagreements effected the development of the CCP's organization in Wuxiang, but, as Chapter 7 details, became even more apparent as the local party moved to initiate social and economic reform.

The Wuxiang CCP County Committee was formally established in February after approval from the Hebei-Henan-Shanxi CCP Provincial Committee had been given at Liaoxian: the county committee was placed under the newly established East Shanxi Special Committee which reported to the provincial committee. Table 3.2 provides an overview of its organizational development during 1938–1945, as well as comparative data for later years. The county party continued to grow rapidly during both 1938 and 1939, particularly as it operated more openly with success in its social campaigns and the attempt to gain political power.

By the end of 1938 the Wuxiang CCP had almost 3,000 members; and by July 1939 when the 1st Congress of the Wuxiang CCP met the county party had 5,708 members and 271 branches. The extent of this growth can be put in some perspective by reference to the figures provided in Table 3.2 indicating the organizational size of the county CCP organization in both 1949 and 1956. By the party congress of 1939, the county organiza-

Table 3.2 CCP Organizational Development in Wuxiang, 1937–1945

Year	Wuxiang Branches	Wuxiang CCP members	West Wuxiang Branches	West Wuxiang CCP members
1938	57	2999		
1939	271	5708		
1940	118	3784	37	1370
1941	105	2629	40	635
1942	147	3170	81	1093
1943		3166		756
1944	144	2765	71	1060
1945	186	3925	77	1251
1945	263	5176	(both counties)	
1949	213	5348		
1956	294	5577		

Source: WOH pp.90–91, p.136, p.172–74.

tion of the Wuxiang CCP had reached about the same dimensions it was to achieve after the establishment of the PRC. Indeed, the proportion of the population who were members of the county CCP in 1939 (4.4 percent) was not to be exceeded in Wuxiang until 1976. Moreover, in 1939 this was at a time when the CCP Central Committee had stipulated that party membership should not exceed 3 percent of the population.

At the July 1939 Wuxiang CCP Congress the CCP leadership itself recognized that there would have to be a formal consolidation of its membership. There were concerns about the political standing and motivations of some of those who had joined during the previous eighteen months. Membership had to be surrendered and granted again after assessment by the Organization Department.[51] There was nothing unusual in this procedure; at the time every county party organization was moving in an identical direction. The county CCP leadership's views were echoed even more firmly by senior CCP leaders at the base area CCP Congress when it was held in Wuxiang in September.[52]

At the base area CCP congress in September, Li Xuefeng proposed that Wuxiang become an 'experimental county' in the Taihang Region to test and refine programs and practices.[53] Given its experiences during Red May, the Wuxiang CCP was invited to make proposals for basic-level democracy and the implementation of village elections; and to develop ideas for introducing a program of rent and interest reduction. The latter had been a commitment in the CCP program since 1937 and the abandonment of more radical land reform, but generally in the Taihang region during 1937–39 there had been little progress, not least because other concerns were uppermost. As a result in Wuxiang during the last few months of 1939 the CCP's party consolidation and trial policy implementation of this aspect of agrarian policy were attempted simultaneously.

Precise details of what happened in the following few months are difficult to ascertain. However, it is certain that the Wuxiang CCP ran into problems with its trial implementation of a rent and interest reduction campaign, and was formally censured with its leadership being replaced. As these difficulties and the subsequent leadership changes are inherently related to the Wuxiang CCP's attempts at social reform, they will be discussed in detail in Chapter 7. From the criticisms of past behavior that were raised by the incoming leadership it would seem likely that there had been an overemphasis on the revolutionary nature of the campaign, which indeed characterized Wuxiang's CCP politics generally at this time. The county party organization, or parts of it, were criticized, for example, for having suggested that the revolutionary stage of the proletariat had arrived; having advocated the elimination of landlords and rich peasants; and having proposed the abolition of private property.[54]

At the Licheng Meeting of senior cadres in April 1940 organized by the North China Bureau of the CCP Central Committee, the Wuxiang CCP was severely censured, and its leadership reorganized.[55] The formal reprimand at the Licheng Meeting was largely confined to questions of the infringement of human rights, which was one of the major issues to emerge from this meeting as a matter of concern that required readjustment. In particular, there were concerns that arbitrary arrest and even the summary execution of those described as 'class enemies'—particularly landlords—would have severe repercussions on the ability of the CCP to draw on a broad coalition of social support for the war effort.[56]

The immediate consequence of censure in April 1940 was that a Wuxiang Experimental County CCP Committee was formally established. However, this time the emphasis was more on restructuring and redirecting party activities, and making sure that activities in Wuxiang were more under the control of the county party leadership, which itself was brought more closely under the direct supervision of the base area CCP leadership. Wen Jianping was appointed secretary of the CCP county committee; the former party secretary, Li Youjiu, and his deputy Wei Xiaoquan (who was also director of the Organization Department) were both demoted; and every other member of the county party committee lost their position, including the veteran peasant leader Wu Sanyou.[57] The operation of the experimental county as a whole was placed under the supervision of Peng

Tao, a member of the base area CCP committee and Director of its Mobilization Department.

The tasks of the new Wuxiang CCP committee were clear. They had to restructure the local party leadership; sort out membership through a further party consolidation; ensure some form of organizational efficiency; and continue with the trial implementation of policies for the rent and interest reduction campaign in a more moderated way.[58] However, the new leadership rapidly also ran into difficulties during the second half of 1940. They were unable to exercise adequate internal control over the county CCP organization, either over the new cadres they recruited to subordinate positions or over those they had inherited. Moreover, whilst the worst excesses of arbitrary arrest and personal aggression toward landlords, rich peasants, and middle peasants may have stopped, the broad direction of policies seems not to have been dramatically adjusted. One result was that social dislocation continued with even the smaller-scale wealthier landowners continuing to leave the area.[59]

The Taihang Base Area CCP committee investigated the work of the Wuxiang CCP in January 1941,[60] and the experimental county was wound up in February 1941 after its leadership finally admitted responsibilities explicitly for both 'leftist' errors of overenthusiasm in policy implementation, and 'liberalism' within the county party organization.[61] When the new (experimental) county party leadership had taken up office in April 1940, it had been particularly heavy in its criticism of its predecessors and the local organization they had previously developed even before 1937. There is more than a hint in the problems it encountered before February 1941 of local resistance to a perceived intrusion from outside, though equally some of the problems it encountered certainly had a separate existence. The experimental county party leadership had expelled over five hundred members of the CCP during the party consolidation it executed in the middle of 1940, and recruited a large number of landless laborers and poor peasants, together with to a lesser extent artisans and industrial workers. The county party secretary, Wen Jianping left office and was replaced by the man he had replaced in April 1940, Li Youjiu. Moreover, other local members of the county party committee dismissed in early 1940 were also restored to the leadership. Once again these included the long-term peasant leader, Wu Sanyou.[62]

There was no further attempt to restructure the Wuxiang CCP in these ways again during the war, though in July 1941 West Wuxiang held its 1st CCP Congress, and in August 1941 Wuxiang its 2nd CCP Congress to discuss the organizational consequences of the division of the county. However, as Chapter 7 relates, issues of interpretation of the appropriate relationship between class and revolution, which lay at the heart of the

1940 and early 1941 reorganizations of Wuxiang CCP leadership, were to remain matters of difference and discussion between the Wuxiang CCP and the Taihang Region's leadership until late 1943. All the same, this did not prevent cadres who were recruited in Wuxiang from serving elsewhere.[63] In addition to supplying large numbers of troops to the main-line Eighth Route Army forces, Wuxiang was also a major source of cadres during the war: it is reported that some 5,400 cadres who eventually worked outside the county came from Wuxiang.[64]

POLITICAL CHANGE IN WUXIANG

The process of political change in Wuxiang was in considerable contrast to that of Liaoxian, and generally atypical of the Taihang Base Area, because of the strength of the local CCP organization. The CCP's fitful organization during the 1930s bequeathed an organizational presence and party membership that were to shape Wuxiang's social and political revolution during the war. As elsewhere the first stage in political change was the replacement of the former ruling elite by a resistance government based on a new social coalition. However, in Wuxiang the CCP rapidly became the lead organization in the Sacrifice League. During 1938 and 1939 the CCP achieved political power through mass mobilization and local elections.

One consequence of these developments was that the Wuxiang CCP was almost always able to act fairly autonomously. Though the base area leadership attempted to tighten its control over the county CCP during 1940, the attempt proved ultimately futile and local leadership was eventually restored and given its head for the rest of the war.

NOTES

1. 'Wuxiang xian' ['Wuxiang County'] in Xu Guosheng and Chen Ninghua (ed) *Shanxi xian qu jingji fazhan shilue* [Historical outline of the economic development of counties and regions in Shanxi] Taiyuan, Shanxi jingji chubanshe, 1992, p.256.

2. Before the War the county town was located at Guxian. As a result of Japanese action in April 1938 the county government moved to Duancun, further west, which the Japanese later occupied.

3. See, for example, Kojima Seiichi *Hoku Shi keizai tokuhon* [An Economic Primer of North China] Tokyo, 1937, vol.1, p.40; quoted in Donald G Gillin *Warlord Yen Hsi-shan in Shansi Province, 1911–1949* Princeton, New Jersey, Princeton University Press, 1967, p.86.

4. BZZM p.454. During the War there was no road from eastern Wuxiang to southern Liaoxian, though the distance is not very far. Indeed, at that time there was no road to Wangjiayu. A rudimentary, narrow and easily defendable path led from the valley floor up the sides of the mountain.

5. Li Zhikuan 'Wuxiang xian geming jiuzhi' ['Wuxiang County Revolutionary Sites'] in *Weiwei Taihang* [The Towering Taihang Mountains] no.2, 1989, p.50.

6. See, for example, KZW p.3; and Li Zhikuan and Song Ruzhen 'Balu mama' ['Mother of the Eighth Route Army'] in WF vol.2, p.535.

7. WX p.346.

8. IHW pp.5–6.

9. For example, Peng Tao 'Yinian zhuanbian Wuxiang gongzuode jinyan jiaoxun' ['Work Experience Transforms Wuxiang in a Year'] May 1941, in TDZH vol.4: 1941, p.342. The Wuxiang CCP Committee was either contemporarily or later criticized for its conduct of the 1939 village elections; the 1939 expansion of CCP membership; its organizational behavior and policies at the end of 1939 and the beginning of 1940; the 1940 CCP consolidation; the implementation of different aspects of land policy in each of 1940, 1941, 1942, and the 1943–44 campaign against spies and traitors; as well as after 1945 during the land reform movement.

10. For an example of a contemporary comment, see the Wuxiang CCP Committee's own admission, in Zhonggong JinJiYu qudangwei 'Wuxiang shiyanxian gongzuode jiantao yu zhuanbian fangxiang' ['A Self-criticism of Wuxiang Experimental County's Work and its Change of Direction'] 7 January 1941, in TDZH vol.4: 1941, p.9. For a recollection, see Cheng Rong 'Huishou wushinian' ['Looking Back Fifty Years'] in WF vol.1, p.56.

11. Shangdang is the name of the Changzhi area, and is sometimes used to refer to the whole of Southeast Shanxi. Safflower is used in Chinese medicine.

12. Li Yisan 'Zhonggong Wuxiang dixia tang zuzhide chuangjian jingguo' ['After the Establishment of the CCP's Underground Organization in Wuxiang'] in *Weiwei Taihang* [The Towering Taihang Mountains] no.4, 1986, p.60; and Wu Guangtang 'Zai baise kongbude rizili' ['In the Days of the White Terror'] in Wu Guangtang bianshen weiyuanhui (ed) *Wu Guangtang wenji* [Collected Works of Wu Guangtang] Taiyuan, Shanxi renmin chubanshe, 1993, p.9. Others included Zhao Xiangrong, who worked in the Taiyue Base Area during the War and then worked in the CCP Central Committee's Organization Department; and Cheng Rong, who worked in the Central Party School in Yan'an during the War and later in the All-China Marketing and Supply Coopetative, and The People's Bank.

13. WOH p.16.

14. Wu Sanyou 'Huiyi zhongde nongmin kangzhaituan' ['Recalling the Peasants Refusal League'] in WF vol.1, 1985, p.63.

15. Donald G Gillin *Warlord Yen Hsi-shan in Shansi Province, 1911–1949* Princeton, New Jersey, Princeton University Press, 1967, p.229.

16. Wang Yutang 'Zhengdun huifu Wuxiang dangzhuzhi jianyi' ['A Concise Recollection of the Resumption and Restoration of the CCP's Organization in Wuxiang'] in WF vol.1, 1985, p.87.

17. Liang Zhixiang and Zhang Guoxiang 'Dierci guogong hezuo zai Shanxide chenggong shixian' ['The Achievements of the Second United Front in Shanxi'] in *Shizhi yanjiu* [Historical and Archive Research] no.1, 1996, p.4.

18. IHW p.25.
19. Li Chunfang 'Gaizao jiuzhengquande douzheng' ['The Struggle to Transform the Former System of Political Power'] in WF vol.1, 1985, p.92.
20. The factory workers were from the rural iron works and coal mines. There were large numbers of shepherds because, unlike most of China, Shanxi raises and consumes large amounts of lamb. WX p.285ff; IHW p.42ff.
21. IHW p.44.
22. See, Edward Friedman, Paul Pickowicz and Mark Selden *Chinese Village, Socialist State* New Haven, Connecticut, Yale University Press, 1991, p.41.
23. Li Yisan 'Dixiadang zuzhi chuangjian jingguo' ['The Experience of Establishing an Underground Party Organization'] in WF vol.1, 1985, p.15.
24. See, for example, Wang Dapin (ed) *Taihang mubiao xuanji* [A Selection of Taihang Woodcuts] Taiyuan, Shanxi renmin chubanshe, 1991, p.230.
25. Even in the elections of March 1943, 6.5 percent of the elected representatives at village level had the class status of 'landlord.'
26. Yang Wei 'Taihangshan beiqude tudi wenti' ['Land Issues in the Northern Part of the Taihang Mountains'] May 1940, in TDZH vol.3: 1940, p.311.
27. Tian Youru 'Shanxi tudi zhidu gaige lishi gaiyao' ['Outline History of Reform of the Land System in Shanxi'] in *Shanxi dangshi tongxun* [Bulletin of Shanxi Party History] no.2, 1993, p.4.
28. The consequences of this aspect of Wuxiang's environment will be discussed in greater detail in Chapter 8. These data come from TJSD1 p.1349.
29. Zhonggong JinJiYu qudangwei 'Guanyu Wuxiang gongzuode yijian' ['Opinions on Wuxiang's Work'] July 1940, in TDZH vol.3: 1940, p.509.
30. There are different versions of this same intent. See, for example: IHW p.3.
31. 'Cong jige dianxinghu kan shehui caifu he tudide jiju yu bianhua'['The Transformation of Social Wealth and Land Concentration as Seen in Several Case Studies'] in TW p.178ff.
32. Jiang Shunxing and Li Liangyu (ed) *Shanxi wang Yan Xishan* [Yan Xishan, King of Shanxi] Henan renmin chubanshe, 1990, p.146.
33. WX p.293.
34. Zhonggong JinJiYu qudangwei 'Wuxiang shiyanxian gongzuode jiantao yu zhuanbian fangxiang' ['A Self-criticism of Wuxiang Experimental County's Work and Its Change of Direction'] 7 January 1941, in TDZH vol.4: 1941, p.9.
35. Xu Zirong, comments on 28 June 1941, in FOC p.24.
36. WX p.286.
37. IHW p.135 ff.
38. Li Wuzi's comments at CCP Shanxi-Hebei-Henan Regional Committee, 5 September 1943, in ZJY p.13. Li Wuzi was a Wuxiang CCP Committee member at this time; he later became Secretary.
39. WOH p.64 ff, p.76 ff.
40. IHW p.127; WX p.287.
41. Donald G Gillin *Warlord Yen Hsi-shan in Shansi Province, 1911–1949* Princeton, New Jersey, Princeton University Press, 1967, p.3; Jing Zhankui *Yan Xishan guanliao ziben yanjiu* [A Study of Yan Xishan's Bureaucratic Capitalism] Taiyuan, Shanxi jingji chubanshe, 1993, p.49 ff.

42. IHW p.30 ff.

43. Shanxisheng Wuxiangxian funu lianhehui (ed) *Wuxiang funu yundong shiliao xuanbian* [Selected Materials from the Women's Movement in Wuxiang] Wuxiang, 1982.

44. WX p.303.

45. KZW p.25; and WX p.287, p.323.

46. WX p.299.

47. The Wuxiang County record has a section on the battle history of the Eighth Route Army, WX p.323 ff.

48. KZW p.51 ff. A guerilla intelligence training unit was established that functioned into the 1970s. During the 1960s and 1970s it was employed to train international guerillas who came to China under the PRC's foreign policy.

49. Wuxiangxian zhihuibu 'Weikun Panlong di wo douzheng bageyuede jiandan huigu' ['A Brief Memoir of the Eight-Month Siege of Panlong'] November 1943, in DWD p.405.

50. LXH p.34 ff.

51. IHW p.67.

52. Yang Shangkun 'Zhonggong JinJiYuqu diyici daibiao dahui shangde zhengzhi baogao' ['Political Report to the 1st Congress of the Shanxi-Hebei-Henan CCP'] in TDZH vol.2, 1939, p.480 ff.

53. LXH p.106 ff.

54. Wen Jianping (Jian Ping) 'Wuxiang shiyanxian shouci huodong fenzi dongyuan dahui zongjie' ['Summary of the Conference of Advanced Activists in Mobilization in Wuxiang Experimental County'] 25 April 1940, in TDZH vol.3: 1940, p.266.

55. WOH p.22.

56. The report of the meeting listed human rights as the first issue highlighted, in Zhonggong zhongyang beifangju 'Licheng huiyi guanyu zhengquan jianzheng wentide jielun' ['The Licheng Meeting's Conclusions on Political Development'] April 1940, in TDZH vol.3: 1940, p.253. According to Li Xuefeng, Deng Xiaoping had been particularly insistent on this point. Li also suggested that this emphasis on human rights had caused problems during 1940–43 as local cadres felt constrained thereafter to take any kind of determined action against landlords and rich peasants; in LXH p.99. For Deng Xiaoping's speech, see: 'Deng Xiaoping zai Zhonggong zhongyang beifangju Licheng huiyi shangde fayan' ['Deng Xiaoping's opening speech at the Licheng Meeting of the CCP Central Committee's North China Bureau'] 11 April 1940, in TDZH vol.3: 1940, p.248. On the significance of the CCP's appeal to a broad coalition as part of its overall strategy, see also Mark Selden *China in Revolution: The Yenan Way Revisited* New York, M E Sharpe, 1995, pp.169–170.

57. WOH p.22.

58. 'Wuxiang shiyanxian shouci huodong fenzi dongyuan dahui zongjie' ['Summary of Wuxiang Experimental County's First Activists' Conference'] in WX, April 1940, p.853 ff.

59. Peng Tao provided a relatively comprehensive overview of the 1940 problems in 'Yinian zhuanbian Wuxiang gongzuode jinyan jiaoxun' ['Work Experi-

ence Transforms Wuxiang in a Year'] May 1941, in TDZH vol.4: 1941, p.342. He also alluded to the Wuxiang difficulties in 'JinJiYu qude xinxingshi yu xinrenwu' ['New circumstances and new tasks in the Shanxi-Hebei-Henan area'] 27 June 1941, in TDZH vol.4: 1941, p.479.

60. Peng Tao 'Yinian zhuanbian Wuxiang gongzuode jinyan jiaoxun' ['Work Experience Transforms Wuxiang in a Year'] May 1941, in TDZH vol.4: 1941, p.343.

61. Zhonggong JinJiYu qudangwei 'Wuxiang shiyanxian gongzuode jiantao yu zhuanbian fangxiang' ['A Self-criticism of Wuxiang Experimental County's Work and its Change of Direction'] 7 January 1941, in TDZH vol.4: 1941, p.9.

62. WOH p.22.

63. Those who went on to achieve senior cadre status are listed by with information about their date and place of birth, together with a brief description of their later positions, in WX p.688 ff.

64. KZW p.67.

4

Licheng: Food and Factories

Licheng is even deeper into the Taihang Mountains than either Liaoxian or Wuxiang. Until the building of a railway during the 1980s and of a new highway in the 1990s between Handan and Changzhi, the county had been fairly remote and inaccessible from either Hebei or major urban centres in Shanxi. Surrounded by other areas of concentrated resistance activity, Licheng's experience during the war was consequently somewhat different from that of either Wuxiang or Liaoxian (Zuoquan.) Although the Japanese managed to occupy the county town on four separate occasions they were unable to sustain a long-term operation in Licheng.

Licheng was also one of the wealthier counties in the Taihang region, based solely on its agricultural output. Its natural advantages for a defensive operation together with its grain surplus meant that the county was rapidly developed during 1939 and after by the CCP as the base area's source of military supplies. In particular its more mountainous northern part, neighboring areas of CCP strength in Wuxiang and Liaoxian, became the small-scale industrial hub of the base area. A number of munitions factories were established here, of which the largest and most famous was at Huangyadong, but the north of the county also had chemical plants, iron works, uniform and furniture factories.

The development of North Licheng—which became a separate county in late November 1943 as part of the support arrangements for the Siege of Panlong in Wuxiang—was made even more secure by the ability of the Licheng resistance from a fairly early stage in the war to mobilize the population for defense. The Sacrifice League and the CCP did not produce the large numbers of either regular soldiers or militia that were generated in Wuxiang, nor did they for that matter fight as many engagements, but the resistance was successful in its organization of defence and had a record against Japanese troops that led the Central Committee of the CCP to commend the county armed forces and their organizers in November 1941.[1]

The paradox in Licheng's wartime experience is that whilst it was less engaged in military operations against the Japanese than either Liaoxian or Wuxiang, it also seems to have been relatively more susceptible to internal problems. A new political order was ensured first through the Sacrifice League in mid-1938, and then by the CCP at the beginning of 1940. However, Licheng's wartime experience, especially after 1940, is characterized by a record of political difficulties both between the CCP and some parts of the local population, and within the CCP. On three separate occasions there were armed uprisings against the resistance government: in 1938, 1941 and 1942. The Taihang Base Area party committee restructured the Licheng CCP organization in both 1938 and 1943, and in 1940 the Licheng CCP leadership itself acted, restructured its own organization, and expelled most of its members. Although some of the resistance to the Licheng government in and after 1940 is related to the manner of the local CCP's separation from the Sacrifice League and its supporters, most resulted from its attempt to implement social reform and is consequently discussed in Chapter 8.

SECURITY AND SUCCESS

Questions of military strategy and indeed the wider military environment played a substantial role in the CCP's involvement in Licheng from a very early stage. The Sacrifice League organization in Licheng was one of the strongest in the Taihang region. Nonetheless, organizing a resistance government in the county under its leadership at the end of 1937 and into 1938 required the additional presence of troops from the Eighth Route Army before the existing county head was prepared to cede office even in favor of a new united front government. At that time and later the Eighth Route Army took the opportunity to recruit heavily in Licheng. Starting with 1939 the Eighth Route Army developed its military production activities in the high mountain area in the north of the county.

Moreover, both the later divisions of the county were determined by strategic concerns outside Licheng. The establishment of a separate Piancheng County at the beginning of 1940 was designed to assist CCP activities in Shexian and Wu'an Counties to the east. Piancheng was in any case somewhat administratively anomalous. It had been a subdistrict under the county but physically separated from the rest of the county by both Liaoxian and part of Shexian, in Henan. The creation of a North Licheng County in October 1943 was designed to help the CCP forces in the campaign laying siege to Panlong in Wuxiang to the west.[2]

Although Licheng was to become a county that produced a large number of cadres who went on to serve elsewhere in the CCP and PRC,[3] unlike Wuxiang, which also supplied many later cadres, it had no CCP organization before the War of Resistance. Moreover, there were also almost no Licheng natives who had become members of the CCP when working or studying outside the county before 1937. One of the few was Huo Fan, who had joined in the mid-1930s when a student in Beiping, and who went on to become the secretary of the county CCP committee on two separate occasions during the war. Indeed, the CCP was to remain fairly weak until the end of 1939. The route to establishing a Resist Japan Government, as well as a CCP organization in Licheng, was through the Sacrifice League. However, despite considerable popular support for both the idea of a resistance government and the Sacrifice League, its takeover was to prove surprisingly difficult.

Opposition to the development of a Sacrifice League-led government in Licheng came from the existing county government, under Tian Jijiao and his supporters. Sacrifice League sources claimed that Tian was unwilling to fight the Japanese, and instead was prepared to stay and govern Licheng even after invasion.[4] Whilst that explanation is not totally beyond the bounds of possibility, it is also possible that the conflict between Tian Jijiao and the Sacrifice League organizers was as much about leadership of the county. On the one side was a traditional county establishment based on the ownership of land. On the other, was a new aspirant modernizing elite based in the Sacrifice League who were teachers and largely emerging middle class intellectuals. All had studied and trained outside the county during the 1920s and 1930s and returned home, either to work or just with the start of war, as was the case with Huo Fan. Undoubtedly this conflict also reflected a generation gap: nearly all the teachers and intellectuals were themselves children of the establishment.[5]

In his role as Director of the 3rd District of Shanxi under Yan Xishan's government, Bo Yibo had set about appointing members of the Sacrifice League as the new heads of county governments under his jurisdiction during October and November 1937. In Licheng, He Gongzhen was appointed to replace Tian Jijiao, but the latter refused to accept his removal from office. The Eighth Route Army dispatched a work team of the 344th Brigade of the 115th Division (which had accompanied the 129th Division into the Taihang region) to Licheng to assist.[6] The work team supported a group of about a hundred members of the Sacrifice League as they stormed the government office, confiscated the county seal of office and assisted the new county head to take office with a new Licheng Resist Japan County Government under Sacrifice League leadership.[7]

Wang Fengwu's work team was joined in Licheng by another from the 129th Division led by Wang Qian and together they assisted with the development of both the Sacrifice League and the CCP, and recruited soldiers for their units. Two guerilla troops were rapidly raised: the Zhang River Guerillas and the Sacrifice League Guerilla Troop, each with about 500 people recruited locally. The Zhang River Guerillas left in December for the Shandong-Henan borders, whereas the Sacrifice League Guerilla Troop stayed to assist with the defence of Licheng.[8] However, this was far from the end of military recruitment in the county. As Table 4.1 indicates, Licheng was a regular source of soldiers to the ranks of the Eighth Route Army, as well as of part-time fighters for the local militia. In addition, the military factories later established in North Licheng were all staffed almost totally from the local population.

The Japanese invasion of 16 February 1938 established a pattern to be followed for the rest of the war. As Japanese forces troops invaded, the resistance forces and the government agencies retreated to the north of the county and roughly the area beyond Nanweiquan and around Xijing. When Japanese troops withdrew or were defeated then the resistance moved back to the area around the county town, though it rarely occupied the county town itself, preferring to locate itself just outside in Beishe. This was to be repeated in the second half of 1939 when the Japanese took up occupation of the county town for a six-months stretch; for three weeks in November 1941 when the armaments factory at Huangyadong was under siege; and again in May and June 1942 when occupation only lasted

Table 4.1 Annual Recruitment to Eighth Route Army and Militia in Licheng, 1937–1945 (numbers of people)

Year	Eighth Route Army recruits	Militia force (total)
1937	950	1590
1941	345	2006
1942	299	3306
1943	377	3943
1944	434	5155
1945	855	

Source: LX p.441.

20 days.[9] On this first occasion the occupation lasted until the 25 April, when the Japanese withdrew as part of the general mobilization of their forces away from Southeast Shanxi toward the south of the country.

The absence of Japanese activities provided the opportunity for the Eighth Route Army to develop its industrial sites in the north of Licheng. The attraction must really have been one of suitable defensive positions rather than any other available resources. The largest munitions factory, at Huangyadong, for example, is sited high in the mountains in a ravine where the only access is a fairly easily defended one-person-wide, twisting and rising path that then passes through nothing more than a very narrow crack in the rocks. Other plants and factories—the Chiyu Cartridge Factory, the Shibei Paper Factory, the Eighth Route Army Uniform Factory, the Yuanquan Chemical Plant, the Taihang Engineering School, the Shiwei Medicine Factory and a large number of other munitions works[10]—were established in similar, defendable locations, including large caves, hidden depressions and within other ravines. In all cases there were almost no resources other than labor locally available for some distance around, and sometimes not even that. Everything for production would have to be carried in, including coal, and that in itself was a logistical feat. Unlike most counties in Shanxi Province, let alone in the Taihang Mountains, Licheng has no coal deposits. There is iron ore there, but this had not been exploited until the advent of the Eighth Route Army.

On the other hand, the defensive strategy does appear to have worked. Huangyadong, for example, was the object of three major campaigns of attack by Japanese troops: in July 1939, in September 1940, and again in November 1941. The 1940 attack was particularly destructive of resistance resources, with more than a hundred people being killed as part of the uniform factory and a hospital were destroyed. In 1941 the Japanese first occupied the county town, then sent a force of 7,000 soldiers on to the north of the county to attack Huangyadong. The CCP forces under Zuo Quan were outnumbered six to one, but eventually within eleven days were able to turn the attack back.[11]

The longest period of Japanese presence in Licheng was the whole second half of 1939 when the county town was occupied. It ended in December 1939 with a military action by the Eighth Route Army not only to liberate Licheng, but also to control the mountain sections of the Handan-Changzhi Highway that the Japanese had been fortifying. This too proved to be a successful action, and the road between Licheng and Shexian to the east was largely under the control of the CCP's forces for the rest of the war.[12] Whilst Licheng and the CCP's activities there were clearly not totally secure from external attack after 1939, they were immeasurably better off in this regard than other parts of the base area. In September 1943 its relative safety was reflected in the decision to develop an airstrip for the base area at Changningchuan, in the east of Licheng County. This was the first airfield under the control of CCP forces outside of Yan'an, and provided the senior CCP leaders stationed in Matian with both a more convenient means of communication with the outside world, and for many of them their first taste of air travel.[13]

NEW INTELLECTUALS, OLD ESTABLISHMENT

One of the attractions of Licheng to the CCP was its defensive position. Another equally as important was its surplus grain production. Licheng on the eve of war was unusual in a number of ways compared to other parts of the Taihang region. Quite apart from the lack of coal deposits, before 1949 there had been no industrial development and few commercial enterprises in Licheng. As a result, unlike other parts of the Taihang Region, and notably Wuxiang and Liaoxian, almost everyone in Licheng was engaged in farming, not least because it was relatively productive. Table 4.2 provides data from 1935 on the composition of the workforce by their type of employment.

Agricultural production was mainly grain and sheep (80 percent and 13 percent of total production by value respectively).[14] The main crops were millet, wheat and corn (in that order) and despite the lack of industry and commerce, the county was a net exporter. In 1933 for example, there was a 44 percent trade surplus.[15] Licheng was not a fabulously wealthy county, but it was considerably richer per capita than any other

Table 4.2 Employment in Licheng County, 1935 (percentage of individuals employed)

Employment	Percentage of population
Army	1.4
Artisans	1.1
Traders	1.5
Farming	92.6
Government offices	0.1
Teachers	3.3
Total	100.0 (49,417 people)

Source: Statistics calculated from LX p.501.

county in the Taihang Region.[16] Moreover, wealth was probably more evenly distributed than in most parts of the Taihang region. There was a low concentration of landholdings, many fewer poor peasants than in other Taihang counties and a larger proportion of middle peasants, even though the Taihang region at that time was largely characterized by the large size of its middle peasantry.[17]

Licheng had been a long-term producer of agricultural wealth. In the twentieth century this had not led as in other parts of the Taihang region to either industrial or commercial development, possibly because of the distances and difficulties involved in reaching external markets. However, during the 1920s and 1930s money had been invested in education. By 1934, 60 percent of the eligible year cohorts were attending primary school in the county.[18] At least one school, the First High School in the county town had more than 1,000 students in 1937, and there were 187 established primary schools.[19] As Table 4.2 indicates there were some 1,600 teachers in the county, and studying to become a teacher outside the county in Changzhi, Taiyuan and Beiping was a well-established career path for the county's youth. One of those who had followed that path was a founder of the Sacrifice League in Licheng, Zhang Buying, who by 1936 had become the head teacher of the First High School; another (as already noted) was Huo Fan, the secretary of the county CCP committee during most of 1940–44.

Licheng's society before the war was also remarkably religious, or at least a large proportion belonged to religious organizations or sects. County records from the last pre-war years list five large Buddhist monasteries that had over a hundred full-time monks and nuns; and a major temple complex in the county town with 121 monks. There were many fewer established Daoist priests, who operated in a more localized way; as did the various communities established in the eighteenth century by Dutch Catholics, and the Christian protestant church established in the county town.[20] However, some 20 percent of the population actively belonged to a sect. (By 1942 it was reported that everyone over the age of thirty participated, including CCP members.[21]) County records indicate that twenty-nine sects were active in Licheng during the War of Resistance, including the 'Sixth Trigram Movement,' 'Long Hairs,' 'Village Restorationists,' the 'Confucius Sect' (a local sect not to be confused with the sometime state-encouraged religion), the 'Nine Officials,' 'Bright Eyes,' 'Black Tea,' the 'Shouyang Sect,' 'Eight Trigrams,' 'Red Spears,' and 'Heavenly Gates.'[22]

Both sects and teachers were to play an important role in Licheng during the war. Teachers were the initial organizers of resistance, and played the central role in the development of the Sacrifice League, and initially the CCP. The sects became important as vehicles for the opposition to the CCP-led government, especially after 1939, and as discussed in Chapter 8.

One of the results of Licheng's educational development was that starting in the mid-1920s a whole succession of students from the county started going on to study elsewhere, notably Changzhi, Taiyuan and Beiping. Many were interested in political activities, as well as discussing questions of nationalism and revolution, all of which were key issues for students at that time. In 1928 when more than forty of these students were back in Licheng for the Spring Festival, they formed the Licheng Returned Students Federation. The Federation was led by Li Yurui, Yang Jiaopu, Shi Jixin, Shi Bingqian, and Wang Ting all of whom were later to be active in both the Sacrifice League and the CCP. At first they arranged to meet every year to discuss politics but soon found themselves drawn into campaigns against corrupt officials, illegal activities by business people and overexploitative landowners.[23] Even at this early stage their activities brought them into conflict with the county establishment and the local government.

The Returned Students Federation had a first highly publicized success in 1930 when they managed to force the county government to prosecute a local salt shop for using faulty scales that short-changed customers by about 10 percent; and in 1931 they first became active in the movement to resist Japanese aggression. In 1936 even before the establishment of the Sacrifice League, the Returned Students Federation, which by now had grown to several hundred members, started travelling around the county and organizing political rallies in the villages and small towns. These meetings included not only speeches but also performances of plays and local opera specifically written or adapted for the occasion with suitable content on themes of nationalism and resistance.

A group of members of the Licheng Returned Students Federation were instrumental in establishing the local branch of the Sacrifice League at the start of 1937, together with some of the students currently studying at the First High School, and most of the other members of the Federation subsequently joined. In June 1937 the provincial office of the Sacrifice League sent Li Xuhua (a CCP member originally from Wuxiang) and Lu Fengcai (also a CCP member, but from Jiaocheng) to Licheng to establish a branch more formally under the leadership of its Qinxian Committee. Several hundred intellectuals, teachers and former students attended at a foundation ceremony in the Temple of Confucius, in the county town, and afterwards the Sacrifice League set about establishing local branches and organizations throughout the county. Right from the start there was opposition from the county government and its agencies who apparently resented the Sacrifice League's involvement in areas which they saw as their responsibility.

The Sacrifice League grew rapidly during the second half of 1937, building on the Returned Students Federation's earlier networks not only in the county town, but also in the villages and around the county. As already noted, despite widespread popular support the county establishment were reluctant to cede power, and the county head particularly resistant to his replacement. Even after his forced removal problems continued. The new Licheng government was dominated by the former members of the Returned Students Federation and was very much a Sacrifice League operation. However, it had also inherited many of the officers and staff of the previous regime, even though it tried to replace senior officials and restructure activities as it could. It seems likely that Tian Jijiao's remnant supporters who were officials and members of the local elite resented the activities of the Sacrifice League, not only because the latter were usurping their own social and political position in Licheng society, but also simply because they were young, and this too went against their worldview.[24]

During February to April the county government had been forced north and underground, but with Japanese withdrawal it was able to start being more active within the county. Government branch offices were established in all the major townships of the county—in Xijing, Piancheng, Shangyao and Dongyangguan (roughly north, northeast, west and east)—and Departments of Grain and Mobilization were established under the county offices in the county town.[25] It also started a mass mobilization campaign to encourage a more equal tax burden, which rapidly brought it into conflict with the local county establishment since they were now being asked to provide more public grain and support for the war effort. Once again Sacrifice League and CCP sources claimed there was talk amongst 'a group of people within the county government' (meaning former supporters of Tian Jijiao and the county establishment) that if the public burden was going to be this high they might as well adopt a policy of passive resistance to Japan.[26]

The conflict between the establishment elite and the younger intellectuals grew rapidly and finally came to a head in two incidents during the middle of 1938, both of which led to armed confrontation. The first in Xijing during late April escalated very quickly and threatened the unity of the county government and the Sacrifice League. When the county government had returned from Xijing (after the Japanese withdrawal) it had deliberately left some sections of its operation behind, including two headed by former appointments of Tian Jijiao. Public security under the county government was organized by a Sacrifice League member and teacher, Zheng Yifeng[27] who tried to establish a local branch agency in Xijing but was refused entry. Li Xuhua, as a Sacrifice League organizer, tried to sort the situation out but a violent confrontation resulted. The section heads complained to He Gongzhen who decided that his authority was under attack, perhaps because Li Xuhua was a Sacrifice League organizer and had no formal position in the county government. He took an armed group and arrested a number of leading members of the Sacrifice League branch, threatening to punish them for their interference. Rescue and clarification was apparently effected by the intervention of Wang Qian and his work team from the 129th Division.[28]

The second, which was even more serious, led to a direct attempt to depose the county government, and centered around the question of who organized and had the right to organize the county's self-defense militia. County government maintained that though it might ask others to participate in a number of ways and even on occasion organize self-defense activities, nonetheless the authority for those kinds of responsibilities was its alone, as the county government. Against this some of the former supporters of Tian Jijiao argued that organization of public security was their social duty, separate from any government authority. They not only had the right to carry arms, but the duty to protect Licheng regardless of any specific government. At the end of April a number of them established a Licheng Protection Regiment in Baiguan Village, where they kidnapped He Gongzhen and declared the creation of a new county government with a new head.[29] Zheng Yifeng took emergency action, calling for assistance, once again, from Wang Qian, and trying himself to talk the kidnappers out of any over hasty action. However, as the troops arrived the rebellion seems to have crumpled, with most of its leaders escaping to Qinxian and leaving He Gongzhen behind.[30]

The actions of those members of the former county government who had supported armed opposition necessarily had repercussions for any of Tian Jijiao's former supporters still in the government service, or even those thought likely to share those perspectives by virtue of their common background. Five heads of department in the county government were replaced, together with an untold number of more minor officials.[31] Moreover, with this consolidation of the Sacrifice League's hold on power came a more concerted attempt to establish the framework for future social change. Village elections were held at the end of the year; and various occupation-based associations were established for the first time in the county, including Patriotic Associations for (separately) Workers and Teachers.

The first six months of 1939, before the second Japanese invasion of the county, proceeded under the Sacrifice League's leadership. The CCP continued to grow as local members were recruited. However, there was little organizational structure and little need for organizational discipline as the CCP worked almost completely within the framework of the Sacrifice

League. The Sacrifice League presented a case for the maintenance of a united front that even permitted the Nationalist Party to reestablish a branch in the county. The Nationalist Party had about eight hundred members at the beginning of the year and this grew to several thousand within a relatively short time.[32] In the meantime, superior CCP organizations started both to organize the Eighth Route Army's industrial operations in the north of the county; and to establish the headquarters of the note-issuing South Hebei Bank in Xijing, which was close at hand.

The resistance government first established by the Sacrifice League in November 1937 theoretically continued in office to the end of the war. However, in January 1940 the Licheng CCP moved decisively to replace the Sacrifice League-led government, and indeed completely closed down the Sacrifice League's local organization.[33] Ma Jianzhi, an open CCP member was appointed to head the county government. The leading positions in most of the departments of the county government, and all the leading personnel of the departments of finance, civil affairs, armed personnel, and public security were changed, as were all the district heads within the county. Most spectacularly this included several of the founders of the Sacrifice League in Licheng, who were all dismissed.

In the process of this takeover the local party organization also dramatically restructured itself. The essence of both changes was that most, though by no means all, the teachers and intellectuals from the Returned Students Federation who had joined the Sacrifice League, established the resistance government and then also later joined the CCP were excluded from politics. A large part of the explanation of the dramatic decrease in the membership of the Licheng CCP—from 2206 to 802[34]—during the party consolidation of 1940 was that almost every member who was an intellectual was expelled.

The extent to which this attack on the Sacrifice League and the Returned Students Federation alienated support from some groups in Licheng—particularly rich peasants and intellectuals—would be hard to overestimate. Indeed, many intellectuals simply left the county and did not return.[35] As Chapter 8 discusses, it was certainly a major contributory factor in the development of armed opposition to the resistance government in 1941. However, it engendered resentment even amongst those members of the CCP who were not expelled at this time, but who nonetheless recognized the contribution and role of teachers and intellectuals in the Licheng CCP.[36]

Economic problems started in 1940 in Licheng, which only served to heighten the political uncertainties. However, after that year the county government was not seriously challenged by either environmental or economic concerns as was the case elsewhere in the Taihang Region. Nor for that matter, despite its political problems in the wake of separation from the Sacrifice League and with the implementation of programs of social reform, was it ever in danger of being replaced by the internal opposition that emerged. All the same, as Chapter 8 indicates, the ability of the resistance government and the CCP to mobilize popular support was almost matched by the potential for difficulties to emerge within the county and to pose problems for its leadership.

The environmental challenges to government in Licheng were clearly much less than those faced in either Wuxiang or Liaoxian. Climactic conditions were no less severe: there was a famine in 1940, a poor harvest in 1941, severe drought in 1942 and no rain fell between May and August 1943. However, Licheng's relative wealth and lack of economic depression before 1937 meant that that there was much less rural emiseration on which disaster could build, whilst as already noted natural conditions permitted the production of a food surplus in normal harvest years.

Local government did not remain inactive in the face of drought. Licheng became an early experimenter in the cooperativization of agriculture. Mutual-aid Teams that involved about 14,000 people were started in June 1941. During the Great Production Movement of 1944, 38 percent of the rural population were organized into Mutual-aid Teams, and experiments started with the development of five semi-socialist rural cooperatives at that time.[37] With help from the Eighth Route Army a number of large-scale irrigation projects were started along the northern and southern branches of the Zhang River in 1942, as a result of which agricultural output increased by 31 percent.[38] One result was that refugees flooded in during 1942–43 from Hebei and Henan as famine and then disease increased dramatically in those areas.[39] Another result was that the aquaducts and bridges built as part of the irrigation projects were named to celebrate the 'unity between party, government, army and the people' after specific leaders of the base area. At a ceremony in 1943 the Bocheng, Xiaoping and Xiufeng Bridges (after Liu Bocheng, Deng Xiaoping, and Yang Xiufeng) were unveiled.[40]

Local government also acted to ensure that the county's grain surpluses did in fact go in large measure to support base area activities. Perhaps the most dramatic indication of this imperative in action was the county's repeated reductions in the numbers of officials and cadres supported in nonproductive occupations. Three times during 1941–43 the county implemented a program of 'Better Troops, Simpler Administration.' By the end of the second round of reductions at the end of 1942, the number of those publicly supported had been reduced by 53 percent, from 730 to 346 people.[41] In the third round, the number was reduced a further fifth, and the number of subdistricts under county direction was reduced from 42 to 35.[42]

ORGANIZATION AND RECTIFICATION

The CCP was slow to establish an organizational presence in Licheng, although shortly after the outbreak of war there were already a number of CCP members in the county. These included a number of the earliest Sacrifice League organizers, as, for example, Li Xuhua; as well as others who had joined the CCP elsewhere and who had just returned home, such as Huo Fan. However, the further development of a local CCP organization had to wait until November and the arrival of the work team from the 115th Division of the Eighth Route Army. Once the problems of removing the recalcitrant head of the county government had been solved, and the Resist Japan Government established the work team turned to party and military recruitment.

A Licheng CCP Work Committee was established to prepare for the later establishment of a county party committee. A number of former members of the Returned Students Federation now active in the Sacrifice League were the first local members. Indeed, the first secretary (of the Work Committee) was Yang Jiaopu, one of the original members of the Returned Students Federation in 1928 and already a member of the Sacrifice League. She was joined in the leadership of the local CCP by Zheng Yifeng, Zheng Lilu, and Li Xuhua.[43] Small teams were then organized with the help of the Eighth Route Army work team, and sent out to the towns and villages, with branches being established in first Beishe, and then Qiaojiazhuang, Langzhuang, Pingdou, Xijing, and Dongyadi.[44]

The first rural party branch was established at Beishe, just outside the county town, almost immediately, and that rapidly became the principal site of its activities. There was a former temple there which served as headquarters, training center, and meeting space. It was here, for example, that the April 1940 meeting of senior cadres in the Shanxi-Hebei-Henan Border Region (also known as the Licheng Meeting) convened, as well as the Licheng CCP Congresses of August 1938 and September 1941. Beishe itself was to become and remain a model village in a variety of campaigns during the next several decades.

The initial membership of the Licheng CCP during 1937–38 drew heavily on intellectuals and middle peasants.[45] The party's initial recruitment base followed the pattern of the Sacrifice League and encouraged teachers and members of the Returned Students Federation to join. Indeed, the Licheng CCP followed a strategy of political inclusivity from within the Sacrifice League until after 1939. According to Xu Zirong, the first rural recruits to the Licheng CCP were mainly middle peasants. They were apparently not only keen to join, but also very generous in providing money. Poor peasants on the other hand, were more reticent, though some did join. Where they did join it was on the condition that they did not have to contribute money as well. Probably of significance in the light of later events, when rich peasants became organized in resistance to Japan, as through the Sacrifice League, they were often even at this stage fairly hostile to the CCP.[46]

A start had been made with recruitment and the development of party branches during late 1937 and early 1938. However, the Licheng CCP was not immediately a high profile organization, and throughout 1938–39 was all but indistinguishable from the Sacrifice League, though it had started to publish its own local newspaper—*The Taihang Mountain Daily*—in 1938. From August 1938 to March 1939 the Licheng CCP also became responsible for the development of party operations in neighboring Xiangyuan County. During 1938–39 the Licheng CCP attempted to guide the work of the Sacrifice League through a United Front Work Department (under Zhao Bokang)[47] and through a Patriotic Teachers Association (under Wang Daoshi)[48] both of which closed with the changed arrangements of 1940. The strategy of inclusivity from within the Sacrifice League was an obvious organizational approach for the CCP to pursue at the time. However, in the longer term these common origins and development were also to create problems. After 1939 as the CCP sought to ensure the political reliability of its members this earlier relationship made any member of both organizations automatically suspect, and necessarily in social terms suspicion fell greatest on intellectuals.

There were full-scale CCP reorganizations in Licheng in 1938, 1940, and again in 1942–43. Unfortunately, all but the major party consolidation of 1940 remain somewhat obscured. It is far from clear whether and when the difficulties were only within Licheng, or between the base area leadership and the Licheng CCP. Indeed, it is even possible that local problems led to difficulties for the Licheng CCP leadership in its dealings with the CCP committee for the base area, and that the Licheng CCP's local problems were exacerbated by its relationship with the base area CCP. Certainly there is more than a suspicion in the organizational experience of the Licheng CCP that its difficulties were self-sustaining, especially after the major purge of 1940 when many of its original founders were expelled.

One obvious strength of the Licheng CCP was its ability not simply to keep going despite difficulties, but also to grow. Table 4.3 provides an overview of the Licheng CCP's organizational development during 1937–45. Party consolidation in 1940, when aggregate membership dropped by more than 63 percent, and when all members were investigated and required to reapply, is clearly evident. By the end of the war in August 1945 it was reported that North Licheng and Licheng together had 217 branches and a total of 4313 members.[49]

In retrospect the Licheng CCP itself has recognized that it was frequently subject to reorganization and rectification during 1937–45 but

Table 4.3 CCP Organizational Development in Licheng, 1937–1945

Year	Licheng Branches	CCP members	North Licheng Branches	CCP members
1937		32		
1938	108	1775		
1939	141	2206		
1940		802		
1941	115	1764		
1942	147	2199		
1943	110	1962		
1944		2024	46	851
1945	167	2934	50	1043

Source: LOH p.56.

ascribes its organizational strength to the establishment at a very early period in October 1938 of a cadre training program, which later grew into the Licheng County CCP School. Thirty-two classes graduated during 1938–45. Cadres were given training in practical and political skills, and 'had the revolution explained to them.'[50]

The various reorganizations of the Licheng CCP would appear to have resulted from a mixture of local concerns about political reliability together with attempts from the CCP committee of the base area to ensure its control. Neither was necessarily effective and they often conflicted. The first reorganization of the Licheng CCP in August 1938 indicates some of those problems. As already noted, the initial recruits to the Licheng CCP were intellectuals and peasants. The leadership of the CCP base area committee visited Licheng in August and directed the county party committee to broaden the base of its support. Apparently the base area leadership had two concerns. It felt that the Licheng CCP had spent too much time in recruiting for the armed forces, and not put enough effort into the development of the party organization; and it was concerned about the social mix to be found in the local membership.[51] The local party organization duly complied, and recruited over four hundred new members who were laborers: within a very short period, farmhands came to represent a fifth of the total Licheng CCP membership.[52]

This somewhat strange alliance of the exceptionally poor and the somewhat privileged did not survive very long. With the Licheng CCP's assumption of political power in January 1940, it moved decisively against the majority of its members who were teachers and from intellectual backgrounds, not least because it suspected their close relationship with the Sacrifice League-led government that it had just removed.[53] It also moved to ensure the removal of all those who were suspect not only on political grounds but also because of their social and economic backgrounds, such as those who were, or who were from, landlord and rich peasant families.

As already noted, the party consolidation in Licheng was particularly draconian, and certainly much more severe than in either Wuxiang (where the CCP was better established) or Liaoxian (which shared a similar CCP history). It was particularly severe on cadres who were teachers and intellectuals. Though figures are not available for either the ordinary party membership of the Licheng CCP during 1940, or its social composition, a couple of years later the base area's Organization Department did provide statistics for the change in the Licheng cadre force at this time. Before 1940, 47 percent of Licheng's cadres had been teachers and intellectuals, with one percent from a rich peasant background. In 1940 this changed dramatically and only 18 percent of the county's cadres were teachers and intellectuals, and none were from a rich peasant background.[54]

All the same, as these figures suggest, not every member of the Licheng CCP with an intellectual class status was expelled at this time, and there were even former teachers who had been members of the Sacrifice League as well as the CCP who remained within the party. After 1939 the Licheng CCP still had twenty-seven members who were regarded as from an intellectual background.[55] The Licheng county gazetteer provides biographies of some thirty-eight people who had served the county particularly well during the War of Resistance. Of these, fifteen had been teachers in 1937, and four had been students during the war.[56] Of those fifteen teachers, ten are said to have joined the CCP in 1937, when (at the end of the year) the local party organization only had a total of thirty-two members.

The 1940 reorganization of the Licheng CCP was nonetheless fundamental and thorough, and there was a danger of a localist backlash, which (as Chapter 8 indicates) is indeed what happened to some extent with the emergence of the Sixth Trigram Movement. Even before such manifestations, the base area CCP committee had tried to moderate any possible adverse local reaction by sending Huo Fan back to his home county. Huo had been in Licheng again during 1937 and 1938 and served with the Sacrifice League operation in the county. However, in the middle of 1938 he had been sent to work with the Propaganda Department under the Liaoxian CCP. In 1940 as the reorganization of the local CCP deepened, he was appointed secretary of the Licheng CCP committee.

In the meantime, by the second half of 1940 the party consolidation had moved on apace. Every party member was deemed to have resigned. They were all then asked to reapply. Some were permitted to do so without further ado, but the majority were required to undergo a substantial examination process. At that stage the Licheng CCP divided the remaining applicants into four groups who were treated differently: those who would be retained; those where a decision would be delayed; those where the applicants would be counseled; and those who would be expelled. All those who were eventually readmitted, and there were only a couple of hundred, had to undergo a period of reeducation at the county CCP school.[57]

The result was a dramatic change in the social basis of the CCP in Licheng. Most previous members of the Licheng CCP from three separate groups were not permitted to rejoin: those from landlord and rich peasant backgrounds were particularly suspect; people thought to have a strong commitment to Yan Xishan, or even to the former Licheng establishment were also politically suspect; and the attempt to recruit large numbers of landless laborers was abandoned as a mistake.[58] At the same time, poor and middle peasants were encouraged to join without the same kind of detailed assessment.[59]

One of the difficulties the CCP has repeatedly experienced with processes that question the appropriateness of an individual's party membership is that they are often difficult to stop and tend to feed on themselves.[60] Something of that nature appears to have happened on this occasion, though not as dramatically as has sometimes been the case. At the same time as the CCP was restructuring its membership through concerns about potential localism, it also removed many of its cadres from their positions and transferred them to other locations. In particular native cadres were subject to this procedure in order to ensure that any particularistic relationships were disturbed. Huo Fan suddenly found himself under criticism and by the end of the year had been demoted.

As elsewhere in North China, there was a tension between 'insiders' and 'outsiders': local cadres with first-hand knowledge, experience and familiarity; as against cadres from Taiyuan, Beiping and the metropolitan areas of North China who considered themselves more sophisticated. The latter often acted as though they had additional insights into the ways of the CCP; they tended in consequence to regard their local colleagues somewhat as 'turnip-head,' uneducated peasants regardless of their background, experience or standing.[61] As Chapter 7 discusses, something like this seems to have occurred in Wuxiang during 1940. In Licheng this tension was to rumble on for the rest of the war. Local experience was needed, but to many in the base area organization of the CCP local knowledge was also suspect.

The difference had been mediated in the short term. However, the conflict over presumed localism between 'insiders' and 'outsiders' did threaten to get out of hand again at the end of 1942 and into 1943, and eventually became caught up in the unfolding of the national CCP's rectification movement in Licheng. Huo Fan had been serving in the county throughout and was reappointed as secretary of the Licheng CCP during 1942, just as the base area CCP committee was once again becoming more concerned about the dangers of localism. Such concerns were not without some justification, particularly in Licheng. As Chapter 8 indicates, by 1942–43 there were increasing attempts by village cadres to protect their local communities, with landlords and rich peasants actively seeking such protection.

The Licheng CCP acted at first to try and redirect those of its cadres who were suspected of this kind of behavior. However, these activities also coincided with the base area CCP committee's growing concerns about spies and infiltrators, which did increase the climate of suspicion. The base area's Organization Department eventually intervened, reorganizing the leadership of the Licheng CCP once again in 1943, and changing many of its 115 cadres at the county and subdistrict levels. Those suspected of inappropriate behavior were given the chance to 'confess' at a series of inner-party 'confession meetings': a meeting of the CCP Shanxi-Hebei-Henan Committee was told 'We tried to win them over by getting them to confess in party meetings' though apparently without much success.[62]

However, neither the intervention of the base area's CCP committee, nor the opportunity to recant appeared to be able to solve the problem. The whole movement against localist activists rapidly developed its own dynamic and became corrosive. Huo Fan ended up on leave for the whole of 1944, which he spent in study and rectification under the direction of the base area CCP committee. By early 1945 most of the leading members of the Licheng CCP committee and its organizations were all 'outsiders,' as were (unusually for the Taihang Region) the cadres in the county's subdistricts.[63]

POLITICAL CHANGE IN LICHENG

On the surface Licheng would appear to have had many advantages in the development of the base area's base area, and indeed CCP rule. Japanese presence here during the war was considerably less than anywhere else, the exclusively agricultural economy ran a surplus, and there was a local nationalist and resistance organization—the Returned Students Federation—in operation well in advance of the war. However, during the 1940s Licheng was to present the CCP with some of the most serious challenges to its rule in the Taihang Base Area. The CCP was able to establish its political institutions and even to implement its programs of political and social reform. At the same time it also encountered considerable resistance which severely tested the ability of the local CCP organization to maintain operations and to regenerate itself.

The problems encountered by the CCP in Licheng are an excellent example of the potential conflict in the revolutionary process between the drive to create new social and political structures, and the drive to centralize political leadership. The starting point for the CCP's difficulties was the political revolution it engineered in January 1940 that ended the resistance coalition. The Returned Students Federation had been the organizational source for the foundation of both the Sacrifice League and the CCP, and had led the somewhat protracted movement to remove the local ruling elite in the early stages of the political revolution in Licheng. However, when the CCP assumed control of the county government it turned on not only the Returned Students Federation, but also intellectuals in general and the former supporters of the Sacrifice League. It thus effectively alienated both the county's previous ruling elite and a particularly strong alternative and modernizing elite. At the same time the CCP further weakened its own political capacity in the county by carrying out a party consolidation that expelled most of its own members, and which was particularly suspicious of those with local knowledge and expertise. As problems multiplied during the 1940s this lack of local knowledge and experience then not only became more acute, but developed further into a distrust of local cadres by the base area CCP.

NOTES

1. 'Shiba jituanjun zongsilingbu fayanren guanyu Huangyadong baoweizhande tanhua' ['A Spokesman for the 18th Army Group Talks about the Battle to Protect Huangyadong'] in *Xinhua ribao* [New China Daily] North China Edition, 27 November 1941, p.1.

2. LOH p.21.

3. LX pp.813–879 lists more than 1,000.

4. See, for example, LGD p.5; and Liu Huan 'Licheng jiandang chuqide yidian qingkuang' ['A View of the Early Establishment of the Party in Licheng'] 4 January 1987, in DJ p.644.

5. The official Licheng County Record lists forty-four celebrated individuals who served in the county during the War of Resistance. Nineteen of these in 1937 had been either teachers or students. None are described as having come from poor or even middle peasant background, whereas three are explicitly described as having been born into landlord families. See LX p.734 ff.

6. LGD p.7. Ironically the work team was led by Wang Fengwu who himself later defected to the Japanese side.

7. LOH p.43.

8. Li Daqing and Dong Weifa 'Balujun yierjiushi Licheng gongzuotuan yu Zhanhe youjiduide chuangjian' ['The Licheng Work Team of the Eighth Route

Army's 129th Division and the establishment of the Zhan River Guerilla Unit'] in *Shanxi dangshi tongxun* [Newsletter of Shanxi Party History] no.3, 1987, p.33. Li Daqing was himself a member of the second work team that arrived from the 129th Division in November 1937.

9. LZ p.14.

10. Licheng xian' ['Licheng County'] in Xu Guosheng and Chen Ninghua (ed) *Shanxi xian qu jingji fazhan shilue* [Historical outline of the economic development of counties and regions in Shanxi] Taiyuan, Shanxi jingji chubanshe, 1992, p.232.

11. 'Shiba jituanjun zongsilingbu fayanren guanyu Huangyadong baoweizhande tanhua' ['A Spokesman for the 18th Army Group Talks about the Battle to Protect Huangyadong'] in *Xinhua ribao* [New China Daily] North China Edition, 27 November 1941, p.1.

12. LX p.451.

13. Li Da *KangRi zhanzhengzhongde balujun yierjiushi* [The 129th Division of the Eighth Route Army in the War of Resistance to Japan] Beijing, Renmin chubanshe, 1985, p.382.

14. 'Licheng xian' ['Licheng County'] in Xu Guosheng and Chen Ninghua (ed) *Shanxi xian qu jingji fazhan shilue* [Historical outline of the economic development of counties and regions in Shanxi] Taiyuan, Shanxi jingji chubanshe, 1992, p.231.

15. The Shanxi Province *Ten Year Plan* prepared for Yan Xishan, and quoted in LGD p.3.

16. 'Licheng xian' ['Licheng County'] in Xu Guosheng and Chen Ninghua (ed) *Shanxi xian qu jingji fazhan shilue* [Historical outline of the economic development of counties and regions in Shanxi] Taiyuan, Shanxi jingji chubanshe, 1992, p.231.

17. Tian Youru 'Shanxi tudi zhidu gaige lishi gaiyao' ['Outline History of Reform of the Land System in Shanxi'] in *Shanxi dangshi tongxun* [Bulletin of Shanxi Party History] no.2, 1993, p.8.

18. LX p.499.

19. LZ p.477 and p.485.

20. LX pp.681–82.

21. LGD p.5.

22. LZ p.196.

23. Liu Huan 'Licheng jiandang chuqide yidian qingkuang' ['A View of the Early Establishment of the Party in Licheng'] 4 January 1987, in DJ p.644 ff.

24. Liu Huan 'Licheng jiandang chuqide yidian qingkuang' ['A View of the Early Establishment of the Party in Licheng'] 4 January 1987, in DJ p.645.

25. LOH p.32.

26. Liu Huan 'Licheng jiandang chuqide yidian qingkuang' ['A View of the Early Establishment of the Party in Licheng'] 4 January 1987, in DJ p.647.

27. LX p.415.

28. Liu Huan 'Licheng jiandang chuqide yidian qingkuang' ['A View of the Early Establishment of the Party in Licheng'] 4 January 1987, in DJ p.649.

29. LX p.377.

30. Liu Huan 'Licheng jiandang chuqide yidian qingkuang' ['A View of the Early Establishment of the Party in Licheng'] 4 January 1987, in DJ p.649.

31. LOH p.32.

32. LX p.140.

33. By comparison the organization of the Sacrifice League in Wuxiang, where it was considerably less active or significant, remained extant to the end of 1940.

34. LOH p.56.

35. LGD p.5.

36. See, for example, the comments of Liu Huan complaining about the mistreatment of colleagues at this time, and pointing out that 'there is a historical lesson to be learnt from this'; in 'Licheng jiandang chuqide yidian qingkuang' ['A View of the Early Establishment of the Party in Licheng'] 4 January 1987, in DJ p.650.

37. LX p.212–213.

38. Licheng xian' ['Licheng County'] in Xu Guosheng and Chen Ninghua (ed) *Shanxi xian qu jingji fazhan shilue* [Historical outline of the economic development of counties and regions in Shanxi] Taiyuan, Shanxi jingji chubanshe, 1992, p.231; LX p.227.

39. CHL p.145.

40. LX p.584. These bridges stayed with their nameplates intact until the Cultural Revolution. The Bocheng Bridge (after Liu Bocheng, the Commander of the 129th Division) remains to this day, but the Xiaoping Bridge (after Deng Xiaoping) was completely destroyed at that time. However, its nameplate was secreted away and now adorns the courtyard of a peasant fan in Baiyu Village.

41. LX pp.381–82.

42. CHL p.130.

43. Liu Huan 'Licheng jiandang chuqide yidian qingkuang' ['A View of the Early Establishment of the Party in Licheng'] 4 January 1987, in DJ p.645. Liu Huan's first-hand account of events conflicts with the official record. See LOH p.24.

44. LOH p.22.

45. Xu Zirong 'Guanyu bage xiande zhibu gongzuo' ['Work on Party Branches in Eight Counties'] 30 August 1942 in DJ p.237.

46. Xu Zirong 'Guanyu bage xiande zhibu gongzuo' ['Work on Party Branches in Eight Counties'] 30 August 1942 in DJ p.238.

47. LZ p.130.

48. LX p.467.

49. LOH p.3.

50. Wang Xintai 'Jianshu xinminzhu zhuyi geming shiqi Licheng dang zuzhi de jianshe' ['An Overview of the Development of the Party's Organization in Licheng during the New Democratic Revolution'] in *Shanxi dangshi tongxun* [Newsletter of Shanxi Party History] no.3, 1991, p.41.

51. LXH p.73 ff.

52. LOH p.56.

53. The problem of CCP members working with the Sacrifice League, and developing a 'Sacrifice League Mentality' was felt more widely than just Licheng. See He Yingcai 'JinJiYu bianqu gonggu dangde jige wenti' ['Several Issues in the Consolidation of the Party in the Shanxi-Hebei-Henan Border Area'] 6 December 1940, in TDZH vol.3: 1940, p.808.

54. Comments by Lai Ruoyu, 1 March 1945, in SOC p.33.
55. LOH p.56.
56. LX p.734 ff.
57. Wang Xintai 'Jianshu xinminzhu zhuyi geming shiqi Licheng dang zuzhi de jianshe' ['An Overview of the Development of the Party's Organization in Licheng during the New Democratic Revolution'] in *Shanxi dangshi tongxun* [Newsletter of Shanxi Party History] no.3, 1991, p.41.
58. Wang Xintai 'Jianshu xinminzhu zhuyi geming shiqi Licheng dang zuzhi de jianshe' ['An Overview of the Development of the Party's Organization in Licheng during the New Democratic Revolution'] in *Shanxi dangshi tongxun* [Newsletter of Shanxi Party History] no.3, 1991, p.41.
59. CHL pp.79–83.
60. Frederick C Teiwes *Politics and Purges in China* New York, M E Sharpe, 1979, p.27; and Frederick C Teiwes 'Establishment and consolidation of the new regime' in *The Cambridge History of China* Vol. 14, The People's Republic of China Part I, The Emergence of Revolutionary China 1949–1965, Cambridge, Cambridge University Press, 1987, Chapter 2, p.61.
61. Mao Zedong discussed this problem in 'Rectify the Party's Style of Work' 1 February 1942, in *Selected Works of Mao Tse-tung* Beijing, Foreign Languages Press, 1967, Vol.3, p.45.
62. Summary of discussion on research into party branches, in ZJY p.8.
63. Wang Qian's comments at the Sixth Organizational Conference of the Taihang Base Area, 20 February 1945, in SOC p.3.

Part II

Social Reform

5

The Revolutionary Imperative

At the start of the War of Resistance the CCP had most definitely put aside its revolutionary agenda in order to support a united front coalition with Chiang Kai-shek and the Nationalist Party against Japan. It not only played down its own revolutionary rhetoric and emphasized the importance of Sun Yat-sen's 'Three People's Principles' but agreed to end its calls for the confiscation and redistribution of landlords' property,.as well as armed revolt.[1] The CCP successfully built on this wider nationalist appeal throughout the war, and there were certainly times when the party leadership attempted to rein in moves by part of its organization that might jeopardize its political position in this respect. In particular in Shanxi after the break with Yan Xishan, the party Central Committee went to great lengths to advise its membership that though a united front with that province's warlord might have broken down, the principle of the united front for all classes and kinds of people to support the CCP against the Japanese had not.[2]

During the War of Resistance and even shortly thereafter there were accounts of CCP activities in North China which suggested that the party had been less than concerned with a fundamental social revolution during the war.[3] However, the CCP had temporarily shelved its revolutionary goals at the beginning of the war, it had not abandoned them completely. As the war developed, leaders in the CCP's central institutions and even more the party's activists in the base areas became increasingly concerned with programs of social change. Particularly in the Taihang region the CCP's commitment to radically reshape the sociopolitical environment was not abandoned for very long. Once political order was established the CCP set about developing the political space in which social and economic reform could be implemented, both for its own sake and in order to develop a social base of support. That process is the subject of the second part of this study of the Taihang Base Area, and in particular Liaoxian, Wuxiang and Licheng Counties.

The first part of this book has detailed how the CCP's political order was established at different times in each of the three counties: during the first few months of 1939 in Wuxiang; in January 1940 in Licheng; and by April 1940 in Liaoxian. However, at the level of the base area, though a CCP Committee had existed since October 1937, the establishment of political order was not begun until well after the Licheng Meeting, organized by the CCP's North China Bureau during April 1940. The Joint Office for the Taihang, Taiyue and South Hebei Base Areas was slow to become administratively functional, and it could be argued that from this perspective the CCP's rule was not institutionalized even in those few small areas it then controlled unreservedly until the second half of 1941.

Even allowing that the establishment of political order is a process rather than a specific moment, these differences of timing are of more than passing concern. A coordinated base area may not have been fully functional, but nonetheless the leadership of the CCP in the base area as well as its constituent parts had already started to experiment with programs of radical social change. In the case of Wuxiang this would seem to have started on a large scale as early as May 1939. Indeed the search for an appropriate revolutionary strategy and its implementation are a large part of the explanation of some of the problems within the CCP, as well as between the CCP and society that have already been encountered. There were essentially two dimensions to the CCP's revolutionary imperative, and they were sometimes in conflict: there was a drive to create new structures of wealth, power and status; and there was also a drive to homogenize and unify, not least under its own central leadership. Much depended on the cadre force, which was necessarily variable in its abilities, and sometimes, as in the case of Licheng, found wanting.

The process of social reform in the Taihang region started with early attempts at social engineering that were extremely problematic. Attempts to radicalize landless laborers and poor peasants failed to achieve their goals and in the process resulted in (sometimes extreme) rural class conflict, and the alienation of parts of the CCP's rural base of support. The CCP's attempts to adapt to the challenges of its environment led to a major debate within the party on class and revolution, and specifically the role of the middle peasant. Adaptation and then further adaptation by the CCP eventually resulted in both a changed social environment and a social base of support for the CCP which centered on the middle peasantry. However, in that process the concept of middle peasant was elaborated and politically transformed.

The process of social change was uneven, even in those secure parts of the base area firmly under CCP control. It was also often chaotic, uncoordinated and violent. There were problems between the CCP, in its many different organizational forms, and the wider society; but there were also social tensions that emerged within the peasantry as expectations became frustrated. Equally, there were difficulties that emerged in the relationships within the CCP, particularly between levels and most particularly between the leadership of the base area and those of the county party committees.

SOCIAL ENGINEERING

The Taihang region as a whole had been predominantly rural on the eve of the War of Resistance, though far from a subsistence economy. Across the region, landlords and middle peasants sold half their total product at market; even poor peasants sold on average about a fifth of their output.[4] Moreover, as already noted, neither Liaoxian, Wuxiang nor Licheng had remained untouched by modernization. Liaoxian had become a rapidly expanding commercial center during the 1920s, based on coal and sheep; Wuxiang had established a rural-based small-scale industrial sector; and Licheng's prosperity had been reflected in high levels of education.

The economic changes of the 1920s and 1930s in the Taihang region had led to the development of a rural society increasingly characterized by a large group of wage earners, as well as widespread landowning. Though some areas had experienced large-scale commercial development and land concentration—Wuxiang was a notable example—the more usual pattern was an increasing number of smaller-scale landholders who farmed their own land, and might both rent out some land and rent in other. In addition, members of their households might hire themselves out as workers to other landowners as well as working their own family's land. Mortgages were usually raised on land, both for the original purchase and to raise capital, less for further development than to cope with the economic recession of the 1930s. By 1937 debts from interest repayments were as much of a problem as rent, with landowners and peasants increasingly mortgaging all kinds of property to meet interest payments on accumulating debts. The danger for the peasant was that if they defaulted on either loan repayments or indeed rent, the landowner could repossess.

In terms of the CCP's sociopolitical classification, there were fewer poor peasants, and more middle peasants in the Taihang region than elsewhere. There were few absentee landlords, except in the immediate Changzhi area where living in the city and having other business interests whilst owning land in the surrounding counties was a local landlord characteristic.[5] Unlike some parts of North China there were few managerial landlords in the region; and in general a decreasing number of rich peasants.[6] As already noted, there had also been the emergence of a substantial rural working class during the two decades before the War of Resistance.

Urban Intellectuals and Peasants

Those who came into the Taihang region in 1937 and then organized the base area, were for the most part not in any sense locals, and few had little experience of rural China at all. The CCP's first organizers and the earliest recruits to the resistance cause were almost exclusively urban intellectuals.[7] Quite apart from their reactions to the local physical environment, they were often shocked by both the poverty they encountered, and cultural differences which local people took for granted. Chen Dadong, who had been working in the base area with the Shanxi-Hebei-Henan Peasant Association since 1939, went to Shuangfengchuan Village in Heshun County in 1941 to set up a pilot project for the rent and interest reduction campaign. His urban middle class values were shocked to find 'Shuangfengchuan was so poor some peasants couldn't afford to get married: two brothers even shared the same wife.'[8] They were fundamental 'outsiders' who had trouble communicating with local people, their use of language and pronunciation in the county towns, let alone the often totally uneducated poor peasants in the villages.

Under these circumstances the task they faced to mobilize the local population for resistance let alone social reform would have been organizationally and politically uphill even if they had received considerable training beforehand. Of course some, perhaps as many as thirty at base area level and a half dozen or so in Wuxiang, had been CCP organizers before the outbreak of war. However, the evidence suggests that many who were recruited in 1937 had sometimes only very cursory inductions into the CCP, let alone as cadres. By August 1940, 38.7 percent of county-level cadres, for example, had still not attended any kind of training program even at the county-level let alone entered the more formal system of party schools; and of the 61.3 percent who had, more than half had only attended local county-level short-term programs.[9]

The incoming organizers and urban intellectuals certainly recognized the need to learn about their new environment, and for training. However, they also came from a background that provided them with both a moral superiority toward the peasantry, and an almost messianic belief in the role of the intellectual as savior as well as political leader.[10] The potential for misunderstandings, difficulties and mistakes in attempting mobilization and social reform was high. Li Xuefeng, who was the ranking secretary of the base area CCP committee and himself an urban intellectual, often commented during 1937–45 on the organizational and political problems facing cadres because of their own backgrounds. On occasion he even complained about what he clearly thought was their unreasonable behavior or unrealistic political expectations. Looking back on the course of the base area's development from early 1945 he was particularly pointed:

> Many leading cadres are urban intellectuals. When they first came they knew little about the rural areas and the peasants, and nothing about peasant cadres or worker-peasant cadres. Whether deliberately or not, they hurt the worker-peasant and local cadres through their city views and absolutist interpretations of Marxism.[11]

However, the problems Li was referring to in March 1945 were not immediately apparent in October 1937. Until the second half of 1939 base area activities concentrated on dealing with the military threat; working within the united front, particularly with Yan Xishan and the Sacrifice League; and on building a CCP organization. There was little time or opportunity for concerns about implementing a program of social change. Indeed, to have done so might readily have jeopardized other activities, and particularly the development of the united front.

All the same, war and social movements had an impact on local structures of wealth and power during the first two years of the base area. Some landlords fled and where that happened their landholdings became public land that were redistributed within the village. However, landlords and rich peasants for the most part stayed in place, though the depression of the 1930s followed by Japanese invasion and political uncertainty had left some of the them economically exposed. During 1938–39 across the Taihang region as a whole landlords and rich peasants started to sell the less profitable parts of their land. One of the pressures in this direction came from local government, which particularly during 1939 encouraged both landlords and rich peasants to shoulder a disproportionate amount of the tax burden from their savings: roughly two-thirds of the total. The land they sold was for the most part bought by owner-cultivators who were more able to afford it not least because they were largely exempt from tax as local governments turned to donations from those who had savings. Poor peasants, tenants and landless laborers, however, found themselves becoming markedly poorer at this time, largely as the wage economy which they had come to depend on before the war started to contract.[12]

In the first two years of the war the CCP grew dramatically. Recruitment patterns varied greatly with location, though in general it recruited heavily amongst teachers and the educated generally, as well as amongst the young. Owner-cultivators joined in large numbers, as did 'vagrants.' Landlords and rich peasants also joined, but on the whole not the old (people over 40), poor peasants or rural tenants. These last two categories were always difficult to mobilize during the war, but at this time they were particularly inactive.[13] All the same, the result was that the social basis of the CCP started to change as these new recruits began to take on additional responsibilities. At a base area CCP meeting to discuss party branch development during July 1942 someone pointed out that 'Those who joined the party early were middle peasants, vagrants and landlords, and most of them have become and remained cadres.'[14]

The first attempts to introduce a program of social change locally came toward the end of 1939 in the form of a campaign to reduce rents and interest payments on debts initiated by Yan'an. This 'double reduction' policy had been part of the CCP's national agenda since its abandonment of more radical land reform in 1937. It was to prove markedly unsuccessful, and created further problems for the base area's CCP leadership. The details of the attempted campaign are not readily available, but it would appear to have foundered on a mixture of cadre inexperience and peasant resistance. Its results were not only class conflict, violence and social dislocation, but also a major reassessment of the base area's strategy, which itself was to prove problematic.

The essence of the various political movements to introduce social change was a series of public meetings—struggle meetings—at which landowners were called to account. Earlier in 1939 this technique had been used very successfully in a number of places, notably Wuxiang in the middle of the year, to reach a more politically acceptable distribution of the tax burden. The exercise centered on mediated conflict between landowners and peasants, which had to be carefully managed if local situations were not to get out of hand. In this and subsequent campaigns the focus moved particularly to peasants who had lost either land-use rights or ownership of land through debt, who were now encouraged to request restitution, especially where the rent and interest rates charged were now considered excessive. In general, the Peasant Associations usually tried to negotiate agreements between landowner and renter, creditor and debtor, beforehand on the grounds of community solidarity (especially in wartime) and indeed most accumulated debts were cleared in this way. However, if agreement could not be reached then disputes would be publicly aired.

In general at the end of 1939 and into 1940, the politics of rural social change were extremely impatient. The Peasant Associations and their activities were organized from the top down, by the CCP committees and local governments at various levels, rather than as would later be the case by cadres who emerged from within the land redistribution movement. They were often inexperienced, untrained and anxious for political success. Landless tenants and poor peasants had been and remained resistant to change and hard to mobilize. Whilst it was clear they were more concerned about the availability of work, land taxes and land rents than landownership, once the landless tenants and poor peasants became involved in political action the cadres found them unpredictable and hard to control.

One result was that local situations did rapidly get out of hand and turn to violence: those with land and property were sometimes surrounded, beaten up and even killed by those without.[15] Another consequence was that local cadres sometimes just went ahead and either directed or ensured that land was first confiscated, and then redistributed from not only landlords, but also rich peasants.[16] In addition, though the extent of such activity is not known, there were calls from county-level as well as village cadres for the poor and the landless to get organized for immediate land reform: the confiscation of land and property and their redistribution. The Liaoxian CCP called for a rural revolution precisely along these lines in October 1939.[17]

The extent to which the rent and interest reduction campaign escalated out of control, the numbers and distribution of landlords and rich peasants under attack, as well as the length of time the drive for land seizure continued are all not known. It would seem that Liaoxian experienced the most severe land reform at this time, though problems of this kind are currently most readily documented and acknowledged for Wuxiang.[18] Peng Tao, Director of the Mobilization Department for the CCP committee of the base area openly admitted that on occasion the lines had been drawn too sharply, and the campaigns were unbalanced: 'We made mistakes and there was chaos in our handling of the transformation of class relations.'[19] The regional Joint Government Administrative Office went further admitting breaches of human rights through zealousness in mass mobilization during 1940.[20] Indeed, the Licheng Meeting of the North China Bureau, held in April 1940, explicitly censured the Wuxiang CCP for its handling of the rent and interest reduction campaign on these grounds.[21] The Liaoxian leadership of the CCP was also heavily criticized at the Licheng Meeting for its land reform.

The potential economic and political consequences of this attempt at social reform were great and a major threat to the base area. In the short-term, where those who felt threatened could leave, they did. The Peasant Association acknowledged that large numbers of the 'rural social elite' had fled to the Japanese-occupied territories at this time.[22] Quite apart from the threat to continued CCP attempts to maintain a post-Yan Xishan broad coalition of political support outside the base area, these dislocations also threatened an already precarious economic situation.

The Theory of the Unique Influence of Class Status

At the beginning of 1940 the base area faced its first major crisis. The united front with Yan Xishan had collapsed in civil war, Japanese pressure was increasing, and economic problems loomed large. A review of party membership—a party 'consolidation'—had long been on the agenda, after the rapid expansion of 1937–39. Now it was needed additionally to remove any remnant sympathetic attitudes to Yan Xishan, and to ensure greater political reliability in the wake of the unsuccessful rent and interest reduction campaign. In general, it needed a new mobilizatory strategy, to build on the support already gained through the united front but to assist with the new political environment.

The response was to turn to class analysis and to consolidate the CCP, as had been originally suggested when the topic was first discussed in November 1939, by developing its proletarian membership. The practical problem even at that date had been that the base area had already evacuated the urban centers of Southeast Shanxi and southwest Hebei for the Taihang Mountains. There had been industrial workers in the base area: about 2565 were in CCP-led unions before 1940.[23] However, by late 1939 most were either in the Eighth Route Army or in guerilla areas. By 1940, for example, Wuxiang had thirty-five former unionists, Liaoxian ten and Licheng twenty.[24]

In CCP usage the European concept of 'proletariat' was not unreasonably rendered as 'the class without property.' The search for the working class could then be extended to include not only rural industrial workers, but also craftsmen of all kinds (for example, house builders and repairers, shoemakers, ironsmiths); shepherds (sheep were and are a major industry in the Taihang region); farmhands; and tenant peasants, because they did not own the land they worked. Because they were forced to sell their labor to live all these social categories were effectively landless laborers or 'peasant-workers.' Similarly because, even though they might own a small amount of land, poor peasants were forced to rent from a landowner they could also be regarded as part of the category of the 'exploited.' In practice the proletariat thus became 'industrial workers, farmhands and poor peasants.'[25]

In his discussion document right at the end of 1939 that summed up the local CCP's development during the previous two years, Lai Ruoyu—then a member of the base area CCP committee and later Director of its

Organization Department—had highlighted 'the issue of class status' as the most significant question for the immediate future.[26] He was far from alone in highlighting this concern to determine the social groups to be targeted not only for recruitment to the CCP but also for the development of wider support. Many in the leadership of the CCP at base area and county level explained the failures of late 1939 as a result of poor class analysis. In their view the CCP's program was not at fault but rather its implementation because of the poor quality of party cadres and the political unreliability of party members. Some reflected on the CCP's over-reliance on intellectuals and middle peasants for leadership; all bemoaned the lack of workers in the Taihang base area CCP.[27] The Wuxiang CCP in particular criticized the role of middle peasants in its leadership; the Licheng CCP pointed to its intellectuals as the cause of failure.

Discussions within the base area CCP in the first few months of 1940 led to a 'theory of the unique influence of class status' which reached even beyond the ideological formulations of November 1939. Recruitment to the CCP would now not only favor poor peasants, industrial workers and landless laborers, but exclude for the most part members of the rural social elite, rich peasants, middle peasants, and intellectuals.[28] Moreover, these discriminations would also be extended into the CCP's policies as they affected the wider community. The immediate results of debate were a review of party membership that decreased the numbers from those social categories in the local organizations, and quite a serious attack on the base area's cadre force.[29] This outcome also meant a basic continuation of the same policies on social reform that had characterized the previous few months, even if some attempt was now being made to reduce the potential for uncontrolled violence.

The 'theory of the unique influence of class status' was more than simply an application of a set class analysis. It resulted from a discussion of the principles of the CCP's class analysis, and led to a crude form of Marxism that held political beliefs and actions to be determined and predicted exclusively by social background. The theory seems to have originated with the urban intellectuals who had joined the CCP at an early stage in the war. These perspectives left little if any room for the transformative power of consciousness in encouraging a process of political change, and seems to have asserted that only the proletariat as now defined could have genuine revolutionary potential.

However, the articulation of the 'theory of the unique influence of class status' not only privileged the working class, it discriminated against privilege and wealth. It clearly discriminated against the privilege and wealth of the old society—landlords, rich peasants, the traditional intellectual stratum—and extended its critique to embrace new privilege, those who had been able to profit from the war and earlier social dislocation particularly to buy land, and even more particularly the owner-cultivators. It even promised to 'Turn workers and peasants into intellectuals, and to make intellectuals practical.'[30] The importance of this dividing line is graphically reflected in the base area's 1940 report on its party consolidation campaign: this presented its results by demonstrating the increase in the ratio between CCP members who were workers and poor peasants, on the one hand, as against those who were middle peasants or higher status, on the other, district by district.[31]

The formal process of party consolidation—in which members were required to reapply and be reassessed—meant that the impact of the 'theory of the unique influence of class status' on the composition of the local CCP was dramatic. A minimum 30 percent quota for workers to be new recruits to all CCP branches had been introduced in 1939.[32] Various kinds of workers were now recruited to the CCP: the number of industrial workers increased by a factor of nine, and of craftsmen by a factor of four though the absolute numbers remained small at 1.8 and 1.9 percent, respectively, of the base area party's membership. The proportion of CCP members who were middle peasants decreased considerably.

By the middle of 1940, 72 percent of the county-level cadres under the Taihang Base Area CCP committee were still intellectuals. However, only 23.7 percent of cadres at the subdistrict level were now middle peasants, whereas the proportion of workers had risen to 17.1 percent, and of poor peasants to 37.3 percent.[33] The consolidation campaign was used to exclude many of those landlords, rich peasants, middle peasants and intellectuals who were not also established cadres[34]; and even those who were cadres were subject to investigation meetings where their political credentials were tested. Leadership of the Peasants' Associations, which had been dominated by middle peasants, passed overwhelmingly to poor peasants.[35]

The base area CCP's determined attempt to develop a large number of poor peasant and worker cadres proved a problematic experiment almost immediately. Quite apart from any other difficulties there was a question of literacy. A large part of the responsibilities of CCP and other cadres, even in the rural areas of the Taihang Mountains, involved paperwork and these new poor peasant and worker cadres were almost universally illiterate. One who was appointed as secretary of a county party committee at this time found himself 'promoted' rather rapidly, first to a position in the base area, and then to Yan'an. Though he later learnt to read, he always attributed his meteoric rise to having been an illiterate peasant-worker cadre.

Economic and Political Consequences

The base area leadership did move to moderate excess during 1940, but remained committed to its general program of radical reform. Even whilst emphasizing the need to respect 'human rights' and providing guarantees to landlords and rich peasants that their land would not be confiscated, they continued to pressure them both politically and economically. Politically, the pressure was maintained for landowners to reduce rents and interest rates, and to regularize debts and tenancy arrangements. As a result the number of land disputes of various kinds escalated dramatically during 1940.[36]

However, the economic pressures placed on landlords, rich peasants and increasingly owner-cultivators served to depress further an already depressed economy, and eventually led to further political resistance. Land sales rose steeply as landlords and rich peasants divested themselves of less-profitable assets that carried a high political risk. Whilst land redistribution was a politically desirable goal, particularly if it could occur through the operation of market forces rather than political confiscation and reallocation, the economic impact of such a sudden change was severe. In 1940 the base area economy nosedived and inflation increased dramatically. Two years later, Li Dazhang, the Director of the base area's Propaganda Department was highly critical of those of the base area's earlier leadership who had not understood that political success depended on ensuring the economic livelihood of ordinary people.[37] The increasing shortage of economic opportunity for both poor peasants and landless rural laborers was effectively worsened, rather than ameliorated by pushing them into positions of political leadership. In consequence, tensions between poor peasants and owner-cultivators increased, to be added to the potential conflict between landlords and rich peasants, on the one hand, and the rest of the peasantry on the other.

The reform of the tax system introduced at the beginning of 1940 was a disincentive to production, and encouraged landlords, rich peasants and owner-cultivators to sell their land rather than to farm it. A key part of the CCP's reform program at this time concentrated on the taxation system and ensuring a more equitable sharing of the tax bill. As already noted in discussion of Wuxiang's development during 1939, tax was even more of a concern to peasants than land ownership since the tax apportionment system was based on a poll tax rather than a wealth or property tax. The CCP was committed to a more progressive income tax but could not immediately introduce a new system, not least because it lacked the administrative infrastructure.

The compromise in 1940, which was intended as a short-term measure, was to prove almost economically disastrous.[38] Landownership was taxed, but with no direct reference to income. As a result a large proportion of the tax burden was to be paid by landlords and rich peasants. However, the amount to be paid by the middle peasants—who had been the major purchasers of land during the previous two years—came as a considerable shock, not least because their margins were much lower than those for landlords and rich peasants and because they had not (for the most part[39]) paid tax in the preceding years.

Given the social origins of the Taihang Base Area CCP's leadership, there were of course economists on hand to explain why 12.6 percent of the farming land in the region was going on the market at this time, why production was declining, and why rural labor wages were about 40 percent of what they had been before 1937.[40] One of their solutions was a new form of taxation based on income, but this required other political and institutional developments before it could be introduced.[41]

The potential for disaster was great. The rural social elite who had fled earlier were now being followed by others much less privileged. The economic depression made it difficult often for tenants to find the resources to meet their rents, even under the new system. As Lai Ruoyu acknowledged 'When tenant peasants can't cope with the rent problems they just go to the enemy for shelter. We will lose our mass power for guerilla war if we're not careful.'[42] Even intellectuals and cadres were feeling the pinch and opting out politically. A discussant at the Taihang Base Area's Organizational Conference in 1941 complained that 'Some of the primary school teachers have given up teaching to go to work in coal mines or to go back to their villages to work farmland. Cadres have developed 'get-rich' ideas.'[43] In the longer term, these economic and political problems led to wider political resistance, and even on one occasion contributed to an armed uprising, in Licheng during October 1941, as Chapter 8 details.

Toward the end of 1940 and into early 1941 as the base area CCP leadership realized the extent of the emerging difficulties, it tried to remedy the situation.[44] An attempt was made in February 1941 to reorganize the Peasants' Associations (and indeed all mass organizations) so that they operated more from within society than as state or political agencies.[45] In most counties, intellectuals were allowed back into the CCP once again and by mid-1941 soon outnumbered the workers. The proportion of middle peasants who were party members, however, continued to fall.[46]

Table 5.1 provides data on the tax rates as a proportion of income by social category for 1940–42 in the Taihang region. As it indicates, in 1941 and again 1942 the tax system was modified so that the burden on all

Table 5.1 Taxation Rates by Social Category, Taihang Region, 1940–1942 (percentage of income)

Year	Social category Landlord	Rich peasant	Middle peasant	Poor peasant
1940	28	22	19	11
1941	23	18	14	5
1942	36	23	10	4

Source: Zhonggong Taihang qudangwei *Taihangqu yinhang gongsheng gongzuo: cankao ziliao* [Commercial Work of the Taihang Base Area Banks: reference materials] Vol. 2: *Liunianlai zhongyao jingji jianshe huiyi jueyi huiyi* [Important Economic Development Meetings, Resolutions, and Recollections during the last Six Years] Huabei Xinhuashudian, 1946, p.121.

social categories, but particularly middle peasants, was lightened. Debt, rent and interest reduction procedures were regularized. Land could now only be reclaimed by peasants from landlords where the amount they owed in interest on a loan was more than double the original principal borrowed. Where the amount of the interest and the principal were roughly the same then the accumulated interest might be completely discounted but the peasant was still required to repay the original loan to the lender.

A substantial proportion of the landlords and rich peasants did return, and inevitably there were reactions to the excesses of 1939–40. Some of the land that had been confiscated was returned. When approached about rent and interest reduction landlords might well accept a measure of change but were cautious and less open than they had generally been earlier. It seems likely that they tried to maintain some of the political initiative individually. A fairly common complaint from poor peasants, and a reason given for their lack of activism at this time, was that they believed any arrangements struck now would only be temporary.[47] Moreover a two 'rent' system rapidly developed. There was the 'real rent'—a sum the landlord required them to pay. Then there was the 'nominal rent'—the original amount of the rent that the landlord required them to declare during the rent reduction movement.[48] For their part, local cadres were excessively careful, and tended to go to the other extreme of not exercising political direction at all rather than getting involved in an uncertain political movement.

CLASS AND REVOLUTION

Though there may have been differences within the base area CCP over the ways in which the policies of 1940–41 were applied, and the appropriate intensity of their implementation, there is no evidence of any difference of opinion about the general direction of those policies. However, this unity of purpose was to change dramatically during 1942–43 as the base area CCP attempted to revive its program for social reform. The catalyst was criticism from the CCP Central Committee of the implementation of land policy in the Taihang region during 1941, followed by a renewed attempt to implement rent and interest reduction. Within the base area CCP this led to discussion of the 'middle peasant question'—a debate about the centrality and appropriateness of the middle peasant as an agent of revolutionary change,[49] which when combined with other difficulties in the base area at the time of the campaign to reduce rent and interest effectively resulted in its partial implementation and postponement.

Rent and Interest Reduction

For the leadership of the base area CCP, and even more presumably for lower level cadres, the readjustments of 1941 represented a compromise between their longer-term revolutionary goals and what was immediately achievable. All the same even the readjustments of 1941 led to the Taihang CCP being criticized by the CCP Central Committee. In the words of the letter from the CCP Central Committee to Li Xuefeng (as Secretary of the base area's CCP committee) 'We feel that it is possible your land policies are a bit too far to the 'left'.' The CCP Central Committee was particularly critical of the Taihang CCP's attempts to regularize the arrangements for reducing, abolishing and maintaining rent and interest payments, both because it felt these were not consistent with activities elsewhere in North China (notably the Shanxi-Chahar-Hebei Border Region) and because it felt they continued discrimination against landlords and rich peasants, which prevented 'development of a capitalist economy.'[50]

Li Xuefeng's response was to prepare the base area CCP for the relaunching of a campaign centered on achieving rent and interest reductions, once the immediate military problems that beset the base area at the beginning of 1942 had at least temporarily been dealt with.[51] The Taihang CCP's guidelines on the implementation of land policy for 1942 highlighted some new departures for the base area. The most important were its approach to united front tactics, the recognition of regional difference within the base area, and the role proposed for the middle peasant in the implementation of rent and interest reduction.[52]

The guidelines unequivocally accepted the CCP Central Committee's criticisms from the previous year. Landlords and rich peasants were now not only to be treated as suppliers of agricultural output, but in the war situation they could become correctly politicized. If the peasants were to be allowed land, so then too should the landlords and rich peasants be allowed to own land. The aim, according to the guidelines, was 'to weaken but not to eliminate the feudal forces.' To this end it was crucial that any struggle stayed within the law.

Crucially the base area's new analysis also moved to concentrate on middle peasants as the principle agent of social change. Poor peasants and laborers were not abandoned as part of the revolutionary coalition, but it was now the middle peasants to whom the base area CCP looked for local leadership, and it would be changes in their socioeconomic status that would be used to judge the success of the campaign. The only concession to earlier politics in the Taihang Base Area that were reflected in the rent and interest reduction campaign guidelines was a differentiated strategy that allowed different procedures according to local conditions at various stages between those that had almost completed the proposed reforms and those where the process of change had barely started.

Any political campaigns were put on hold in the base area during May-July 1942 as the Japanese attacked south Liaoxian and in particular Matian. However, the drive for a rent and interest reduction campaign was resurrected after Liu Shaoqi visited in September. This time in attempting to reform the rural social environment the Taihang CCP attempted to establish a social contract between landlords and peasants. Essentially debts could be cleared, and rents reduced in return for permanency: the landlords would retain permanency of ownership and the peasants would not only acknowledge that right but also commit themselves to standard rents.[53] Simultaneously, a further administered reform of the tax system was attempted that set a target tax budget for the base area as well as a guideline payment rate for each social category. Cadres were explicitly told: 'Don't overdo it (this time)!'[54]

As before, the public meeting was at the heart of the local implementation of rent and interest reduction. As before too, whilst there certainly were occasions when the principles of 'large democracy'—landlord and peasants coming together in a village-based no-holds barred discussion of their mutual problems—were followed, there were equally occasions when local situations went beyond the bounds of the permissible. In Yangwei Village, Pingshun County, for example, the largest landlord in the village Song Fulu, attended a struggle meeting that lasted five days and which was resolved reasonably when other landlords in the village eventually joined with the peasants and persuaded Song to surrender ownership of both debt and much of his land in the interests of all.[55] However, speaking in 1983 of their earlier participation in the 1942 campaign both Zhang Shuxin (in Lucheng) and Yuan Jingwu (in Xiangyuan) recalled more violently struggle meetings where landlords were killed and their property redistributed.[56]

On the whole though, the insistence of both the Border Region Government and the base area CCP committee on the recognition of human and economic rights in the 1942 rent and interest reduction campaign would appear to have had an impact. It was after all this insistence that allowed landlords and rich peasants to stand their ground and even on occasion more surreptitiously to resist, notably through reaching accommodations with the new village political leaders, as appears to have happened extensively in parts of Licheng. Later investigations of the 1942 rent and interest reduction campaign revealed instances of agreed rent reductions not having been maintained through legalistic interpretations; landlords evicting peasants because they had not formally signed a tenancy agreement; and landlords introducing new tenancy contracts outside the rent and interest reduction campaign process.[57]

All the same, where the campaign was implemented it resulted in substantial reductions in the landholdings of both landlords and rich peasants, though there were different patterns to redistribution according to each locality's socioeconomic environment.[58] As before the primary mechanism of redistribution was land sales rather than confiscation (though there was also some local government involvement in reallocation of land[59]) as landlords and rich peasants needed to realize additional assets or made judgments about the continued profitability of land. The problem from the Taihang CCP leadership's point of view was that it had only been implemented in 60 percent of the villages in its secure areas, and had only involved 26 percent of the population.[60]

The Middle Peasant Question

Conditions of war, alongside landlord and rich peasant resistance are the more obvious explanations for the incomplete implementation of rent and interest reduction. At the same time it would seem that the campaign's concentration on the middle peasant as the chosen agent of social change was both a matter of confusion and led to some opposition within the Taihang CCP.[61] Confusion and even opposition are not hard to understand. As already noted, some cadres were concerned that middle peasants had been the major beneficiaries from land sales as a result of the rent and interest reduction campaign of 1939. To them, the middle peasant was a landowner, and possibly even a landlord in the sense of renting out land to poor peasants and landless tenants, if usually on a smaller scale than suggested by the categories of landlord and rich peasant.

The resultant discussion of the 'middle peasant question' within the CCP either halted the campaign in its tracks or slowed it down so much that postponement was the only option. It is not difficult to identify the different arguments that were espoused, though it is somewhat difficult to attribute specific positions to individuals or organizations. In general there would seem to be a difference between a base area CCP leadership trying at the very least to come to terms with the restrictions from above and to sell the idea of the middle peasant as an agent of change to some within the local party who could not understand what was going on, and some more local leaders who were presented (and to some extent presented themselves) as wanting to be more principled and 'revolutionary.'

The essential problem for many cadres that the rent and interest reduction campaign highlighted was their unease about the role of the middle peasant as a suitable agent of revolutionary change. For some who objected the problem was clearly ideological and their preferences drew them to emphasize the roles of either (or indeed both) landless laborers and poor peasants. For others there were more practical concerns, that surrounded the apparent corruptibility of middle peasants, or their reliability in political struggle. One of the latter would seem to have been Peng Tao, who in a subtle analysis pointed out that though it was more difficult to create activists out of poor peasants than middle peasants, nonetheless poor peasants were more active in struggle sessions against landlords and rich peasants (when required) than middle peasants.[62]

The base area CCP committee had started to explain its new strategy on social reform in detail at a series of inner-party meetings during July and August 1942. Landlords and rich peasants were only to be struggled against if they resisted measures to settle debts or to reduce rents. The campaign was to be put in the hands of the middle peasants, who would then mobilize support from the poor peasants and landless laborers. The most significant shift in policy was the decision to encourage middle peasants as basic-level cadres. In large part this was a recognition of the situation on the ground. Poor peasants and landless laborers had been tried as village cadres during 1940–41 and been found wanting.

Many middle peasants had indeed already become cadres in the villages not only because they had become the largest social category as a result of the social changes that had occurred after 1938, but also because they tended to be literate, and perhaps more importantly, because they had the economic wherewithal to do the job. Village cadres were expected to continue their own work as well as taking a leadership role, and owning and farming land was often an informal prerequisite. However, even the base area CCP leadership accepted that encouraging middle peasants to take these roles would not be as easy as had once been the case. As Xu Zirong, the Director of the Organization Department, pointed out, the political events of 1940–41 had turned the middle peasants generally into political 'waverers'—people who were uncertain about their own political direction, and particularly their attitudes to the CCP—and the task for the CCP was to renew their support.[63]

Explaining this to county and subdistrict level cadres, and ensuring their compliance was not an easy task either. At the various meetings of July and August 1942, Xu Zirong urged party cadres to take a balanced view on this program of social reform and to avoid deviations to the 'left' (overenthusiasm) or to the 'right' (accepting the status quo): he asked them 'to proceed from reality, rather than principle' and to remember that 'people and situations change: the enemy as well as ourselves.'[64] In discussing the development of CCP branches, Xu quite candidly accepted that the significance of 'class status' had become and remained confused. The key issues were the point at which an individual's class status was assessed; the extent to which individual consciousness might effect political behavior; and the relationship between group and individual behavior. Through a survey of CCP members in twenty-nine branches across eight counties, Xu argued that individuals had not only changed their socioeconomic status through the war—those who were now middle peasants also included large numbers of those who had previously been poor peasants, those who had been landless laborers had become poor peasants and even middle peasants—but had been able to raise their consciousness through political education.[65]

Xu Zirong placed great emphasis on the need for and the power of political education. In the process there is more than a hint that he was trying to address some of the concerns of those within the Taihang CCP who might have been concerned about what they saw as an abandonment of the working class and the revolution:

> Our purpose is to educate party members to understand communism, and to help them understand the relationship between today's concerns and long-term interests, as well as the relationship between personal and class interests. We need to remould the ideology of party members, strengthen their sense of organisation, and overcome their individualism. However, this education has to take the experience of different kinds of party members into account. Peasants understand communism differently from workers and intellectuals. The workers are born communists; the intellectuals learn communism from advanced knowledge; but it is difficult for the peasants to understand communism. The peasants are not satisfied with their present situation, but on the other hand they have a mentality of private ownership. They are used to private ideology, private habits and private customs. They are also very conservative.[66]

All the same, it seems likely that some opposition was raised even in July and August 1942. The survey Xu had used to develop his arguments was published together with a commentary that explicitly discussed the question 'What is this revolution for?'[67]

Discussion of the 'middle peasant question' continued for over a year. During 1940–41 the base area CCP had a membership dominated by poor peasants, and a village-level leadership of poor peasants and workers. By the end of 1942 the membership was comprised of poor and middle peasants in roughly equal proportions, but its cadre force in the villages was now largely one of middle peasants. However, the change had been achieved at the cost of not only delay in the rent and interest reduction campaign, but also an attack on many village-level middle peasant cadres from their county and subdistrict superiors.

County and subdistrict cadres, and many can be assumed to have been poor peasant and worker cadres promoted earlier, objected to the way the rent and interest reduction campaigns were being implemented. They took the middle peasant village cadres to task for their class status which they held to be 'degenerate'; and accused middle peasants of being more interested in making money than revolution, taking advantage of the rent and interest campaign to buy land themselves, and having too much personally to lose by engaging in reform. Once again the blanket critique of privilege was applied, as it had been during 1940, though this time to middle peasant behavior. The relative wealth of the middle peasants within the village led some to regard them as 'the agents of the landlords in the exploitation of the peasants,' as well as susceptible to bribery and corruption.[68] In consequence, at least in some locations county and subdistrict cadres declared the rent and interest reduction campaign to have been invalid, sought to have the campaign completely restarted, and effectively brought it to a premature halt.[69]

There was more than an element of class conflict reflected in the politics of the 'middle peasant question,' in addition to the tension between levels within the CCP. For example, at one meeting where the 'middle peasant question' was discussed in detail, one cadre was minuted as having described some of the difficulties:

> In villages where middle peasants dominate, relations between middle peasants and poor peasants are bad. Middle peasants think that poor peasants are poor just because they don't work, and that they are doomed to be ruled. The poor peasants and the landless labourers, on the other hand, have lived a miserable life for a long time. This has resulted in antagonism between middle and poor peasants. In such villages, it is not easy for us to carry out our policies. The poor peasants are neglected and oppressed. They can only gamble and visit prostitutes.[70]

Another cadre was even more pointed:

> Why can't the initiative of poor peasants and farmhands be brought into full play? It's because village leaders are mostly middle peasants, and selfish. They look down on ordinary people and pay little attention to encouraging poor peasants and workers.[71]

Even given that this was a discussion of county and district-level cadres, few were prepared to speak up strongly for the middle peasant. On the whole, the most that was said in their defense was that class status was a complicated issue, and that the real problem facing the CCP was one of political affiliation rather than a problem of class status. Middle peasants could become revolutionary because they too had been exploited in the past, but because they were interested in status and wealth they had to be intellectually remolded by the CCP.[72]

There was, however, one county leader who begged to differ, and instead of agreeing with his peer group he agreed with the senior leadership of the base area. In his view

> Middle peasants can serve as a bridge in mobilising the masses in the countryside. They are capable and can play an important role in changing rural class relations. In Wu'an there are more middle peasants than poor peasants and workers. It is easier for party members who are middle peasants to build a broad coalition of support than for those who are poor peasants and workers. Middle peasants are also able to bring intellectuals into that broad coalition. Middle peasants can carry out the united front policy efficiently, while poor peasants and farmhands tend to be more radical. Middle peasants can assist in the education of workers. Therefore, middle peasants should become an essential part of the party.[73]

In part this conflict reflected the division in the CCP's strategy between the need for economic production and the need for political control. Middle peasants were presented by many as the entrepreneurs who wanted to develop the local economy, whilst poor peasants were seen as having the moral authority for revolution. As one organizer put it, expressing the problem in the villages somewhat ironically: 'Middle peasants are selfish, demanding further economic development; but many people within the party take poverty as an honour.'[74]

Whilst there were clearly ideological, social and organizational differences behind discussion of the 'middle peasant question' nonetheless the Taihang CCP had moved toward resolution by September 1943. Lai Ruoyu (by this stage Director of the Organization Department under the Taihang Region CCP Committee) outlined the base area leadership's position on the 'middle peasant question' in a speech at that time. In this view, people did change their class status as their socioeconomic status changed; and moreover the socio-economic status of many middle peasants had altered considerably since 1937. However, as part of that process there were now in any case different kinds of middle peasants with different kinds of socioeconomic status, different experiences and most likely different and new types of class status that needed to be recognized, not the least of which were upwardly mobile poor peasants and landless laborers. For Lai and the regional party leadership, middle peasants were activists and therefore even if they had problems they could nonetheless be properly educated. Indeed, Lai even went so far as to suggest that at that time and in that place it was his hope that it would be possible for the middle peasants to assist in 'the proletarianization of the workers.'[75]

THE CCP AND THE PEASANT SMALL-HOLDER

The final stage in the Taihang CCP's wartime program of social reform came during 1944–45 when a more widespread rent and interest reduction campaign effectively reduced the economic status of landlords and rich peasants to that of the rich middle peasant of the pre-war era, and established the peasant small-holder as the dominant mode of production. In the process, by early 1945 the CCP had developed a considerable social base of support amongst those peasant small-holders. Moreover, peasant small-holders—predominantly middle peasants, but also including poor peasants—now led its local organization, even above the village level.

The opportunity to reach resolution of the inner-party discussion on class and revolution in the Taihang Region came with the national rectification movement, implemented locally during late 1943 and 1944.[76] Although it was still locally incomplete by early 1945, the rectification of the CCP went much further than earlier party consolidations particularly in its attention to ideological education and enabled the base area CCP committee to control its own organization more effectively. It also brought most parts of the Taihang CCP even more closely into the orbit of the CCP nationally, and not just the base area leadership, the regional CCP committee or activities in the southern part of Liaoxian (Zuoquan.)

The warnings that local cadres would be expected to conform had been issued quite clearly in discussions of party development during 1943. Base area leaders were continually warning that cadres needed further training and education, and these views were even echoed by some county and subdistrict level cadres who were (presumably) having difficulties with their subordinates.[77] The Taihang rectification movement itself started in October 1943 and tranche by tranche cadres were required to attend party school for reeducation and reassessment.[78]

Few details are available of individual histories during the Taihang rectification movement. Nonetheless it is quite clear that the local issues that surfaced echoed earlier inner-party debates on class and revolution. However, this later discussion was designed either to ensure that cadres changed their views or were marked for no further responsibilities. In his report on the rectification movement during 1945, Zhang Panshi (Director, Propaganda Department) himself originally also an urban intellectual (and one who was educated in Japan) made frequent references to the inappropriate 'background influences' of cadres and their 'unrelated perspectives.' Indeed ensuring no further 'leftist' excess was clearly one of the more important goals of the exercise, though somewhat paradoxically this was said to have been achieved by ensuring that individuals changed their 'essential nature.' The emphasis was on learning from local situations, though of course under the direction of CCP authorities.[79]

Some of the difficulties the rectification movement encountered in trying to convince local cadres of the need to change are clear from Li Xuefeng's remarks at various stages of the movement in 1943 and 1944. Change management specialists at the end of the twentieth century would not have envied Li or his colleagues their task. One particular difficulty seems to have been in persuading local cadres that revolutions not only needed revolutionary organizations, but that sometimes those revolutionary organizations had to be more pragmatic than revolutionary manifestos sometimes suggested. Another was a degree of intransigence on the relationship between group and individual interests.[80] It was with an almost palpable sense of relief that Li Xuefeng finally brought the curtain down on the 'middle peasant question' at the base area's Sixth Organizational Work Conference in March 1945.[81]

The rectification movement not only ensured that the Taihang CCP now had (or was about to have) an organizational discipline it had sometimes previously lacked, but now allowed the party committee for the base area to return to the social reform program it had previously attempted during the second half of 1942. The middle peasant was now unreservedly at the center of this program. However, in order both to ensure ease of policy implementation on the ground and to placate concerns within the party organization, there was now no longer a single category of middle peasant, but several. In outlining the various types of middle peasant at the end of 1943, Lai Ruoyu readily accepted the social and political existence of 'a serious anti-middle peasant sentiment.'[82] Partly in consequence, he made it perfectly plain that whilst all middle peasants were to be regarded as politically acceptable, some were clearly to be more acceptable than others.

There were those who had been owner-cultivators before the war and remained middle peasants: these were the so-called 'old middle peasants.' Lai regarded the old middle peasants as politically reliable because 'they had no political status before the war and were economically exploited.' Then there were the 'new middle peasants': those who had only become owner-cultivators during the war. They were inherently politically suspect, according to Lai, and needed ideological remoulding either after economic improvement which made them easy prey for bourgeois tendencies, or because they had previously been wealthier. These new middle peasants covered a number of fairly important subcategories. There were former poor peasants, and even some landless laborers and tenant farmers, who had become new middle peasants. There were former owner-cultivators who had become richer through the recent past and were now referred to as 'new rich middle peasants.' There were also former landlords and rich peasants who had become déclassé through land sales.

At the end of 1943 and beginning of 1944, CCP membership in the Taihang Region was 56.3 percent middle peasant: 30.4 old middle peasant and 25.9 new middle peasant; 27 percent were poor peasants. However, there was an even higher proportion of middle peasants (60 percent) to be found as cadres: 31.8 percent were old middle peasants, 27.2 percent were new middle peasants. Only 20.7 percent of cadres were poor peasants.[83] In some counties the proportions of middle peasant members and cadres were even higher. Wu'an for example, had a membership described as 88 percent middle peasant—50 percent new middle peasant and 38 percent old middle peasant. Wu'an's cadre force was similarly described as 91 percent middle peasant—57 percent new middle peasant and 34 percent old middle peasant.[84]

The base area's attempt to bring social reform through its land policy was relaunched in August 1944.[85] The aim was to introduce rent and interest reduction in those villages that the 1942 program had not reached (now considerably greater in number because of the expansion of the base area) or where politics at that time had delivered solutions now considered unsound. In the process it was also hoped to remedy some of the practices subsequently developed by landowners to avoid compliance with the rent and interest reduction, not least to try to ensure that they did not recur. Middle peasants were once again regarded as the main agent of social change, though probably with more confidence in their ability to manage the politics of the situation than had been the case two years earlier. Certainly newspaper reports on the campaign gave them every reason for feeling that way. At the end of 1944 the *New China Daily* commented: 'It was a loss that we did not previously pay attention to the mobilization of the middle peasants. It was wrong that some cadres thought tenancy issues had nothing to do with middle peasants.'[86]

In the campaign of 1944–45, the village struggle meeting was largely, though not exclusively, replaced by a series of government-sponsored local arbitration committees that attempted to resolve issues through discussion before more formal procedures began.[87] Even so there were contemporary reports that cadres had sometimes taken too radical an approach to their task of redistribution.[88] However, the main mechanism for land redistribution remained sales by landlords and rich peasants, though as before some was also allocated by government action. There were two further significant differences in the process of the 1944 campaign. One was that the campaign placed considerably more emphasis on the role of village cadres in the process than had previously been the case. More emphasis in particular was placed on the need for cadres to lead peasant activities. The lesson of possible cadre passivity, especially in the face of any possible resistance, was learnt from the 1942 campaign. At the same time, in an attempt to offset any tendency to commandism inherent in that emphasis, criticism of cadre weakness, or even dissatisfaction with cadre performance was also encouraged, though critics were reminded to make allowances for difficulties in the daily lives and work of cadres.[89]

The other significant difference between the land policy campaigns of 1942 and 1944 was that the latter had to deal with the development of a chronic rural labor shortage. Even allowing for regional differences, which remained acute,[90] by 1945 it was clear that across the base area as a whole fewer peasants were exclusively dependent on wages as the number of peasant small-holders increased.[91] The former rural workers and landless peasants were now beginning to become peasant small-holders themselves, working for each other as well as farming their own small-holdings. Landlords and rich peasants were thus further deprived of their ability to work larger tracts of land in the ways they had previously done, increasingly having to rely on labor from within their households. This too undoubtedly led to increased land sales.

The 1944–45 land campaign, and its consequent changes in landownership, resulted in both the emergence of a peasant small-holder economy, and political leadership at village level passing further into the hands of the peasant small-holder. By the end of the war, two-thirds of all landholding households were identified as those of middle peasants, who owned about two-thirds of the land. Middle peasants also dominated the local level membership of the CCP, and provided more than two-thirds of all village level cadres. Alongside those designated as middle peasants, a quarter of the landholding households were those of poor peasants who owned about one-seventh of the land. Poor peasants additionally provided just under a quarter of the CCP's local membership and about a fifth of the cadres.

At village level almost everyone now lived in a peasant small-holder household, regardless of their formal class status. Though it is somewhat misleading to generalize across the whole base area, average landholdings for each social category had decreased and had become more equal. There were now very few landless laborers, and particularly in the most secure parts of the base area those landlords who had stayed in place and wanted to maintain their social position had basically traded in wealth for security. In socioeconomic terms, those who were still designated as landlords and rich peasants had essentially become rich independent small-holders.

All the same, the degree of homogeneity in this peasant small-holder society should not be overstated. It was dominated by those designated as middle and poor peasants yet fairly recent experience had suggested differences between those two social categories as well as their shared concerns. The social category of middle peasant had come to include a number of significant subdivisions, with different backgrounds and expectations. By the end of the war, in terms of the CCP's categorization, just under two-thirds of the middle peasants had not changed their class status; about 30 percent were former poor peasants and landless peasants; whilst about 5 percent were former landlords and rich peasants.[92] Moreover, even by mid-1945 the patterns of landholding and social stratification remained uneven across the base area, and were largely determined by the local situation.

NOTES

1. Lyman Van Slyke 'The Chinese Communist Movement during the Sino-Japanese War, 1937–45,' in *The Cambridge History of China* Vol. 13, Republican China, 1912–1949, Part II, Cambridge, Cambridge University Press, 1986, Chapter 12, p.610.

2. See, for example, Yang Shangkun 'Zai Zhonggong zhongyang beifangju Licheng huiyishangde baogao' ['Report to the Licheng Conference of the CCP Central Committee Northern Bureau'] 16 April 1940, in TDZH vol.3: 1940, p.195; and in wider context, Liu Shaoqi 'Resolutely Smash the Onslaughts of the Die-hards' May 1940, in *Selected Works of Liu Shaoqi* vol.1, Beijing, Foreign Languages Press, 1984, p.169.

3. See, for example, Jack Belden *China Shakes the World* Penguin Hanrmondsworth, Penguin, 1973, especially p.108 ff; Stuart Gelder *The Chinese Communists* London, Victor Gollancz, 1946, especially p.213 ff for a description of landlord-peasant relations; and George Hogg *I See a New China* London, Victor Gollancz, 1945.

4. TJSD1 p.1348.

5. Information derived from *Banianlai Riben faxisi cuihui Taihangqu renminde gaishu* [General Description of the People of the Taihang Region after Eight Years of Japan's Fascist Destruction] 1945, in CJZX vol.1, p.534; and TGCG p.1334.

6. Some contemporary sources claimed that increased rich peasant bankruptcies during the 1930s had revolutionized the intellectuals who later joined the CCP. The available evidence would seem to suggest that the children of landlords and rich peasants were revolutionized through participation in higher education, which could only be achieved because their families were not bankrupt.

7. According to Chi Biqing, the urban intellectuals became cadres, the workers became guerilla fighters: in Chi Biqing 'Chi Biqing tongzhi tan Taihang qunzhong yundong' ['Comrade Chi Biqing Talks about the Taihang Mass Movement'] 22 July 1986, in QY p.262. Chi Biqing, himself originally an urban intellectual, was a peasant organizer at this time and later became Chair of the Taihang Region Peasant Association.

8. Chen Dadong 'Yijiusiyinian zai Heshun Shuangfengchuan jianzu jianxi shidiande huiyi' ['A Memoir of the Rent and Interest Reduction Trial in Shuangfengchuan, Heshun County'] in TW p.201.

9. By August 1940, 43 out of 111 county level CCP cadres had still not participated in any political training program. See, Zhonggong JinJiYu qudangwei 'Zuzhibu gei Beifangjude gongzuo baogao' ['Organization Department Report to North China Bureau'] August 1940, in *Shanxi geming genjudi* [Shanxi Revolutionary Base Areas] no.1, 1989, p.3; and in TDZH vol.3: 1940, p.572.

10. See, for example, Martin M C Yang *Chinese Social Structure* Taipei, The National Book Company, 1969, p.143 discusses this tradition in some detail. See, also Jerome B Grieder *Intellectuals and the State in Modern China* New York, The Free Press, 1981.

11. Li Xuefeng, 8 March 1945, in SOC p.67.

12. The most detailed contemporary account of socioeconomic changes during October 1937-May 1940 is to be found in '1937 nian—1940 nian wuyue xinzhengce yiqian' ['1937 to May 1940: Before the New Policy'] in TJSD1 pp.1364–1367.

13. Xu Zirong 'Guanyu bage xiande zhibu gongzuo' ['Work on Party Branches in Eight Counties'] 30 August 1942, in DJ p.236.

14. Comments recorded in minutes for 29 July 1942, in XZJY p.7.

15. JinJiYuqu nongjiu zonghui 'JinJiYuqu nongjiu zonghui liangnianlai gongzuo cailiao' ['Materials on the work of the Shanxi-Hebei-Henan region peasant's association during the last two years'] June 1941, in TDZH vol.4: 1941, p.386 ff.

16. See, for example, reports on confiscation of land from rich peasants in Zhudou Village, a mountain area in Liaoxian, in LDB p.42.

17. See Chapter 6.

18. To be discussed in Chapter 7. At a later CCP meeting that discussed party branch development in 'advanced areas,' it was reported that both Zanhuang and Wuxiang had basically completed class struggle at this time, see XZJY p.1.

19. Peng Tao 'Qunzhong yundong de fazhan yu jieji guanxi de bianhua' ['The

development of mass movements and the transformation of class relations'] February 1943, in TW p.229.

20. 'Guanyu gongan gongzuo de baogao' ['Report on Public Security Work'] in *JiTai lianban diyici zhuanyuan xianzhang huiyi tekan* [Special Pronouncement of the Joint Office, First Meeting of Commissioners and County Heads] February 1941, p.189.

21. WOH p.22.

22. JinJiYuqu nongjiu zonghui 'JinJiYuqu nongjiu zonghui liangnianlai gongzuo cailiao' ['Materials on the work of the Shanxi-Hebei-Henan region peasant's association during the last two years'] June 1941, in TDZH vol.4: 1941, p.387.

23. According to Ke Han, the majority were coal miners. See Ke Han 'Jindong bianjing' ['East Shanxi's Borders'] 11 June 1938, in *Xinhua ribao* [New China Daily, North China edition] 4 July 1938, p.4. Further details in Zhonggong JinJiYu quwei 'Zhigong weiyuanhui gongyun gongzuo baogao' ['Workers Union Report on Workers Mobilization Work'] 10 May 1940, in TDZH vol.3: 1940, p.333.

24. Yang Jue 'JinJiYuqude gongren yundong' ['The Worker's Movement in the Shanxi-Hebei-Henan District'] April 1941, in QY p.283.

25. Zhonggong JinJiYu quwei 'Guanyu gonggu zuzhide zhishixin' ['Letter of Instruction on Consolidating Organization'] 2 November 1939, in TDZH vol.2: 1939, p.685. In his report to the CCP congress in September Li Xuefeng had emphasized the need for cadres with 'proletarian class status': Li Xuefeng 'Zhonggong JinJiYu diyici daibiao dahui shangde gongzuo baogao' ['Report to the 1st Representative Assembly of the CCP in Shanxi-Hebei-Henan'] September 1939, in TDZH vol.2: 1939, p.494.

26. Lai Ruoyu 'Liangyuelai Jindong gongzuode zongjie' ['Summary of Work in the East Shanxi District during the last two months'] January 1940, in TDZH vol.3: 1940, p.53.

27. See, for example, Xu Zirong 'Zhengfeng yu jiandang shi muqiande yanzhong renwu' ['Rectification and development of the Party is the immediate most important task'] 15 April 1940, in DJ p.186; and He Yingcai 'JinJiYu bianqu gonggu dangde jige wenti' ['Several Issues in the Consolidation of the Party in the Shanxi-Hebei-Henan Border Area'] 6 December 1940, in TDZH vol.3: 1940, especially p.801 ff. Xu Zirong was Director, Propaganda Department and He Yingcai had been Director, Organization Department under the base area CCP committee.

28. Li Xuefeng provided an overview of trends in party recruitment in his summary report to the Taihang Base Area's Sixth Organizational Meeting on 8 March 1945, in SOC p.63.

29. Liu Jianxun 'Baogao' ['Report'] to Taihang Sixth Organizational Work Conference, in SOC p.14 ff.

30. 'Yijiusanjiunian gongzuo zongjie yu yijiusilingnian gongzuo jihuade baogao' ['Report on 1939 Work Summary and 1940 Work Plan'] 6 January 1940, in TDZH vol.3: 1940, p.13.

31. Zhonggong JinJiYu qudangwei 'Zuzhibu gei Beifangjude gongzuo baogao' ['Organization Department Report to North China Bureau'] August 1940, in TDZH vol.3: 1940, p.557.

32. Zhonggong JinJi diwei 'Sangeyueneide gongzuo yaoqiu yu gongzuo rili' ['Work Agenda and Requirments for the Next Three Months'] 30 May 1939, in TDZH vol.2: 1939, p.122.

33. Zhonggong JinJiYu qudangwei 'Zuzhibu gei Beifangjude gongzuo baogao' ['Organization Department Report to North China Bureau'] August 1940, in *Shanxi geming genjudi* [Shanxi Revolutionary Base Areas] no.1, 1989, p.3; and in TDZH vol.3: 1940, p.570 ff.

34. The North Zhang River District of the base area (the Fifth District) is instructive in this respect. It seems that 36 percent of its cadres were landlords or rich peasants (9 percent and 27 percent, respectively) throughout the War. See JinJiYuqu 'Yijiusi'ernian zhengzhi gongzuo zongjie' ['Summary of Political Work in 1942'] 8 January 1943, in Zhonggong Henan shengwei dangshi ziliao zhengji bianzuan weiyuanhui (ed) *Taihang kangRi genjudi* [The Taihang Anti-Japanese Base Area] Zhonggong Henan dangshi ziliao congshu, Henan renmin chubanshe, 1986, vol.1, p.236.

35. JinJiYuqu nongjiu zonghui 'JinJiYuqu nongjiu zonghui liangnianlai gongzuo cailiao' ['Materials on the work of the Shanxi-Hebei-Henan region peasants' association during the last two years'] June 1941, in TDZH vol.4: 1941, p.446.

36. JinJiYuqu nongjiu zonghui 'JinJiYuqu nongjiu zonghui liangnianlai gongzuo cailiao' ['Materials on the work of the Shanxi-Hebei-Henan region peasants' association during the last two years'] June 1941, in TDZH vol.4: 1941, p.363.

37. Li Dazhang 'Jiang qunzhong gongzuode jiandan huiyi' ['A Brief Overview of the Mass Movement'] 1943, in TW p.198.

38. Rong Zihe 'Jiajin jinxing heli fudan zoushang tongyi de suode leijinshui' ['Strengthen implementation of the "reasonable burden" so that it becomes a progressive income tax'] 18 September 1940, in CJJ vol.2, p.540.

39. For example, the different politics of social change in Wuxiang also entailed that middle peasants there were contributing to the public burden even in 1938 and 1939.

40. Zhen Yuan 'Tantan heli fudan leijinshuide fenpei dingfen wenti' ['Discussion of Problems in the Distribution and Determination of a Reasonable Burden Progressive Tax'] August 1940, in TDZH vol.3:1940, p.589.

41. Rong Zihe 'Jinyibu jiaqiang caijing jianshe, kaizhan dui di jingji douzheng' ['Advance Financial and Economic Construction, Develop the Economic Struggle against the Enemy'] February 1943, in CJJ vol.1, p.152.

42. Lai Ruoyu (Ruo Yu) 'Qunzhong yundong yu qunzhong youji zhanzheng' ['The Mass Movement and Mass Guerilla Warfare'] December 1941, in TDZH vol.4: 1941, p.980.

43. Lu Hong'an in a comment on 30 June 1941, FOC p.59.

44. A catalog of excess may be found in Yin Feng 'Tudi zhengce zhongde jige juti wenti' ['Several Specific Issues on Land Policy'] June 1941, in TDZH vol.4: 1941, p.363.

45. Zhonggong JinJiYu qudangwei 'Guanyu jiaqiang qunzhong gongzuode jueding' ['CCP Shanxi-Hebei-Henan regional committee decision concerning strengthening mass work'] 15 February 1941, in TDZH vol.4: 1941, p.151. These moves followed after Li Xuefeng's directive, in 'Genjudi jianshe yu qunzhong

gongzuo—dang yu qunzhong gongzuo' ['The Development of the Base Area and Masses Work—the Party and Masses Work'] 5 December 1940, in TDZH vol.3: 1940, p.787.

46. By June 1941 the Taihang Base Area's membership was 2.4 percent intellectuals and 1.8 percent workers. A year earlier intellectuals had only accounted for 0.02 percent of the base area's CCP membership. Over the same year the proportion of CCP members who were middle peasants decreased from 39.4 percent to 34.3 percent. Details from Zhonggong JinJiYu qudangwei 'Guanyu gonggu dangde gongzuode zongjie' ['Summary of the Work of Consolidating the Party'] 8 October 1941, in TDZH vol.4: 1941, 1994, p.828.

47. Peng Tao 'JinJiYu qude xinxingshi yu xinrenwu' ['New circumstances and new tasks in the Shanxi-Hebei-Henan area'] 27 June 1941, in TDZH vol.4: 1941, p.479.

48. Lai Ruoyu (Ruo Yu) 'Qunzhong yundong yu qunzhong youji zhanzheng' ['The Mass Movement and Mass Guerilla Warfare'] December 1941 in TDZH vol.4: 1941, p.980.

49. Li Xuefeng provided a detailed history of the 'middle peasant question' in his summary report to the Taihang Base Area's Sixth Organizational Meeting on 8 March 1945, in SOC p.62. For an earlier and detailed discussion of the 'middle peasant question,' see session led by Lai Ruoyu at the meeting of the regional party committee on 5 September 1943, in ZJY p.21.

50. Zhonggong zhongyang 'Zhonggong zhongyang guanyu nongmin tudi wenti gei Li Xuefeng de zhishi' ['Instruction to Li Xuefeng on the question of peasants and land from the CCP's Central Committee'] November 1941, in TDZH vol.4: 1941, p.919.

51. LXH p.133. The CCP Central Committee issued a 'Decision on Land Policy in the Anti-Japanese Base Areas' on 28 January 1942; and an 'Instruction on Implementing the Decision on Land Policy' on 4 February 1942.

52. Zhonggong JinJiYu qudangwei 'Guanyu ruhe shixing tudi zhengcede zhishi' ['Instructions in carrying out land policy'] 15 April 1942, in LXH p.135. See also: JinJiYuqu nonjiu zonghui 'Nongmin tudi douzheng gangling' ['The Peasants Program to Struggle for Land'] 19 March 1942, in *Xinhua Ribao* [New China Daily—North China Edition] 7 April 1942.

53. Peng Tao 'Qunzhong yundong de fazhan yu jieji guanxi de bianhua' ['The development of mass movements and the transformation of class relations'] February 1943, in TW p.227.

54. Zhonggong JinJiYu qudangwei 'Guanyu shixing fudan zhengcede zhishi' ['Instruction on Implementing (Tax) Burden Policy'] 10 August 1942, in TW p.213.

55. 'Tabeiqu tudi zhengcede shixing ji nongmin douzheng celuede cailiao huibian' 1 September 1942 ['Collection of Materials on the Implementation of Land Policy and the Strategy for Rural Struggle in the (North) Taihang Region'] in *Shanxi geming genjudi* [Shanxi Revolutionary Base Areas] no.2, 1991, p.17.

56. Zhang Shuxin (p.460) and Yuan Jingwu (p.463) in 'Taihang laoqu tugai qianhou nongcun jingji biange kaocha zuotanhui fayan gangyao"['Outline of Discussion Meeting on the Investigation of Rural Economic Change in the Taihang Areas of the Revoluton before and after Land Reform'] 7 July 1983, in TW.

57. Gao Yuangui 'Dizhu fandui jianzude banfa he womende duice' ['The Methods of Landlords in Opposing Rent Reductions and our Policy Response'] 31 December 1942, in CJZX vol.2, p.548.
58. TJSD1 p.1379 ff.
59. Though some of this was land confiscated from landlords because they had sided with the Japanese, most was mainly land that had been lying idle and not farmed. A substantial proportion was poor quality, mountain 'boundary land' enclosed by landowners with Imperial permission at an earlier period when migration was being encouraged, and which previously had not been tradable.
60. Zhonggong JinJiYu qudangwei 'Guanyu shixing Zhongyang tudi zhengce zhishide baogao' ['Report on Implementing the CCP Central Committee's Directive on Land Policy'] 30 October 1942, p.217; and Li Dazhang 'Jiang Yijiusi'er nian qunzhong gongzuode jiandan zongjie' ['Brief Summary of Mass Work during 1942'] 1943, p.224, both in TW.
61. Li Xuefeng, in his report to the Taihang Base Area's Sixth Organizational Meeting on 8 March 1945, in SOC p.63 ff.
62. Peng Tao 'Qunzhong yundong de fazhan yu jieji guanxi de bianhua' ['The development of mass movements and the transformation of class relations'] February 1943, in TW p.227.
63. Xu Zirong 'Guanyu bage xiande zhibu gongzuo' ['Work on Party Branches in Eight Counties'] 30 August 1942, in DJ p.247.
64. Xu Zirong, 9 August 1942, in XZJY p.60.
65. Xu Zirong 'Guanyu bage xiande zhibu gongzuo' ['Work on Party Branches in Eight Counties'] 30 August 1942, in DJ p.279 ff. Details of the survey may be found in: 'Shisanxian sanshijiuge zhibude chubu yanjiu' ['Preliminary Research on 39 Branches in 13 Counties'] 20 September 1942, in DJ p.266.
66. Xu Zirong, 9 August 1942, in XZJY p.60.
67. 'Shisanxian sanshijiuge zhibude chubu yanjiu' ['Preliminary Research on 39 Branches in 13 Counties'] 20 September 1942, in DJ p.288.
68. Comments by Guo Zong 5 September 1943, in ZJY p.14.
69. Li Xuefeng, in his report to the Taihang Base Area's Sixth Organizational Meeting on 8 March 1945, in SOC p.63.
70. Comments by Guo Zhong, Taihang 3rd District, 5 September 1943, in ZJY p.22.
71. Comments by Meng Xiangguang, member of an investigation group in Shexian, 5 September 1943, in ZJY p.31.
72. Comments by, amongst others, Cai Lingcheng, of the Taihang 2nd District, 5 September 1943, in ZJY p.77.
73. Liu An, from Wu'an, 5 September 1943, in ZJY p.13.
74. Comment by Guo Zhong, on East Xiyang, 5 September 1943, in ZJY p.23.
75. Lai Ruoyu 'Muqian shiqide zhibu jianshe wenti—zai di'erci zhibu yanjiuhuide zongjie zhiyibu' ['The Current Question of Party Branch Development—Section of a Summary at the 2nd Research Conference on Party Branches'] September 1943, in DJ p.298 ff.
76. Base area leadership cadres had undertaken rectification on a number of occasions during 1942 and early 1943. The Taihang CCP had been criticized for

inadequate attention to the rectification process by Deng Xiaoping and Peng Dehuai in February 1943. The whole process started again, first at senior levels and then working its way down through the administrative hierarchy. See LXH p.196.

77. For example, a whole section of the discussion on party branch development at a meeting of the regional CCP committee in September 1943 had been devoted to the subject of 'How to ensure unity of ideology within the party,' and the demands for cadre training and education are clearly recorded in its minutes. See ZJY p.52 ff.

78. Zhonggong Taihang qudangwei 'Guanyu jinmingnian liangnian qiedi wancheng quanqu zhengfeng renwu ji muqian jieduande jihua' ['Tasks for the next two years to complete rectification throughout the region and plans for the current stage'] 21 October 1943, in GSX vol.3, p.658.

79. Zhang Panshi 'Guanyu ganbu jiaoyu gongzuo' ['On Cadre Education Work'] February 1945, in DJ p.396 ff.

80. See, for example, Li Xuefeng 'Qudangwei dangxiao di'erqi zhengfengde sixiang yu sixiang lingdao zongjie' ['Summary of Ideological Leadership and Ideological Rectification in the Regional Party School's Second Group'] January 1944, in DJ p.358.

81. 8 March 1945, in SOC p.60 ff.

82. Summary of Party Branch Research at meeting of the CCP Shanxi-Hebei-Henan Regional Committee, 5 September 1943, in ZJY p.3.

83. Lai Ruoyu 'Muqian shiqide zhibu jianshe wenti—zai di'erci zhibu yanjiuhuide zongjie zhiyibu' ['The Current Question of Party Branch Development—Section of a Summary at the 2nd Research Conference on Party Branches'] September 1943, in DJ p.303 ff.

84. ZJY p.11.

85. Zhonggong Taihang qudangwei 'Guanyu shiqie jianzu yundongde zhishi' ['Directive on Implementing the Rent Reduction Movement'] 17 November 1944, in TW p.257.

86. Yu Yichuan 'Yijiusisinian dongli jianzu yundong jiben jingyan' ['The Basic Experience of the Winter 1944 Rent Reduction Movement'] in TW p.270.

87. JinJiLuYu bianqu zhengfu 'Jige tudi wenti chuli banfade jueding' ['Several Decisions on the Methods for Managing Land Issues'] October 1944, in CJZX vol.2, p.1466.

88. TJSD2 pp.1426–27.

89. 'Yijiusisinian kaizhan jianzujianxi douzhengde dianxing ziliao' ['Typical Cases of Rent and Interest Reduction'] 20 December 1944, in TW p.274.

90. See, for example, TJSD2 p.1426 ff.

91. Zhonggong Taihang qudangwei 'Guanyu muqian jianzuzhong yixie wentide jiejue banfa de zhishi fujian' ['Supplementary Directive on Current Methods for Resolving Several Questions in Rent Reduction'] 5 February 1945, in CJZX vol.2, pp.1467–69.

92. TJSD2 p.1415.

6

Liaoxian: Land and Social Reform

After November 1940 the location of the headquarters units of the Taihang Base Area, the Eighth Route Army, and its 129th Division, as well as of the CCP North China Bureau in Matian and Tongyu (in the southern part of the county) necessarily affected the ways in which the Liaoxian (after September 1942, the Zuoquan) CCP went about its task of implementing a program of social reform. There was, for example, little resistance from county or subdistrict level cadres to the accommodations they were forced to make during 1941 with local landlords and rich peasants, or to the promotion of the middle peasant as an agent of change which started in 1942. Indeed, it seems likely that the middle peasant strategy was trialed here first before being encouraged elsewhere in the base area. As Chapter 2 indicated, during 1942–45 security and stability within the area of CCP control were the prime concerns. Though there were tensions here too between middle peasants and poor peasants, as well as between landlords and peasants, in general CCP presence ensured the more rapid mediation of conflict and the emergence of a peasant smallholder society.

On the other hand, the Liaoxian CCP's attempts to revolutionize the county before the arrival of Deng Xiaoping, Yang Shangkun and the Eighth Route Army would suggest that its cadres were quite capable of being radical if left to themselves. At the end of 1939 when the local CCP was not even in unreserved control of the county government, let alone of Liaoxian as a whole, it had called for an immediate and radical land reform. The impact of this on the local community was dramatic and not only led to land confiscations from landlords and rich peasants, as well as the redistribution of their property, but also contributed to the flight of capital from Tongyu and open conflict within the united front. It also led to a severe reaction during the second half of 1940 and 1941, which set back the CCP's program of social reform.

INITIAL MOBILIZATION

The nucleus of the CCP in Liaoxian had grown under the auspices of the Sacrifice League, and was originally based on personnel from the Liaoxian First High School. Many of its teachers, recent graduates and students joined not only the Sacrifice League, but also the CCP. One of these was Li Xiuren, who was the first propaganda organizer for the new party organization, and later went on to become the Secretary of the West Liaoxian CCP committee. In his recollection, these initial recruits were initially committed nationalists but not immediately revolutionaries, who became radicalized by the Japanese invasion. Li had been a student at the Liaoxian First High School and recalled a revolutionary student from Northeast China coming to give a talk once in 1936 and being met with stunned silence.[1]

The CCP recruited at first almost exclusively from the ranks of the Sacrifice League, the Patriotic Women's Association and the Liaoxian Teacher's Federation. Its initial membership was in consequence composed of teachers, young women from the county town, and students. Its first committee had four members with an average age of twenty-two, all of whom were either recent graduates, or current students who had returned to Liaoxian at the start of the war.[2]

This initial group of recruits became the core of the CCP's local organization and set the tone for much of the local leadership throughout the war. The membership of the CCP in Liaoxian had a well-above the average proportion of women members (10–12 percent, where few other county party organizations reached 5 percent) and a large number of women activists. These included three later women secretaries of the Liaoxian CCP Committee: Chen Shunying, Yang Yangyu and Zhai Ying.[3] Indeed, when Liaoxian became an 'experimental county' party organization at the end of 1939 its CCP committee has nine members, three of whom were women: Zhai Ying, Yang Yangyu and Zhang Ling.[4]

The local CCP also had fairly high levels of education and came largely from an urban background. In August 1940, well after the demise of the Sacrifice League-led government and Japanese occupation of the county town, and even after the party's first major consolidation—in which CCP members were required to reapply, and which was used elsewhere to significantly alter the social composition of membership—little had changed. Though it was to alter during 1941–42, at that stage only 13 percent of the membership of the Liaoxian CCP came from a rural background, 17 percent of its membership were either students or had already graduated from school or college, and 60 percent were under thirty years old.[5]

At the start of 1938 the CCP started to recruit around the county's villages using the Sacrifice League's network of organizers and the graduates from the Peasants Training Institute. 'At that time all the talk was of class status and the need to recruit rural workers' according to Li Xiuren.[6] One 20-year-old farm-laborer remembered being recruited by a 'fresh-faced 18- or 19-year-old university student from Northeast China' and rapidly found himself on a training program to become a cadre himself.[7]

This young farm-laborer's recruitment method may have been usual but he was unusual. The Liaoxian CCP recruited few farm-laborers or poor peasants at this time, and those that did join generally 'failed to play a major role in their branches' and usually left quite quickly.[8] Until the end of 1939 the Liaoxian CCP remained dominated by its urban and intellectual base, with a growing proportion of middle peasant youth. There was also apparently a group of forty or so bandits who were recruited at this time, some of whom not only became cadres but also eventually established and maintained the security force for the county.[9]

One result of the location of the base area headquarters in Liaoxian, as well as so many central CCP organizations, was that those areas controlled by the CCP, particularly in the south of the county, were the subject of a number of social and economic surveys by the Taihang Investigation Unit. Though the information does not necessarily accurately reflect the situation across the whole of the county, it does provide data on those small towns and villages, which the CCP regarded as the secure part of its local operation. The information may not be totally reliable, not least because of the conditions of war, and as the investigators frequently reported, their own inexperience.[10] Nonetheless, the Investigation Unit's survey data does provide much useful material that assists the examination of social change. Table 6.1, for example, provides survey data on the distribution of households by CCP class status for 1937. Unusually, this distribution is for all households, and not just landowning households.

Liaoxian's economy had become highly commercialized during the 1920s. Tongyu for example had a large commercial distillery and flour mill before the war, and it was quite a small town of just under 20,000 people. It also had a number of silversmiths in addition to a range of other artisans' workshops and commercial enterprises.[11] The south of the county was the richest part, largely because of the strength of its agricultural production, whereas the north had better communications with the outside world. The best farming land was around Tongyu and Matian, not least because (by Shanxi standards) it was usually well-watered.

Liaoxian was particularly heavily surveyed in 1942 as the base area prepared to introduce a new rent and interest reduction campaign. In the process the survey differentiated villages according to their dominant landlords, in order to assess the potential for mobilization. It identified three basic types of village: those dominated by commercial landlords and land usage, those still dominated by native landlords, and those dominated by traditional landlords but from outside the village. Villages dominated by commercial landlords were those close to main routes of transport, where (usually) financial enterprises had invested in cash crops during the 1920s. Villages influenced by commercialization were regarded as the prime target for the rent and interest reduction campaign, because class conflict was assumed to be the most acute there as a result of land concentration and land sales over tenants' heads. Villages dominated by native landlords were regarded as difficult places to mobilize peasants; whereas it was said to be easy to mobilize peasants in those villages with landlords from somewhere else. The survey asked people to recollect their previous status and estimated that as of 1937, 62 percent of households had been in villages dominated by commercial landlords; 26 percent in villages dominated by native landlords; and 12 percent in villages dominated by landlords from somewhere else entirely.

The first two years of the war in Liaoxian variously affected the different kinds of landholders according to their type of village. In general, during 1937–39 landlords sold and otherwise disposed of land under the pressures of war and tax burden pressures brought to bear by local government. In villages dominated by commercial landlords, the use-right and ownership of land passed largely to rich peasants. In villages dominated by commercial landlords, landownership became more concentrated, particularly as middle peasants and poor peasants found their debts being called in under the pressures of war and taxation. The pat-

Table 6.1 Social Composition of Liaoxian, 1937 (percentage of households by social category)

Landlord	2.7	Tenants and farmhands	28.0
Rich peasant	8.2	Trader	3.2
Middle peasant	35.8	Artisan	2.3
Poor peasant	18.4	Vagrant	1.6

Source: Calculated from data presented in LDB pp.27–33.

tern of redistribution in villages dominated by both native and out-of-village landlords was different with rich peasants tending to decrease their holdings, whilst middle and poor peasants were able to obtain sometimes quite large amounts of land of their own, some of which they even started renting out themselves.[12]

The CCP's first two years of development in Liaoxian were slow and not very successful. There was resistance from both the local population and the local government. A campaign to ensure a more equitable tax burden in 1938 fizzled out, in the eyes of one participant because its proponents were being too radical.[13] One CCP cadre in a village-region had problems with the head of that village-region, appointed by county government. He thought to use the opportunity to campaign for popular elections, then part of the CCP program. He organized a demonstration of a 1,000 people which petitioned the county government. Though the county government removed the recalcitrant administrator they refused to introduce elections.[14]

A Peasant Association was established almost immediately and was regarded as well-organized[15] but beyond providing a base of operations to middle peasant youth appears to have done little. Attempts to start a rent and interest reduction campaign were similarly rapidly abandoned. It was hard to mobilize the middle peasants as well as the poor peasants, who all had misgivings about joining in this kind of activity. As before it was possible to recruit middle peasant youth, but not their parents, or the elderly more generally. The only exception was that the rent and interest reduction campaign identified a number of peasants who had been forced to return their land through getting into too much debt, and they were recruited to the CCP.[16] One possible reason for the difficulties encountered in mobilization was suggested by a later Liaoxian CCP report on this period which observed that there had been a need to tackle literacy before starting to 'imbue the peasants with terminology that had nothing to do with their actual lives.'[17]

Toward the end of 1939 the Liaoxian CCP remained small by comparison to other neighboring party organizations. Its leaders at county and subdistrict levels were still largely urban intellectuals, as were the leading officials in the county government. Of the seven people who formed the county CCP committee, one was a poor peasant, the other six were 'intellectuals'—one was a landlord, four were rich peasants and one was a middle peasant. Two were natives to the county and another two were from neighboring counties. All had only joined the CCP since the end of 1937, and all were under thirty. Four of the seven were graduates and everyone was literate. Of the CCP cadres at subdistrict level, there was a landless tenant, eight poor peasants, four middle peasants, one rich peasant, and five intellectuals. All had only been in the CCP two years at the maximum. All seven county government officials were intellectuals, as were most of the leaders of the various mass organizations.[18] In the Liaoxian CCP's own view there was a concern that its political balance was misplaced: there was 'a lack of proletarian backbone and a lack of rural basic masses; a distinct failure to mobilize the basic masses.'[19]

REVOLUTIONARY MOVES

The Liaoxian CCP seems to have decided to act more radically round about October 1939. The county party leadership introduced a program of fundamental land reform, and attempted to recruit large numbers of landless tenants and poor peasants to its cause. There is no reason to believe that it acted against the leadership of the base area CCP. Both county and base area CCP later acknowledged the outbreak of excess; and Deng Xiaoping and Yang Xiufeng (for the Joint Office for the South Hebei, Taiyue and Taihang Base Areas) heavily criticized the Liaoxian CCP leadership in speeches to the Licheng Meeting of the CCP's North China Bureau in April 1940. However, no one within the local CCP was formally disciplined. Moreover Liaoxian remained an 'experimental county' for the CCP throughout this period, which not only placed its operation directly under the base area, but also suggested that it was a test bed for possible future policies and procedures.

The base area was generally increasingly beleaguered by both the Japanese forces and its rapidly deteriorating relationship with Yan Xishan. In the county the CCP committee was moving increasingly into conflict with its former allies, local notables and the Nationalist Party. It had also notably failed to establish a toehold amongst the poorer peasantry and farmworkers.

In October 1939 the Liaoxian CCP committee called for the organization of a peasant association based solely on farm laborers and poor peasants, unlike the middle peasant dominated peasant association that was already in existence. Its membership was to be two-thirds farm laborer and one-third poor peasant. The Liaoxian CCP's instructions then exhorted the poor and the landless to implement 'a complete and utter land reform . . . and to determinedly exterminate the landlords and rich peasants.'[20] The formulation of land reform as confiscation of land and property, followed by their redistribution was precisely the concept the CCP had explicitly foresworn in its agreements with the Nationalist Party Government in 1937.

The exact extent of this early attempt at land reform in terms of how many people were affected, how long it lasted and how much land was redistributed are not known. However, it has the reputation of being the most severe in the Taihang Base Area at this time, and there certainly were land confiscations from both landlords and rich peasants. In one village, for example, at the beginning of 1940, 52 *mu* of temple land was redistributed to poor peasants; whilst 114 *mu* of land belonging to a landlord, and 66 *mu* of land formerly with a rich peasant and a middle peasant, were redistributed to landless laborers and poor peasants.[21]

Rich peasants were a prime target because they had been disproportionately active in the commercial market in the two years beforehand. Many landlord families, in contrast, had divided up their land holdings amongst themselves in response to the county government's attempts to tax land holdings rather than families, and were consequently less open to immediate attack. In addition to confiscations, landlords and rich peasants were forced by government decree to lease land at low rents and on long contracts to middle and poor peasants.[22]

The results of these various actions were fairly predictable. Landless laborers and tenants did join the Liaoxian CCP in great numbers, almost doubling the size of the membership within three months. However, the costs were also high. Inflation soared as both political and military uncertainties combined to threaten a deteriorating economy. The large business enterprises that had followed the resistance government to Tongyu in July 1939 returned north.[23] It is not known how many landlords went with them, or how many rich peasants also fled. At the beginning of 1940, the prices of millet, salt, cotton cloth and matches doubled virtually overnight. The price of kerosene increased by a factor of five.[24] There can also be little doubt that these events ensured the outbreak of more open conflict within the Sacrifice League-led county government.

Despite these developments, the Liaoxian CCP was somewhat reluctant to modify the general direction of its strategy, even as it modified the manner of its appeal to change. As Li Xiuren confirmed explicitly in his memoir, at this stage in early 1940 the Liaoxian CCP became infected by the 'theory of the unique influence of class status.'[25] It moved to encourage poor peasants and landless tenants in ways other than simply supplying land, as had been attempted with the land reform movement. Farmworkers' wages had fallen 39 percent since the start of the war,[26] much to their complaint.[27] Once control of the county government was assured, in February 1940, the CCP moved to assist by immediately doubling wage rates.[28]

Despite being originally led and dominated by intellectuals and middle peasant youth, the Liaoxian CCP moved against those two social groups in general. (Individuals in leadership positions seem, however, for the most part, to have remained in position.) Reflecting later in the year on this early part of 1940, one county cadre talked about 'a certain village' in the county that had not (in his opinion) treated its intellectuals appropriately at this time. The village had found itself with three university graduates, three high school graduates and twenty other graduates of junior and primary schools, whom it then 'forced' to establish and run a 'Rural Night School.' In his opinion this was demeaning and they could have been put to better use teaching and propagandising more widely.[29] On the other hand, the development of women remained firmly on the Liaoxian CCP's agenda for social reform, as it had been even during 1939. At the meeting where the clarion call for land reform had been issued the commitment was made to turn Liaoxian into a 'model county for its work in the development of young women.'[30]

The Liaoxian CCP party consolidation of early 1940 seems likely to have reflected the leadership's new desiderata. Details of the social composition of the Liaoxian CCP are not available for the beginning of 1940, only for October 1940. Table 6.2 provides information about the social composition of the general membership of the Liaoxian CCP for 1940–42. Given earlier information about the composition of the Liaoxian CCP it would seem that the figures for 1940 confirm a dramatic influx of farmhands and poor peasants. Since the figures for 1940 also include the changes that were made after about June, when the Liaoxian CCP started admitting that it had been overenthusiastic in its pursuit of laborers and landless tenants, at the expense of other social categories, the extent of the radical change earlier in the year was probably even greater.

Certainly these trends are confirmed by the changing social composition of village heads and council members elected in 1939, before Liaoxian's radical phase started, and during 1940, again after it had passed. Table 6.3 provides information on individuals who were village leaders in terms of the CCP's sociopolitical classification.

Table 6.2 Social Composition, Liaoxian CCP, 1940–1942 (percentage of members)

Year	Social category				
	Workers	Poor peasants	Middle peasants	Intellectuals	Others
1940	14	55	26	3.6	1.4
1941	11	51	35	1.4	1.6
1942	10	36	50	2.3	1.7

Source: Data for 1940: Yang Daifu 'Liaoxian shiyanxian gongzuo zongjie' ['Summary of Work in Liaoxian Experimental County'] October 1940, in TDZH vol.3: 1940, p.713. Data for 1941: ZOH p.23. Data for 1942: LDB p.177.

Table 6.3 Social Composition of Village Heads and Council Members in Liaoxian, 1939–1940 (percentage of individuals)

Year and Status	Social category Worker	Poor peasant	Middle peasant	Rich peasant	Intellectual	Landlord	Trader
1939 Head	10.0	29.2	30.0	6.7	13.3		
1940 Head	4.2	57.7	25.0	4.2	8.5		
1940 Member	3.6	35.0	34.0	11.2		1.1	0.9

Source: Yang Daifu 'Liaoxian shiyanxian gongzuo zongjie' ['Summary of Work in Liaoxian Experimental County'] October 1940, in TDZH vol.3: 1940, pp.718–19.

Once again the pattern would seem to suggest that the Liaoxian CCP turned increasingly to farmhands and poor peasants as its social allies during the first half of 1940, and against middle peasants and intellectuals. Certainly there was a great push to 'cleanse' the Liaoxian CCP of 'the new aristocracy'—those party members who had profited from land sales during 1937–39 and most of whom were middle peasants.[31]

By April 1940, when the new county government under its leadership was established, the Liaoxian CCP leadership remained in no hurry to pull back from the general direction of the program of social reform it had begun the previous year. According to Yang Daifu, the Secretary of the county party committee 'Things haven't gone exactly to plan, but they have been in the spirit of what we intended.'[32] In his view any problems had occurred through the failings of party members and cadres whose understandings were faulty—they understood that they needed to mobilize the population but were less clear about the end and the means. From the tone and content of his remarks it would seem that there had been differences of opinion between county-level and local cadres, with the latter unwilling to accept on occasion the discipline of the county leadership.

THE MIDDLE PEASANT ALTERNATIVE

After the Licheng Meeting of the North China Bureau in April 1940, the Liaoxian CCP did eventually decide to restrain itself more completely.

Change was signaled clearly in June 1940 when the Liaoxian CCP accepted that there had been 'leftist' excesses in the previous nine months, and that impetuousness and excess would now have to stop.[33] Most possibly change was further necessitated by the wider military situation and a decision to move the headquarters of the Eighth Route Army here. However, in terms of the internal situation within the county the cost of this decision was a severe and understandable reaction from landlords and rich peasants who demanded the return of land and property, as well as greater legalism in the handling of land transactions. The county government felt it had no choice but to comply as far as possible in order to try and rebuild both the local economy and any possible basis to a broad social coalition of support.

In the second half of 1940 alone 11,804 land disputes were settled in the wake of the Liaoxian CCP's changed perspectives.[34] The second half of 1940 and all of 1941 saw a determined move by landlords and rich peasants to regain as many of their assets as possible. Most of the land that had been confiscated at the end of 1939 and early 1940 appears to have been returned. That was certainly the case with the village whose confiscations were reported in detail earlier. Indeed, poor peasants in that village were later reported as pleading for help: "We were supported in the past but no one backs us up now.'[35] Similarly, land that landlords and rich peasants had been forced to lease to poor peasants by government decree was returned in 1941 and 1942. The exception to this general pattern of returned land was temple and church land, which apparently stayed reallocated as of early 1940.

The Liaoxian CCP's regularization of land relationships during 1941 attempted to build on its demand for reduced rents and interests, though in a more legalistic way. It aimed to establish tenancy contracts for all land, including land which was previously nontradable, such as 'boundary land.' Certain kinds of rent, such as those which shared land output regardless of the quality of the harvest, were outlawed. However, at this stage in its dealings with landlords and rich peasants bruised by the events of 1940 the county government was not in a strong position, and there was little if any recognition of tenant's rights: in particular the poorer peasants complained about the lack of permanence in their tenure.

From the tenants' point of view the only bright spot was that middle and poor peasants who had leased land from small-scale landowners who were from outside their village were allowed to retain the possession they had been granted, and not just land use.[36] This generally happened where landlords were not able to raise resources to return that portion of a rent received in the past at a rate higher than those now in operation. In these cases, difficulties in communication with landlords from other villages were either assumed or proven and led to tenants being granted possession.

Selling the changed strategy to the Liaoxian CCP was clearly no easy matter in 1941. In the middle of the year Li Xuefeng addressed a party meeting and emphasized once again the need to avoid 'leftist excesses' not least in order to ensure the internal security of the base area. He concluded by sending his audience off to read Deng Xiaoping's recently written 'The party and the anti-Japanese democratic government,' targeted at resurrecting the practice of a united front, not least through the introduction of the 'Three-thirds' election system.[37]

Despite previous arguments made by landlords and rich peasants for a more rational economic environment, there was plenty of evidence that they either found it equally as hard to understand new formal tenancies, or would if they could avoid any formal agreements and attempt to rent out their land in previously traditional ways. There were reported cases of landlords terminating tenancies early if their tenants attempted to enforce village government contracts.[38] In many cases the tenancy contracts were simply ignored by both landlord and peasant tenant in agreement that a village government contract was best left alone, or not something that involved them: it was 'village government business.'[39]

Taxation was the only effective weapon still at the Liaoxian CCP's disposal during 1941 for pushing forward its commitment to greater equalization in land usage. Table 6.4 lists differential tax burdens by social category for 1941.

Of course, in contrast to earlier years the percentage of the tax burden was generally higher because of the intensity of the war effort and the increased number of mouths to feed in south Liaoxian now that the

Table 6.4 Tax Burden by Social Category, Liaoxian, 1941 (percentage of income)

Landlord	55
Managerial landlord	41
Rich peasant	37
Middle peasant	30
Poor peasant	10
Average for total population	37

Source: LDB p.69.

various headquarters' units were all based here—an additional 20,000 people according to Li Xuefeng.[40] In one sense the strategy worked. Land sales rose dramatically in 1941. Most of the land sold (51 percent) was by landlords and former landlords divesting themselves of land they now regarded as uneconomic or not worth the risk. Middle peasants were responsible for 30 percent of land sales, rich peasants 15 percent, and poor peasants 4 percent.[41]

The relatively high rate of middle peasant land sales during 1941 is a key to one of the problems that resulted from the CCP's attempts to use tax rates to redistribute land. The tax burden in 1941 was still land and not income based. Middle peasants had, despite the setbacks of 1940 still seen their landholdings increase overall since 1937. For many, though, it became financially impossible to both afford public grain contributions in 1941 and accept the government regulated rent reductions. The returns on rent were not covering even their marginal costs for renting out land. The same problem also faced many rich peasants and landlords, though usually they were working on larger margins.[42]

In addition, sales of land by landlords and rich peasants during 1941 resulted in many landless laborers finding themselves without work; and in the villages dominated by commercial capital, poor peasants lost their land altogether as it was sold over their heads.[43] Moreover, land sales were not the only viable option for well-endowed landlord families. One strategy that emerged clearly on all kinds of land in Liaoxian was for landlord families to divide their households within the family. As a result landlord households did not decline as a proportion of the population, though their average landholdings had roughly halved between 1937 and the end of 1941.

The net result of all the various changes in landownership from 1937 to the beginning of 1942 was complex across the county, and largely dependent on village conditions. For example, in villages previously dominated by commercial landlords there was a fall in average rich peasant landholdings even more dramatic than that experienced by landlords. Table 6.5 summarizes the proportions of landholding households by social category at the beginning of 1942, according to the type of landlord-dominated village (as of 1937).

Table 6.6 summarizes the changes in average landholding for each household by social category at the beginning of 1942, according to the type of landlord-dominated village (as of 1937.)

By the end of 1941 it was clear that despite land sales during the preceding year middle peasants had been the main beneficiaries of the various changes since the start of the war in all the different kinds of villages identified by the Liaoxian CCP. At this stage the Liaoxian CCP embraced the strategy of building a program of social reform on the role of the

Table 6.5 Social Composition of Landowners, Liaoxian, Early 1942 (percentage of landholding households)

Village dominated by landlord type	Social category Landlord	Rich peasant	Middle peasant	Poor peasant	Trader	Other
Commercial	3.8	7.7	43.1	20.2	14.4	10.9
Native	5.7	9.7	55.8	27.1	0.4	1.3
Non-native	3.9	6.1	45.3	38.7	4.4	1.7

Source: LDB pp.73–75.

middle peasant. The change was purposeful and deliberate. The CCP's county-level leadership once again highlighted the importance of class status, but pointed out this time that consciousness was a defining feature of political correctness, and that consciousness came through political education. Whilst recognizing that intellectuals had an important and positive contribution to make, it implicitly criticized some of their earlier actions and behavior. It criticized their work style: emphasizing that mass mobilization did not just mean able individuals leading or telling a group

Table 6.6 Average Landholdings by Social Category in Liaoxian, 1937 and Early 1942 (*mu* per household)

Village dominated by landlord type	Social category Landlord	Rich peasant	Middle peasant	Poor peasant	Trader
Commercial					
1937	255.6	62.0	12.8	2.7	5.0
1942	111.7	31.3	13.1	3.5	1.1
Native					
1937	149.3	63.7	11.9	4.3	3.6
1942	82.4	43.1	12.1	5.8	5.0
Non-native					
1937	70.7	34.2	13.3	4.3	7.1
1942	32.8	40.0	14.3	5.1	9.0

Source: LDB p.29, p.32, p.33.

of people what to do, but required the development of a movement which would use group dynamics to transform local communities from within. It also stressed that formal education, whilst not unimportant, had to be regarded as secondary to political education.[44] Reflecting on that strategic shift some years later, Li Xiuren saw it as the watershed in the development of CCP rule. In his view once the middle peasants 'were educated . . . to realise that their interests no longer rested with the landlords, their raised consciousness was brought to bear to assist in meeting the needs of the poor peasants and landless tenants' and enabled them to combine to make revolution.[45]

The Liaoxian CCP's change of direction was presumably with the approval of the leadership of both the base area and the central CCP's institutions, if not at their command. Certainly, the impact of the decision was immediate. By the middle of 1941 middle peasants were already coming to dominate the Liaoxian Peasant Association and its branches. In the Taihang Base Area as a whole, the almost five hundred village representatives of the county Peasant Associations and their local level branches differentiated by class status were 8 percent rich peasant, 34 percent middle peasant, 44 percent poor peasant, 10 percent peasant tenants, and 4 percent farm laborers. In Liaoxian the composition of the county's just under a hundred village representatives in the Peasant Association leadership was 17 percent rich peasant, 38 percent middle peasant, 36 percent poor peasant and 9 percent tenant-farmers.[46] As Table 6.2 indicates, by early 1942 the majority of CCP members in Liaoxian were middle peasants; by later in the year this had grown to an overwhelming majority.[47]

RENT AND INTEREST REDUCTION CAMPAIGNS

The September 1942 rent and interest reduction campaign in Zuoquan was clearly intended as a model for emulation by other parts of the base area. Examples of its procedures and work style were propagandized quite heavily. The county CCP's proximity to the base area leadership, and its embrace of the middle peasant strategy may help explain why its views on the 'middle peasant question' were sometimes more muted than most. However, it too experienced the tensions between middle and poor peasants more openly articulated by cadres from other counties.

The Zuoquan's CCP appeal to the middle peasant was increased still further during 1942–43. However, during 1937–39 it managed to be more successful in recruiting the youth of middle peasant families rather than their parents, and indeed was more successful generally amongst young people from wealthier backgrounds.[48] It also deliberately maintained its emphasis on recruiting women and attempting to encourage women's participation in the workforce and politics.[49] Though the Zuoquan CCP leadership did not abandon the poor peasants and landless tenants—and was mindful of the need to provide help and assistance to those who were less well-off[50]—the response was not encouraging. Agricultural loans were supplied overwhelmingly to poor peasants as opposed to middle peasants (in a ratio of 4:1),[51] but still as Li Xuefeng commented in 1943 it was both difficult for the CCP to mobilize them or recruit them to the party.[52] Even once recruited they often remained inactive, or left after a while.

The Zuoquan CCP tried to persuade landowners to renegotiate rent rates and accept government-sponsored tenancy agreements (including the tenant's guarantee of long lease) without necessarily organizing a struggle meeting. Later records suggest they were successful in two-thirds of the cases.[53] However, a struggle meeting could also become more like a struggle week. One such that was heavily publicized at the time to both instruct cadres and to encourage peasants was the case of Gui Hechen in Matian, which provides an example of the struggle meeting process.[54]

Matian originally had one landlord—Gui Hecheng—who leased out about a quarter of the land, and a number of smaller-scale landlords, whilst one-fifth of its households were tenants. Few of the tenancies in Matian by late 1942 were governed by tenancy contracts and indeed most tenancies were still based on traditional production-sharing rentals, now considered inappropriate. When the county government started trying to enforce the border region government's 1942 decree on rent and interest reduction, there was a distinct lack of response. Peasants in particular did not see the point since it seemed likely that the move would only at best be temporary. According to the cadres of the Peasant Association, they had unsuccessfully approached every landlord to try and negotiate the introduction of tenancy agreements and a 25 percent reduction in rents. At this stage in the war it seems likely that many landlords can have believed that the local CCP regime was not going to last: certainly many CCP cadres appear to have also believed it, according to reports elsewhere by the Zuoquan CCP Organization Department.[55]

Reports of the event suggest the Peasant and Women's Associations called a meeting in the village square which was attended by about six hundred people, who came with sticks, shovels and grain sacks, presumably because they expected some direct action. The Chair of the Peasant Association addressed the meeting, as did the village head who emphasized that the rent and interest reduction campaign was the result of both border region and county government action. Members of an Eighth Route Army unit were also in attendance and they went off to look for landlords to answer to the peasant demands for lower rent and interest rates as well as the introduction of tenancy contracts.

The soldiers came back in the afternoon with three landowners who rented out land, and the three ran the gauntlet of the mass meeting. In public the landowners accepted the need to follow government decrees, and made a commitment to ensure that contracts were agreed with their tenants. However, the peasants at the meeting were a little uneasy about this, not least because they felt the landlords were more literate and numerate and might use that superiority to their advantage. The meeting then formed a rent reduction committee that would examine all proposed contracts before final approval by landlord and tenants, and lodgment with the county government.

Apparently, the Eighth Route Army detachment had not been able to find Gui Hecheng and the Peasant Association decided that on the second day they should take further action. The Peasant Association leadership and a group of Gui Hecheng's peasants went to his house and confronted him. Gui was told that the tenants were not leaving until he had agreed to their demands for lower rents, based on a fixed rate, and the return of the surplus rent (over and above the 25 percent rate) that he had taken as his share in that year. The confrontation lasted all day until eventually Gui conceded that he would return some of the surplus rent he had received and provided first 3 *dan* of grain; then 7 *dan* and 2,700 dollars; and then finally 30 further *dan* of grain through repeated negotiations.

When the Peasant Association met the next day there was a distinct feeling of anti-climax and after further discussion the association's leadership, the soldiers who had been involved two days earlier, the rent reduction committee and Gui's tenants first met in the village square and then marched to his house in even more belligerent mood. It was reported that on this occasion angry tenants attacked Gui Hecheng even more furiously and demanded in no uncertain terms that he not only agree acceptable tenancy arrangements, but that he return more grain and money that more accurately reflected his overcharging of rent. This time apparently confrontation was more intense but for a shorter period, and resulted in Gui Hecheng agreeing to comply. Over the next few days the rent reduction committee made a through examination of Gui's assets and property, which then resulted in the surrender of '55 *dan* of corn, 36 *dan* of wheat, 7 *dan* of beans, 762 *jin* of millet straw, 200 *jin* of peanuts, and 4,098 dollars of South Hebei Bank currency.'

Although this incident and other aspects of the 1942 rent and interest reduction campaign were regarded as being successfully completed at the time, in the following year some of the solutions which had been negotiated or enforced appeared to have come undone or not been maintained. In January 1944 the county CCP initiated a survey of how the two-year arrangements to reduce rent and interest had progressed. This found that in some cases the agreements and procedures of 1942 were still in place, but argued that arrangements could be tightened and that in the process rent and interest rates could be lowered further. As in 1941 contracts had often been set aside by landlord and tenant through agreement, not least because tenants were often more familiar with previous tenancy practices. The rent and interest reduction campaign was rerun starting in the autumn of 1944, continuing into 1945.[56]

Whilst the rent and interest reduction campaigns were specifically targeted at mediation of class conflict between landlord and peasants, the CCP's choice of the middle peasant as an agent of social change also resulted in tensions locally between middle peasants, on the one hand, and poor peasants and landless tenants on the other. In 1943 Li Xuefeng blamed county cadres for their lack of leadership and inadequate assertion of party discipline.[57] This was an understandable reaction but not one that addressed the real causes of the social tension. In the villages, the wealth and status of some people were rising rather rapidly largely as a result of the policies being followed by the CCP. As one Zuoquan cadre commented at a base area CCP meeting in 1943 that discussed the 'middle peasant question': 'our activists and cadres are mostly rising middle peasants [i.e., former middle peasants who are becoming richer]. The poor peasants and the farm-hands are relatively inactive and silent . . . The middle peasants are most active because they benefit most from the struggle.'[58]

According to the head of the Zuoquan CCP Organization Department, 'The mentality of privilege and factionalism exists everywhere.' Even allowing for exaggeration on her part because she was encouraging party members to modify their behavior, it would seem that tensions between middle and poor peasants had increased. She reported on the complaints from poor peasant and farmhands that suggested they felt they were losing out in the current processes of social change. In her words 'All peasants want land first, and then a wife' but whereas poor peasants and landless laborers could see that these were available for middle peasants, they themselves felt they were not getting their just desserts. Even where land and property was being allocated to poor peasants and farmhands, they felt that the quality of the land they were receiving was not as good as that going to the middle peasants. She was not unsympathetic to this view, accepting that CCP members who were middle peasants did increase their wealth under the defense of increasing production for the public good.[59] However, she pointed out that forbidding them from wealth creation would be somewhat self-defeating, and instead requested moderation.[60]

The class status gap between middle peasants on the one hand, and poor peasants and landless laborers on the other was particularly acute in the organizational operation of the county CCP. Middle peasants were frequently accused of not consulting their poor peasant and farmhand colleagues, and wanting to be 'in control'; whilst both middle peasant and poor peasant cadres were criticized for finding it easier to issue orders rather than to work alongside cadres and party members from different backgrounds. Another local cadre, Xu Tiangui, was extremely critical. He censored village cadres, who were usually middle peasants, for taking a 'perfunctory attitude towards their work in order to have more personal time for their own production'; and he castigated subdistrict level cadres, more usually poor peasants or landless laborers, for bypassing village cadres in order to carry out their own projects in the villages.[61]

Xu Tiangui's cynicism came from an investigation of three party branches. In his report he identified three ideological pathologies. One was that of building a personal fortune—party members showed great enthusiasm in production campaigns but were reluctant to be involved in the CCP's activities. A second was paradoxically, the fear of building a personal fortune: party members ceased to be engaged in production lest they be expelled from the CCP, and their property redivided after an increase in wealth. The third new ideology was described as an 'ultra-left deviation' in which cadres tried to prove their revolutionary credentials by not having anything to do with landlords or former landlords. They were not prepared to consider reeducation for those who had been dispossessed by the recent political campaigns, or even contact with their families. As a result, in such cases the children of former landlord families 'didn't dare to go out (of their homes) for fear of being beaten up.' Xu observed that middle peasants dominated all three party branches and all local branches of the Peasant Association, and concluded that these ideologies all resulted 'from class status and impure motives for joining the party.'[62]

Zhai Ying was noticeably reticent in passing any comment on the revolutionary potential (or otherwise) of the middle peasant. However, both county organizers who spoke at the 1943 party meeting that discussed the 'middle peasant question' in detail, believed any problems were largely those of cadre management, best resolved through ideological rectification.[63] The advocacy of rectification was indeed a major finding in general of the 1943 meeting that discussed the 'middle peasant question.' Given the decision had already been taken that Taihang Base Area cadres would soon participate in the national CCP rectification, it is likely that such an outcome was an important part of the exercise.

SOCIAL CHANGE IN LIAOXIAN

Social change in Liaoxian during the War of Resistance proceeded anything but evenly. During November 1939 to March 1940, the Liaoxian CCP had encouraged rural class conflict which resulted in land confiscations from landowners and redistributions to poor peasants and the landless. Following criticism of the county CCP leadership at the Licheng Meeting of the North China Bureau in April 1940 these policies were reversed almost totally with for a while poor peasants feeling discriminated against as landlords and rich peasants regained much of their lost property.

Starting in 1941 the county's renewed program of social reform was not so much typical of the Taihang Base Area as a deliberately crafted model for emulation. Its advocacy of the middle peasant strategy was as much an initiative of the base area leadership as of the county CCP. Although the program met with some success, particularly in ensuring that middle peasants became the social base for the CCP and Liaoxian's village leadership, there were nonetheless problems and resentments in its implementation. As throughout the base area this resentment generally stymied the full implementation of the middle peasant strategy until after the CCP rectification that started in late 1943.

NOTES

1. Li Xiuren 'Wo liaojiede Liaoxian (Zuoquan) Heshun dangde jianshe he fazhan' ['Comments on the Establishment and Development of the Party in Liaoxian (Zuoquan) and Heshun'] in DJ p.572.
2. ZOH p.17.
3. HCZ p.211.
4. HCZ p.34.
5. ZOH p.23.
6. Li Xiuren 'Wo liaojiede Liaoxian (Zuoquan) Heshun dangde jianshe he fazhan' ['Comments on the Establishment and Development of the Party in Liaoxian (Zuoquan) and Heshun'] in DJ p.573.
7. Zhang Shufan 'Zai Zuoquan gongzuode huiyi' ['Memoir of Work in Zuoquan'] in DJ p.584.
8. LDB p.172.
9. Xu Zirong 'Guanyu bage xiande zhibu gongzuo' ['Work on Party Branches in Eight Counties'] 30 August 1942, in DJ p.237 (comments on Liaoxian) and p.247 (comments on subsequent careers).
10. They were, for example, conscious that their interviewees were sometimes providing the answers they thought the interviewers wanted to hear. See, for example, the introduction to LDB.
11. LDB pp.140–42.
12. LDB pp.27–34.
13. Li Xiuren 'Wo liaojiede Liaoxian (Zuoquan) Heshun dangde jianshe he fazhan' ['Comments on the Establishment and Development of the Party in Liaoxian (Zuoquan) and Heshun'] in DJ p.574.
14. Zhang Shufan 'Zai Zuoquan gongzuode huiyi' ['Memoir of Work in Zuoquan'] in DJ p.584.

15. JinJiYuqu nongjiu zonghui 'JinJiYuqu nongjiu zonghui liangnianlai gongzuo cailiao' ['Materials on the work of the Shanxi-Hebei-Henan region peasants' association during the last two years'] June 1941, in TDZH vol.4: 1941, p.400.
16. Li Xiuren 'Wo liaojiede Liaoxian (Zuoquan) Heshun dangde jianshe he fazhan' ['Comments on the Establishment and Development of the Party in Liaoxian (Zuoquan) and Heshun'] in DJ p.575.
17. LDB p.180.
18. Zhonggong JinJiYu qudangwei 'Zuzhibu gei Beifangjude gongzuo baogao' ['Organization Department Report to North China Bureau'] August 1940, in *Shanxi geming genjudi* [Shanxi Revolutionary Base Areas] no.1, 1989, p.9.
19. LDB p.176.
20. 'Liaoxian shiyanxiande dongyuan baogao' ['Report on Mobilization in Liaoxian Experimental County'] October 1939, in TDZH vol.2: 1939, p.666.
21. LDB p.55.
22. LDB pp.38–42.
23. LDB pp.140–41.
24. LDB p.166.
25. Li Xiuren 'Wo liaojiede Liaoxian (Zuoquan) Heshun dangde jianshe he fazhan' ['Comments on the Establishment and Development of the Party in Liaoxian (Zuoquan) and Heshun'] in DJ p.577.
26. TW p.113.
27. Li Xiuren 'Wo liaojiede Liaoxian (Zuoquan) Heshun dangde jianshe he fazhan' ['Comments on the Establishment and Development of the Party in Liaoxian (Zuoquan) and Heshun'] in DJ p.576.
28. TW p.23.
29. Yang Daifu 'Liaoxian shiyanxian gongzuo zongjie' ['Summary of Work in Liaoxian Experimental County'] October 1940, in TDZH vol.3: 1940, p.716.
30. 'Liaoxian shiyanxiande dongyuan baogao' ['Report on Mobilization in Liaoxian Experimental County'] October 1939, in TDZH vol.2: 1939, p.666.
31. Li Xiuren 'Wo liaojiede Liaoxian (Zuoquan) Heshun dangde jianshe he fazhan' ['Comments on the Establishment and Development of the Party in Liaoxian (Zuoquan) and Heshun'] in DJ p.578.
32. Yang Daifu (Dai Fu) 'Liaoxian shiyanxian juti lingdaode jidian jingyan' ['Aspects of Concrete Leadership in Liaoxian Experimental County'] April 1940, in TDZH vol.3: 1940, p.275.
33. 'Chuangzao Liaoxian mofan xiande zhandou renwu ji gongzuo biaozhun' ['Realise the Important Tasks and Standards of Liaoxian Model County'] Summer 1940, in TDZH vol.3: 1940, p.513.
34. Yang Daifu 'Liaoxian shiyanxian gongzuo zongjie' ['Summary of Work in Liaoxian Experimental County'] October 1940, in TDZH vol.3: 1940, p.721.
35. LDB p.55.
36. LDB p.34.
37. Li Xuefeng 'Guanyu Liaoxian gongzuode fayan' ['Speech about Liaoxian's Work'] 1 June 1941, in TDZH vol.4:1941, p.351. Deng's speech may be found in Deng Xiaoping 'Dang yu KangRi minzhu zhengquan' ['The party and the anti-Japanese democratic government'] 15 April 1941, in Deng Xiaoping *Deng Xiaoping*

Wenxuan, 1938–1965 [Selected Works of Deng Xiaoping 1938–1965] Beijing, Renmin chubanshe, 1989, p.8.

38. See, for example, cases cited in Tongyu, in LDB p.148.
39. LDB p.57.
40. LXH p.176.
41. JinJiYuqu nongjiu zonghui 'JinJiYuqu nongjiu zonghui liangnianlai gongzuo cailiao' ['Materials on the work of the Shanxi-Hebei-Henan region peasants' association during the last two years'] June 1941, in TDZH vol.4: 1941, p.418.
42. LDB p.57.
43. LDB pp.39–40.
44. Yang Daifu 'Liaoxian shiyanxian gongzuo zongjie' ['Summary of Work in Liaoxian Experimental County'] October 1940, in TDZH vol.3: 1940, p.715.
45. Li Xiuren 'Wo liaojiede Liaoxian (Zuoquan) Heshun dangde jianshe he fazhan' ['Comments on the Establishment and Development of the Party in Liaoxian (Zuoquan) and Heshun'] in DJ p.581.
46. JinJiYuqu nongjiu zonghui 'JinJiYuqu nongjiu zonghui liangnianlai gongzuo cailiao' ['Materials on the work of the Shanxi-Hebei-Henan region peasant's association during the last two years'] June 1941, in TDZH vol.4: 1941, p.460.
47. 'Shisanxian sanshijiuge zhibude chubu yanjiu' ['Preliminary Research on 39 Branches in 13 Counties'] 20 September 1942, in DJ p.282.
48. LDB p.174.
49. LDB p.185.
50. LDB p.77.
51. 'Linianlai Taihangqu jinrong huobi tongji ziliao' ['Historical Statistics on Banking and Currency in the Taihang Region'] 18 February 1946, in TYG vol.4, part I, p.76.
52. Li Xuefeng 'Zuoquan sinian gongzuo jianjie ji jinhou gongzuo yijian' ['Overview of Work in Zuoquan during the last Four Years and Ideas for the Future'] 1943, in DJ p.309.
53. HZ p.120.
54. 'Jianzu jianxi zhongde dianxing nongcun' ['Case Studies of Rent and Interest Reduction'] 1943, in Zhonggong Taihang qudangwei *Taihang dang shiliao biancun* [Collection of Historical Party Materials on Taihang] Huabei Xinhua shudian, 1944, vol.1, p.403.
55. Zhai Ying, 5 September 1943, in ZJY p.34.
56. HZ p.240.
57. Li Xuefeng 'Zuoquan sinian gongzuo jianjie ji jinhou gongzuo yijian' ['Overview of Work in Zuoquan during the last Four Years and Ideas for the Future'] 1943, in DJ p.315.
58. ZJY p.31.
59. ZJY p.54.
60. ZJY pp.58–59.
61. ZJY p.60.
62. ZJY p.56.
63. Xu Tiangui (pp.43–44), Zhai Ying (p.57) in ZJY.

7

Wuxiang: Radical Politics and Revolutionary Conflict

Despite Liaoxian's brush with land reform in late 1939 and its later close relationship with the base area CCP leadership, Wuxiang was considerably more in the forefront of the attempt to introduce programs of social reform in the Taihang region during the war. Wuxiang was the first location in the Taihang region chosen in late 1939 for the experimental implementation of a rent and interest reduction campaign. Though criticized for some aspects of its experience at that time, it went on to become regarded as a model within the base area not only for rent and interest reduction, but also more generally for developing programs of social reform. By the middle of 1942 Wuxiang was regarded as having already completed 'class struggle' despite the problems it had encountered.[1]

In addition, the Wuxiang CCP was also right at the center of the inner-party discussions about class and revolution that accompanied the attempt to develop a program of social reform within the Taihang Base Area during 1940–43. In particular, the leadership of the Wuxiang CCP became some of the most vocal critics of the middle peasant strategy adopted by the base area leadership in early 1941. This particular stance may well have been related to the county CCP's experience during 1940 when in the wake of problems with the 1939 rent and interest reduction campaign it encountered further problems with middle peasants and middle peasant cadres, as the Wuxiang CCP leadership tried to restore balance and direction to its program of social reform. However, the Wuxiang CCP leadership's stance on the 'middle peasant question' may also be more widely related to the county's socioeconomic composition at the start of the War of

Resistance, where unusually for the Taihang region there was a high degree of concentration of landownership, and in consequence far fewer middle peasants.

RADICAL MOBILIZATION

As already detailed in Chapter 3, the redevelopment of the Wuxiang CCP at the beginning of the War of Resistance lay in the hands largely of a group of teachers and urban intellectuals. Most of these were natives, some of them returning for the first time since the local CCP's closure and their flight in 1936. In addition, their ranks were supplemented by other organizers for the CCP and the Sacrifice League at the end of 1937. Together they were to form the nucleus of the Wuxiang's leadership for all the next eight years.

Comprehensive name lists are not extant below the county-level. However, there is some incomplete information available about Wuxiang's long-term and full-time party and local government activists. Later comments (including at the end of the war itself) indicate that Wuxiang's permanent cadre force was dominated by a group of 56 organizers. These included those who had first gone into the (then) districts and village-regions of the county in 1938 and 1939, and who in large number stayed wherever they had been sent for the duration of the war, as well as some who remained part of the county-level operation.

Most of the cadres were from Wuxiang itself: only about one-fifth were not native to the county. However, most were not from the locality where they ended up working through the war; only about one in ten were natives of the locality within Wuxiang where they were now based. Twenty-nine of those original fifty-six organizers were teachers or students, and almost all (26) were still in Wuxiang at the end of the war.[2] A locally produced 1986 record of Wuxiang natives who were part of the county's cadre force during the War of Resistance listed fifty-two individuals. Of these, sixteen had been too young to be involved in other activities before 1937; two are acknowledged as from peasant backgrounds; and seventeen had previous careers as teachers (one of whom was also said to have been from a peasant background).[3]

The Wuxiang CCP's early recruitment pattern was somewhat different to that experienced in Liaoxian, or indeed generally in the Taihang region. During late 1937 and into 1938 it was particularly successful in recruiting both extremes of the rural social spectrum, but not the center. A substantial number of rich peasants joined at the first opportunity, and became long-term village and even subdistrict cadres.[4] Similarly, recruitment was extremely successful in attracting large numbers of farmhands, landless tenants and poor peasants. As one of those recruited at this time later commented, they may not have 'been literate, but they were politically reliable' and again in contrast to the experience elsewhere in the Taihang region, large numbers stayed in the CCP.[5] It made no great headway in recruiting middle peasants at this time, nor does it seem to have wanted to move particularly in that direction.

Table 7.1 provides information on the social composition of the Wuxiang CCP during the war. The extent to which the Wuxiang's CCP recruitment pattern during 1938–39 was unusual is highlighted by contrast with that for the Taihang Base Area as a whole, and in particular for the proportions of recruits who were landless tenants, farmhands and middle peasants. Whilst about 40 percent of the membership of the base area CCP at this time were categorized as middle peasants, in Wuxiang the proportion was never greater than 10 percent. Where in the Taihang Base Area CCP as a whole, workers of all kinds (including farmhands, tenant farmers, artisans and industrial workers) only accounted for under 10 percent, in the Wuxiang CCP they provided 20 percent and more of the party membership.[6]

The explanation of these differences is almost certainly to be found in Wuxiang's different socioeconomic environment, as well as the party leadership's previous experience of organization in the county during the 1930s which allowed it to develop both faster and more surely at an early stage of the war. As already noted, Wuxiang's agriculture had not only been heavily commercialized before the war, there was also a high degree of concentration of landownership. In consequence, there was a large number of very poor peasants and farmhands, especially in the eastern part of the county, where the Wuxiang CCP settled after mid-1939. Table 7.2 provides information on the number of households and their share of landownership by social category before the war, and at its end.

There was also a high degree of poverty. One of the urban intellectuals who was sent to Wuxiang by the base area CCP committee (in 1939) later recalled his reactions: 'Everything is relative but these poor peasants were not just poor, they were dirt poor; and even the fairly well-off peasants were really poor.' Certainly Wuxiang was and remains one of the poorest counties in the Taihang region, and was markedly poorer than both Liaoxian and Licheng during the War of Resistance (as Table 0.1 indicates).

The process of land concentration was a fairly recent phenomenon. Interest had started to rise with commercial and industrial development in the county: from 1 to 2 percent per annum around 1901 to 3 to 5 percent per annum by the 1920s.[7] Commercialization and increasing debt had resulted in land sales in Wuxiang during the first part of the twentieth century. However, the economic depression that started in 1931 had a dramatic effect. Rapidly rising interest rates and debt coupled with a string

Table 7.1 Social Composition of Wuxiang CCP, 1937–1945 (percentage of members)

Year	Social category								
	Workers				Peasants			Intellectuals	Others
	All	Industrial worker	Handicraft worker	Landless laborer	Poor peasant	Middle peasant	Rich peasant		
Wuxiang									
1938	27.6	2.3	5.9	19.4	50.0	10.0	6.5	5.9	
1939	20.7	1.7	7.0	12.0	53.8	8.6	9.1	7.7	
1941	15.2	2.8	3.2	9.2	42.9	35.8		3.7	2.4
1943	12.9	1.6	3.1	8.2	46.7	32.9	4.0	2.6	1.0
1944	9.5	2.1	1.6	5.8	38.9	46.5	3.0	1.9	0.2
West Wuxiang									
1941	12.9	1.4	4.3	7.2	42.5	31.8	3.2	7.6	2.0
1943	22.0	0.6	6.0	15.3	37.3	30.0	4.5	1.2	5.0
1944	4.3		2.8	1.4	49.5	40.0	5.0	1.0	

Source: Calculated from statistics in WOH pp.90–91.

Table 7.2 Landholding and Households by Social Category, Wuxiang, 1935 and 1945 (percentage)

Year Social category	Households	Landownership
1935		
Landlords and Rich peasants	4.9	54.0
Middle peasants	19.1	16.5
Poor peasants	76.0	29.5
1945		
Landlords and Rich peasants	2.3	1.6
Middle peasants	57.4	52.5
Poor peasants	40.3	45.9

Source: WX p.291.

of poor harvests had resulted in land being turned over to creditors in large quantities. In one village in the eastern part of the county during 1934–36, 85 households, including 3 landlords, 11 rich peasants, 39 middle peasants, 28 poor peasants, 3 farmhands and 1 tenant farmer, all had their land and property sequestered by creditors.[8]

A 1939 survey undertaken in Wuxiang to prepare for the trial implementation of a campaign of rent and interest reduction found that commercial debt was of far more serious concern than rent, or indeed landownership. Its estimate was that about 23 percent of land was rented by peasants, and that less than a fifth of all rural households were landless. Even when rent could not be paid because of poor harvest there was a tendency for landowners to maintain their relationship with their tenants. This was a common practice in the neighboring areas of eastern Wuxiang and northern Licheng and necessarily created complications when the CCP attempted its rent reduction campaign.[9]

Interest rates and rising debt had proved more corrosive. The 1939 survey estimated that 40 percent of peasants had commercial debts, and came across villages where almost every household carried a debt. In particular, it highlighted the extent to which poor peasants had borrowed from rich peasants. It uncovered a total of 144 debts across 79 households in the 10 villages it surveyed. Of these debts, 101 were not for repayments on land but for tools and assistance to work the land.[10]

In 1938 and 1939 the Wuxiang CCP deliberately ensured it recruited in large numbers from the poor peasants, landless tenants and farmhands. It regarded these social categories as most readily mobilized because of their antagonism toward landlords as a class, and the concentration of landownership, which had taken place largely since 1921. At the same time, it had different criteria for the selection of its cadres. Particularly at the village level, cadres had to be 'knowledgeable and capable of dealing with landlords and the powerful; resourceful and capable of handling outsiders; wealthy enough to be self-supporting and to understand financial matters; communicative and able to deal easily with people from the upper strata of society.'[11]

Partly in consequence, one of the features of the Wuxiang CCP throughout the war was that it not only had a solid phalanx of rich peasants amongst its cadres, but also a number of landlords, or more accurately, soon-to-become former landlords. The precise number is not known but there are several examples of small-scale landlords who became involved with the CCP and then decided to surrender the majority of their landholdings.[12]

As already noted, the Wuxiang CCP's early attempts at popular mobilization were all largely successful, and undoubtedly help explain the invitation from the base area CCP leadership for the county party organization to trial policies and practices for a rent and interest reduction campaign at the end of 1939. The trial implementation went badly awry, though it is difficult to assess the relative contributions of poor planning at the county and subdistrict levels, and overenthusiasm by village cadres and peasants. The details of the problems that emerged remain largely obscured and are mainly only visible through later criticisms. However, on balance it would seem that the problems faced by the Wuxiang CCP in the first few months of 1940 resulted from the heady mixture of revolutionary idealism by some subdistrict cadres, political expressivism by landless laborers, and attempted land seizures by some peasant smallholders.

Following investigation by the base area CCP leadership and the North China Bureau of the CCP Central Committee it was acknowledged that there had been problems in Wuxiang. In April 1940 the Wuxiang CCP was reorganized and its leadership replaced.[13] Wen Jianping was appointed as the new Secretary of the Wuxiang CCP. Wen had been a student at the outbreak of war and had become a protégé of Liu Shaoqi's. He had previously worked in the Taiyue Base Area and immediately before appointment to Wuxiang had been the Director of the Propaganda Department at the district level under the Shanxi-Hebei-Henan CCP regional committee for the district which included Wuxiang. The base area CCP and the North China Bureau specifically criticized the county party committee for the abuse of human rights; concerns which were certainly uppermost nationally for the CCP as it sought to ensure the continuation of a broad coalition of support against Japan in the context of the ruptured relationship with Yan Xishan. Certainly many sources have acknowledged that struggle meetings did indeed become uncontrollable at this time in Wuxiang.[14] However, the available evidence would seem to suggest that some subdistrict leaderships or groups within the county party organization, had some greater responsibility than not keeping overenthusiastic village cadres or peasants in check.

With the reorganization of the Wuxiang CCP leadership, Wen Jianping read local cadres and activists a very stiff lesson in April 1940. Addressing a meeting of local cadres and activists, he listed the mistakes the previous county party organization was held to have made, and pointed out the error of its ways in no small detail.[15] He certainly made the attempt at social reform of the last few months appear more like full-scale revolution than the trial implementation of a program of rent and interest reduction. According to this interpretation of the events of the past few months, parts of the previous county party organization had indeed proceeded from an analysis of a revolutionary situation. Wen castigated an unnamed subdistrict committee within the previous county party organization for suggesting that the proletarian stage of history had arrived, and that as a result economic growth was no longer a priority. He also criticized the apparently more generally held views that the dictatorship of the proletariat should now be used to exterminate the landlord and rich peasant classes; that private property should be abolished; and that the united front was finished and unsustainable, not least because landlords and rich peasants were not really prepared to resist Japan.

Certainly Wen Jianping's view of events would appear supported to some extent by Peng Tao's later confirmation that in the course of more than 700 struggle meetings in Wuxiang at this time, more than 80 landlords and rich peasants had been physically attacked, and that most of them had died.[16] Given that there were probably about 6,000 landlords and rich peasants in the whole county, and that CCP activities were concentrated in the eastern parts of the county, these figures represent a very high proportion of the total numbers of landlords and rich peasants in that area. Land was confiscated from both landlords and rich peasants, and redistributed: indeed as Wen Jianping complained, peasants were thinking more about land redistribution than production during the spring ploughing. Again the extent of confiscations and redistributions is not known, though it would appear that the pretext for seizure was often that the landowner was a 'traitor' or engaged in enclosing or farming land illegally. Under those circumstances Wen Jianping's comment that 'At present the landlords and rich peasants are uniting to oppose us' seems somewhat understated, and there can be little doubt that many fled the area.[17]

The encouragement of rural class conflict was the responsibility of the Wuxiang CCP leadership. However, it is unlikely that the belief in immediate proletarian revolution emanated from the county CCP. Although almost all its leaders were demoted once the Wuxiang Experimental CCP Committee was established, they were not otherwise disciplined. Far from being expelled from the party, many of them returned to the leadership after the experimental committee itself was terminated.

Moreover, Wen Jianping's opening speech to the Wuxiang CCP's local cadres and activists certainly indicates that a number of subdistricts and CCP branches were being held more responsible than others for some of the revolutionary beliefs that had been articulated. He divided party branches into broad groups according to his prescription for their future. One group, including branches in Hongshui, Shangsi, Dongbi, Jianzhang, Jiahe, Panlong and Lanting were told that the revolution was not simply a matter of attacking and removing landlords and rich peasants. In Wen's view these branches needed reorganizing. A second group, including branches in Dayou, Donggou, Shuqin, and Yukou were accused of having followed policies but excessively, and were said to require political education. A third group, including party branches in Hongshui and Shimen were held to be thoroughly deficient because of their 'bad class status,' with no further details, and were earmarked for closure.[18]

EXPERIMENTAL INTERLUDE

Although the Wuxiang experience had its unique characteristics, the county party organization had not been alone in running into difficulties of this kind with its rent and interest campaign at the end of 1939 and beginning of 1940.[19] Quite apart from the unpredictability of struggle meetings the contemporary political situation was more than a little uncertain for CCP cadres, especially in the middle of a civil war in addition to the resistance to Japan. Greater direction was provided generally to the CCP organization in March 1940 with the end of the civil war in Shanxi when the CCP Central Committee provided an 'Instruction on Problems of Political Power in the Base Areas,' which indicated the continued need for a broad coalition of social forces against Japanese aggression.

In Wuxiang the new CCP leadership moved quickly to stamp its authority on the county party organization—backed by the leaderships of both the base area and the CCP North China Bureau. Wen Jianping warned the meeting of local cadres and activists in April 1940 'We're going to uncover all the hidden problems' as he moved from an examination of past problems to discuss the practical measures needed to restructure and develop the CCP organization. His starting point was class status: in his view leadership and cadre work style had been at fault because of inadequate attention to questions of class status. In particular, Wen emphasized the need to recruit 'lots of workers'[20]: in his view because there had been too few workers, there had been a lack of inner-party democracy, too much bureaucracy and commandism. Moreover, there is a strong suggestion in his speech that some of the excessive activities, especially the seizure of landlord and rich peasant land and property, was driven by middle peasants anxious to benefit from their leadership of the redistribution.

Wen Jianping reached back into the CCP's traditions to find solutions for the current problems and referred to the organizational development of the CCP's Jiangxi Soviet and its policies as a suitable model for emulation. He set an agenda for the future that concentrated on production, in particular land usage (he recommended the development of cotton and other cash crops), the raising of livestock and the organization of mutual aid teams. The more immediate concerns were organizational: reeducating village cadres; restructuring and strengthening party branches; and the formal reassessment of everyone's CCP membership.

The party consolidation campaign was the Wuxiang CCP's main concern during May-July 1940. Every member had to reapply and have their class status examined in detail. As part of this process they were required to attend study classes of twenty to thirty people to discuss three topics: the role of the CCP as the vanguard of the proletariat, and not a mass organization; Communism and the Three People's Principles; and the nature of classes and strata in China's villages, as well as the CCP's policies towards them.

In detailing the procedures for the forthcoming party consolidation, Wen Jianping highlighted a need to ensure that the class status of young women was thoroughly examined. Since this was the only social category specifically targeted in this way, it suggests there might be some connection with the events of late 1939 and early 1940, though quite why is unclear and there is no further information available.[21] One possible explanation, that would also seem to have been the case in Licheng (though manifested later) was that CCP mobilization in general raised expectations of women's involvement in public life to a level that the CCP was either unable or unwilling to meet. In Licheng, as will be discussed later, young, rich women felt excluded from the CCP and joined the Sixth Trigram Movement.

The new leadership of the experimental county adopted a narrow interpretation of revolutionary class status. Indeed, in the words of a later history of the Wuxiang CCP, in this party consolidation it 'overemphasized the importance of class status.'[22] In broad terms the aim of the party consolidation appears to have been to develop a substantial working-class basis for the Wuxiang CCP. In practical terms this meant denying ordinary CCP membership to anyone with any kind of property—not only landlords, and rich peasants, but also middle peasants—and encouraging mainly landless laborers, tenants and poor peasants, as well as artisans and industrial workers to a lesser extent. One celebrated party branch had 31 members: 17 poor peasants, 7 landless tenants and 7 farmhands. Its 6-person committee included 4 poor peasants and 2 landless tenants.[23] Cadres and members who came from landlord and rich peasant backgrounds were necessarily suspect in this process, but by no means always expelled, particularly if they could justify a change in their class status.

During May-July 1940, the Wuxiang CCP rejected the party membership of 554 people (about 10 percent) whom it regarded as unsuitable, or at least, no longer regarded as suitable. At the same time it accepted a large number of new members, possibly even more than were being rejected, who were either laborers of various kinds or very poor peasants. As already noted in Chapter 3, the Wuxiang CCP had gloried in its ability to have workers, shepherds, landless laborers, and farmhands elected in the elections of Red May. Certainly, there had been a growing though still small industrial working class in Wuxiang before the war. In the 1920s and 1930s several cotton spinning factories had been established, and hemp spinning and weaving was a well-established industry based on domestic outworking. A large paper company had started operations in 1925, and in 1937 just before the outbreak of war the county government had established its own large-scale iron works. A rural coal-mining industry was well-established in the east of the county, though the industry had been badly depressed during the 1930s because of the general economic decline in the region, falling prices, and oversupply. By 1937 there were already more than thirty large-scale enterprises who each employed more than fifty workers.[24] Whilst the local CCP recruited from and mobilized these industrial workers, the largest numbers of those now regarded as 'workers' for recruitment purposes were rural landless forced to labor to live, farmhands, and artisans.

As Table 7.1 indicates, details of the social composition of the Wuxiang CCP are not available for 1940. Clearly even allowing for the particular pattern of landholding in Wuxiang, the county CCP had already well before 1940 gone out of its way to recruit from the less privileged in society, and particularly those it regarded as various kinds of workers and laborers. Though there may well have been a limit in the county to the number of additional workers and laborers that the Wuxiang CCP could recruit, it continued to be exhorted to do better. By the end of the year, when the county leadership was again in trouble with the base area CCP leadership, it was once again being told that it had too few workers and not paying enough attention to their recruitment. He Yingcai at that time pointed out critically that there were more than 900 industrial workers in the county, but only 30 of them were members of the CCP.[25]

Compared to Wen Jianping's veiled threats and highly structured agenda when he assumed the leadership of the Wuxiang CCP in April, the formal report to the base area CCP committee toward the end of the party consolidation in July 1940 was considerably more circumspect.[26] In large part this change in enthusiasm probably reflected the increasing seriousness of the military situation as the Japanese pressed further into the county. However, the county party leadership had clearly found it more difficult than it had previously imagined to solve the problems that had emerged earlier in the year. It apparently remained difficult to stop peasants attacking landlords and rich peasants, party branches were proving remarkably resistant to the county leadership's attempt at reorganization, and the county level organization itself was experiencing its own problems. In retrospect a year later, Peng Tao, who was the member of the base area CCP committee supervising the Wuxiang Experimental CCP Committee, criticized its leadership for not having established an appropriate balance between its needs and popular demands.[27]

Once again, the problems faced by the Wuxiang CCP during the second half of 1940 are not immediately visible. However, the county party leadership's self-criticism, when it admitted defeat at the beginning of 1941,[28] and later comments from the leadership of the base area CCP committee, provide evidence of developments. The county party committee which had been reorganized in April in order to trial policies for rent and interest reduction, abandoned this task in July in favor of economic revival. However, it still continued to concentrate on the task of party restructuring with a vehemence that proved counterproductive. The CCP's organization in Wuxiang started to self-destruct, and at the same time the county party leadership apparently made little attempt to guide economic renewal.

By the middle of 1940 there was clearly an urgent need to implement a new policy toward landlords, rich peasants and even intellectuals. Economic production had been severally disrupted both by the course of the war, and by the political campaigns earlier in the year. In the county party leadership's own estimate there was not a single village (presumably in its area of jurisdiction) that had not experienced some form of political struggle during 1939 and 1940. Those landlords and rich peasants who had been persuaded back remained concerned for their safety and economic futures and needed reassuring. Intellectuals were similarly somewhat uncertain of their political standing.[29]

Despite earlier misgivings about middle peasants, they now appear to have been targeted as the benchmark for economic revival. It was argued that setting an appropriate tax burden for middle peasants and from that then calculating taxation for other social categories would reassure landlords and rich peasants. Middle peasants were also encouraged to become village level cadres, and were recruited in large numbers to the CCP, for the first time in the county since the start of the war. The precise figures for the second half of 1940 are not available, though as Table 7.1 indicates, by 1941 middle peasants represented almost 36 percent of the local CCP membership. The impact on the Peasant Association was even more dramatic. By 1941 there were more middle than poor peasants who were cadres of the Peasant Association in Wuxiang: 53 percent, whereas in the Taihang region as a whole only 48 percent of peasant association cadres were middle peasants.[30]

Whilst encouraging middle peasants, the county party leadership seems to have struggled with its own internal organizational problems. In its defense it claimed that the county party organization had no discipline, that cadres were unwilling to change or to work together. At the beginning of 1941 it was recommending closing some branches down altogether and sending most of the cadres off on training and political reeducation programs.[31] The base area CCP leadership later held the county party leadership, in contrast, to have been far too critical of the cadre force. In its view, the county party leadership had created an atmosphere of suspicion and blame in which upper and lower levels, and colleagues of the same rank were set against each other.[32]

It is also more than possible that the local cadres were reacting adversely to being disciplined so severely by a leadership so obviously marked as that of 'outsiders.' Many village and subdistrict cadres had little more than two years' membership of the CCP and were relatively inexperienced. They had little notion of CCP discipline and probably a restricted knowledge of the wider CCP organization. In addition, they were fiercely proud of the Wuxiang CCP's own revolutionary tradition before 1937. Some probably resented being told about a need to learn from the Jiangxi Soviet, and others were probably a little confused about that kind of reference.

In the villages the new middle peasant cadres rapidly came into conflict with the stalwarts of the CCP organization who had survived the party consolidation. In January 1941 the Wuxiang CCP leadership referred to this clash as one between two 'deviations': the 'ultra-left' deviation of the middle peasant cadres who were trying to prove their political credentials by being even more overenthusiastic in the pursuit of current policies, and the 'left' deviation of other (presumably poor peasant and landless laborer) cadres who were unwilling to have anything much to do with them.[33] Whilst the base area CCP leadership accepted that changed social policies and lack of political attention during the latter part of 1940 had allowed some land profiteering, and permitted 'unscrupulous elements' to join the CCP, it also held that these were soluble problems, particularly through the 'raising of middle peasant consciousness.'[34] In January the CCP committees of the base area and the base area's 3rd District (which was reponsible for Wuxiang) conducted an inquiry into the Wuxiang CCP Experimental County and its leadership and decided to reorganize once again, restoring the previous county party leadership into the bargain.

MIDDLE PEASANT CONCERNS

The restoration of a more locally based leadership appears to have had a considerable positive impact on the Wuxiang CCP, despite the difficulties of the military situation. Paradoxically, given the closure of the experimental county, 1941 saw the renewed trial implementation of rent and interest reduction in Wuxiang. However, at the same time the county leadership made some limited moves to attempt to reassure the rich, largely through the recently reformed electoral system at village, subdistrict and county levels.

Peng Tao encouraged the Wuxiang CCP in its attempts to introduce new forms of political contestation. He praised the Wuxiang CCP leadership for its implementation of the electoral system based on the 'Three-thirds' principle, and pointed out to them that 'The struggle for the realization of democratic politics is very complicated. It doesn't work if one tries to oppress, control and monopolise everything.'[35] All the same, the Wuxiang CCP was either not willing to surrender its control of positions, or not able to find suitable candidates to support the activity: at both subdistrict and county level just under half of those candidates elected were CCP members, instead of the quota of a third.[36]

All the same, rents were substantially reduced during the first six months of the year.[37] One noticeable innovation practiced in the county, and later adopted elsewhere in the Taihang region, was the method of calculation. Rent had usually been calculated in grain, measured in *dou*, a traditional measure equivalent to anywhere between 25 and 50 kilograms. The amount of the *dou* was standardized at 5 kilograms, and this new, reduced 'small *dou*' as it rapidly became known, was used to calculate rent, immediately cutting rents to at least one-fifth. Similarly, a start was made on debt clearances. County authorities estimated that the number of peasant households in debt had also been reduced by about a half, and in the process that all the available arable land was now being farmed. Previously one of the consequences of debt and default had been the growth of 'waste' or unfarmed land, as tenants and mortgagees had been forced to return land they could no longer pay for to either its owners or the holders of the collateral. These creditors were sometimes unable for various reasons to cultivate the land themselves and much lay idle.[38]

One result was that there was a more sustainable land redistribution than had occurred in early 1940: landlords sold, middle and poor peasants bought. The first half of 1941 saw 1,246 land transactions, with middle peasants buying 50 percent of the land being made available, and poor peasants 30 percent.[39] Another result was that peasants reduced the amount of time they spent in work for others for wages, and in the words of Liu Jianxun (a member of the CCP committee for the Taihang region) 'It is very difficult to get hired labour these days.' A third result was that whilst there were still some individuals classified as landlords for political reasons, the size of their landholdings were now quite small, often equivalent only to that of rich or middle peasants.[40]

These changes led to a considerable growth in the number of middle peasant households. Speaking at the base area 4th Organizational Work Conference in June 1941, Liu Jianxun cited one village in the county which had 20 middle peasant families before the war, but now had sixty-two. He also cited land sales in another village where 467 *mu* had been sold to thirteen middle peasants and sixteen poor peasants.[41] Moreover, this growth in the number of middle peasant households was reflected in the composition of the county party organization, and particularly in the growth of the number of cadres who were middle peasants in the villages. Table 7.1 provides full details of the county's CCP membership during 1941. Table 7.3 provides data on a smaller survey of the social composition of the members and cadres of CCP branches in six sub-districts.

Many of the middle peasants coming to positions of authority during 1941 were necessarily former poor peasants and landless laborers. As the opportunities came for them to acquire their own land, through purchase or government-organized redistribution, they had jumped at the chance. However, this upward mobility was not without its ability to create social tensions in a village, as indeed were other aspects of the 'middle peasant question.' Those who were middle peasants wanted to be rich peasants, and resented poor peasants trying to become middle peasants. Those who had been owner-cultivators, or rich peasants, and who were downwardly mobile resented the change. There was apparently a 1942 study of social change in Wuxiang which suggested that 'it was the middle peasant elements who were responsible for making trouble.'[42] Certainly it

Table 7.3 Social Composition of Members and Cadres of Party Branches in Six Subdistricts, Wuxiang CCP, 1942 (percentage of individuals)

Political category	Social category Farm-hands	Poor peasants	Middle peasants	Rich peasants	Other
Members	2.0	48.0	34.5	5.0	0.5
Cadres	2.3	40.0	50.0	3.0	4.5

Source: 'Shisanxian sanshijiuge zhibude chubu yanjiu' ['Preliminary Research on 39 Branches in 13 Counties'] 20 September 1942, in DJ pp.278–79.

would appear that the leadership of the Wuxiang CCP thought that way. In their description of both rural social tensions and difficulties with cadres within the CCP, they frequently returned to this problem.

Ma Guishu, who was secretary of the Wuxiang CCP during 1942–44, and had been Director of its Propaganda Department beforehand, had a completely negative view of middle peasants which he articulated forcefully at a base area CCP committee meeting in September 1943. Possibly his attitude was shaped by his experience of middle peasant behavior during the radical phase of 1939–40, in addition to any difficulties that might have emerged with the changed strategy in the county since the middle of 1940. He was prepared to accept that there were different kinds of middle peasants, but in his view they all posed substantial problems. He differentiated new middle peasants, old middle peasants, and new rich middle peasants, as well as separating out middle peasant youth for specific criticism.[43]

According to Ma Guishu those who were 'new' middle peasants now because they had been poor peasants were suspect because 'Their ascent was due to our policy rather than their labour.' Whilst he accepted that they had been exploited in the past, he now suspected both that they were perfectly willing to exploit others themselves, and that they were prone to speculative behavior. Because they were the 'new rich' and precisely because they were upwardly mobile, he considered them more susceptible to bribery and corruption from richer people, attracted by both the wealth and the association with higher social status. Those who were new middle peasants because they were bankrupted former middle peasants, rich peasants or landlords were certainly not to be considered politically reliable, in his view, because they held the current system responsible for their pauperization.

Ma Guishu's analysis of the 'old' middle peasants was no more sympathetic. In his interpretation those who had been middle peasants before the war were narrow-minded, status conscious and only out for themselves. Old middle peasants were authority conscious, and would make overtures equally to the rich or the CCP if they thought such alliances would benefit them personally. On top of everything, they were politically unreliable because they suspected that they were being discriminated against for their wealth. At the same time they were very hesitant to engage further in production for fear of becoming rich peasants and discriminated against further. Where old middle peasants had joined the CCP they were doubly suspect in Ma Guishu's view because they had only done so in order to raise their political status. Many of the old middle peasants were not only politically conscious in this way, but feeling that they should be afforded a high status were prone to engage in behind-the-scenes factionalism.

Rich middle peasants—that is, former middle peasants who had gained in economic wealth, landholding and laborer-hiring capacity—had started to emerge in Wuxiang in 1942. Ma's view of these rich middle peasants was predictably straightforward. He considered them selfish and incapable of 'proletarian awareness.' Ma Guishu singled out middle peasant youth as sharing all their parents' problems, but in addition considered their behavior even more reprehensible because they were work-shy but liked being in the limelight. In response to this last criticism Lai Ruoyu is recorded as having said "Middle peasant youth don't like work? Is that a characteristic of middle peasant youth or just all young people?'[44]

There was little doubt where Ma Guishu's political sympathies lay. He suggested that party branches where middle peasants dominated were more liable to be influenced by the rich and powerful. In contrast, in his view party branches dominated by poor peasants and workers 'would have better and close ties with the masses.' He argued that middle peasants could and should be part of the new politics, but only provided that they were led by poor peasants and workers. He proposed that middle peasants should be restricted to half the total membership in any one branch, and that only under rare circumstances should they be allowed to lead party branches. However, even in Wuxiang, Ma was fighting an uphill battle. By March 1943, as Table 7.4 demonstrates, village government in Wuxiang was considerably more dominated by middle peasants, and the rather wealthier, than by poor peasants and landless tenants.

Similarly, by Ma Guishu's calculation in September 1943, old middle peasants dominated 35 percent of the county's CCP branches; poor peasants dominated 34 percent; and new middle peasants (who had been poor peasants) dominated 6 percent.[45]

Table 7.4 Social Composition of Candidates Elected to Village Governments, Wuxiang, March 1943 (percentage of individuals)

Landless tenants	7.0
Poor peasants	28.1
Middle peasants	43.0
Rich peasants	15.4
Landlords	6.5

Source: KZW p.24.

A central part of the middle peasant strategy, and one observed in Liaoxian (Zuoquan) in Chapter 6, was that the middle peasants were expected to lead the poor peasants and landless laborers. This too was clearly not Ma Guishu's preference. On the contrary he argued the opposite: that middle peasants should be remolded politically by those with proletarian consciousness—the poor peasants and rural laborers. Ma was very clear about the relative merits of laborers and peasants as far as the social basis of politics went: 'Labourers are firm in any political struggle, while peasants have worries and are less easily organized because they have to care for their families.'[46] Perhaps too this difference in Wuxiang was because here it had proved possible to mobilize laborers and poor peasants more effectively from the early part of the war. Certainly there were villages, such as Xialiang, where workers were leading the Peasants Association.[47]

Ma Guishu's analysis though fairly strident was not totally unbalanced. He recognized the need to encourage middle peasants, not least for economic reasons. He also argued that middle peasants, and rich peasants too for that matter, should be made to feel more economically and politically secure so that their production would increase. He particularly criticized the influence of 'leftist' problems in Wuxiang which had left many rich and middle peasants feeling they would be punished if they became wealthier.[48] Moreover, during 1940–45 at least he was one of those who consistently advocated more open but regulated political conflict. In his own words: 'A democratic struggle is a struggle to reason things out.'[49]

Ma Guishu's views on the 'middle peasant question' were not unique in the Wuxiang CCP. An investigation of Wuxiang party branches in 1943 reported that upwardly mobile new middle peasants soon began exploiting others, and that established middle peasant cadres were more interested in the pursuit of privilege. It detected a dominant ideology in

Wuxiang party branches where middle peasants led local organizations characterized by individuals 'scrambling for leadership, status and fame.'[50] One of Ma's colleagues from within the Wuxiang CCP accused middle peasants of lacking a democratic work style: only being prepared to give orders, not to listen.[51] Another highlighted the difficulty of getting middle peasants into the production-oriented campaign to organize mutual-aid teams and suggested that if they would not participate they should be treated politically as if they were rich peasants.[52]

CLASS CHANGE

A key issue highlighted by the comments of Ma Guishu was that by late 1943 and moving into 1944, it had become necessary to manage rural class conflict in a more sophisticated way. Social tensions were never far below the surface and despite all attempts to ensure otherwise, in the 1942 rent and interest reduction campaign in Wuxiang, there were once again examples of struggle meetings becoming unruly and leading to excess.[53] As Table 7.1 indicates, middle peasants and poor peasants were coming to dominate the local CCP, if in different proportions to elsewhere in the Taihang Base Area. However, from the point of view of the CCP's ability to work with individuals it was becoming as important to know their past background, as well as their current socioeconomic status.

The extent of social tensions showed clearly in a survey of different types of peasants in Wuxiang undertaken during 1943.[54] It identified five different kinds of peasant: rich peasants, middle peasants, landless tenant peasants, landless peasants, and farmhands, and was based on a survey of 500 people.

According to the survey, rich peasants had land and property; could marry early (thirteen years old is cited); had savings to tide them through natural disasters; and could lend money, hire labor and engage in commercial activities. They resented high tax rates and the dislocations of the war, but they were also resentful of poor peasants demanding rent and interest reductions. The middle peasants interviewed did not generally need to either rent land or work for others. They wanted either to become rich or to be treated as though they were rich peasants. They tended to explain their position in life in terms of fate, and were said to be more than somewhat fearful of change. They resented the upwardly mobile poor peasants and landless tenants and accused them of being economically dependent on landlords. They also regarded landless tenants and farmhands as aggressive and excessive in politics; and criticized the latter in particular for their 'indecent lifestyle.'

The tenant peasants interviewed were found to rent the land they worked from landowners, but to have their own livestock and tools. They were able to get married. They usually needed to borrow money, often from the middle peasants, with whom they came to have an ambivalent relationship. They were found to have low expectations of life and seemed happy enough if they could provide enough food for themselves and their families without having to beg. The landless peasants interviewed were somewhat similar, only poorer. They did not own their own tools and livestock, leased but small plots and usually had to work for others as well as tilling their own land. They resented the relatively wealthy even more markedly than the tenant peasants. The farmhands in the survey had no home or family, and were too poor to afford medicine. Their only goal in life was to establish a home and to get married.

In 1942 Wuxiang had been designated as a model for 'advanced' areas in the rent and interest reduction campaign in recognition of both its potential for local mobilization and its past experience with the implementation of the CCP's land policy. Few details of the 1942 campaign are available for the county as a whole, though by the end it was reported that the landholdings of those designated as landlords had been reduced by 35 percent.[55] By 1945 it was reported that the landholdings of landlords had been reduced by a further 50 percent.[56] As Table 7.2 indicates, the rent and interest reduction campaigns of 1942, and then of 1944–45 resulted in a much less concentrated land distribution in Wuxiang. In a real sense, Wuxiang's intense land concentration before the war had made the task slightly easier for the CCP by ensuring, even without the extreme politics of 1939–40, that there was land that would be confiscatable and which could then be redistributed to poor peasants and landless tenants. Landlords who had left at the start of the war or who had sided with the Japanese authorities, or who were thought to be sympathetic to the Japanese regime, lost their land in this way during 1944–45. It is claimed that by 1945 one-third of all poor peasants and farmhands in the county had become middle peasants.[57]

Increasingly, however, the social categories of the CCP's analysis were becoming attenuated. A new approach was required both to mediate social tension and to answer the concerns of cadres about the revolutionary status of the middle peasant. As indicated in Chapter 5, when introducing the middle peasant strategy during the middle of 1942, Xu Zirong had suggested that an individual's class status could change. It would then be possible, and sometimes perhaps desirable to assess an individual's past class status in addition to their current class status. In a sense this was a response to objections to the middle peasant strategy, designed to convince doubters within the party about the revolutionary potential of

Table 7.5 Social Composition of Model Workers, as of 1937 and 1944 (number of model workers, 1944)

Year	Social category: Farm-hand	Shepherd	Tenant peasant	Poor peasant	Middle peasant	Rich peasant	Trader
1937	37	2	12	95	66	5	1
1944	1		2	41	166	7	1

Source: Lai Ruoyu 'Shengchan yundongde chubu zongjie' ['Preliminary Summary on the Production Movement'] August 1944, in QY p.210.

the middle peasant. The experience of someone who had been a poor peasant or landless tenant but who was now a middle peasant tended to undermine both the 'theory of the unique influence of class status' as well as some of the other objections to the middle peasant strategy.

Wuxiang CCP was a major proponent of the 1944 production campaign—known as the Great Production Campaign—a major mobilization attempt to overcome the economic problems the base area faced, and based on the organization of mutual-aid teams. It produced two of its own model worker heroes whose experiences were widely publicized throughout the base area—Wang Haicheng and Li Mabao.[58] The campaign climaxed with awards for those who had become model workers. Lai Ruoyu took the opportunity to demonstrate one message of the middle peasant strategy. He explained that Wuxiang's 218 model workers of 1944 might now seem to be predominantly middle peasants, but their roots were substantially to be found amongst poor peasants and landless laborers. Table 7.5 presents information about the class status of Wuxiang's 218 model workers in 1944 as of 1937, as well as in 1944.

Statistically questionable as it may be, Lai Ruoyu's point was that the revolution and the CCP's future was safe in the hands of middle peasants and upwardly mobile poor peasants and farmhands.[59]

HANBI VILLAGE

A vignette of the process of social change in Wuxiang during the War of Resistance is provided by the experience of Hanbi Village, in the mountain area of eastern Wuxiang.[60] Hanbi Village was right at the center of the CCP-controlled area, and was close to villages where the Eighth Route

Army located its headquarters operations in 1939. It was a fairly large village even in 1937, with 776 people in 207 households. Of these, Hanbi had a larger proportion of middle peasants than was normal in Wuxiang: some 45 percent of households owning 22 percent of land. Poor peasants accounted for 35 percent households and owned 22 percent of land.[61]

Hanbi Village had a high level of land concentration. There were six landlords who owned 44 percent of the village's land. However, the largest of these—Wei Xiaoshan—dominated, owning 41 percent of the land of the village. His landholdings had grown during the 1920s and 1930s as a result of land purchases, as well as transfers resulting from defaulting loans and debts. The Wei Family rented out 40 percent of the land of the village to its inhabitants.

Hanbi Village also had twenty-four rich peasant households in 1937. However, their average landholding were not much greater than those of the middle peasants: 10 *mu* compared to 7.2 *mu*. Of these 24 rich peasant families, 19 were headed by individuals who were still members of the Peasants Association at the end of the war, and at least 5 were leading members of the CCP in the village. Of the six landlords, two were executed in 1943, two disposed of their property and joined the CCP at an early stage, and the other two joined the Peasants Association.

The Eighth Route Army first arrived here at the end of 1937 on a recruiting exercise. A Peasant Association was established and its first leader was Wang Haicheng, who was to become a model worker in 1944. In the short-term little changed in the village. However, in 1939 a factory worker, Bai Houru, was elected village head. Wei Xiaoshan objected strongly and tried to force Bai to stand down, but he was protected by the Peasant Association which organized a twenty-person bodyguard. At the same time about 300 people marched to the district offices of the county government and presented a petition of complaint against Wei, which was upheld.

The rent and interest reduction campaign started at the end of 1939 with two of the village's landlords surrendering the lands they had previously rented out. With the escalation of the campaign, Wei Xiaoshan left the village temporarily at the beginning of 1940. The surrendered land, referred to as 'enlightened land' because it was said to have come from 'enlightened' landlords, was redistributed to landless laborers in the village.

Wei Xiaoshan returned later in 1940, but relations were not good between his family and the Peasant Association during that year and the next. In 1942 the Peasant Association stepped up the attack on the Wei Family. There was a series of struggle meetings over forty days that first prepared the case against the Wei Family landlords and then proceeded to attack Wei Xiaoshan, Wei Wenlai and Wei Jing.[62] Wei Wenlai was chosen as the most vulnerable first target.

On the day before the campaign went public, Wei Wenlai was asked about his possible reactions. At that stage he agreed to cancel debts and surrender his rights to rented land. At the struggle meeting the next day he kept to his word. He apologized for his past transgressions and surrendered both some of his savings and most of his rented land. Whilst he was greeted as an 'enlightened' landlord, the struggle process continued, and a series of peasants aired their complaints about his behavior to the public meeting.

The target of the struggle meetings then turned to Wei Xiaoshan, but with less success. He was much more obdurate, refusing at first to cancel any tenancy agreements at all. As the meetings became stormier he finally agreed to surrender about 15 percent of the village's total land. At that point the Peasant Association turned the spotlight off tenancy agreements and on to tax, demanding to know why Wei Xiaoshan was not providing any public grain. Wei claimed not to have any grain and procrastinated. However, a group of eighty from the Peasant Association eventually stormed his granary and confiscated 70 *dan* of grain.

The result of the 1942 rent and interest reduction campaign in Hanbi Village was that through land and property transfers 29 poor peasant households became middle peasants, 8 households of landless tenants became poor peasants, as did 3 worker households. The amount of land in the village owned by landlords and rich peasants together decreased to 47 percent of the total; and middle peasant landholdings increased to 38 percent. By this stage the Peasant Association had 67 members: 31 poor peasants, 27 middle peasants, 9 rich peasants and 2 landlords. The village's party branch had 20 members: 11 poor peasants, 5 rich peasants, and 4 middle peasants. It was led by a 6-person committee, 3 of whom were rich peasants.

In 1943 the Peasant Association finally settled accounts with Wei Xiaoshan. He and Wei Jing were accused of having organized a 'New People's Society' in opposition to the village government, and of not having disclosed all the family's property and land during the previous year's rent and interest reduction campaign. Both were tried and executed.

During 1944 Hanbi Village was active during the nearby siege of Panlong; and as part of the Great Production Campaign became an 'advanced model village' for its organization of mutual-aid teams. Thirty-two new middle peasants participated in these teams, as did 46 poor peasants, 77 middle peasants and 18 rich peasants. At the same time, most of the land confiscated from the Wei Family, amounting to 28 percent of the total village land, was redistributed to the villagers. The remaining 10 percent of the land which had previously belonged to Wei Xiaoshan was donated to thirteen families of demobilized soldiers who had settled in the village.[63]

By the end of the war there were only two landlord households left in the village, though now reduced to only 10 *mu* of land each. Farmhands had completely disappeared in the village as a social category; and forty-three households of formerly poor peasants had become new middle peasants.

SOCIAL CHANGE IN WUXIANG

Wuxiang's process of social change was different in a number of ways from that which occurred in Liaoxian, though it too was inherently incremental. The Wuxiang CCP built the broad appeal that brought it to power in 1939 on a program of social reform, and was an early experimenter with campaigns of rent and interest reduction. Its encouragement of rural class conflict at the end of 1939 and beginning of 1940 led to severe dislocation, criticism from the base area CCP and the reorganization of the county CCP leadership.

However, in the aftermath of reactions to these events the Wuxiang CCP also discovered the usefulness of the middle peasant as catalyst of social change and continued economic growth. By 1945 Wuxiang had become an exclusively peasant small-holder economy with almost no landlords or rich peasants. While the Wuxiang CCP was willing to embrace the middle peasant as the appropriate standard for social equalization, it was considerably more hesitant on political grounds about the promotion of middle peasants as village leaders.

The success of Wuxiang's drive for social reform is largely attributable to its specific socioeconomic conditions, which were unusual for the Taihang Base Area. In Wuxiang, agricultural commercialization before the war not only led to peasant pauperization, but also a readily apparent class conflict that the CCP could exploit, especially given the scale of land concentration that developed in the county. Absentee landlords and landlords siding with the invading Japanese forces provided large amounts of confiscated land for redistribution. This not only eased the CCP's ability to implement programs of social reform more generally, but also ensured the development of a significant social base of support.

NOTES

1. Minutes of the Conference on Party Branches in Advanced Areas, 29 July 1942, in XZJY p.3.
2. Lai Ruoyu provided details in his comments to Taihang Sixth Organizational Work Conference, 1 March 1945, in SOC p.30.

3. WX pp.667–688.
4. Xu Zirong 'Guanyu bage xiande zhibu gongzuo' ['Work on Party Branches in Eight Counties'] 30 August 1942, in DJ p.238.
5. Comments by Ji Xijian, in 'Taihang laoqu tugai qianhou nongcun jingji biange kaocha zuotanhui fayan gangyao' ['Outline of Discussion Meeting on the Investigation of Rural Economic Change in the Taihang Areas of the Revolution before and after Land Reform'] 7 July 1983, in TW p.437.
6. Zhonggong JinJiYu qudangwei 'Zuzhibu gei Beifangjude gongzuo baogao' ['Organization Department Report to North China Bureau'] August 1940, in *Shanxi geming genjudi* [Shanxi Revolutionary Base Areas] no.1, 1989, p.3; and in TDZH vol.3: 1940, p.544.
7. Liu Jiansheng *Shanxi jindai jingjishi* [Modern Shanxi's Economic History] Taiyuan, Shanxi jingji chubanshe, 1997, p.835.
8. TW pp.86–88.
9. Huang Yuan 'Jindongnande poqie jianzu jianxi wenti' ['The Urgent Issue of Reducing Rent and Interest in Southeast Shanxi'] March 1940, in TDZH vol.3:1940, pp.121–24.
10. Huang Yuan 'Jindongnande poqie jianzu jianxi wenti' ['The Urgent Issue of Reducing Rent and Interest in Southeast Shanxi'] March 1940, in TDZH vol.3: 1940, p.125.
11. 'Wuxiang nongmin gejieceng shenghuo tedian jiqi ganbu shengzhangde diaocha' ['Survey of Various Categories of Peasants in Wuxiang and Their Characteristics'] July 1943, in CJZX vol.2, p.1398.
12. See, for example, the cases of two landlords cited in Wei Xiaoquan 'Hanbicun tudi wentide dianxing diaocha—shinian douzheng fanxiushen' ['Investigation of a Case Study of the Land Question in a Village in Hanbi—Ten Years of Struggle and Transformation'] April 1947, in WX p.879.
13. WOH p.22.
14. See, for example, the comments by Chi Biqing, Chair of the Taihang Peasants Association, in Chi Biqing 'Tan Taihang qunzhong yundong' ['Mass Mobilization in the Taihang'] 22 July 1986, in QY p.266.
15. Wen Jianping (Jian Ping) 'Wuxiang shiyanxian shouci huodong fenzi dongyuan dahui zongjie' ['Summary of the Conference of Advanced Activists in Mobilization in Wuxiang Experimental County'] 25 April 1940, in TDZH vol.3: 1940, p.260. Detail of the past leadership's misunderstanding of the revolutionary situation is provided on p.266.
16. Peng Tao 'Sanfenqu qunzhong yundongde yiban gaikuang yu jingyan jiaoxun' 10 March 1942 ['The circumstances of the masses movement in the Third District and the lessons to be learnt'] in Zhonggong Taihang qudangwei *Taihang gefenqu tangde wenjian xuanbian* [Selected Party Documents of Districts in the Taihang] Huabei Xinhuashudian, 1944, vol.3: 1942, p.130.
17. Wen Jianping (Jian Ping) 'Wuxiang shiyanxian shouci huodong fenzi dongyuan dahui zongjie' ['Summary of the Conference of Advanced Activists in Mobilization in Wuxiang Experimental County'] 25 April 1940, in TDZH vol.3: 1940, p.260. Detail of the past leadership's misunderstanding of the revolutionary situation is provided on p.263. See also: JinJiYuqu nongjiu zonghui 'JinJiYuqu nongjiu zonghui liangnianlai gongzuo cailiao' ['Materials on the work of the

Shanxi-Hebei-Henan region peasants' association during the last two years'] June 1941, in TDZH vol.4: 1941, p.387.

18. Wen Jianping (Jian Ping) 'Wuxiang shiyanxian shouci huodong fenzi dongyuan dahui zongjie' ['Summary of the Conference of Advanced Activists in Mobilization in Wuxiang Experimental County'] 25 April 1940, in TDZH vol.3: 1940, p.270.

19. Tian Youru 'Shanxi tudi zhidu gaige lishi gaiyao' ['Outline History of Reform of the Land System in Shanxi'] in *Shanxi dangshi tongxun* [Bulletin of Shanxi Party History] no.2, 1993, pp.20–21.

20. Wen Jianping (Jian Ping) 'Wuxiang shiyanxian shouci huodong fenzi dongyuan dahui zongjie' ['Summary of the Conference of Advanced Activists in Mobilization in Wuxiang Experimental County'] 25 April 1940, in TDZH vol.3: 1940, p.260.

21. Wen Jianping (Jian Ping) 'Wuxiang shiyanxian shouci huodong fenzi dongyuan dahui zongjie' ['Summary of the Conference of Advanced Activists in Mobilization in Wuxiang Experimental County'] 25 April 1940, in TDZH vol.3: 1940, p.272.

22. IHW p.67.

23. He Yingcai 'JinJiYu bianqu gonggu dangde jige wenti' ['Several Issues in the Consolidation of the Party in the Shanxi-Hebei-Henan Border Area'] 6 December 1940, in TDZH vol.3: 1940, p.802.

24. 'Wuxiang xian' ['Wuxiang County'] in Xu Guosheng and Chen Ninghua (ed) *Shanxi xian qu jingji fazhan shilue* [Historical outline of the economic development of counties and regions in Shanxi] Taiyuan, Shanxi jingji chubanshe, 1992, p.256.

25. He Yingcai 'JinJiYu bianqu gonggu dangde jige wenti' ['Several Issues in the Consolidation of the Party in the Shanxi-Hebei-Henan Border Area'] 6 December 1940, in TDZH vol.3: 1940, p.801.

26. Zhonggong JinJiYu qudangwei 'Guanyu Wuxiang gongzuode yijian' ['Opinions on Wuxiang's Work'] July 1940, in TDZH vol.3: 1940, p.509.

27. Peng Tao 'Yinian zhuanbian Wuxiang gongzuode jinyan jiaoxun' ['Work Experience Transforms Wuxiang in a Year'] May 1941, in TDZH vol.4: 1941, p.342.

28. Zhonggong JinJiYu qudangwei 'Wuxiang shiyanxian gongzuode jiantao yu zhuanbian fangxiang' ['A Self-criticism of Wuxiang Experimental County's Work and its Change of Direction'] 7 January 1941, in TDZH vol.4:1941, p.9.

29. Peng Tao 'JinJiYu qude xinxingshi yu xinrenwu' ['New circumstances and new tasks in the Shanxi-Hebei-Henan area'] 27 June 1941, in TDZH vol.4: 1941, p.479.

30. JinJiYuqu nongjiu zonghui 'JinJiYuqu nongjiu zonghui liangnianlai gongzuo cailiao' ['Materials on the work of the Shanxi-Hebei-Henan region peasants' association during the last two years'] June 1941, in TDZH vol.4: 1941, p.462.

31. Zhonggong JinJiYu qudangwei 'Wuxiang shiyanxian gongzuode jiantao yu zhuanbian fangxiang' ['A Self-criticism of Wuxiang Experimental County's Work and Its Change of Direction'] 7 January 1941, in TDZH vol.4: 1941, p.10.

32. Peng Tao 'Yinian zhuanbian Wuxiang gongzuode jinyan jiaoxun' ['Work Experience Transforms Wuxiang in a Year'] May 1941, in TDZH vol.4:1941, p.343.

33. Zhonggong JinJiYu qudangwei 'Wuxiang shiyanxian gongzuode jiantao yu zhuanbian fangxiang' ['A Self-criticism of Wuxiang Experimental County's Work and its Change of Direction'] 7 January 1941, in TDZH vol.4: 1941, p.9.

34. Peng Tao 'Yinian zhuanbian Wuxiang gongzuode jinyan jiaoxun' ['Work Experience Transforms Wuxiang in a Year'] May 1941, in TDZH vol.4: 1941, p.343.

35. Comments on 27 June 1941, in FOC p.17.

36. At subdistrict level in Wuxiang, twenty-four out of forty-nine elected candidates were CCP members; at the county level, fourteen out of sixteen. Zhonggong JinJiYu qudangwei 'Qu xian cun "sansanzhi" qingkuang tongjibiao' ['Table of the "Three-thirds system" in Counties, Sub-districts and Villages'] 1941, in TDZH vol.4: 1941, p.990.

37. JinJiYuqu nongjiu zonghui 'JinJiYuqu nongjiu zonghui liangnianlai gongzuo cailiao' ['Materials on the work of the Shanxi-Hebei-Henan region peasants' association during the last two years'] June 1941, in TDZH vol.4: 1941, p.411.

38. Comments by Liu Jianxun on 30 June 1941, in FOC p.58.

39. Comments by Liu Jianxun on 30 June 1941, in FOC p.56.

40. Comments on 30 June 1941, in FOC p.58.

41. Comments on 30 June 1941, in FOC p.56.

42. According to Lai Ruoyu, in his summary report to the 6th Organizational Work Conference of the Taihang Base Area on 1 March 1945, in SOC p.38.

43. ZJY pp.6–8.

44. ZJY p.21.

45. ZJY p.7.

46. ZJY p.32.

47. Sympathetic comments by Lai Ruoyu who agreed that workers had the best chance of uniting all classes, in ZJY p.32.

48. ZJY p.82.

49. Comments on 30 June 1941, in FOC p.60.

50. Comments by Guo Zhong, in ZJY p.53.

51. Comments by Li Wuzi, in ZJY p.61.

52. ZJY p.27.

53. Comments by Ji Xijian, in 'Taihang laoqu tugai qianhou nongcun jingji biange kaocha zuotanhui fayan gangyao"['Outline of Discussion Meeting on the Investigation of Rural Economic Change in the Taihang Areas of the Revolution before and after Land Reform'] 7 July 1983, in TW pp.438–39.

54. 'Wuxiang nongmin gejieceng shenghuo tedian jiqi ganbu shengzhangde diaocha' ['Survey of Various Categories of Peasants in Wuxiang and their Characteristics'] July 1943, in CJZX vol.2, p.1395 ff.

55. IHW p.81.

56. TSJD2 p.1431.

57. IHW p.147.

58. Ma Guishu 'Wuxiang dashengchanzhong lingdao yu qongzhong jiehede jingyan' ['The Experience of Unity between Masses and Leadership in Wuxiang during the Great Production Campaign'] in WX p.870 ff.

59. Lai Ruoyu 'Shengchan yundongde chubu zongjie' ['Preliminary Summary on the Production Movement'] August 1944, in QY p.209 ff.

60. Based on a history of Hanbi Village prepared in 1947, and supplemented by additional documentary and oral information. Wei Xiaoquan 'Hanbicun tudi wentide dianxing diaocha—shinian douzheng fanxiushen' ['Investigative Case Study of the Land Question in Hanbi Village—Ten Years of Struggle and Transformation'] April 1947, in WX p.876 ff.

61. Despite these statistics poor peasants were considerably poorer than middle peasants in Hanbi: their households had roughly twice as many people.

62. An account of the 1942 events in Hanbi may also be found in 'Jianzu jianxi zhongde dianxing nongcun' ['Case Studies of Rent and Interest Reduction'] 1943, reprinted in Zhonggong Taihang qudangwei *Taihang dang shiliao biancun* [Collection of Historical Party Materials on Taihang] Huabei Xinhua shudian, 1944, vol.1, p.397.

63. IHW p.148.

8

Licheng: Resistance and Rebellion

Licheng's socioeconomic environment at the start of the War of Resistance had been different from that of both Liaoxian and Wuxiang. The county had no heavy industry and few commercial enterprises, but, as outlined in Chapter 4, was wealthier and had higher levels of education. Equally, after the Licheng CCP established its political order in January 1940 the county's experience was markedly different. Licheng achieved relative military security at the same time and this facilitated its implementation of programs of social reform. However, particularly by comparison with Wuxiang and Liaoxian, the Licheng CCP encountered more and more serious problems both within its own organization and with some sectors of the local population as a result of those attempts to bring social reform.

The most obvious explanation of that paradox was the lack of a sense of organizational continuity in the Licheng CCP, unlike the experience of county party organizations in Wuxiang and Liaoxian. Before 1940, the Licheng CCP had been dominated by teachers and intellectuals from the earlier Returned Students Federation, and had operated as part of the Sacrifice League. In 1940 it not only severed this relationship with the Sacrifice League, it also expelled the vast majority of its members, especially those who were teachers and intellectuals. The Licheng CCP's seizure of power in early 1940, and the policies that accompanied that change, seriously alienated some politically active and articulate sectors of the local population, well beyond the membership of the former Returned Students Federation.

In addition, the Licheng CCP's break with the past in January 1940 also denied the local party the benefit of a trained cadre force for its future reform program. Indeed, in many respects the lack of a reliable group of cadres probably caused the Licheng CCP more problems than the Sixth Trigram Movement's attempted seizure of power in October 1941, or any of the other various armed conflicts that emerged in reaction to social reform during 1941–43. The 1940 and subsequent restructuring of the cadre force at county and subdistrict levels denied the party organization the benefit of local intelligence and some ability to manage these and other adverse reactions. Moreover, it also encouraged village cadres to rely more on their relationships with local landowners than the county party organization, and to establish mutually supportive networks for protection against the encroachments of the developing party-state.

A NEW REGIME

Those who had formed Licheng's initial resistance government and staffed both the Sacrifice League and local CCP on their establishment were largely teachers. Most were natives of the county but all had trained and lived for some time in the larger cities of Shanxi and North China. The successor membership of the CCP after 1939 was clearly different. Although a few, perhaps as many as a dozen, of the earlier intellectuals in the Returned Students Federation and the Sacrifice League, were not expelled, the local party organization was now overwhelmingly comprised of poor and middle peasants and a new leadership for the county was appointed by the base area CCP committee.

Detailed figures are not available for the membership of the Licheng CCP, or its social composition before 1942. Table 8.1 provides information on the social composition of the Licheng CCP during 1942–45. To provide comparative data, the figures for Licheng and North Licheng counties during 1944–45 have been combined. Compared to the situation before 1940 it is clear that there had been significant changes by 1942, with no intellectual members listed, and much less than a fifth (as reported in 1940) who were farmhands.

A clearer and more immediate guide to the changing trends in the social composition of the Licheng CCP is provided by information about the cadre force during 1940. By the middle of 1940 there were still five members of the county-level leadership in Licheng regarded as intellectuals, though one was designated that way because he came from a landlord background and only two were educated beyond the primary level. At the subdistrict level, only four out of twenty cadres were regarded as intellectuals: fifteen were poor peasants, middle peasants or tenant farmers.

Table 8.1 Social Composition of Licheng CCP, 1942–1945 (percentage of individual members)

Year	Social category Farm-hand	Artisan	Poor peasant	Middle peasant	Rich peasant	Intellectual	Other
1942	2.9	0.9	42.3	49.4	4.6		0.4
1943	4.5		34.7	55.9	4.4	0.5	
1944	3.3	0.7	35.6	56.3	3.4	0.5	0.2
1945	1.6	1.3	36.0	58.8	2.9	0.5	0.2

Source: LOH pp.56–57. Data for North Licheng and Licheng are combined for 1944 and 1945.

Perhaps even more indicative of change, at the county-level only one of Licheng's leading cadres had been a CCP member longer than two years, and all were under twenty-five years old.[1]

At the start of 1940 the new Licheng resistance government made few concessions to its opponents amongst the landlords and rich peasants, or the former supporters of the Sacrifice League. Almost its first task was to launch a political campaign to encourage a more equitable share of the tax burden. As part of that process it approached landlords and rich peasants and asked for donations of grain, seed, farm tools and livestock to both help the war effort and the poor who were suffering because of the war. A contemporary report (from May 1940) frankly admitted that some of these donations in Licheng had been extracted forcibly by cadres.[2]

In addition, the resistance government started redistributing some of the land which it had at its disposal, or could bring under its jurisdiction, to poor peasants and tenant farmers. This included land which had been illegally enclosed by landowners, or not registered, as well as land belonging to village associations. Licheng's specific practices in this regard were similarly almost immediately criticized by the base area leadership. However, the redistributed land also included a number of different categories of land which unreservedly belonged to landowners and which exercised the base area leadership even more vigorously.[3]

There was land which was lying fallow because it had previously been sold or leased to peasants by landowners but then reclaimed by the latter once the rent or loan repayments were not maintained. There was also the land of absentee landlords which the CCP was committed to farming, but not to confiscating and redistributing. Confiscation was only permitted if a landowner was a known traitor, specifically if they had sided with the Japanese. Apparently, according to the base area's criticism, in Licheng 'labels such as "spy" or "stubborn element" have been used to scare people away so as to confiscate their land.'[4] It is not clear how the land of the former county establishment supporters of Tian Jijiao who had mounted armed resistance to the Sacrifice League-led government in 1938 was categorized in these terms. However, in its criticisms of the Licheng CCP the base area CCP committee confirmed that their land had been confiscated and redistributed at this time.[5]

A 1940 survey of a single village in Licheng charted the resulting changes in landownership as a result of this campaign. Its process is summarized in Table 8.2, which provides information of the source and recipients of the redistributed land.

Table 8.2 highlights the contemporary emphasis on assisting poor peasants and tenants, as well as the extent of land confiscations from those who were politically suspect. Even allowing that the village under survey was almost certainly far from the average in any sense, the amount of land involved is substantial for a single village. These were precisely the kind of measures which elsewhere in the Taihang Base Area at this time, nota-

Table 8.2 Land Redistribution in Licheng, 1940 (number of households, percentage and amount of land redistributed, in one village)

	Number of households	Percentage of land	Land in *mu*
Source of redistributed land			
Traitors			616
People with no offspring			22.9
Village Association			10
Recipient of redistributed land			
Landless poor becoming poor peasant	14	35	
Poor peasant	15	36	
Landless poor becoming middle peasant	10	23	

Source: TW p.113.

bly Xingtai and Shahe, were causing not only landlords and rich peasants but also middle peasants to pack up and leave. The impact in Licheng, as elsewhere, was to worsen the economic situation as production faltered and inflation came to the county for the first time since the outbreak of war. During 1940 in Licheng, the price for rice increased almost three times, the price of cotton increased almost four times, and the price of cloth increased ninefold.[6]

The warnings from the base area CCP committee certainly made the Licheng CCP a little more circumspect in the manner of its activities but did not generally alter the direction of policies during the remainder of 1940 and into 1941. In particular it attempted to assist middle and poor peasants to position themselves more effectively economically and politically through debt clearances and the introduction of village elections. In both cases these attempts at social reform were to alienate certain sections of the local society still further, and whilst it led some to either leave the county altogether or just not participate further in wider political activities, it also drove others to attempt a more radical form of resistance.

As already noted, Licheng had a large middle peasantry and a low degree of land concentration. In 1937 the average landlord household in the county had about 60 *mu* of land,[7] which was about a third of the average for the Taihang region as a whole.[8] Most rural households owned some land, and though rents could create conflicts, the bigger problem was debt. Many poor and middle peasant households were in debt locally to landlords, rich peasants and other middle peasants, and had been for some time. The regular practice was that landholdings were used as collateral, and debt could and often did result in their loss. Table 8.3 provides

Table 8.3 Social Composition of Debt and Loans, Licheng, 1941 (percentage of debtors and creditors)

Social category	Debtors	Creditors
Landlord		29
Rich peasant	4	38
Middle peasant	20	26
Poor peasant	75	7
Farmhand	1	

Source: JinJiYuqu nongjiu zonghui 'JinJiYuqu nongjiu zonghui liangnianlai gongzuo cailiao' ['Materials on the work of the Shanxi-Hebei-Henan region peasants' association during the last two years'] June 1941, in TDZH vol.4: 1941, p.414.

information of the social composition of debtors and creditors in Licheng during 1941 based on a survey of four subdistricts.

The role of the rich peasant as a major lender at village level is clearly demonstrated in Table 8.3, and probably explains some of the more intense antagonism felt in Licheng toward rich peasants, as opposed to landlords as a class. As elsewhere in the Taihang Base Area, the attempt to introduce social reform through a new policy on land usage first concentrated on clearing debts in unpaid interest that had previously accumulated, and reclaiming land that was not being farmed. Again, as elsewhere, the actual mobilization of the peasants for large, public meetings where debts and land usage were discussed was not organized by the CCP itself, but through the newly organized Peasants Association.

The antagonism toward middle peasants from both the county party organization and poor peasants that was so noticeable in Wuxiang was certainly not visible in Licheng, perhaps because of the different pattern of landholding. In Licheng the membership and the leadership of the Peasants Association were increasingly dominated by poor and middle peasants, as was the local party organization itself. During the first half of 1941, 38 percent of representatives to the Licheng Peasants Association were middle peasants, and 36 percent were poor peasants; 40 percent of its committee were middle peasants and 36 percent poor peasants; and 53 percent of its cadres were middle peasants, and 41 percent poor peasants.[9]

The Licheng Peasants Association attempted to resolve some of the debt and land problems facing its members during the spring ploughing period at the beginning of 1941. The principles it adopted were precisely those of the base area: if the interest was twice the principal then the debtor could ask for the debt to be cleared, but if less than that then the debt had to be honored. Where debts and rents were considered to have been excessive, then landowners would be required to return the excess, and in order to find those resources they would usually sell land or provide land to their creditors in place of this new debt. By its own admission, and even before the open emergence of the Sixth Trigram Movement, the Peasants Association felt it had not organized itself particularly well for the political campaign at the start of 1941. Indeed, it criticized itself for having engaged in 'leftist' overenthusiasm, and in the middle of the year was somewhat presciently claiming inadequate support, regarding its position in the county as 'rather wobbly.'[10]

There is certainly evidence to suggest that it had been somewhat aggressive in its pursuit of landlords and rich peasants, and had discriminated heavily in favor of poor peasants. According to one estimate, four percent of total land in the county was redistributed as a result of these debt clearances in early 1941.[11] Information on the social composition of

Table 8.4 Social Composition of Land Transfers, Licheng, 1941 (percentage of land sales and purchases)

Social category	Sold land	Purchased land
Landlord	27	
Rich peasant	36	12
Middle peasant	37	35
Poor peasant		53

Source: JinJiYuqu nongjiu zonghui 'JinJi-Yuqu nongjiu zonghui liangnianlai gongzuo cailiao' ['Materials on the work of the Shanxi-Hebei-Henan region peasants' association during the last two years'] June 1941, in TDZH vol.4: 1941, p.417.

land transfers in one subdistrict of Licheng at the beginning of 1941 is provided in Table 8.4.

There had been 429 struggle meetings in 144 villages involving about three-quarters of the county's population.[12] Some of the landlords effectively being dispossessed were absentee landlords. For example, in Qiushuyuan Village, there had been three landlords at the start of the year owning 8 percent of the land. Two of these had been absentee landlords from Shexian owning 5 percent of the village's land which they now sold.[13] All the same, landlords and indeed rich peasants seemed somewhat shell-shocked by the campaign of debt clearances at the start of 1941. Some landlords in particular obviously could not understand what was going on. One complained loudly to the head of the county CCP committee's Organization Department, 'Since you're not abolishing landlords or private ownership, why aren't we allowed to reclaim our land where rents have not been paid.'[14]

Elections held in the first part of 1941 told a similar story of social change that was perhaps too rich for the landlords and rich peasants to accept or to understand so quickly. By May 1941 Licheng's village elections had provided a radically different local leadership largely in the hands of middle and poor peasants. Middle peasants accounted for 40 percent of the successful candidates on village councils, poor peasants 44 percent, rural and landless laborers 12 percent. Rich peasants now only accounted for 3 percent and landlords only 1 percent of village councilors.[15]

THE SIXTH TRIGRAM MOVEMENT

The social and political changes of 1940–41 go a long way toward explaining the emergence of the Sixth Trigram Movement in Licheng, which grew during those two years and became a vehicle for opposition to the resistance government. It was largely a movement of those who had been disadvantaged by the Licheng CCP's changed strategy at the beginning of 1940, or who otherwise felt themselves threatened by subsequent CCP and resistance government action. In particular, its leadership expanded to include a number of former senior officials in the Sacrifice League-led government who had been dismissed when the Licheng CCP assumed power, and its social base appears to have been amongst the more privileged sectors of society.

At the time, the Licheng CCP tried to suggest that the Sixth Trigram Movement's armed attack on the Licheng county government offices in October 1941 was the result of enemy *agents provocateurs*.[16] However, any such explanations are unconvincing not least because no specific agents were ever identified and the local organization of the Nationalist Party was equally excluded by the Sixth Trigram Movement.[17] As one of the CCP's cadres said later about the emergence of the Sixth Trigram Movement: 'We knew something was going on, but we didn't know where they were meeting or what they were doing.' Certainly it would seem more likely that the base area CCP committee's reorganization of the county leadership, which as Chapter 4 detailed, replaced native party cadres with 'outsiders,' impaired its ability to obtain intelligence.

Many aspects of the development of the Sixth Trigram Movement and its attempt to seize power from the Licheng County government were unusual, not the least that the CCP allowed its activities to develop to the point of armed rebellion, that it publicized the uprising almost immediately[18] and that whilst it summarily executed the ringleaders it dealt with the movement's other participants more openly. The CCP's response was doubly unusual because by the time the Sixth Trigram Movement attempted to seize power, it had 3,321 members, whereas the local CCP itself only had 1,764.[19] The Sixth Trigram Movement was also unusual in that almost half its members were female, and largely females from better-off backgrounds, though only a few women were involved in the specific attempt to seize power in October 1941. Perhaps the only aspect of the Sixth Trigram Movement that is fairly standard was the mystery surrounding its origins before 1939 and its development after that date.

A close reading of the investigation report prepared by the Taihang Base Area's Investigation Unit during 1941–42 as well as other sources suggests very strongly that the growth of the Sixth Trigram Movement after 1939 was related directly to the end of the Sacrifice League-led government and the CCP's assertion of political leadership in Licheng.[20] At both the leadership level and in society as a whole, that assertion of political presence by the CCP set matters in motion leading directly to the October 1941 assault on the county government headquarters in Beishe Village. At the same time, the development of the Sixth Trigram Movement and its attempt at rebellion must be kept in perspective. As serious as it was, it at no time threatened to dislodge the CCP in Licheng: it was poorly armed and organized, and largely confined to the southern part of the county.

By all accounts the Sixth Trigram Movement was originally one of exactly the same kind of sects that were numerous in North China at this time. As already noted, a large proportion of Licheng's population actively belonged to such organizations and the Sixth Trigram Movement was one of twenty-nine in the county. Established in Licheng in or about 1936 it remained just another one of those sects and fairly small until 1940, with its headquarters at Gangdong, the next door village to Beishe. Its leader was Li Yongxiang, the local landlord (and relative of Tian Jijiao, the one-time county head) and its origins are otherwise shrouded in mystery. Even former adherents interviewed in Licheng during the 1990s were unable to recall any more precise a genesis.

In addition to being known as the Sixth Trigram Movement it was also referred to as the *Salvationist Sect of the Goddess from the Southern Sea* and was a secret society which amongst other things instructed its potential members that if they discussed its activities with nonmembers they would disappear into thin air. It offered self-cultivation, invincibility and an ideology of restoration. According to the 1942 Investigation Report, the growth of the Sixth Trigram Movement all occurred during 1940–41, and was concentrated in the more prosperous southern part of the county, in 66 villages, all within 8 kilometers of Licheng County town, though in total it extended to 120 villages.

The social causes of its growth would appear to have been precisely the first tentative steps toward social reform that were attempted during 1940–41, as the CCP sought to come to terms with its post-Yan Xishan environment. Increased tax being carried by landlords and rich peasants, as well as the campaign of debt clearances, coincided with the growth period of the Sixth Trigram Movement, and its social composition at the time of its closure suggest a close correlation. Table 8.5 provides a comparison of the social structure of the memberships of the Licheng CCP and the Sixth Trigram Movement, and provides wider comparative data for the populations of Licheng County and the Taihang Region as a whole.

Table 8.5 suggests that the contrasting appeals of the Licheng CCP and the Sixth Trigram Movement were to poor peasants and rich peasants,

Table 8.5 Comparative Social Structure of CCP and Sixth Trigram Movement Members, Licheng, 1941 (percentage of individual members)

Social category	CCP	Sixth Trigram Movement	Licheng County	Taihang Region
Male	96.6	53		
Female	3.4	47		
Rich peasants (and landlords)	4.6	21.0	13.4	10.5
Middle peasants	49.2	53.0	57.3	37.8
Poor peasants	42.1	26.0	29.3	49.0
Others	4.1			

Sources: Percentages for Licheng County and the Taihang Region are based on proportions of peasant households. LOH p.56; LGD p.26; and TSJD2 p.1408.

respectively. Both shared a middle peasant membership approximately in proportion to the Licheng population. The Licheng CCP was an organization whose membership was mainly poor and middle peasants; the Sixth Trigram Movement was more one of middle peasants, rich peasants and landlords. This clearly cannot be an exact relationship since there were both poor peasants in the Sixth Trigram Movement as well as rich peasants and indeed landlords in the CCP. However, the impression that the Sixth Trigram was a movement of the more affluent is reinforced by an analysis of its leadership. Of the Sixth Trigram Movement's 29 senior officials, 5 were landlords, 13 rich peasants, 10 middle peasants, and one a merchant.[21]

The changed county government policies of 1940–41 may have created a social base for the Sixth Trigram Movement to exploit. However, it was the changes in the CCP's recruitment policies and attitudes toward participation in the county government that were even more directly to lead to the emergence of the Sixth Trigram Movement as a political force. As Chapter 4 has outlined, before 1940 there had been little differentiation made between the CCP and resistance activities more generally by either the party organization itself or by the wider community in Licheng. The CCP had grown rapidly after the middle of 1938 and had adopted a policy of inclusivity. Leaders of villages and the heads of the various traditional village associations were recruited to the CCP, as often were complete village associations. One notable example was the village association of Beishe Village, which became the first rural party branch of the Licheng

CCP. Another, which was expelled as a result of its involvement with the Sixth Trigram Movement was the West Land Association of Lubao Village.[22]

The Licheng CCP's strategy of political inclusivity ended with the beginning of 1940, the seizure of power and a reorganization of the county government and its structures that saw many Sacrifice League supporters dismissed. These changes effectively alienated a substantial element of the previously more progressively minded local elite who had become involved with the CCP at the start of the War of Resistance. While not all of them would have had the same degree of involvement with the expansion or operation of the Sixth Trigram Movement, it does seem likely that a group of them were instrumental in attempting to use the sect as a vehicle for the recovery of power. In particular, this included three former county government officials who had been removed from their positions of leadership in departments of the county government at this time and who then became senior leaders of the Sixth Trigram Movement: Sui Qi and Zhao Liancheng from the Department of Armed Personnel, as well as Chang Huating from the Department of Public Security.

Discontent at the CCP's new policies was also evident in the comments made by those interviewed at lower levels of the Sixth Trigram Movement by the Investigation Unit during 1941–42. Yang Xiantang from Wangjiazhuang, for example, was a rich peasant who had been village head and a staunch supporter of Yan Xishan. He believed the latter had been unfairly supplanted by the CCP in 1940. On his own admission his decision to join the Sixth Trigram Movement was completely political and he became the commander of one of its district organizations. Li Wuting was a university engineering graduate who thought the debt clearances campaign unfair since, in his view, landlords had not been able to speak in their own defense and whatever the peasants wanted was done. He argued very strongly that the 'government's progressive programs are not suitable for the backward life of the masses.' Qiao Hongtai of Qiaojiazhuang had previously worked in the Licheng County Government and 'participated in resistance activities' at the start of the war. However, he was disaffected by the CCP's tax policy and refusing an offer of work in the new government in 1940 he took up a teaching position in the Licheng First High School.[23]

The Sixth Trigram Movement made its push to take over the county government on 10 October 1941. Five hundred of its members in five groups prepared to attack the county government and two subdistrict government offices. Four of the five groups were either rapidly dispersed or otherwise persuaded by the militia to go elsewhere. The fifth and largest group gathered at Gangdong, and marched on the office of the county government in neighboring Beishe where they clashed with the local public security forces. Li Yongxiang, the leader of the Sixth Trigram Movement led the charge and was killed almost immediately by a grenade. Another three members of the Sixth Trigram Movement were killed along with seven defenders of the county government in the assault.[24] Seven of the Sixth Trigram leaders were executed immediately, and over a hundred followers arrested though later released. The remaining leaders of the attempted insurrection burnt their houses and together with about a hundred followers marched south to Lucheng and ultimately Changzhi. Over 3,000 participants of the Sixth Trigram Movement were investigated by the county's public security officers but no further arrests or punishments followed.[25]

One of the more long-time consequences of the Sixth Trigram's activities was the attention to women's issues later provided by the Licheng CCP. As already noted, the Sixth Trigram Movement was unusual in the extent of its female membership. By contrast as Table 8.5 indicates, the Licheng CCP had less than 4 percent of women members. The 1941–42 investigation of the Sixth Trigram Movement paid particular attention to the question of women's participation. It revealed that the Sixth Trigram Movement had not only been a movement of women to a degree not previously experienced in the county, but also one that attracted young women from wealthier, more privileged backgrounds. Table 8.6 presents details from the Investigation Unit's survey of women in the Sixth Trigram Movement.

The Investigation Unit questioned the Sixth Trigram Movement's women followers about their motivations for participation. The overwhelming desire for greater freedom and self-expression emerges clearly from their interviews. Freedom of choice in marriage, and the ability to

Table 8.6 Age and Social Class of Women Members of the Sixth Trigram Movement, Licheng, 1941 (percentage of female of members)

Age category	Social category			
	Poor peasant	Middle peasant	Rich peasant	Total
Young	3	11	23	36
Middle-aged	6	17	17	40
Old	9	11	3	23
Total	18	39	43	

Source: LGD p.48.

move beyond the confines of either the parental or the family home were the most frequently cited goals for former women members in joining the Sixth Trigram Movement. It would appear that some women even joined just because membership and the compulsory attendance at various meetings presented an opportunity for women to move around outside the home without requiring the permission of parents, husbands or mothers-in-law.

Once the dust had settled on the Sixth Trigram Movement the Licheng CCP made determined moves to redress its low level of female participation by recruiting more women members. It doubled the number in the county party during 1942, and by 1945 they amounted to 10.3 percent of the membership.[26] For its part the Licheng Patriotic Women's Association also attempted to address some of the issues raised by the women participants in the Sixth Trigram Movement, and renewed attempts to reform marriage practices and to increase women's participation rates in politics.[27]

Similarly, the base area moved rapidly to change policy on taxation in the wake of the attempted insurrection. There had always been a realization that the base area's policy on supply and taxation was inadequate, and had been neither thoroughly considered nor adequately developed. The Joint Office for the Taihang, Taiyue and South Hebei Base Areas had new draft legislation in preparation and the Border Region Government was able to accelerate the introduction of a new tax system almost immediately. It was followed the next year by the preparation of a 'universal progressive tax' which still taxed wealth but as calculated on the productive capacity of property over an average number of years.[28] Moreover, as was noted in Chapter 4, concerted and repeated attempts were made to reduce the numbers of people engaged in nonproductive occupations in Licheng, exempt from tax and needing to be supported themselves. Certainly, after 1941 Licheng's tax burden as a proportion of its income remained noticeably lower than other counties, as for example Wuxiang, for the remainder of the war.[29]

SOCIAL REFORM AND COMMUNALISM

Although the Sixth Trigram Movement posed a dramatic challenge, it was in some ways not the most serious the Licheng CCP had to face. The attempt to further social reform in 1942 through the introduction of rent and interest reduction, though partly successful, encountered even more serious resistance which was considerably more effective for being restrained and trying to act within the evolving party-state system. There were indeed additional public order problems that the resistance government had to face as a result of its continued reform program. However, the social reform program was more effectively delayed by the emergence of local protection networks that developed between village cadres and landowners.

In July 1942 the Licheng CCP chose four test areas for the implementation of its rent and interest reduction campaign: Xiacun, Shangyao, Quzhuang and Pengzhuang. These were safe choices at a time when the Japanese had just completed what turned out to be their last invasion of the county. All are located off main lines of communication and were in villages considered extremely secure and where the CCP was well organized. By the end of the year these test areas were able to report that they had successfully reduced the number of poor peasant households from 49 percent to 30 percent, and to have increased the number of middle peasant households from 31 percent to 48 percent.[30]

However, this choice of test areas largely avoided the hard choice that village cadres were being asked to manage in the 1942 and indeed subsequent rent and interest reduction campaigns. The campaign's political and economic goals were sometimes seen as being in conflict by village cadres, who were unsure whether they should be pursuing landowners to surrender land the latter did not farm themselves, or to ensure that their land was used most productively. This problem was by no means unique to Licheng, and particularly not during 1942 when Japanese pressure was at its height.

Similarly, there was also a danger that landowners would see their own interests as being in direct conflict with these kind of campaigns. Whilst the landowners were more than willing to accept the county government's imperatives to support the production for war effort, they were less than enthusiastic about accepting the CCP's more political agenda designed to bring about radical social change, particularly when the logic of the latter was ultimately destructive of their own positions. Their response was often to attempt to retreat into their own local communities and ignore aspects of the CCP's political program. Where this proved impractical it led to other forms of resistance, sometimes outside the activities of the CCP's party-state in the making, and sometimes inside.

The introduction of the new tax system in 1942, as well as of rent and interest reduction campaigns in both late 1942 and again in 1944, were all intended to encourage property redistribution as well as political participation from poorer peasants and landless laborers. A key feature of these campaigns was the public meeting where criticisms could be raised against landlords and rich peasants. As in the campaigns to reduce debt during 1940 and 1941 those with property and wealth often seemed not to understand. Landlords who had shown themselves the most sympathetic towards the CCP politically and prepared to contribute the most economically sometimes articulated a total disbelief that they were still being persecuted.

Xie Haoli was a particularly good example of this kind of behavior in Licheng. Xie was a Japanese-educated landlord who by all accounts was a humanitarian and pro-CCP sympathizer. He was an elected member of both the county council, and of the Border Region Provisional Assembly. All the same, as a landlord, he, too, was not exempt from the political pressures that resulted from the CCP's desire to introduce social change, and he was subject to both all the campaigns to redistribute land and their struggle meetings. His bewilderment was expressed clearly at a struggle meeting in 1942, when he is reported to have said 'Now that I have agreed to comply with what you ask me to do, why do you still want to struggle against me? I oppose your struggle against me!'[31]

One strategy adopted by some less articulate or politically well-placed landlords and rich peasants was to resort to localist organization, perhaps in a belief that they could defensively control their immediate environment. Although the county government had closed down the Sixth Trigram Movement after October 1941, it could do little about the other 28 sects that were active in Licheng at the time. To do so without provocation might have threatened the willingness of the wealthier peasants and landlords to ensure the maximum agricultural production from their land, particularly given the widespread membership in those various sects throughout the county.

Whilst some of those activities were fairly harmless, others seemed to pose a threat to a public security department that was somewhat justifiably nervous after its inability to take more long-term preventive action against the Sixth Trigram Movement during 1940–41. On a number of occasions during 1942–45, the county government's public security officers moved to defuse the association of more wealthy local landowners and local branches of sects. In the middle of 1942 there was even another reported attempt at armed uprising, only this time in Dongyangguan, and led by a local sect known as the Confucius Sect. One hundred sixty-eight people were arrested on this occasion, of whom thirteen were executed. Altogether during 1942–43 about a hundred people were arrested and accused of having engaged in preparations for various armed uprisings associated with sects and secret societies.[32]

However, by far the most serious reactions against the CCP's program of social reform came from landowners who attempted to protect themselves and their property through cooperation and alliances with their village cadres. For the landowners this was in effect an attempt to buy political protection with economic production. They would ensure maximum agricultural output for the new local political leadership in a village if in return the leadership protected them against further encroachments by the expanding party-state in the making. Landlords were classified as rich peasants or even middle peasants. Landlords, rich peasants and middle peasants were allowed to nominally divide their households whilst the family as a whole maintained, or even in some cases expanded its landholdings.[33] Perhaps most importantly, landowners were not required to run the gauntlet of a struggle meeting. Such practices appear to have been widespread in Licheng and would certainly explain many of the defects in the 1942 rent and interest reduction campaign, and why much of the campaign had to be repeated during 1944–45 in the county.

A particularly extensive case of such behavior came to light during 1943, with the Taihang Base Area CCP Committee eventually forced to intervene to ensure the dismissal of a new village cadre who had succumbed to this kind of localism.[34] Li Furong was not a middle peasant but a former landless laborer. He had proved himself to be a dynamic and well-intentioned village head during 1940 in Nanweiquan, in the north of Licheng. He was particularly good at ensuring that the village met its production-related tasks and quotas, but was less observant of directives in campaigns designed to redistribute wealth and property, such as the 1942 rent and interest reduction campaign, which he apparently chose largely to ignore. Both the subdistrict and county-level CCP committees attempted to discipline him at the time, but with no success.

When the county CCP committee formally attempted to remove Li Furong from office for his lack of attention to its directives on land policy, it met opposition from two directions. The predictable source of opposition was from Li Furong's village, where ingenuous landowners provided the county party committee with glowing testimonials about their village cadre. However, it also met opposition from the Department of Production of the Border Region Government, which was more than happy with Nanweiquan's agricultural output which it saw as being an important public asset. The county party organization then appealed to the base area CCP committee, which after investigation eventually supported the Licheng CCP Committee and agreed that whilst Li Furong's localism might have been economically well-motivated, it was politically unacceptable.

An investigation undertaken during 1943 revealed the mixed impact of the previous year's rent and interest reduction campaign. In some places, such as Quzhuang and Xijing it appeared to have met the CCP's desired aims of making poor peasants richer and swelling the number and landholdings of the middle peasantry. In Quzhuang there had been fifty-six households of poor peasants and thirty-six households of middle peasants; there were now thirty-three poor peasant households and fifty-nine middle peasant households. In Xijing, fifty peasant households had all become middle peasants through debt clearances.[35]

However, it was also clear that in much of the county landlords and rich peasants had been allowed more room for maneuver, particularly to avoid the consequences of the rent and interest reduction process, and especially by comparison with the situation elsewhere in the base area, even though there had also been difficulties elsewhere. In Licheng the problem was not that the campaign had stopped because county and sub-district cadres did not trust middle peasant cadres, but rather that village cadres, many of whom were indeed middle peasants, had one way or another subverted the entire process. Much of the apparent change brought by the 1942 rent and interest reduction campaign was consequently misleading, and these difficulties seem likely to have been the major reason for the subsequent restructuring of the county party organization by the base area CCP committee.[36] The new Licheng CCP leadership then set about relaunching the rent and interest campaign, as throughout the base area.[37]

The 1944 rent and interest reduction campaign in Licheng certainly seems to have achieved some of its global aims. Table 8.7 provides data on the proportions of households in a survey of 42 villages who rented out land, according to their social category. These villages were all said in 1944 not to have carried out the 1942 rent and interest reduction.

As Table 8.7 indicates one result of the 1944 rent and interest reduction campaign in Licheng was then that an increased proportion of rentier activity was being undertaken by middle peasants, as landlord and rich peasant landholdings decreased. As might be expected in Licheng, an even larger proportion of the new middle peasants were déclassé landlords and rich peasants than was to be found elsewhere in the base area. One estimate suggests that 40 percent of all middle peasants who rented land out at this time in Licheng were former landlords and rich peasants.[38]

Second time around, the Licheng CCP might have been attempting a more thorough process but it was necessarily fraught with many of the

Table 8.7 Social Composition of Rentiers, Licheng, 1942–1944 (percentage of all households renting land, 42 villages)

Social category	1942	1944
Landlord	36.7	20.3
Rich peasant	29.9	25.3
Middle peasant	27.4	48.8
Poor peasant	6.1	5.7

Source: TSJD2 p.1437.

problems that previous campaigns had encountered. In particular, mediating class conflict remained difficult both at and outside the struggle meeting. In Licheng by 1944 a particular problem was that most landlord's landholdings were already quite small. The Border Region Government's regulations for rent and interest reductions included provisions for the return of land to former tenants where they had been dispossessed as a result of not maintaining rental payments to a landlord.[39] In general, this was only likely to occur in the southern part of Licheng; in the north, as in eastern Wuxiang, the established practice was for landlords and tenants to continue a tenancy relationship even when the tenant defaulted.[40] In the south of the county there had been little recognition of either a sustainable relationship, or tenants' rights before 1944. Landlords had reclaimed land and under the pressure of war and a CCP-led government had then sold it on the open market. However, the regulations for the return of land had not been devised for a socioeconomic environment where there were a large number of not fabulously wealthy landlords, rich peasants and middle peasants. As a result some Licheng landlords were being instructed to return land not only that they no longer had, but also that was in excess of their current assets. For example, one Li Wuting was required to return 15 *mu* of land to former tenants, even though he now only owned 14 *mu* all of which he was farming himself.[41] Village cadres found themselves caught in the middle, between poor peasants demanding tenants' rights and landlords demanding their right to subsistence.

Accounts of struggle meetings in Licheng during 1944 reflect a degree of cadre training to ensure that their proceedings were better managed. For example, in one four-day session of struggle meetings, disputes between seventy-six tenants and thirteen landlords were processed. It was more like a series of arbitration meetings than earlier examples of struggle meetings, with all parties being expected to make concessions.[42]

One of those to be required to attend a struggle meeting was once again Xie Haoli, who had been somewhat bewildered at his earlier 1942 struggle meeting. On this occasion the reports of the struggle meeting against him are instructive on a number of counts. In the first place, they suggest that it was possible for the theory of conflict reconciliation by public meeting to be put into practice, though underlining the need for both sides to be prepared to participate and to reach a solution. Xie and his accusers had a lively meeting where he was asked about his attitudes to the rent and interest reduction campaign. He explained that he was opposed to it because he did not agree with the notion of guaranteed tenant rights. The Peasant Association then asked him why he had supported the Border Region Government's legislation at the time a decision was taken if he was so opposed. Xie explained that there would have been no point to have spoken out since most of his fellow members of the Border Region Provisional Assembly were in favor.

A second instructive aspect of Xie Haoli's struggle meeting was that although it was reported that he had been treated with explicit leniency 'because of his honesty,' he was still required to return 2 *mu* of land to tenants whose land he had earlier repossessed. This reduced his own landholdings to 8 *mu* of self-farmed land, and 15 *mu* of leased land: an amount which was equivalent to a middle peasant in his own village before 1937. At the same time, a third instructive aspect of his struggle meeting was the continued deference afforded to Xie Haoli. Despite the forced decline in his economic circumstances he was still regarded as a senior figure in society, partly because of his education, and partly because of his political standing as a member of the Border Region Provisional Assembly.[43]

As Table 8.1 indicates, the Licheng CCP had developed a solid base of support in the middle and poor peasantry during 1942–45. It had also achieved some of its other goals of social reform. Table 8.8 provides information on the social composition of landownership in Licheng at the end of the war: specifically data on the proportion of households owning land; the proportion of land owned; and the average land holding all for each social category.

A complete set of comparative data for before the War of Resistance in Licheng is not available. However, in 1937 Licheng's landlords and rich peasants are reported to have owned 30.4 percent of the county's land; poor peasants are reported to have owned 1.7 percent. The programs of social reform during 1940–45 would appear to have brought an additional 9.4 percent of the county's population into the ranks of the landowners who had previously been tenants and farmhands.[44] The figures presented in Table 8.8 suggest not only that landowners remained slightly wealthier

Table 8.8 Social Composition of Landownership, Licheng, 1945

Social category	Percentage of households owning land	Percentage of land	Average *mu* per household
Landlord	3.6	7.7	33.0
Rich peasant	11.0	14.0	20.0
Middle peasant	50.5	48.5	15.2
Poor peasant	34.8	29.8	1.6

Source: Statistics calculated from information presented in LZ p.209.

in Licheng at the end of the war, but also that the process of social change had proceeded slightly slower in comparison not only with the Taihang Base Area as a whole, but also particularly by comparison with a county more radical in its pursuit of social reform such as Wuxiang. These differences presumably reflected the specific socioeconomic conditions in the county, as well as the difficulties the Licheng CCP encountered in implementing and gaining acceptance for its programs of social reform during 1940–45.

SOCIAL CHANGE IN LICHENG

Where the experience of Wuxiang clearly indicates the potential success open to the CCP under conditions of significant class polarization, the case of Licheng exemplifies the complexities of the revolutionary process in a very different social environment. Licheng's social structure on the eve of war was more dominated by rich peasants, in the CCP's categorization, than by landlords. It was both more equal and somewhat wealthier than other parts of the Taihang region. The attempt to implement similar policies in Licheng as in Wuxiang was not only less successful, it also had potential to be counterproductive in the short-term, at times leading to considerable resistance and opposition. At the same time, the experience of Licheng also demonstrates the capacity of the CCP's tactics of polarization to sustain the drive for its desired goals under less favorable circumstances, and this too is a necessary part of the process of revolutionary incrementalism.

NOTES

1. Zhonggong JinJiYu qudangwei 'Zuzhibu gei Beifangjude gongzuo baogao' ['Organization Department Report to North China Bureau'] August 1940, in *Shanxi geming genjudi* [Shanxi Revolutionary Base Areas] no.1, 1989, p.3; and in TDZH vol.3: 1940, p.569.
2. Yang Wei 'Taihangshan beiqude tudi wenti' ['Land Issues in the Northern Part of the Taihang Mountains'] May 1940, in TDZH vol.3: 1940, p.329.
3. Yang Wei 'Taihangshan beiqude tudi wenti' ['Land Issues in the Northern Part of the Taihang Mountains'] May 1940, in TDZH vol.3: 1940, p.324.
4. Yang Wei 'Taihangshan beiqude tudi wenti' ['Land Issues in the Northern Part of the Taihang Mountains'] May 1940, in TDZH vol.3: 1940, p.325.
5. Yang Wei 'Taihangshan beiqude tudi wenti' ['Land Issues in the Northern Part of the Taihang Mountains'] May 1940, in TDZH vol.3: 1940, p.329.
6. TYG vol.1, part II, p.231.
7. LZ p.209.

8. See Table 0.4.

9. JinJiYuqu nongjiu zonghui 'JinJiYuqu nongjiu zonghui liangnianlai gongzuo cailiao' ['Materials on the work of the Shanxi-Hebei-Henan region peasants' association during the last two years'] June 1941, in TDZH vol.4: 1941, p.460.

10. JinJiYuqu nongjiu zonghui 'JinJiYuqu nongjiu zonghui liangnianlai gongzuo cailiao' ['Materials on the work of the Shanxi-Hebei-Henan region peasants' association during the last two years'] June 1941, in TDZH vol.4: 1941, p.400.

11. TW p.117.

12. LX p.378.

13. JinJiYuqu nongjiu zonghui 'JinJiYuqu nongjiu zonghui liangnianlai gongzuo cailiao' ['Materials on the work of the Shanxi-Hebei-Henan region peasants' association during the last two years'] June 1941, in TDZH vol.4: 1941, p.392.

14. Reported by Xu Zirong, in FOC June 1941, p.31.

15. CHL p.101.

16. Zhonggong JinJuYu qudangwei 'Licheng Liguadao bodongde jingguo ji jingyan jiaoxun' ['The Experience and Lessons of the Licheng Sixth Trigram Rebellion'] 12 October 1941, in GBG p.100.

17. Contrasting explanations of the Sixth Trigram Movement may be found in Xiao Feng and Yao Fei 'Licheng Liguadao Bodong shishiqi jiaoxun' ['The Lesson of the History of the Liguadao Uprising in Licheng'] in *Shanxi geming genjudi* [Shanxi Revolutionary Base Areas] no.2, 1991, p.30; and David S G Goodman 'The Licheng Rebellion of 1941: class, gender and leadership in the Sino-Japanese War' in *Modern China* Vol.23 no.2 April 1997 p.216.

18. The public security department and base area party committee commented immediately in Zhonggong JinJuYu qudangwei 'Licheng Liguadao bodongde jingguo ji jingyan jiaoxun' ['The Experience and Lessons of the Licheng Sixth Trigram Rebellion'] 12 October 1941, in GBG p.100.

19. LOH p56.

20. Zhonggong JinJiYu qudangwei Licheng kaochatuan *Li Gua Dao shijian diaocha baogao* [Report of the Investigation into the Sixth Trigram Movement Incident] April 1942. There is a brief summary of the report's introduction in Licheng kaochatuan 'Lichengxian Liguadao baoluan' ['The Sixth Trigram Movement Insurrection in Licheng County'] April 1942, in GBG p.106.

21. LGD p.27.

22. LGD p.89.

23. LGD p.36 (Yang Xiantang); p.62 (Li Wuting); and (p.75) Qiao Hongtai.

24. CHL pp.108–112; and LX p.379.

25. In 1968 one of Li Yongxiang's brothers, Li Xiaolao, who had fled the area in 1941 and returned was arrested and punished for his involvment. See, LZ pp.197–98.

26. LOH p.56.

27. JinJiYu qu funu qiuguo lianhe zonghui 'Guanyu "Fandui maimaihun zhengqu zizhuhun" de chubu zongjie' ['Preliminary Summary on "Opposing the trade in brides and striving to ensure freedom of choice in marriage"'] 31 August 1942, QY p.419.

28. 'Jin Ji Lu Yu Bianqu zhengfu zhuxi gei zhuanyuan, xianzhang de zhishixin' ['Letter of Instruction from the Chairman of the Shanxi-Hebei-Shandong-Henan

Border Region Government to District Commissioners and County Heads'] 26 June 1943, in CJZX vol.1, p.1051.

29. JinJiLuYu Bianqu zhengfu diaocha yanjiushi *Taihangqu yijiusisinian guomin jingji diaocha chubu yanjiu* [Preliminary Investigation and Research on the Economy of the Taihang Base Area in 1944] 1945, in CJJ vol.2, p.451.

30. LZ p.210.

31. 'Taihang laoqu tugai qianhou nongcun jingji biange kaocha zuotanhui fayan gangyao"['Outline of Discussion Meeting on the Investigation of Rural Economic Change in the Taihang Areas of the Revoluton before and after Land Reform'] 7 July 1983, in TW pp.455–56.

32. LZ p.197.

33. Gao Yuangui 'Dizhu fandui jianzude banfa he womende duice' ['The Methods of Landlords in Opposing Rent Reductions and our Policy Response'] 31 December 1942, in CJZX vol.2, p.548.

34. Zhonggong JinJiYu qudangwei 'Jiancha Nanweiquan wenti houde jueding' ['Resolution after an Investigation of the Nanweiquan Question'] 25 May 1943, in DJ p.295.

35. LZ p.210.

36. Summary of discussion on research into party branches, in ZJY p.8.

37. LX p.382 ff.

38. TW p.138.

39. JiTai lianban 'Jianzu jianxi zanxing tiaolie' ['Provisional Regulations for Rent and Interest Reduction'] 29 October 1940 (p.568); JinJiLuYu Bianqu zhengfu 'Jianzu jianxi bugao' ['Notice of Rent and Interest Reduction'] 1 October 1942 (p.545); and JinJiLuYu Bianqu zhengfu 'Guanyu jianzu gongzuode shishi' ['Instructions on Rent Reduction'] 17 October 1942 (p.546), in CJZX vol.2.

40. Huang Yuan 'Jindongnande poqie jianzu jianxi wenti' ['The Urgent Issue of Reducing Rent and Interest in Southeast Shanxi'] March 1940, in TDZH vol.3: 1940, p.124.

41. 'Yijiusisinian kaizhan xiaozuxiaoxi douzhengde dianxing ziliao' ['Typical Cases of Rent and Interest Reduction'] 20 December 1944, in TW pp.278–79.

42. 'Yijiusisinian kaizhan xiaozuxiaoxi douzhengde dianxing ziliao' ['Typical Cases of Rent and Interest Reduction'] 20 December 1944, in TW pp.281–82.

43. 'Yijiusisinian kaizhan xiaozuxiaoxi douzhengde dianxing ziliao' ['Typical Cases of Rent and Interest Reduction'] 20 December 1944, in TW pp.280–81.

44. LZ p.209.

Conclusion

Revolution in Southeast Shanxi

On occasion the recent history of the War of Resistance has challenged the notion that there was a revolution in the base areas of North China. The experience of the Taihang Base Area certainly does not support that view: its development was revolutionary in both intent and impact. Whilst the extent of change should not be exaggerated, the Taihang Base Area saw a fundamental revolution during the war, not least in the categories of village level social and political discourse. By the end of the war there were new political institutions in place in the villages, at county level, and as part of the Shanxi-Hebei-Shandong-Henan Border Region. In the villages at the heart of the base area the peasant small-holder had become the dominant form of economic production, and this too had altered other aspects of social and political interaction.

Rural society changed under the joint pressures of war and political campaigns, if less than the contemporary rhetoric suggested. However, the changes in rhetoric are important for understanding the extent to which the old structures of wealth, status and power had been challenged. The process of revolutionary change may now appear incomplete because land reform and the establishment of the PRC followed. All the same at the time the transformation of social and political institutions appeared considerable, and seemed confirmed by the ease with which land reform was speedily completed once introduced the following year.

Change was fairly ubiquitous. The CCP had been the harbinger of revolution, but this was no one-way process: more even than fighting a guerilla war, the sustained search for social reform led to fundamental changes in the party's organization. It eventually became both more united and more complex, and widened its social appeal as well as its membership, particularly developing a significant rural base of support. In addition, this account of the Taihang Base Area has also highlighted the personal transformations inherent in the process of social change, as individuals—cadres, members of the CCP, teachers, urban intellectuals, landlords and peasants—have struggled to come to terms with both social dislocation and the rapidly changing micropolitics of their immediate environment.

REVOLUTION AND SOCIAL CHANGE

All the elements for the description of revolution would appear to be visible in the emergence of the Taihang Base Area during the War of Resistance. There was the overthrow of government; the creation of new political institutions; and a process of revolutionary social transformation. All of which was accompanied by immense social upheaval, dislocation and violence; and shaped by the development of a revolutionary movement. However, two events tend to detract from an assessment of its activities and the impact on society in revolutionary perspectives. The first is the outbreak of war and the development of a united front with Yan Xishan in Shanxi through the operations of the Sacrifice League, which bequeathes an aura of broad-based gradual reform rather than more dramatic change. The second is the establishment of the PRC, and the series of far greater revolutions that followed the end of the War of Resistance and which further transformed rural and urban society.

Before 1940 the Taihang Base Area had an institutional form more related to party and military affairs than to local government. However, control of local government was important to the CCP, especially county government. The CCP had come to power early in Wuxiang, but in Liaoxian and Licheng at the beginning of 1940 it moved rapidly to ensure its control of county government as the alliance with Yan Xishan crumbled. Whilst there is little detailed information available on the precise nature of these moves, in Liaoxian the seizure of power appears to have been largely external, supported by military force; in Licheng the CCP's takeover was more like an internal coup.

In Liaoxian and Wuxiang the assumption of governmental authority during the civil war with Yan Xishan at the end of 1939 and beginning of 1940 was accompanied by more radical calls for change, such as immediate land reform, the abolition of private property and proletarian uprising. To some extent these have been presented as the result of confusion on the part of local and overenthusiastic cadres, and indeed in Wuxiang that may be the case. However, in at least Liaoxian the violent overthrow of the landlord and rich peasant classes was advocated by the county party leadership itself.

The intrigue in the more extreme events of 1939–40 that must remain for the present unresolved is the extent of senior CCP complicity in those events. In general, many of the CCP's national leaders based physically in the Taihang Base Area were fairly frequently involved in its development. Moreover, at about the same time the call for radical land reform was launched in Liaoxian, Deng Xiaoping had just returned to the county after his marriage in Yan'an,[1] though it would seem likely he had other matters of greater importance on his mind at the time, such as the continuing crisis facing the CCP in South Hebei. Given the organizational arrangements within the CCP at the time it is unlikely Deng would not have known about some of these activities. The base area CCP committee was co-located with the headquarters of the 129th Division of which he was the political commissar.

It is possible that for a short time even fairly senior leaders were content to let these matters run their radical course, and at the time it might have seemed like a less risky strategy.[2] The political and military situations were extremely uncertain and there was no guarantee of any particular outcome. Had a truce with the Nationalist Party's forces not been possible, or had Yan Xishan been able to act more aggressively in Southeast Shanxi other solutions might have been required, including withdrawal. Leaving a radicalized peasantry behind might then have seemed like a marker for the future.

In the event, drastic solutions were not required and the base area CCP leadership moved both to dampen the revolutionary enthusiasm of local cadres and to establish new political institutions during April 1940. Liaoxian was fairly easy to restrain given the proximity of the various CCP headquarter activities. The Wuxiang party organization was overhauled, though not as it transpired with any great degree of success. With the resolution of the crisis at the beginning of 1940 the Taihang Base Area also moved rapidly, together with other adjacent CCP areas of activity to create a series of new economic and political institutions. As political instruments the Shanxi-Hebei-Shandong-Henan Border Region Government, and its associated assembly, may have been rather low key. However, their greater significance was in first stabilizing and then beginning to develop the economy of the Taihang region. This was to prove crucial not only for supporting military and political activities, but also in meeting the severe environmental challenges the region faced during the first half of the 1940s.

The social revolution of these years is most clearly seen through the results of the CCP's programs of social reform on landownership and usage. In terms of the social categories employed by the CCP, across the Taihang region as a whole a rural economy that had been dominated by landlords and rich peasants in 1937, had become one in which middle peasants predominated by 1945. At the end of the war two-thirds of all landholding households were those of middle peasants, who owned about two-thirds of the land.[3] In addition, a quarter of landholding households were those of poor peasants who owned about one-seventh of the land.

As the average size of landholding decreased for each of the CCP's social categories and became more equal, the majority of villagers in the Taihang Base Area came to live in peasant small-holder households. To the majority of those designated by the CCP as middle peasants who had remained owner-cultivators throughout the war were added a variety of upwardly and downwardly mobile social groups. Landless laborers and tenants had become poor independant small-holders who usually still needed to rent land and to work for others, but were nonetheless now landowners. Similarly, a substantial proportion of those who had changed their class status from that of poor peasant to that of middle peasant during the war, were now also poor independent small-holders. In socio-economic terms, landlords and rich peasants now had landholdings equivalent to those of rich independent small-holders on the eve of the war.

There were of course variations in these patterns of social and economic change, as the cases of Liaoxian, Wuxiang and Licheng bear witness. Indeed, at the end of the war both Wuxiang and Licheng were recognized by the CCP as having a below average preponderance of middle peasants, if for different reasons. In Wuxiang, land had been more concentrated in the hands of exceptionally large-scale landlords before the war with fewer owner-cultivators and more poor peasants compared to the rest of the Taihang region. Wuxiang's politics of change had tended to the radical end of the spectrum, and a greater emphasis had been maintained on the role of the poor peasant. Licheng had been a richer county with less land concentration, fewer poor peasants and more owner-cultivators at the start of the war. Partly in consequence, there was a more broadly based local elite that proved somewhat resistant to the CCP's programs of social reform. Nonetheless, even in Licheng, and in Wuxiang too for that matter, the new social structure was dominated by peasant small-holders.

Political change accompanied the changes in landownership and the social composition of rural society. Landlords and rich peasants, and particularly the former, might still have substantial residual social status, but their control of village politics had largely passed to village cadres who were drawn overwhelmingly from the ranks of those described as middle peasants. Across the Taihang Base Area as a whole, these middle peasants dominated the local membership of the CCP, and provided more than two-thirds of all village level cadres by the end of the war. Poor peasants provided under a quarter of the CCP's local membership and about a fifth of the cadres. Again there was variation: in Wuxiang a higher proportion of the membership were poor peasants, and the Wuxiang CCP had more poor peasant cadres, though there were also rich peasant cadres too in quite some number. In Licheng on the other hand, whilst the party membership had a majority of middle peasants, there was also a large number of poor peasants; a larger proportion indeed than in the county as a whole, which again perhaps explains some of the Licheng CCP's long-term problems.

At the same time the extent of both social and political change in the Taihang Base Area should not be exaggerated. Despite the occasional attempt at land reform during the war, and the redistribution in landholdings that did take place, social change had challenged the economic and political power of landlords, it had not challenged the power of land. On the contrary, to a large extent the revolutionary aspects of social change had been based on the promise of land to poor peasants, farmhands and landless tenants, as well as the promise of more land to owner-cultivators.

By no means the whole of the Taihang Base Area as of mid-1945 had developed at the same pace or in the same ways. There was a substantial difference between the social change effected in those parts of the base area where a CCP presence had been maintained throughout the war, especially where CCP-led government had remained operational, and those which had only been incorporated with reexpansion in and after 1943. There were also major differences between long-term secure parts of the base area—including eastern Wuxiang, the southernmost part of Liaoxian (Zuoquan) and Licheng—and those districts which had been more contested—including West Liaoxian.

Even within some well-established and secure parts of the Taihang region the pattern of change was uneven. The contrast between Licheng and Wuxiang is fairly obvious, but even within Wuxiang's secure area in the mountainous east of the county there were villages such as Hanbi, where the CCP had no problems in implementing programs, and villages in other areas, such as that round Hongshui, where the county party organization encountered problems throughout the first half of the 1940s. The acceptance of, or resistance to, programs and policies was usually determined village-by-village, and often by highly local and idiosyncratic factors. As Ma Guishu, the CCP secretary of Wuxiang noted in 1943, 'Village cadres do things their own way based on their own experience and customs.'[4] In Licheng, in general, the county government after 1939 found its policies had easier purchase in the north of the county. Yet, Beishe Village, the county party organization's first rural branch and site of the Licheng CCP headquarters, which became a model party organization, was in the south of the county not far from the county town.

The social reform program was clearly secondary to military and political concerns. Indeed, the emergence of a middle peasant strategy was as much determined by the political considerations of the need for a broad social coalition of landowners and peasants, as it was by questions of village leadership. Moreover, though social reform was central to the CCP's agenda in the Taihang Base Area, it did tend to be narrowly defined in terms of land policy, and the CCP was sometimes not conscious of other forms of social change. In Liaoxian (Zuoquan) an independent Patriotic Women's Association had been part of the origins of the resistance movement and had quite some impact on the later development of the county, markedly increasing the proportion of women involved in politics and education. However, elsewhere local authorities were slow to be prepared to acknowledge the possibility of women's participation in social life outside the home. This clearly was a source of conflict for the daughters of rich peasants, and their mothers, in Licheng during 1940–41 and led to the growth of the Sixth Trigram Movement.

Accompanying social and economic change was a change in the vocabulary of social and political activities that was equally important. New categories of social and political discourse started to change the way people thought about their lives and work, not least as these categories came to be invested with authority to determine wealth, status and power. The CCP's descriptions of land-related class status are the most obvious example of these new categories, especially landlords as exploiters and poor peasants as the exploited. Even the CCP's commitment to the concept of the proletariat exerted an influence, though perhaps not always as dramatically manifested as the early 1940 events in Wuxiang. At the same time, the new language of politics also provided ideas about both the goals of reform, and the means that might be employed to effect change, such as struggle and revolution. In that context, revolution was not just political or social change, but became the catalyst of change itself.

The identification of class status and the ramifications of the CCP's class analysis might have been of greater concern to cadres and party members. However, new village-level political institutions such as struggle meetings, mass campaigns, and village elections effected everyone regardless of social category or political activism. Full-scale land reform in the Taihang Base Area was completed so quickly once introduced in 1946 not only because the process of land equalization had been well underway during the first half of the 1940s, but also because the categories of change were well understood.[5]

The CCP developed considerable social roots in the Taihang Base Area, and particularly its secure areas, during the War of Resistance. A social contract was forged that brought together party, peasant small-holders, rural workers, and landless tenants. Quite apart from the impact of this social contract on the Taihang region, the wartime experience generated several thousand cadres who with the establishment of the PRC went on to staff the institutions of party, state and military throughout the rest of the country.

THE TAIHANG CCP

Rural society changed as a result of the CCP's intervention, however, in the process the party itself had not only grown considerably but also changed both institutionally and associationally. Perhaps the single most important characteristic of change was the development of a significant rural social base for party membership. The CCP in the Taihang region started the war as a disparate series of activists in various locations, coordinated militarily by the 129th Division of the Eighth Route Army, and politically by its editorial department, which became the Taihang Base Area CCP committee. The Taihang Base Area CCP ended the war as a complex administrative hierarchy characterized by its organizational unity and discipline.

The genesis of the Taihang Base Area CCP was a number of different activities in Shanxi, Hebei and Henan that included a variety of united front coalitions and independent actions, in a range of political and military involvements in specific locations. From the CCP headquarters' perspective (in North Shaanxi) the 129th Division of the Eighth Route Army was the initial starting point for the Taihang Base Area. Other participants in early areas of CCP and resistance activity might, however, have been a bit more reluctant to privilege the 129th Division either at the time, or in retrospect, even whilst accepting the centrality of its role. Across the Taihang Base Area the Sacrifice League played a major role in most of the counties of Southeast Shanxi without which the development of the CCP's organization would have been considerably more problematic. In southwest Hebei and North Henan local Resist Japan governments formed at the start of the war provided the CCP with significant local foundations.

If the experience of Liaoxian, Wuxiang and Licheng is a reliable indicator it would seem that every county was likely to have even more specific organizational roots for both resistance activities in general and the development of the local CCP organization. In Liaoxian the Patriotic Women's Association and the Liaoxian First High School played pivotal roles, as in an associational sense so did the women's literacy class of the local Presbyterian church. In Wuxiang, the CCP had established earlier branches during the mid-1930s and the development of the Peasants Refusal League, with a measure of support and an organizational infrastructure that were fairly easy to resurrect. In Licheng the Returned Students Federation was initially the origin of both Sacrifice League and the CCP.

The CCP's commitment to revolution included not only ideas about social reform but also a desire to ensure the unification and centralization of its organization in the Taihang Base Area, not least because it was engaged in a national crusade. This organizational imperative often created tensions between the CCP at the base area level, on the one hand, and the local traditions and strengths of activity on the other. In Licheng this tension led to more open conflict and essentially the destruction of the organization responsible for the local revolutionary tradition, the Returned Students Federation; as well as a running battle within the cadre force throughout the early 1940s between 'insider' and 'outsiders'—natives and non-natives—which was eventually only resolved through an overwhelming influx of outsiders. In Wuxiang the local tradition and strength of organization was recognized by the base area leadership of the CCP and readily incorporated into the whole, except for the brief interlude of April 1940 to January 1941 when it too experienced tensions between insiders and outsiders. However, for most of the war the base area leadership turned to Wuxiang as a model of revolutionary experience.

Creating the CCP as a reliable, single revolutionary organization at the county level was difficult enough without considering how the widely different social and political environments across the base area could be brought together. As one county party secretary wryly observed 'Democracy is something party members from poorer backgrounds favor; cadres currently in office are less enthusiastic.'[6] The key to the development of organizational unity and discipline, both within counties and across the base area, was control of the appointment of cadres, an authority which rested exclusively with the superior level in the CCP's administrative hierarchy. Acceptance of this procedure was in some ways even more important to the development of a revolutionary organization than the later rectification movement, which essentially brought CCP cadres in the Taihang Base Area into the national mainstream.[7]

The membership of the Taihang Base Area CCP grew in essentially three phases. The first was rapid expansion from the end of 1937 to October 1939 when the party was at its most inclusive, for a whole range of political and organizational reasons, including the need to establish itself in areas where for the most part the CCP was largely unknown. The second was from late 1939 to mid-1942 when its first became obsessed with questions of class status, and then remained concerned about the need to rely on the political reliability of the landless and the poor. The third and final phase was after mid-1942 when it concentrated on encouraging middle and poor peasants. If the experience of Liaoxian (Zuoquan), Wuxiang and Licheng is a reliable guide, each of these phases would seem to have provided a specific layer of cadres, characterized by a dominant social category, to the Taihang Base Area CCP by the end of the war. Urban intellectuals came to dominate the base area and county level leadership; poor peasants and farmhands to fill the cadres positions in the subdistricts; and village cadres were overwhelmingly middle peasants, with in turn about half of those middle peasants drawn from the ranks of the long-term owner-cultivators.

At the beginning of the war the Taihang party organization was largely led by transposed urban intellectuals. These included the thirty members of the CCP Provincial Committee for the PingHan Railway who accompanied Li Xuefeng to Pingding; the leadership of the various locally established party branches, such as the former Wuxiang CCP leadership; and various individuals who came from the Taihang region but who had gone to study or work in the cities of North China, where they had joined the CCP, such as Huo Fan from Licheng. They were rapidly joined by a large number of school teachers, and displaced students from the colleges and universities of North China: the 'young men from Hebei' that Li Xuefeng and Yang Shangkun often complained about in a light-hearted way.[8] One of those displaced former students was Wen Jianping, who later became the somewhat controversial secretary of Wuxiang during 1940 (though he had actually come from Northeast China, rather than Hebei). Assuming that the experience of Liaoxian, Wuxiang and Licheng was not overly unusual, it does seem that local teachers formed the starting point for organization of the CCP to a remarkable extent.

The attempt to recruit proletarian cadres that started at the end of 1939 proved a mixed blessing. Even when the proletariat was defined in terms of farmhands, landless tenants and poor peasants, they often did not have the economic resources to keep themselves whilst they served as village cadres, nor the literacy or people skills necessary to the tasks they were being asked to perform. Whilst their political reliability to the CCP seemed guaranteed by their impeccable class status, amongst other sectors of society they rapidly developed a reputation for being extreme in political campaigns, which tended to prove counterproductive. In Wuxiang where the local party organization was not faced with much organized resistance and where the socioeconomic environment favored such an approach the reliance on poor peasant and farmhand cadres caused few problems. However, in Licheng where the socioeconomic environment was different, it would seem that the advent of cadres from poor peasant and farmhand backgrounds merely served to exacerbate worsening social and political tensions.

The growth of middle peasant village cadres was a somewhat slow development for the Taihang Base Area CCP. Many cadres in the Taihang CCP were uneasy about recruiting owner-cultivators to the party organization, let alone encouraging them to become cadres. They were regarded as traditional landowners by some, and there were also suspicions as a result of the patterns of land sales that many had become speculators rather than farmers. This was a particular concern at a time when there was apparently a wide-held belief in several communities that CCP members and cadres were gaining land disproportionately through the various processes of redistribution.[9] On the other hand those identified as middle peasants tended also to be those who were economically independent and literate. Moreover, as their introduction even in Wuxiang demonstrated, they were able to deal more effectively with landlords and rich peasants both on their own behalf, and for poor peasants, farmhands and tenants.[10] Some of the concerns about middle peasant cadres within the Taihang CCP were assuaged to some extent by stressing control mechanisms and the need for political education, as well as the realization that many of those described as middle peasants were not as wealthy as the term might once have implied.

The growth of the middle peasant village cadre after the middle of 1942, and indeed the discussion of the whole middle peasant question during 1942–43, is an example of the Taihang CCP's growing organizational and ideological sophistication. Li Xuefeng in looking back from 1945 on the course of developments since 1937 was very harsh in his criticisms of those of his colleagues whom he described as being 'absolutist' in their interpretations of Marxism and its application to the Taihang region. Regardless of any justification to those comments in terms of difficulties with recalcitrant colleagues, or of how their behavior influenced the development of the base area or the party organization, there was a learning process at work in the development of the Taihang CCP. The emphasis on a specific interpretation of proletarian ideology with its rigid application of the determination of class status during 1940 was later replaced by a more complex approach to questions of class and revolution. With time, principles of class analysis were certainly applied with greater sophistication. Considerable emphasis came to be placed on the role of education and consciousness-raising in the determination of class status. Moreover, current class status was increasingly differentiated from previous class status.

There is even a suggestion in the development of the Taihang CCP's ideological formulations that its position on class and revolution might have brought it into conflict with Mao Zedong. In March 1945 when reviewing the course of discussion on the middle peasant question over the preceding years in the Taihang region, Li Xuefeng criticized 'many of our comrades who after having read *Report of an Investigation of the Peasant Movement in Hunan* didn't regard the middle peasants as properly part of "the masses."'[11] The report in question had been written by Mao Zedong in 1927, and was seminal to the development of his political thought. Li Xuefeng's comments were clearly not intended as a criticism of Mao, not least since middle peasants had come to be conceptualized as part of the revolutionary forces throughout the base areas of North China at this time, presumably with his support. However, a number of former cadres have indicated that somewhat earlier they had found Mao's emphasis on the importance of educating poor peasants to be optimistic. As one said 'The peasantry actually have a lot of the landlords' mentality. It's hard to use education simply mechanically.' Another was even more blunt and suggested that Mao's notion of research on the peasantry was not very thorough: 'He did what he wanted to anyhow, and didn't bother about careful research.'

The view that the Taihang Base Area CCP developed greater sophistication during 1937–45 would seem to be contradicted by its apparently constant 'leftism' throughout those years. The base area CCP committee was only criticized openly for being 'leftist' by the CCP Central Committee in November 1941. However, there were a number of occasions when the base area leadership took itself, county leaderships or branches to task for 'leftist' behavior. Most spectacularly the leadership of the Wuxiang CCP was reorganized in March 1940 because some branches had advocated some form of proletarian uprising. 'Leftism' in this context usually refers to actions taken to excess rather than any specific ideological content: CCP activists tending to follow their own political agendas to the exclusion of working well with their own local communities, and even their most obvious support base. 'Leftism' then surfaced so regularly as a criticism in the Taihang Base Area precisely because party cadres at all levels were constantly pushing the bounds of the possible in the attempt at revolution, and overreaching.

PERSONAL TRANSFORMATIONS

Both the principle and the practice of personal transformation were central to the process of social and political change in the Taihang Base Area during the War of Resistance. The CCP's system of class analysis included the possibility that the class status of the individual could change, with the expectation that there would then be a change in their political behavior.

The personal impact of the social dislocation of the times went even further. In particular, urban intellectuals became rural cadres, alongside the former members of the gentry who became peasant small-holders, and the farm laborers who became poor peasants.

From the CCP's point of view during the war, there needed to be a dynamic element to the analysis of class status. This was one of the problems in the Taihang CCP's flirtation with the 'Theory of the unique influence of class status' during 1940. In the short term it resolved this continuing tension about class by adopting an approach to class analysis which left room for class status to change with both economic circumstances and consciousness, and which was applied to both its social policy as well as to inner-party affairs. Individual consciousness could be raised, particularly through education. As Xu Zirong pointed out in the middle of 1942, when he was attempting to explain the base area's new strategy:

> It is not a rule that a person will become bad when their class status becomes higher. The key point is to educate them. They should be educated to understand the relationship between personal interest and class interest. They should understand that they owe their improvement in living to the party's policies. They can't maintain their own interests without maintaining class interests.[12]

The element of personal transformation, of an individual making a choice to change, was considered fundamental. In theory, whilst the CCP could provide various forms of persuasion—political education, assessment of political risk, macroeconomic management—only the individual could decide on their own personal change. This emphasis on personal transformation partly explains the theater of the struggle meeting during the various political campaigns, but especially those to reduce rents and interest. A landlord such as Wei Wenlai in Wuxiang might have agreed to become an 'enlightened landlord' the day before a formal struggle session. However, the CCP still felt that a public statement and criticism the next day were required. Equally within the CCP the process of rectification included a stage in which cadres were expected to connect with their 'essential nature' and achieve personal transformation.

A key theme in the account of social change has been the struggle of individuals trying to understand and sometimes to control their rapidly changing environment. Some succeeded and some did not, some were more able than others, and some were lucky, happening to be in the right place at the right time. Landlords loom large simply because the gentry were a key target of CCP policy. In Licheng, Xie Haoli, a landlord but also a member of the Border Region Provisional Assembly, could not understand why he was the object of one, yet alone several, struggle meetings.

Other landlords, with even greater foresight, luck or political commitment simply gave their land away, as in Hanbi Village, Wuxiang. In Hanbi too, Wei Xiaoshan was not prepared to make a similar sacrifice and was executed.

Peasants too were sometimes surprised by the turn of events, and were possibly even more resistant to change. Poor peasants and tenants were often reluctant to participate in political campaigns fearing retribution. Even later when that hurdle had been passed they remained reluctant, regarding any land settlements as merely temporary. This belief was sometimes reinforced by the behavior of landlords and rich peasants, as, for example, in the wake of the 1942 rent and interest reduction, when such phenomenon were evident, particularly in Licheng.

The struggle to construct personal environments is perhaps an explanation of part of two of the more unusual aspects of the process of social change in the Taihang Base Area. The first is the reported attempt to create a proletarian uprising at the beginning of 1940 in some of the CCP branches of eastern Wuxiang. Admittedly there is little information available. However, it is possible that under the circumstances of civil war and Japanese invasion, village or even subdistrict cadres with only a little knowledge of communist theory and without wider experience of communist organization interpreted proletarian revolution as a millenarianist experience. The second is more certain in that the growth of the Sixth Trigram Movement in Licheng during 1940–41 was definitely fueled by young fairly well-off women who wanted more opportunities to be out of their homes and in public.

The element of personal transformation was considerable for the urban intellectuals who came to the Taihang Base Area at the start of the war and stayed to become its cadre force. The element of surprise and personal struggle at the beginning was even evident for someone like Li Xuefeng, who had already been a CCP organizer for some years. However, there were many amongst these incoming urban intellectuals who had even less experience of the world outside the classroom. Many would have had no experience of rural China, war, politics or the CCP and yet here they were having to manage all together at the same time. Some may have never come fully to terms with their Taihang environment but most survived and were transformed by the experience.

The base area's leadership may have started the war as urban intellectuals, but they became not only peasant organizers and revolutionaries, but also almost universally the leading cadres of the new communist party-state after 1949, as some examples at both base area and county level may indicate. Li Xuefeng, who was the secretary of the Taihang Base Area CCP committee for most of its existence, went on to become a member of the CCP Secretariat of the 8th Central Committee, the First Secretary of the Beijing CCP, and an alternate member of the CCP Political Bureau during the Cultural Revolution before being removed for his leftism in 1970. Xu Zirong, Director of the Taihang Propaganda Department, became a Vice-Minister of Public Security and an alternate member of the 8th Central Committee before the Cultural Revolution. Lai Ruoyu, the Director of the Taihang Organization Department, became a member of the CCP 8th Central Committee and Chairman of the Federation of Trade Unions before his death in 1958. Ma Guishu, the Secretary of the Wuxiang CCP in the 1940s, became a secretary of the CCP in Tibet before the Cultural Revolution, and then a leading cadre in Shanxi afterwards. Huo Fan, the native secretary of the Licheng CCP during the 1940s, became a party secretary in Guangxi Zhuang Autonomous Region before the Cultural Revolution, and later a leading cadre in Shanxi. Zhai Ying, a long-time member of the Liaoxian (Zuoquan) CCP committee and then its secretary, became a leading figure in the Women's Federation after the establishment of the PRC.

REVOLUTION IN NORTH CHINA

The Taihang Base Area was but one of the base areas in North China during the War of Resistance, and Liaoxian (Zuoquan), Wuxiang and Licheng but three of its fifty-eight counties (by mid-1945), albeit three of the most central for most of the first half of the 1940s. A comprehensive history of the War of Resistance in the North China base areas and border regions clearly requires a series of local studies so that longer-range theory can be developed. However, in the interim it is equally as important to attempt to identify key aspects of social and political change at that time, not least in order to inform further research. The observations in this final section concentrate on those actors and processes that have emerged as central concerns throughout this study of the Taihang Base Area. In particular, it considers the parts played in the revolutionary process by localism, teachers, middle peasants, violence and incrementalism.

The CCP's assumption of power in 1949, the establishment of the PRC and the even greater political and social change that followed are often regarded as a response to China's need for modernization rather than as part of a longer process of modernization. Too often a dividing line between the past and the present is drawn at 1949, and even occasionally at 1937. However, the experience of the Taihang region during the War of Resistance draws attention to the social revolution that started there during the 1920s and 1930s. Liaoxian, Wuxiang and Licheng were certainly not Shanghai or Beiping, but nor were they counties dominated by subsistence farming with peasants indentured to absentee landlords. In the

1920s and 1930s each had started to be influenced by modernization in ways that had begun to shape their socioeconomic environment, and which certainly affected the course of the CCP's management of political and social change during the War of Resistance. Liaoxian had become a regional commercial center, not least for the wool trade; Wuxiang was becoming a rural industrial center based on coal, iron and textiles; and Licheng had a highly developed educational system, which in turn led to the Returned Students Federation.

More interesting is the suggestion that the variable impact of modernization on these counties might have been related to the CCP's ability to operate, and to implement its programs of mobilization and social reform. The CCP clearly faced greater resistance in Licheng, once it started to operate openly, than it did in Wuxiang. Even though income per capita in Licheng in 1943 was about 17 percent higher than income per capita in Wuxiang, and wealth was more evenly distributed in Licheng, these kinds of structural relationships cannot provide a total explanation. For a start the county is almost certainly the wrong unit of analysis. CCP support had been developed village by village. In Licheng, CCP support was to be found in both poor and relatively wealthy villages.[13] However, the pattern of life in Licheng had been less affected by economic development in the most recent past than was the case in either Wuxiang or those parts of Liaoxian (Zuoquan) where the CCP settled. Research in Liaoxian during 1942 suggested that the CCP had far more success in mobilizing peasants against landlords where traditional farming relationships in a village had been replaced by commercialized agriculture, and the recent concentration of landownership.[14] In Wuxiang, the degree of land concentration was considerably higher than even in southern Liaoxian, and there too this process had accelerated rapidly since 1928.

Although these environmental factors are likely to have played some role in shaping the development of the base area, their relative influence must be kept in perspective. Certainly the contrast between Licheng and Wuxiang suggests local knowledge and organization may be of even greater significance in determining the CCP's ability to organize, mobilize and implement programs of social reform. The parochialism of the Taihang region, and probably most of rural China, remains intense. The CCP's long-term ability to achieve its aims required local activists with good contacts and a high degree of local acceptability. Where a person did not speak the same local language they would probably have been treated as an outsider and consequently less trusted. A peasant or farmhand in Liaoxian would probably have found it difficult to differentiate between a soldier speaking Japanese and a soldier speaking Fujianese. The Wuxiang CCP had local knowledge, organization and contacts from its earlier activities. It was led initially by local CCP members who were both familiar with the county and its circumstances as well as with the discipline of the CCP as organization. As time went on it was able to produce its own new cadres in large numbers. In Licheng the CCP had local knowledge and organization before 1940. The Returned Students Federation was both local, active and committed to social change, and had begun a program of rural outreach before the war. All this gave the Licheng CCP an exceptional local base at the start of the war. However, the Licheng CCP's reorganization of 1940, when it came to regard anyone associated with the Returned Students League or the Sacrifice League, and intellectuals generally as politically unreliable effectively denied it much local support, and the local skilled leadership it needed.

The importance of local knowledge and acceptability in part explains the emergence of teachers as a revolutionary force in the Taihang Base Area. Teachers were local and were looked up to as community leaders. In each of Liaoxian, Wuxiang and Licheng the locals who first joined and often formed the county CCP organization were almost all teachers, and certainly teachers dominated the early memberships in all three counties. It seems likely that this might be a general pattern elsewhere, at least in the Taihang Base Area. Urban intellectuals clearly came to play a central role from the beginning in the development of the base area. Many of them were teachers or graduates from teacher training establishments, and so might well have been predisposed to recruit teachers. In some cases it is even clear that CCP organizers coming into an area already knew some local teachers from an earlier common experience of work or study. However, it is also likely that teachers wanted to join because they were adventurous and genuinely committed to social change. At this time teachers really were agents of a modernizing ideology. Teaching was a new and modernizing profession. In Shanxi the education curriculum itself was deliberately designed 'to be practical' (to quote Yan Xishan) and to aid modernization, having only fairly recently been introduced.[15] Moreover, the teachers of the 1930s would have been the first generation in their families to have probably any education, but certainly a modern education.

Alongside urban intellectuals and teachers, the other agents of revolutionary change to emerge from the Taihang Base Area seem to have been the middle peasants. The recent rediscovery in the 1980s and 1990s of the role of the middle peasant during the War of Resistance has an in-built tendency to mask the revolutionary changes of those years.[16] In part this is because the middle peasant of the 1940s was rediscovered at a time when China, and particularly the CCP, was not only seeking to regain its history but in the process also searching for new political strategies in the wake of the Mao-dominated years of its politics.

One reading of the concept of middle peasant allows it to be interpreted in a less threatening manner, as the established small landowner of 1937, the equivalent of a yeoman perhaps, encouraging broad popular coalitions of nationalism, as was the case during the War of Resistance. On the other hand, that interpretation was precisely part of the inherent ambiguity in the concept, which became its greatest strength as a category for creating revolution. In socioeconomic as opposed to sociopolitical terms there were significant differences within the ranks of those now identified as middle peasants. In particular, the overwhelming majority of those who found themselves assigned middle peasant class status for the first time during 1942–45 were more accurately smaller-scale, and probably poorer, independent small-holders than the designation of middle peasant implied. From a political perspective it could be presented otherwise, reflecting the conflicting aspirations of a number of social groups.

The advantage of the middle peasant strategy was that it permitted the CCP to proceed with its revolutionary agenda without threatening to alienate a wide range of social groups, as its earlier policies had done. By encouraging middle peasants as village leaders and as the favored mode of economic production it was able to offer each the promise of something they wanted. To the landlords and rich peasants it suggested a less threatening political agenda. To the middle peasants it recognized their socioeconomic worth and potential for village leadership. To poor peasants, tenants and farmhands it offered the possibility of landownership. To cadres pushing for greater and faster change it highlighted the declining value of landownership, and the opportunity for the poor and the landless to benefit economically.

Though it would be possible to regard all those identified by the CCP as middle peasants as agents of revolutionary change because they had contributed to the development of the middle peasant strategy in this way, that would be somewhat misleading. By the end of the war, the CCP's sociopolitical category of middle peasant had come to include a range of socioeconomic groups and significant subcategories even in the CCP's categorization who could not all be considered agents of change, or at least not all equally. The designation of middle peasant came to be applied to owner-cultivators whose circumstances had largely stayed constant during the war; owner-cultivators who had become wealthier, and even a few who had become poorer; déclassé landlords and rich peasants; as well as upwardly mobile former poor peasants, tenants and even farmhands. Of those now middle peasants the most significant agents of revolutionary change would have to have been those who had become local and village leaders of various kinds. Though the statistics are unreliable, it would seem that these were divided in roughly equal proportions between former poor and landless peasants who were upwardly mobile, and former long-term owner-cultivators.

A fairly recent study of Wugong Village, in the Shanxi-Chahar-Hebei Border Region commented on the absence of rural class conflict that accompanied the process of land redistribution during the War of Resistance. It described a 'silent revolution' in which landownership was equalized gradually, through the operation of the market as the prosperous sold land and the poor bought it, unaccompanied by revolutionary violence.[17] Something similar clearly happened in the Taihang Base Area, but here the level of revolutionary violence was considerably higher. Rural class conflict was neither ubiquitous nor constant, but it certainly seems to have never been far away.

The exercise of revolutionary violence was clearly at its height in Liaoxian at the end of 1939 and beginning of 1940; and Wuxiang during 1940, when almost every village in the CCP-controlled eastern part of the county must have been affected. Those occasions were clearly such extreme examples of the exercise of revolutionary violence that it led to censure and political problems for the county party organizations. At the same time, it seems reasonable to assume that for villagers in Wuxiang during the rest of the war, and the subsequent rent and interest reduction campaigns, those events would have become part of the essential context for their participation.

The Liaoxian CCP's call for the extermination of landlords and rich peasants in October 1939, and Wuxiang's experience of rural class conflict in 1940 may have been extreme in scale, but they were not otherwise unusual. In Liaoxian, Wuxiang and Licheng, as well as the Taihang Base Area as a whole, mob violence, attacks on landlords, and the confiscation of land were not everyday events, but they were also not rare, even after 1940. The threat of revolutionary violence was inherent in the operation of the struggle meeting, which could easily escape from anyone's control. It was also inherent in the entire program of social reform based on land redistribution, which was designed to dispossess the wealthy and provide for the poor.

At the same time, the notion of a 'silent revolution' underlines the importance of the CCP's revolutionary incrementalism. The CCP clearly achieved more revolutionary social change, and more effectively, by stages in the Taihang Base Area during 1940–45 than had proved to be the case during 1939–40 when local actions threatened to subvert a sustainable revolution. Despite the problems the CCP encountered within its own organization and with society, it nonethless managed to maintain the momentum of revolutionary change, particularly through the implementation of its middle peasant strategy.

Indeed, even beyond consideration of that aspect of its program of social reform, the incrementalism of the revolutionary process has been central to this account of the Taihang Base Area. This was a complex process of social and political change managed by the CCP, which at the end of the day judged its success more by its continued presence and ability to develop, than by its creation of new structures of wealth, status and power. Managing this complex revolutionary process entailed not only learning from successes and mistakes, and being able to manage revolutionary violence or the threat of revolutionary coercion effectively, it also required, from the CCP's perspective, the creation of conformity and unity under its leadership.

NOTES

1. Benjamin Yang *Deng: A Political Biography* New York, M E Sharpe, 1998, p.90.

2. Mao Zedong's own working style was often to stand back as situations became radicalized (sometimes as a result of his own actions) in order to increase his range of choices. See Frederick C Teiwes *Leadership, Legitimacy and Conflict in China* New York, M E Sharpe, 1984, p.31 ff.

3. Similar processes occurred in the other base areas and border regions of North China. However, the extent of middle peasant predominance in both rural society and CCP membership was higher in the Taihang Base Area. See Tian Youru 'Shanxi tudi zhidu gaige lishi gaiyao' ['Outline History of Reform of the Land System in Shanxi'] in *Shanxi dangshi tongxun* [Bulletin of Shanxi Party History] no.2, 1993, p.17; and comparative data in Shanxisheng shizhi yanjiuyuan (ed) *Shanxi tongzhi* [Encyclopedia of Shanxi] vol.7 *Tudi zhi* [Land] Beijing, Zhonghua shuju, 1998, p.220 ff.

4. ZJY p.31.

5. Zhonggong Taihang qudangwei (ed) *Tudi gaige baogao* [Report on Land Reform] Taihang qudangwei, 1947; Zhonggong Taihangqu sandiwei *Sanfenqu tudi gaige yu qunzhong yundong cailiao jicun* [Collection of Materials on Land Reform and Mass Mobilization in the 3rd District] Taihang sandiwei, 1947.

6. Ma Guishu, CCP secretary of Wuxiang, in ZJY p.32.

7. LXH p.196 ff.

8. Not least because, in their view, there were also 'too few young women.' See their comments in reports to the 1st Representative Assembly of the CCP in Shanxi-Hebei-Henan: Li Xuefeng (p.492) and Yang Shangkun (p.473) in TDZH vol.2: 1939.

9. TW p.132.

10. 'Wuxiang nongmin gejieceng shenghuo tedian jiqi ganbu shengzhangde diaocha' ['Survey of Various Categories of Peasants in Wuxiang and their Characteristics'] July 1943, in CJZX vol.2, p.1398.

11. Summary report, 8 March 1945, in SOC p.65.

12. Xu Zirong, 29 July 1942, in XZJY p.8.

13. For example, Beishe, the site of the Licheng CCP headquarters, was and remains a fairly prosperous village.

14. LDB p.8.

15. Donald G Gillin *Warlord Yen Hsi-shan in Shansi Province, 1911–1949* Princeton, New Jersey, Princeton University Press, 1967, p.68 ff.

16. It had previously been discussed if not so much within China, then in western research by first Isabel and David Crook, and then Victor Nee. See Isabel and David Crook *Revolution in a Chinese Village: Ten Mile Inn* London, Routledge, 1959; and Victor Nee 'Towards a Social Anthropology of the Chinese Revolution' in *Bulletin of Concerned Asian Scholars* Vol.11 No.3, p.40.

17. Edward Friedman, Paul Pickowicz and Mark Selden *Chinese Village, Socialist State* New Haven, Connecticut, Yale University Press, 1991, pp.84–85.

Bibliography

Although the events described in this book occurred some sixty years ago, the sources necessary for its production have only recently been made available. The Bibliography that follows lists primary and secondary sources separately in two distinct sections. The first section includes all primary sources and includes both published and archive material. It provides detail of published collections of documents; specific documents of particular importance; published contemporary serials from the Taihang region; memoirs; and local gazetteers separately. The second section of the Bibliography list secondary sources, both of a general nature and those related to the Taihang Base Area more directly. It includes all accounts of the Taihang Base Area written after 1949, when the Taihang Region formally ceased to exist. In particular it includes accounts of the Taihang Base Area, the Shanxi-Hebei-Shandong-Henan Border Region, and their constituent parts published in the PRC during the 1980s and 1990s.

The publications listed in the first section are mainly of two kinds. They include contemporary material from the Taihang Base Area that was published at the time; and material that has subsequently been republished. Well before the end of the war the Taihang Base Area had prepared its own history.[1] Moreover, toward the end of the Civil War, Tao Lujia, a leading cadre in Pingding County during the War of Resistance, and after the establishment of the PRC the CCP's leading cadre in Shanxi Province, ensured that most of the documents gathered by the Taihang Base Area during its lifetime were deposited in the CCP Taiyuan Archive. In the 1980s the collection and (re)publication of documentation from the Taihang Base Area became a provincial project in the 7th Five-Year Plan.

Much of the material necessarily appears in both types of publication. In all cases an attempt has been made to establish and to cite the fullest and most easily accessible text available for any specific document.[2] Of particular use in that regard, there are three major, openly published collections of documents from the Taihang Base Area that have appeared since the late 1980s. There is a general collection produced under the auspices of the Shanxi History and Archive Research Institute, itself part of the provincial party's organization, which has to date published a series of twelve volumes dealing with different aspects of the base area's development.[3] There is a series of volumes dealing with the development of the CCP, one for each year of the war, being produced by the Shanxi CCP Archive in Taiyuan.[4] The third collection specializes in some detail on financial and economic matters.[5]

The published material from the Taihang Base Area during the war includes not only formal speeches, CCP briefings and position papers, directives, instructions, investigations, reports, conference agendas, records of meetings, investigative reports, as well as a series of eight-year surveys of development that started to appear once the war started to draw to a close. In 1939 the Mobilization Department of the base area's CCP committee established a small Investigation Group that conducted surveys of social and economic change in six counties of the northern part of the region. In 1941 this Investigation Group was enlarged and placed directly under the party committee, becoming an Investigation Unit of more formal standing in 1942. It trained other researchers and altogether carried out some eighty-one formal investigations, that include much detailed investigation of social change at local level. Many of its reports were published at the time and have been republished more recently.[6]

Where no publication details are provided for a document cited in the first section of the Bibliography, this indicates that the document concerned is to be found in the Taiyuan CCP Archive. The Archive includes original and still unpublished material in addition to the earlier histories and collections of documents prepared for the Taihang Base Area before the establishment of the PRC. For example, there are the special reports commissioned by the Taihang authorities through the Investigation Unit, such as that which investigated the 1941 Sixth Trigram Uprising in Licheng, or the summary report on the development of Liaoxian as an experimental county. In addition, the Archive also includes the untranscribed and unpublished minutes of discussion at CCP internal meetings. Those concerned with the base area's organizational work are particularly interesting since they include a record in many cases of the process by which final positions were reached at specific meetings.

The final two parts of the first section of the Bibliography are devoted to memoirs and local gazetteers. Memoirs of the participants are listed first. Many of those active in the Taihang Base Area have written memoirs, either of the war years as a whole or of single or specific events. Perhaps the most comprehensive view of the Taihang Base Area in a memoir is provided by Li Xuefeng.[7] Li was the CCP's leading cadre in the Taihang Base Area from February 1938 for the rest of the war. In addition, a range of other participants at all levels of the base area have written retrospectively of their experiences.

Provincial and county gazetteers have long been a major source of research on China. Before the establishment of the PRC, it was the function of the local or provincial official to ensure the state-approved history of a locality through the production of the gazetteer. Although this aspect of China's statecraft died out during the Cultural Revolution, it has been revived more recently, along with the republication within China of earlier gazetteers. Contemporary county gazetteers have recently appeared for both Wuxiang and Licheng, but not as yet for Zuoquan. During the 1980s each CCP organization at various levels of its administrative hierarchy—central department, ministry, province, district and county—started to prepare an Organizational History to record its development and personnel. These are also listed as primary sources since they, too, are state-approved local histories.

NOTES

1. For details of documentation before 1945, see Tian Youru 'Taihang kangRi genjudi shi yanjiu songshu' ['Research on the History of the Taihang Anti-Japanese Base Area'] in *Dangshi tongxun* [Newsletter on Party History] No. 353 (No. 7 1987) p.39. Party histories for Wuxiang, Cixian and Xingtai were published in 1943, with compendia for the whole region appearing in 1944.

2. Differences between versions of the documents are detailed both here and in notes to the text.

3. Taihang geming genjudishi zongbian weihui (ed) *Taihang geming genjudi shiliao congshu* mostly but not exclusively published by Shanxi renmin chubanshe.

4. Shanxisheng danganguan (ed) *Taihang dangshi ziliao huibian* [Collection of Materials on the History of the Party in the Taihang Base Area] Taiyuan, Shanxi renmin chubanshe. To date four volumes: 1937–38 and 1939, published in 1989; 1940 and 1941, published in 1994. Another four volumes have been scheduled for publication.

5. JinJiLuYu Bianqu caizheng jingji shi bianjizu and Shanxi, Hebei, Shandong, Henan sheng danganguan (ed) *KangRi zhanzheng shiqi JinJiLuYu Bianqu caizheng jingjishi ziliao xuanbian* [Collection of Materials on the Economic and Financial History of the Shanxi-Hebei-Shandong-Henan Border Region during the War of Resistance to Japan] Beijing, Caizheng jingji chubanshe, 1990, 2 vols.

6. Notably the following surveys, all available in JinJiLuYu Bianqu caizheng jingji shi bianjizu and Shanxi, Hebei, Shandong, Henan sheng danganguan (ed)

KangRi zhanzheng shiqi JinJiLuYu Bianqu caizheng jingjishi ziliao xuanbian [Collection of Materials on the Economic and Financial History of the Shanxi-Hebei-Shandong-Henan Border Region during the War of Resistance to Japan] Beijing, Caizheng jingji chubanshe, 1990: *Taihangqu guomin caifu gaikuang* [Outline of national wealth in the Taihang Region] 1944, in vol.2, p.1334; *Taihangqu renmin shenghuode xiaohao* [Everday consumption in the Taihang Region] 1944, in vol.2, p.1341; *Taihangqu shehui jingji diaocha (diyiji)* [Social and Economic Survey of the Taihang Region—First Collection] August 1944, in vol.2, p.1346; *Taihangqu shehui jingji diaocha (dierji)* [Social and Economic Survey of the Taihang Region—Second Collection] 1945, in vol.2, p.1406; *Banianlai Riben faxisi cuihui Taihangqu renminde gaishu* [General Description of The People of The Taihang Region after Eight Years of Japan's Fascist Destruction] 1945, in vol.1 p.534. Further information on the Investigation Unit may be found in 'Bianhouji' ['Editorial Afterthought'] in *Taihangqu shehui jingji diaocha (diyiji)* [Social and Economic Survey of the Taihang Region—First Collection] August 1944, p.1405.

7. Li Xuefeng *Li Xuefeng huiyilu: Taihang shinian* [The Memoirs of Li Xuefeng: Ten Years in the Taihang Mountains]] Beijing, Zhonggong dangshi chubanshe, 1998.

PRIMARY SOURCES

Documentary Collections

Chen Feiqin et al (ed) *Liu-Deng dajun zhengzhan jiwen xuebian* [Study Materials on the Battles of the Liu-Deng Army] [vols] Beijing, Junshi fanwen chubanshe, 1987.

Bo Yibo *Bo Yibo wenxuan (1937–1992)* [Selected Writings of Bo Yibo 1937–1992] Beijing, Renmin chubanshe, 1992.

Chen Yun *Chen Yun Wenxuan, 1926–1949* [Selected Works of Chen Yun 1926–1949] Beijing, Renmin chubanshe, 1984.

Chen Zhuanhai et al (ed) *Rijun huo Yu ziliao xuanbian* [Selected Materials on the Japanese Army's Attack on Henan] Henan shizhi ziliao congbian no.4, Henan renmin chubanshe, 1986.

Deng Xiaoping *Deng Xiaoping Wenxuan, 1938–1965* [Selected Works of Deng Xiaoping 1938–1965] Beijing, Renmin chubanshe, 1989.

Feng Hefa (ed) *Zhongguo nongcun jingji ziliao* [Materials on China's Villages] Shanghai, Li Ming Press, 1935.

Jinan geming genjudishi bianshen weiyuanhui (ed) *Jinan dangshi ziliao* [Materials on Party History in South Hebei] Xingtai, Jinan geming genjudishi bianshen weiyuanhui, 1986 (vol.1), 1987 (vol.2) and 1988 (vol.3).

Jinan Taihang Taiyue xingzheng lianhe banshichu (ed) *JiTai Lianban diyici zhuanyuan xianzhang huiyi tekan* [Special Reports of the 1st Conference of Commissioners and County Heads under the Joint Office for Jinan, Taihang and Taiyue] Jinan Taihang Taiyue xingzheng lianhe banshichu, 1941.

JinJiLuYu Bianqu caizheng jingji shi bianjizu and Shanxi, Hebei, Shandong, Henan sheng danganguan (ed) *KangRi zhanzheng shiqi JinJiLuYu Bianqu caizheng jingjishi ziliao xuanbian* [Collection of Materials on the Economic and Financial History of the Shanxi-Hebei-Shandong-Henan Border Region during the War of Resistance to Japan] [2 vols] Beijing, Caizheng jingji chubanshe, 1990. [CJZX]

JinJiLuYu Bianqu zhengfu (ed) *Faling huibian* [Collection of Laws and Regulations] JinJiLuYu Bianqu zhengfu, 1942.

JinJiLuYu Bianqu zhengfu (ed) *Faling huibian* [Collection of Laws and Regulations] JinJiLuYu Bianqu zhengfu, 2nd edition, 1946.

JinJiLuYu genjudi shiliao xuanbianzhe (ed) *JinJiLuYu genjudi shiliaoxuan* [Selected Materials on the History of the Shanxi-Hebei-Shandong-Henan Base Area] Taiyuan, Shanxi shengwei, 1989, 4 vols (1937–40, 1941–42, 1943–45, 1945–47). [GSX]

Liu Jiang and Lu Qiao (ed) *Taihang xinwen shiliao huibian* [Collection of Historical Materials on the News in Taihang] Taihang xinwen shixuehui, 1994.

Liu Shaoqi *Liu Shaoqi xuanji* [Selected Works of Liu Shaoqi] (2 vols) Beijing, Renmin chubanshe, 1981 and 1985.

Minzhu chubanshe *JinJiLuYu bianqu fenqu xiangjie ditu* [Maps of the Districts of the Shanxi-Hebei-Shandong-Henan Border Region] Huabei xinhua shudian, 1947.

Ministry of Justice, Investigation Department, Republic of China *Zhonggong nongmin yundong yuanshi wenjian huibian* [Collection of Documents from the CCP Peasant Movement] (6 vols) Taipei, Fawubu diaochaju, 1979–82.

Ministry of Justice, Investigation Department, Republic of China *Zhonggong funu yundong yuanshi wenjian huibian* [Collection of Documents from the CCP Women's Movement] (2 vols) Taipei, Fawubu diaochaju, 1980 and 1981.

Ministry of Justice, Investigation Department, Republic of China *Zhonggong dangde jianshe yuanshi wenjian huibian* [Collection of Documents from the Establishment of the CCP] (3 vols) Taipei, Fawubu diaochaju, 1979–82.

Ministry of Justice, Investigation Department, Republic of China *Zhonggong gongren yundong yuanshi wenjian huibian* [Collection of Documents from the CCP worker's Movement] (4 vols) Taipei, Fawubu diaochaju, 1980–82.

Shanxisheng danganguan (ed) *Taihang dangshi ziliao huibian* [Collection of Materials on the History of the Party in the Taihang Base Area] Taiyuan, Shanxi renmin chubanshe, 1989 (1937–38 and 1939 volumes); 1994 (1940 and 1941 volumes). [TDZH]

Shanxisheng wenhuating wenhuazhi bianzuan bangongshi *Shanxi wenhuazhi geming genjudi wenyi yundong shiliao xuanbian* [Selections of Historical Materials from the Culture Movement in the Shanxi Revolutionary Base Areas] Taiyuan, 1983.

Shanxisheng Wuxiangxian funu lianhehui (ed) *Wuxiang funu yundong shiliao xuanbian* [Selected Materials from the Women's Movement in Wuxiang] Wuxiang, 1982.

Taihang geming genjudi huace editorial group *Taihang geming genjudi huace* [Pictures of the Taihang Revolutionary Base Area] Taiyuan, Shanxi renmin chubanshe, 1987.

Taihang geming genjudishi zongbian weihui (ed) *Dang de jianshe* [Party Development] Taihang geming genjudi shiliao congshu No.2, Taiyuan, Shanxi renmin chubanshe, 1989. [DJ]

Taihang geming genjudishi zongbian weihui (ed) *Difang wuzhuang douzheng* [Local Armed Struggle] Taihang geming genjudi shiliao congshu No.3, Taiyuan, Shanxi renmin chubanshe, 1990. [DWD]

Taihang geming genjudishi zongbian weihui (ed) *Zhengquan jianshe* [Political Development] Taihang geming genjudi shiliao congshu No.4, Taiyuan, Shanxi renmin chubanshe, 1990. [ZJ]

Taihang geming genjudishi zongbian weihui (ed) *Tudi wenti* [The Land Question] Taihang geming genjudi shiliao congshu No.5, Taiyuan, Shanxi renmin chubanshe, 1987. [TW]

Taihang geming genjudishi zongbian weihui (ed) *Caizheng jingji jianshe* [Financial and Economic Development] (2 vols) Taihang geming genjudi shiliao congshu No.6, Taiyuan, Shanxi renmin chubanshe, 1987. [CJJ]

Taihang geming genjudishi zongbian weihui (ed) *Qunzhong yundong* [The Mass Movement] Taihang geming genjudi shiliao congshu No.7, Taiyuan, Shanxi renmin chubanshe, 1989. [QY]

Taihang geming genjudishi zongbian weihui (ed) *Wenhua shiye* [Cultural Affairs] Taihang geming genjudi shiliao congshu No.8, Taiyuan, Shanxi renmin chubanshe, 1989. [WS]

Taihang geming genjudishi zongbian weihui (ed) *Gongan baowei gongzuo* [Security and Protection] Taihang geming genjudi shiliao congshu No.9, Taiyuan, Shanxi renmin chubanshe, 1989. [GBG]

Taihang geming genjudishi zongbian weihui (ed) *Yubei zhandou* [The Struggle for North Henan] Taihang geming genjudi shiliao congshu No.11, Taiyuan, Shanxi renmin chubanshe, 1988. [YZ]

Taihang geming genjudishi zongbian weihui (ed) *Jiaotong youzheng* [Communications and Postal Administration] Taihang geming genjudi shiliao congshu No.12, Taiyuan, Shanxi renmin chubanshe, 1995.

Taihang qu yinhang gongshang gongzuo cankao ziliao bianzhe weiyuanhui (ed) *Taihangqu yinhang gongshang gongzuo cankao ziliao* [Reference Materials on Bank and Commercial Work in the Taihang Base Area] Shexian, 1945. [TYG]

Taiyue geming genjudi caizhengshi bianxiezu *Taiyue geming genjudi caizheng ziliao xuanbian* [Selected Materials on Financial Management in the Taiyue Revolutionary Base Area] Taiyue geming genjudi caizhengshi bianxiezu, 1987.

Taiyue geming genjudi gongyeshi bianxiezu *Taiyue geming genjudi gongye ziliao xuanbian* [Selected Materials on Industry in the Taiyue Revolutionary Base Area] Taiyue geming genjudi gongyeshi bianxiezu, 1987.

Taiyue geming genjudi liangshishi bianxiezu *Taiyue geming genjudi liangshi ziliao xuanbian* [Selected Materials on Grain Production in the Taiyue Revolutionary Base Area] Taiyue geming genjudi liangshishi bianxiezu and Shanxisheng liangshiju zhengce yanjiushi, 1987.

Taiyue geming genjudi nongyeshi bianxiezu *Taiyue geming genjudi nongye ziliao xuanbian* [Selected Materials on Agriculture in the Taiyue Revolutionary Base Area] Shanxisheng nongye kexueyuan and Taiyue geming genjudi nongye shi bianxiezu, 1987.

Taiyue genjudi shiliaoxuan bianzhe *Taiyue genjudi shiliaoxuan* [Collection of Historical Material on the Taiyue Base Area] (3 vols) Shanxi shengwei, 1989.

Wang Dapin (ed) *Taihang mubiao xuanji* [A Selection of Taihang Woodcuts] Taiyuan, Shanxi renmin chubanshe, 1991.

Wu Dongcai (ed) *JinJiYu genjudi* [The Shanxi-Hebei-Henan Base Area] Geming genjudi jungong shiliao congshu, Beijing, Bingpin gongye chubanshe, 1990.

Wu Jie (ed) *KangRi zhanzheng shiqi jiefangqu kexue jishu fazhan shi ziliao* [Materials on the History of Scientific and Technical Development in the Liberated Areas during the War of Resistance to Japan] (vols) Beijing, Zhongguo xueshu chubanshe, 1984.

Youdianbu Huabei jiaotong youzheng shiliao bianzhizu Taihang zu (ed) *Huabei jiefangqu jiaotong youzheng shiliao huibian—Taihang quan* [Collection of Historical Materials on Communications and Postal Administrations in the North China Liberated Areas—Taihang volume] (2 vols) Beijing, Youdianbu, 1990.

Zhonggong Hebei Shengwei dangshi ziliao zhengji bianshen weiyuanhui and Taihang (Hebei bufen) shiliao lianhe zhengbian bangongshi (ed) *Jixi minxunchu yu Jixi Youjidui* [The West Hebei Training Regiment and the West Hebei Guerilla Troop] Taihang geming genjudi shiliao congshu No.10, Shijiazhuang, Hebei renmin chubanshe 1989.

Zhonggong Henan shengwei dangshi ziliao zhengji bianzuan weiyuanhui (ed) *Taihang kangRi genjudi* [The Taihang Anti-Japanese Base Area] (2 vols) Zhonggong Henan dangshi ziliao congshu, Henan renmin chubanshe, 1986.

Zhonggong JiLuYu Bianqu dangshi gongzuozu bangongshi and Zhonggong Henan shengwei dangshi gongzuo weiyuanhui (ed) *Zhonggong JiLuYu Bianqu dangshi ziliao xuanbian* [Selected Materials on Party History in the JiLuYu Border Area] Second Part, (3 vols) Henan renmin chubanshe, 1988.

Zhonggong Shanxi shengwei dangshi yanjiushi (ed) *Wenxian xuanbian* [Collection of Documents] (vols) Taiyuan, Shanxi renmin chubanshe, 1986.

Zhonggong Shanxishengwei dangshi yanjiushi and Shanxi Shehui kexueyuan lishi yanjiusuo (ed) *Shanxi geming huiyilu* [Memoirs of the Revolution in Shanxi] (vols) Taiyuan, Shanxi renmin chubanshe, 1983.

Zhonggong Shanxi shengwei dangshi yanjiushi, Shanxisheng danganguan, Taiyue geming genjudi caizheng shiliao bianweihui (ed) *Taiyue geming genjudi caizheng shiliao xuanbian* [Selected Historical Materials on Financial Management in the Taiyue Revolutionary Base Area] (2 vols) Taiyuan, Shanxi jingji chubanshe, 1991.

Zhonggong Taihang qudangwei *Taihang gefenqu tangde wenjian xuanbian* [Selected Party Documents of Districts in the Taihang] (4 vols) vol. 1: 1937-39; vol. 2: 1940-41; vol. 3: 1942; vol. 4: 1943 Huabei Xinhuashudian, 1944.

Zhonggong Taihang qudangwei *Yijiusisannian Taihang dangde wenjian xuanbian* [Collection of Taihang Party Documents, 1943] Taihang dangde wenjian xuanji bianzhe, 1944.

Zhonggong Taihang qudangwei *Taihang dang liunianlai wenjian xuanbian* [Selected Party Documents of the last Six Years in the Taihang] (2 vols with 4 vols appendix) Huabei Xinhua shudian, 1943 and 1944.

Zhonggong Taihang qudangwei *Taihang dang shiliao biancun* [Collection of Historical Party Materials on Taihang] (2 vols) Huabei Xinhua shudian, 1944 and 1945.

Zhonggong Taihang qudangwei *Yijiusiwunian Taihang dangde wenjian xuanbian* [Collection of Taihang Party Documents, 1945] Taihang dangde wenjian xuanji bianzhe, 1946.

Zhonggong Taihang qudangwei *Taihangqu yinhang gongsheng gongzuo: cankao ziliao* [Commercial Work of the Taihang Base Area Banks: Reference Materials] Vol 2: *Liunianlai zhongyao jingji jianshe huiyi jueyi huiyi* [Important Economic Development Meetings, Resolutions, and Recollections during the last Six Years] Huabei Xinhuashudian, 1946.

Zhonggong Taihang qudangwei (ed) *Zhengfeng wenjian huiji* [Collection of Documents on Rectification] Taihang qudangwei, 1947.

Zhonggong Taihangqu sandiwei *Sanfenqu tudi gaige yu qunzhong yundong cailiao jicun* [Collection of Materials on Land Reform and Mass Mobilization in the 3rd District] Taihang sandiwei, 1947.

Zhonggong Taiyuan shiwei xuanzhuanbu, Taiyuan Huayuan *Taihang muban xuanji* [Collection of Taihang Woodcuts] Taiyuan, Shanxi renmin chubanshe, 1991.

Zhonggong zhongyang Beifangju *Kangzhan yilai xuanji* [Selected Documents of the War of Resistance] (2 vols) Huabei Xinhuashudain, 1944.

Zhonggong zhongyang dangxiao dangshi jiaoyanshi (ed) *Zhonggong dangshi cankao ziliao Vol 5: KangRi zhanzheng shiqi* [CCP Reference Materials Vol.5: Period of the War of Resistance to Japan] Beijing, Renmin chubanshe, 1979.

Zhonggong Zuoquan xianweiyuanhui and Zuoquan xian renmin zhengfu (ed) *Balujun zongbu zai Matian* [The Eighth Route Army's HQ in Matian] Taiyuan, Shanxi renmin chubanshe, 1990. [BZZM]

Zhongguo jiefangqu linshi jiuji weiyuanhui JinJiLuYu Bianqu fenhui *Banian kangRi zhanzhengzhong bianqu renmin sunshi zhuangkuang ji jiuji gongzuoshang de liangge zhongyao wenjian* [Two Important Documents on Shortages and Relief in the Shanxi-Hebei-Shandong-Henan Border Region during the Eight Years of the Anti-Japanese War] Zhongguo jiefangqu linshi jiuji weiyuanhui JinJiLuYu Bianqu fenhui, 1946.

Zhongguo zuojia xiehui Shanxi sheng fenhui (ed) *Shanxi geming genjudi wenyi ziliao* [Literature and Art Materials from the Shanxi Revolutionary Base Areas] vol.1 JinJiLuYu volume, Taiyuan, Beiyue Chubanshe, 1987.

Zhongyang danganguan (ed) *Zhonggong zhongyang wenjian xuanji* [Selected Documents of the CCP Central Committee] (vols) Beijing, Zhonggong zhongyang dangxiao chubanshe, 1989– (Volumes 11-15 relate to 1936–1945).

Contemporary Serials

Beifang zazhi [Northern Magazine]
Bianqu zhengbao [Border Region Official Gazette]
Canzhan gongzuo [War Participation Work]
Dang de shenghuo [Party Life]
Gongzuo tongxun [Work Newsletter]

Jiefang [Liberation]
Jiefang ribao [Liberation Daily]
Liandui gongzuo [Company Work]
Minbing [Militia]
Pingyuan zazhi [Magazine of the Plains]
Renmin de Jundui [The People's Troops]
Taihangqu maoyi gongzuo [Taihang Trade Work]
Taihangqu yinhang gongshang gongzuo [Taihang Banking, Industry and Commerce Work]
Xinhua ribao (Huabeiban) [New China Daily (North China Edition)]
Xinhua ribao (Taihangban) [Taihang New China Daily (Taihang Edition)]
Xiangcun yishu [Village Art]
Zhandou [Combat]
Zhanxianshe [Frontline Press]
Zhanyoubao [Comrade in Arms News]
Zhongguo qingnian [China's Youth]

Documents

Bo Yibo 'Jinian Kangzhan yizhounian jiantao Ximeng' ['An Examination of the Sacrifice League on the First Anniversary of the War of Resistance'] 19 June 1938, originally published in *Qingnian zhanqi* [Banner of Youth] no.3 1938, reprinted in *Shanxi geming genjudi* [Shanxi Revolutionary Base Areas] no.4 1986, p.3.

Chi Biqing 'Chi Biqing tongzhi tan Taihang qunzhong yundong' ['Comrade Chi Biqing Talks about the Taihang Mass Movement'] 22 July 1986, in Taihang geming genjudishi zongbian weihui (ed) *Qunzhong yundong* [The Mass Movement] Taihang geming genjudi shiliao congshu No.7, Taiyuan, Shanxi renmin chubanshe, 1989, p.262.

Deng Xiaoping 'Dongyuan xinbing ji xinbing zhengzhi gongzuo' ['Mobilize new recruits and conduct political work among them'] 12 January 1938, in *Deng Xiaoping Wenxuan, 1938–1965* [Selected Works of Deng Xiaoping 1938–1965] Beijing, Renmin chubanshe, 1989, pp.1–7.

Deng Xiaoping 'Deng zhengwei guanyu zai xin de huanjing xia women de gongzuo de zongjie baogao' ['Summary report by Political Commissar Deng on work under the new conditions.'] 10 March 1939, in JinJiLuYu genjudi shiliao xuanbianzhe (ed) *JinJiLuYu genjudi shiliaoxuan* [Selected Materials on the History of the Shanxi-Hebei-Shandong-Henan Base Area] Taiyuan, Shanxi shengwei, 1989, vol.1, pp.245–49.

Deng Xiaoping 'Deng Xiaoping tongzhi zai Taibei junzheng weiyuanhui kuodahui shang de baogao' ['Report by Comrade Deng Xiaoping at enlarged meeting of the North Taihang Military and Administrative Committee'] 3 November 1939, in Taihang gefenqu dang de wenjian xuanji bianzhe *Taihang gefenqu dang de wenjian xuanji* [Selection of Documents on the Party in Each District of the Taihang Region (4 vols)] n.p, 1944, Vol. I, 1939, pp.114–120.

Deng Xiaoping 'Liu Deng guanyu zhengqu wan jun xiaceng guli qi shangceng de fangzhen gei gebu de zhishi' ['Liu and Deng directive to all departments on the policy of winning over the subordinate classes and isolating the upper classes.'] 27 December 1939, in JinJiLuYu genjudi shiliao xuanbianzhe (ed) *JinJiLuYu genjudi shiliaoxuan* [Selected Materials on the History of the Shanxi-Hebei-Shandong-Henan Base Area] Taiyuan, Shanxi shengwei, 1989, vol.1, p.303.

Deng Xiaoping 'Deng Xiaoping zai Zhonggong zhongyang beifangju Licheng huiyi shangde fayan' ['Deng Xiaoping's opening speech at the Licheng Meeting of the CCP Central Committee's North China Bureau'] 11 April 1940, in Shanxisheng danganguan (ed) *Taihang dangshi ziliao huibian* [Collection of Materials on the History of the Party in the Taihang Base Area] Taiyuan, Shanxi renmin chubanshe, 1994, vol.3: 1940, p.248.

Deng Xiaoping 'Yingjie yijiusiyi nian' ['Welcome 1941'] 25 December 1940, in Shanxisheng danganguan (ed) *Taihang dangshi ziliao huibian* [Collection of Materials on the History of the Party in the Taihang Base Area] Taiyuan, Shanxi renmin chubanshe, 1994, vol.3: 1940, p.850.

Deng Xiaoping 'Shengli de huigu yu shengli de qidai' ['Recalling success and looking forward to victory'] 1 January 1941, in Liu Jiang and Lu Qiao (ed) *Taihang xinwen shiliao huibian* [Collection of Historical Materials on the News in Taihang] Taihang xinwen shixuehui, 1994, pp.19–23 (from *Xinhua ribao* 1 January 1941).

Deng Xiaoping 'Deng Xiaoping zai Taihang junqu dierci wuzhuang ganbu kuangda huiyishang de jianghua' ['Deng Xiaoping's speech at the 2nd enlarged meeting of armed force cadres'] 1 February 1941, in Shanxisheng danganguan (ed) *Taihang dangshi ziliao huibian* [Collection of Materials on the History of the Party in the Taihang Base Area] Taiyuan, Shanxi renmin chubanshe, 1994, vol.4: 1941, p.89.

Deng Xiaoping 'Shiju he jige zhengce wenti: zai beiju taolun Jinan gongzuo shi de fayan' ['The current situation and questions of policy: talks at the symposium organized by the North China Bureau (of the CCP Central Committee)'] March 1941, in JinJiLuYu genjudi shiliao xuanbianzhe (ed) *JinJiLuYu genjudi shiliaoxuan* [Selected Materials on the History of the Shanxi-Hebei-Shandong-Henan Base Area] Taiyuan, Shanxi shengwei, 1989, vol.2, pp.13–24.

Deng Xiaoping 'Guanyu chengli JinJiYu bianqu linshi canyihui de tiyi' ['Proposal to Establish the Shanxi-Hebei-Henan Border Region Provisional Assembly'] 16 March 1941, in Zuoquan xian weiyuanhui, Zuoquan xian renmin zhengfu (eds) *Balujun zongbu zai Matian* [The Headquarters of the Eighth Route Army in Matian] Taiyuan, Shanxi renmin chubanshe, 1990, pp.27–33.

Deng Xiaoping 'Dang yu KangRi minzhu zhengquan' ['The party and the anti-Japanese democratic government'] 15 April 1941, in Deng Xiaoping *Deng Xiaoping Wenxuan, 1938–1965* [Selected Works of Deng Xiaoping 1938–1965] Beijing, Renmin chubanshe, 1989, pp.8–21.

Deng Xiaoping 'Fandui mamu dakai Taihangqu de yanzhong jumian' ['Oppose carelessly opening up the Taihang district'] 28 April 1941, in JinJiLuYu genjudi shiliao xuanbianzhe (ed) *JinJiLuYu genjudi shiliaoxuan* [Selected Materials on the History of the Shanxi-Hebei-Shandong-Henan Base Area] Taiyuan, Shanxi shengwei, 1989, vol.2, pp.24–29.

Deng Xiaoping 'Yierjiushi wenhua gongzuo de fangzhen renwu ji qi nuli fangxiang' ['The principals, tasks and orientation for cultural work in the 129th Division'] May 1941, in Deng Xiaoping *Deng Xiaoping Wenxuan, 1938–1965* [Selected Works of Deng Xiaoping 1938–1965] Beijing, Renmin chubanshe, 1989, pp.22–29.

Deng Xiaoping 'Zhengzhi gongshi yu dizhanqu tongbao de guanxi' ['The relationship between the political offensive and followers in enemy-occupied regions'] 20 August 1942, in JinJiLuYu genjudi shiliao xuanbianzhe (ed) *JinJiLuYu genjudi shiliaoxuan* [Selected Materials on the History of the Shanxi-Hebei-Shandong-Henan Base Area] Taiyuan, Shanxi shengwei, 1989, vol.2, pp.215–216.

Deng Xiaoping 'Taihangqu guomindang wenti' ['The Nationalist Party in the Taihang Area'] 23 August 1942, in Taihangdang liunianlai wenjian xuanji bubian bianzhe *Taihangdang liunianlai wenjian xuanji bubian* [Supplement to Collection of Documents on the Taihang Party during the last Six Years] 1944, pp.93–97.

Deng Xiaoping 'Wunianlai duidi douzheng de gailue zongjie yu jinhou duidi douzheng de fangzhen: Deng Xiaoping tongzhi zai Taihang fenju gaogan huiyishang de baogao' ['Summary of conflict with the enemy during the last five years and the consequent policy for struggle: Comrade Deng Xiaoping's report at Taihang Sub-bureau meeting of senior cadres'] 26 January 1943, in JinJiLuYu genjudi shiliao xuanbianzhe (ed) *JinJiLuYu genjudi shiliaoxuan* [Selected Materials on the History of the Shanxi-Hebei-Shandong-Henan Base Area] Taiyuan, Shanxi shengwei, 1989, vol.3, pp.1–31 (from *Zhandou* [Combat] No.15, 15 March 1943, pp.1–50); Selections in 'Wunianlai duidi douzheng de gailue zongjie' ['A general account of the struggle against the enemy over the five years'] 26 January 1943, in Deng Xiaoping *Deng Xiaoping Wenxuan, 1938–1965* [Selected Works of Deng Xiaoping 1938–1965] Beijing, Renmin chubanshe, 1989, pp.33–44; and 'Dizhanqu de zuzhi gongzuo yu zhengce yunyong' ['Organizational work and application of policy in enemy-occupied areas'] 26 January 1943, in Deng Xiaoping *Deng Xiaoping Wenxuan, 1938–1965* [Selected Works of Deng Xiaoping 1938–1965] Beijing, Renmin chubanshe, 1989, pp.45–64.

Deng Xiaoping 'Deng Xiaoping tongzhi zai Taihang fenju gaogan huiyi shang de jielun' ['Comrade Deng Xiaoping's conclusions at Taihang Sub-bureau meeting of senior cadres'] 20 February 1943, in *Zhandou* [Combat] No.19, 25 March 1993, pp.1–92; 'Deng Xiaoping tongzhi zai Taihang fenju gaogan huiyishang de jielun diyierbufen' ['Parts 1 and 2 of the conclusions by Comrade Deng Xiaoping at the Taihang Sub-bureau meeting of senior cadres'] in Taihang dang de wenjian xuanji bianzhe *Yijiusisannian Taihang dangde wenjian xuanji* [Collection of Documents on the Taihang Party in 1943] 1944, pp.107–120; 'Zhailu dier bufen: Zai xin xingshi xia de gongzuo fangzhen' ['Extracts from Part 2: Policies to be implemented in the new circumstances'] in JinJiLuYu genjudi shiliao xuanbianzhe (ed) *JinJiLuYu genjudi shiliaoxuan* [Selected Materials on the History of the Shanxi-Hebei-Shandong-Henan Base Area] Taiyuan, Shanxi shengwei, 1989, vol.3, pp.31–35; 'Genjudi jianshe yu qunzhong yundong' ['The establishment of base areas and the mass movement'] in Deng Xiaoping *Deng Xiaoping Wenxuan, 1938–1965* [Selected Works of Deng Xiaoping 1938–1965] Beijing, Renmin chubanshe, 1989, pp.65–77.

Deng Xiaoping 'Deng Xiaoping tongzhi eryue ershierri zai Taihang fenju gaogan huiyi shang de jielun' ['Conclusions given by Comrade Deng Xiaoping at Taihang Sub-bureau meeting of senior cadres on 22 February'] 22 February 1943, in *Kangzhan yilai xuanji* Vol. II, Part 2, [Selected Documents since the War of Resistance] 1944, pp.103–157.

Deng Xiaoping 'Taihangqude jingji jianshe' ['Economic development in the Taihang Area'] 2 July 1943, in Deng Xiaoping *Deng Xiaoping Wenxuan, 1938–1965* [Selected Works of Deng Xiaoping 1938–1965] Beijing, Renmin chubanshe, 1989, pp.78–86.

Deng Xiaoping 'Deng Xiaoping tongzhi zai fenju dangxiao xuefeng xuexi de zongjie baogao (xuexiao jilu wei jing benren jiaoyue)' ['Summary report on training and study style by Comrade Deng Xiaoping at sub-bureau party school (Party school record; unrevised by the speaker)'] 21 July 1943, in Taihangqu dangwei *Zhengfeng wenjian huiji* [Collection of Documents on Rectification] Taihangqu dangweiyin, 1947, pp.12–30.

Deng Xiaoping 'Nuli shengchan, duguo kunnan, yingjie shengli: Deng zhengzhi weiyuan zai shengchan huiyi shang de baogao jilu' ['Work hard, overcome difficulties and prepare to greet victory: record of a report by Political Commissar Deng at a meeting on production'] 21 September 1943, in JinJiLuYu genjudi shiliao xuanbianzhe (ed) *JinJiLuYu genjudi shiliaoxuan* [Selected Materials on the History of the Shanxi-Hebei-Shandong-Henan Base Area] Taiyuan, Shanxi shengwei, 1989, vol.3, pp.639–641.

Deng Xiaoping 'Zai beifangju dangxiao zhengfeng dongyuanhui shangde jianghua' ['Speech at the mobilization meeting on rectification in the party school of the Northern Bureau'] 10 November 1943, in Deng Xiaoping *Deng Xiaoping Wenxuan, 1938–1965* [Selected Works of Deng Xiaoping 1938–1965] Beijing, Renmin chubanshe, 1989, pp.87–94.

Deng Xiaoping 'Dui jige wenti de yijian' ['Opinions on several matters'] January 1944, in JinJiLuYu genjudi shiliao xuanbianzhe (ed) *JinJiLuYu genjudi shiliaoxuan* [Selected Materials on the History of the Shanxi-Hebei-Shandong-Henan Base Area] Taiyuan, Shanxi shengwei, 1989, vol.2, pp.41–43.

Deng Xiaoping 'Taihangqu guanyu shige wenti de dafu: Deng Xiaoping tongzhi gei dang zhongyang de baogao' ['Taihang Region's response to ten questions: Comrade Deng Xiaoping's report to the CCP Central Committee'] 28 August 1944, in JinJiLuYu genjudi shiliao xuanbianzhe (ed) *JinJiLuYu genjudi shiliaoxuan* [Selected Materials on the History of the Shanxi-Hebei-Shandong-Henan Base Area] Taiyuan, Shanxi shengwei, 1989, vol.2, pp.43–46.

Deng Xiaoping 'Deng Xiaoping tongzhi zai shadi yingxiong laodong yingxiong dahui shang de jianghua' ['Speech by Comrade Deng Xiaoping at a meeting of battle heroes from both the armed and production campaigns'] 23 December 1944, in Taihang dangde wenjian xuanji bianzhe *Yijiusiwunian Taihang dangde wenjian xuanji* [Collection of Taihang Party Documents, 1945] 1946, pp.66–72.

Gao Kefu *Dibalujun zaiShanxi* [The Eighth Route Army in Shanxi] Shanghai, Xinhua shudian, 1938.

Gao Yuangui 'Dizhu fandui jianzude banfa he womende duice' ['The Methods of Landlords in Opposing Rent Reductions and our Policy Response'] 31 December1942, in JinJiLuYu Bianqu caizheng jingji shi bianjizu and Shanxi, Hebei, Shandong, Henan sheng danganguan (ed) *KangRi zhanzheng shiqi JinJiLuYu Bianqu caizheng jingjishi ziliao xuanbian* [Collection of Materials on the Economic and Financial History of the Shanxi-Hebei-Shandong-Henan Border Region during the War of Resistance to Japan] Beijing, Caizheng jingji chubanshe, 1990, vol.2, p.548.

He Yingcai 'Quanqu dangde jianshe wenti' ['Questions in the Development of the Party throughout the Region'] 24 December 1938, in Shanxisheng danganguan (ed) *Taihang dangshi ziliao huibian* [Collection of Materials on the History of the Party in the Taihang Base Area] Taiyuan, Shanxi renmin chubanshe, 1989, vol.1: 1937–38, p.502.

He Yingcai 'JinJiYu bianqu gonggu dangde jige wenti' ['Several Issues in the Consolidation of the Party in the Shanxi-Hebei-Henan Border Area'] 6 December 1940, in Shanxisheng danganguan (ed) *Taihang dangshi ziliao huibian* [Collection of Materials on the History of the Party in the Taihang Base Area] Taiyuan, Shanxi renmin chubanshe, 1994, vol.3: 1940, p.800.

Hua Shanqi 'JiTai lianban Yang zhuren Xiufeng xiang JinJiLuYu bianqu linshi yihuide gongzuo baogao' ['The Work Report of Yang Xiufeng, Chair of the Joint Office for the South Hebei, Taihang and Taiyue Base Areas, to the Shanxi-Hebei-Shandong-Henan Border Region Provisional Assembly'] 21 July 1941, in *Xinhua ribao* [New China News Daily] (North China Edition).

Hua Xingdou 'Dafu Jinzhong dangde jige zuzhi wenti' ['Response to Several Organizational Questions about the Party in Jinzhong'] 30 December 1937, in Shanxisheng danganguan (ed) *Taihang dangshi ziliao huibian* [Collection of Materials on the History of the Party in the Taihang Base Area] Taiyuan, Shanxi renmin chubanshe, 1989, vol.1, p.89.

Huang Yuan 'Jindongnande poqie jianzu jianxi wenti' ['The Urgent Issue of Reducing Rent and Interest in Southeast Shanxi'] March 1940, in Shanxisheng danganguan (ed) *Taihang dangshi ziliao huibian* [Collection of Materials on the History of the Party in the Taihang Base Area] Taiyuan, Shanxi renmin chubanshe, 1994, vol.3: 1940, p.120.

JinJiLuYu Bianqu caizheng jingji shi bianjizu and Shanxi, Hebei, Shandong, Henan sheng danganguan (ed) *KangRi zhanzheng shiqi JinJiLuYu Bianqu caizheng jingjishi ziliao xuanbian* [Collection of Materials on the Economic and Financial History of the Shanxi-Hebei-Shandong-Henan Border Region during the War of Resistance to Japan] Beijing, Caizheng jingji chubanshe, 1990, vol.2, p.568.

JiTai lianban *Diyici zhuanyuan xianzhang huiyi tekan* [Special Pronouncement of the Joint Office, First Meeting of Commissioners and County Heads] February 1941.

JiTai lianban 'Banfa maoyi zanxing tiaoli' ['Provisional Trade Regulations'] 7 June 1941, in Taihang geming genjudishi zongbian weihui (ed) *Caizheng jingji jianshe* [Financial and Economic Development] Taihang geming genjudi shiliao congshu No.6, Taiyuan, Shanxi renmin chubanshe, 1987, vol.1, p.859.

Jia Linfang 'Genju Zuoquanxian Sipingcun tongleishui diaochazhong dui muqian nongmin jingji shenghuo, fudan nengli he tudi jingying fangshi chubu yanjiude wojian' ['Some Personal Comments from Preliminary Research on Peasant Economic Life, Capacity and Land Management at Present from an Investigation of Progressive Income Tax in Siping Village, Zuoquan'] 1 February 1943, in JinJiLuYu Bianqu caizheng jingji shi bianjizu and Shanxi, Hebei, Shandong, Henan sheng danganguan (ed) *KangRi zhanzheng shiqi JinJiLuYu Bianqu caizheng jingjishi ziliao xuanbian* [Collection of Materials on the Economic and Financial History of the Shanxi-Hebei-Shandong-Henan Border Region during the War of Resistance to Japan] Beijing, Caizheng jingji chubanshe, 1990, vol.1, p.1026.

JinJiLuYu Bianqu zhengfu 'Jianzu jianxi bugao' ['Notice of Rent and Interest Reduction'] 1 October 1942, in JinJiLuYu Bianqu caizheng jingji shi bianjizu and Shanxi, Hebei, Shandong, Henan sheng danganguan (ed) *KangRi zhanzheng shiqi JinJiLuYu Bianqu caizheng jingjishi ziliao xuanbian* [Collection of Materials on the Economic and Financial History of the Shanxi-Hebei-Shandong-Henan Border Region during the War of Resistance to Japan] Beijing, Caizheng jingji chubanshe, 1990, vol.2, p.545.

JinJiLuYu Bianqu zhengfu 'Guanyu jianzu gongzuode shishi' ['Instructions on Rent Reduction'] 17 October 1942, in JinJiLuYu Bianqu caizheng jingji shi bianjizu and Shanxi, Hebei, Shandong, Henan sheng danganguan (ed) *KangRi zhanzheng shiqi JinJiLuYu Bianqu caizheng jingjishi ziliao xuanbian* [Collection of Materials on the Economic and Financial History of the Shanxi-Hebei-Shandong-Henan Border Region during the War of Resistance to Japan] Beijing, Caizheng jingji chubanshe, 1990, vol.2, p.546.

JinJiLuYu Bianqu zhengfu 'Yinianlai bianqu zuo wo douzheng xingshi ji Taihangqu dangqian xingzheng gongzuo fangzhen—JinJiLuYu bianqu linshi can huiyi linshi dahui Taihang huiyide gongzuo baogao' ['The Last Year of Struggle between us and the Enemy in the Border Region and Current Work Policy in the Taihang Region—Work Report to the Provisional Taihang Conference of the Shanxi-Hebei-Shandong-Henan Border Region's Provisional Assembly'] 12 September 1943.

JinJiLuYu Bianqu zhengfu 'Taihangqu yijiusi'er, sisan liangniande jiuzai zongjie' ['Summary of Famine Relief in the Taihang District during 1942 and 1943'] 1 August 1944, in Taihang geming genjudishi zongbian weihui (ed) *Caizheng jingji jianshe* [Financial and Economic Development] Taihang geming genjudi shiliao congshu No.6, Taiyuan, Shanxi renmin chubanshe, 1987, vol.1, p.233.

JinJiLuYu bianqu zhengfu 'Jige tudi wenti chuli banfade jueding' ['Several Decisions on the Methods for Managing Land Issues'] October 1944, in JinJiLuYu Bianqu caizheng jingji shi bianjizu and Shanxi, Hebei, Shandong, Henan sheng danganguan (ed) *KangRi zhanzheng shiqi JinJiLuYu Bianqu caizheng jingjishi ziliao xuanbian* [Collection of Materials on the Economic and Financial History of the Shanxi-Hebei-Shandong-Henan Border Region during the War of Resistance to Japan] Beijing, Caizheng jingji chubanshe, 1990, vol.2, p.1466.

JinJiYuqu nongjiu zonghui 'JinJiYuqu nongjiu zonghui liangnianlai gongzuo cailiao' ['Materials on the work of the Shanxi-Hebei-Henan region peasants' association during the last two years'] June 1941, in Shanxisheng danganguan (ed) *Taihang dangshi ziliao huibian* [Collection of Materials on the History of the Party in the Taihang Base Area] Taiyuan, Shanxi renmin chubanshe, 1994, vol.4: 1941, p.377.

JinJiYuqu nongjiu zonghui 'Nongmin tudi douzheng gangling' ['The Peasants Program to Struggle for Land'] 19 March 1942, in *Xinhua Ribao* [New China Daily – North China Edition] 7 April 1942.

Jin Yu 'Heshunxian nongdai dahui tuji gongzuode jiantao' ['Evaluation of the Efforts of the Congress of the Peasants' representatives in Heshun County'] November 1937, in Shanxisheng danganguan (ed) *Taihang dangshi ziliao huibian* [Collection of Materials on the History of the Party in the Taihang Base Area] Taiyuan, Shanxi renmin chubanshe, 1989, vol.1, p.44.

Ke Han 'Jindong bianjing' ['East Shanxi's Borders'] 11 June 1938, in *Xinhua ribao* [New China Daily, North China edition] 4 July 1938, p.4.

Lai Ruoyu 'Liangyuelai Jindong gongzuode zongjie' ['Summary of Work in the East Shanxi District during the last two months'] January 1940, in Shanxisheng danganguan (ed) *Taihang dangshi ziliao huibian* [Collection of Materials on the History of the Party in the Taihang Base Area] Taiyuan, Shanxi renmin chubanshe, 1994, vol.3: 1940, p.53.

Lai Ruoyu (Ruo Yu) 'Qunzhong yundong yu qunzhong youji zhanzheng' ['The Mass Movement and Mass Guerilla Warfare'] December 1941, in Shanxisheng danganguan (ed) *Taihang dangshi ziliao huibian* [Collection of Materials on the History of the Party in the Taihang Base Area] Taiyuan, Shanxi renmin chubanshe, 1994, vol.4: 1941, p.980.

Lai Ruoyu 'Jinzhongqu dui di douzhengde zongjie' ['Summary of the Struggle against the Enemy in Jinzhong (Central Shanxi)'] December 1942, in Taihang geming genjudishi zongbian weihui (ed) *Difang wuzhuang douzheng* [Local Armed Struggle] Taihang geming genjudi shiliao congshu No.3, Taiyuan, Shanxi renmin chubanshe, 1990, p.283.

Lai Ruoyu 'Muqian shiqide zhibu jianshe wenti – zai di'erci zhibu yanjiuhuide zongjie zhiyibu' ['The Current Question of Party Branch Development – Section of a Summary at the 2nd Research Conference on Party Branches'] September 1943, in Taihang geming genjudishi zongbian weihui (ed) *Dang de jianshe* [Party Development] Taihang geming genjudi shiliao congshu No.2, Taiyuan, Shanxi renmin chubanshe, 1989, p.298.

Lai Ruoyu 'Shengchan yundongde chubu zongjie' ['Preliminary Summary on the Production Movement'] August 1944, in Taihang geming genjudishi zongbian weihui (ed) *Qunzhong yundong* [The Mass Movement] Taihang geming genjudi shiliao congshu No.7, Taiyuan, Shanxi renmin chubanshe, 1989, p.207.

Lai Ruoyu 'Jige wentide chubu yanjiu – zai diwei shuji huiyishangde baogao' ['Preliminary Research on Several Questions – Report at a Conference of Secretaries of Party Sub-district Committees'] August 1944, in Taihang geming genjudishi zongbian weihui (ed) *Dang de jianshe* [Party Development] Taihang geming genjudi shiliao congshu No.2, Taiyuan, Shanxi renmin chubanshe, 1989, p.320.

Li Da 'Kaizhan qunzhongxingde shadi yingxun yundong' ['Start a Mass-style Kill the Enemy Movement'] November 1944, in Taihang geming genjudishi zongbian weihui (ed) *Difang wuzhuang douzheng* [Local Armed Struggle] Taihang geming genjudi shiliao congshu No.3, Taiyuan, Shanxi renmin chubanshe, 1990, p.433.

Li Dazhang 'Jiang Yijiusi'er nian qunzhong gongzuode jiandan zongjie' ['Brief Summary of Mass Work during 1942'] 1943, in Taihang geming genjudishi zongbian weihui (ed) *Tudi wenti* [The Land Question] Taihang geming genjudi shiliao congshu No.5, Taiyuan, Shanxi renmin chubanshe, 1987, p.224.

Li Dazhang 'Guoqu qunzhong gongzuode jiandan huigu yu jinhoude gonzuo fangzhen' ['Review of Masses Work in the Past and Policy for the Future'] February 1943, in Taihang geming genjudishi zongbian weihui (ed) *Qunzhong yundong* [The Mass Movement] Taihang geming genjudi shiliao congshu No.7, Taiyuan, Shanxi renmin chubanshe, 1989, p.183.

Li Dazhang 'Jiang qunzhong gongzuode jiandan huiyi' ['A Brief Overview of the Mass Movement'] 1943, in Taihang geming genjudishi zongbian weihui (ed) *Tudi wenti* [The Land Question] Taihang geming genjudi shiliao congshu No.5, Taiyuan, Shanxi renmin chubanshe, 1987, p.197.

Li Xuefeng 'Zhonggong JinJiYu di'yici daibiao dahui shangde gongzuo baogao' ['Report to the 1st Representative Assembly of the CCP in Shanxi-Hebei-Henan'] September 1939, in Shanxisheng danganguan (ed) *Taihang dangshi ziliao huibian* [Collection of Materials on the History of the Party in the Taihang Base Area] vol.2: 1939, Taiyuan, Shanxi renmin chubanshe, 1989, p.485.

Li Xuefeng 'Gonggu Taibei genjudi yu Taibei dangde zhandou renwu' ['Crucial Tasks in Consolidating the Taibei (Taihang) Base Area and the Taibei (Taihang) Party'] 17 March 1940, in Shanxisheng danganguan (ed) *Taihang dangshi ziliao huibian* [Collection of Materials on the History of the Party in the Taihang Base Area] Taiyuan, Shanxi renmin chubanshe, 1994, vol.3: 1940, p.95.

Li Xuefeng 'Genjudi jianshe yu qunzhong gongzuo – dang yu qunzhong gongzuo' ['The Development of the Base Area and Masses Work—the Party and Masses Work'] 5 December 1940, in Shanxisheng danganguan (ed) *Taihang dangshi ziliao huibian* [Collection of Materials on the History of the Party in the Taihang Base Area] Taiyuan, Shanxi renmin chubanshe, 1994, vol.3: 1940, p.787.

Li Xuefeng 'Yijiusiyi niande zhandou gangling' ['1941 Program for Action'] in Shanxisheng danganguan (ed) *Taihang dangshi ziliao huibian* [Collection of Materials on the History of the Party in the Taihang Base Area] Taiyuan, Shanxi renmin chubanshe, 1994, vol.4: 1941, p.1.

Li Xuefeng 'JinJiYu renmin kangRi douzheng ji qi zhengzhi shenghuode xinshiqi' ['The Struggle of People in Shanxi-Hebei-Henan Resisting the Japanese and a New Era in Political Life'] 10 April 1941, in Taihang geming genjudishi zongbian weihui (ed) *Zhengquan jianshe* [Political Development] Taihang geming genjudi shiliao congshu No.4, Taiyuan, Shanxi renmin chubanshe, 1990, p.115.

Li Xuefeng 'Guanyu Liaoxian gongzuode fayan' ['Speech about Liaoxian's Work'] 1 June 1941, in Shanxisheng danganguan (ed) *Taihang dangshi ziliao huibian* [Collection of Materials on the History of the Party in the Taihang Base Area] Taiyuan, Shanxi renmin chubanshe, 1994, vol.4: 1941, p.351.

Li Xuefeng 'JinJiLuYu Bianqu zhengfu chengli yu minzhu yundong' ['The Establishment of the Shanxi-Hebei-Shandong-Henan Border Region and the Democracy Movement'] 2 September 1941, report to Taihang CCP Committee Cadre's Conference, in *Weiwei Taihang* [The Towering Taihang Mountains] no.2 1986, p.15.

Li Xuefeng 'Zuoquan sinian gongzuo jianjie ji jinhou gongzuo yijian' ['Overview of Work in Zuoquan during the last Four Years and Ideas for the Future'] 1943, in Taihang geming genjudishi zongbian weihui (ed) *Dang de jianshe* [Party Development] Taihang geming genjudi shiliao congshu No.2, Taiyuan, Shanxi renmin chubanshe, 1989, p.309.

Li Xuefeng 'Qudangwei dangxiao di'erqi zhengfengde sixiang yu sixiang lingdao zongjie' ['Summary of Ideological Leadership and Ideological Rectification in the Regional Party School's Second Group'] January 1944, in Taihang geming genjudishi zongbian weihui (ed) *Dang de jianshe* [Party Development] Taihang geming genjudi shiliao congshu No.2, Taiyuan, Shanxi renmin chubanshe, 1989, p.358.

Li Yiqing 'Cong Taibei caizheng jingji jianshezhong gonggu Taibei kangRi genjudi' ['Consolidate the Taibei (Taihang) Anti-Japanese Base Area by Developing Economic and Financial Administration'] 1 July 1940, in Taihang geming genjudishi zongbian weihui (ed) *Caizheng jingji jianshe* [Financial and Economic Development] Taihang geming genjudi shiliao congshu No.6, Taiyuan, Shanxi renmin chubanshe, 1987, vol.1, p.79.

Liu Bocheng 'Lun youji zhanzheng' ['On Guerilla War'] in *Balujun junzheng zazhi* [Magazine of the Eighth Route Army] No. 4, 15 April 1939, p.8.

Liu Bocheng 'Zai Zhonggong zhongyang beifangju Licheng huiyishangde baogao' ['Report to the Licheng Conference of the CCP Central Committee Northern Bureau'] 21 April 1940, in Shanxisheng danganguan (ed) *Taihang dangshi ziliao huibian* [Collection of Materials on the History of the Party in the Taihang Base Area] Taiyuan, Shanxi renmin chubanshe, 1994, vol.3: 1940, p.231.

Liu Bocheng and Deng Xiaoping 'Jinian women de zhanyou Zuo Quan tongzhi' ['Remember our Comrade-in-arms Comrade Zuo Quan'] 4 July 1942, in Zuoquan xian weiyuanhui, Zuoquan xian renmin zhengfu (eds) *Balujun zongbu zai Matian* [The Headquarters of the Eighth Route Army in Matian] Taiyuan, Shanxi renmin chubanshe, 1990, pp.341–343.

Liu Shaoqi (Hu Fu) 'Gei JinJiYu shengweide zhishixin' ['Letter of Guidance to the Shanxi-Hebei-Henan Provincial Committee'] 18 August 1938, in Taihang geming genjudishi zongbian weihui (ed) *Dang de jianshe* [Party Development] Taihang geming genjudi shiliao congshu No.2, Taiyuan, Shanxi renmin chubanshe, 1989, p.106.

Liu Shaoqi 'Liunian Huabei Huazhong gongzuo jingyan de baogao' ['Report on Work Experience during the last Six Years in North and Central China'] March 1943, in *Liu Shaoqi xuanji* [Selected Works of Liu Shaoqi] Beijing, Renmin chubanshe, 1981, vol.1, p.263.

Long Ping 'Jieshao JinJiLuYu bianqu' ['Introducing the Shanxi-Hebei-Shandong-Henan Border Region'] in *Jiefang ribao* [Liberation Daily] 23 March 1942.

Stanley Lubman (ed) *Judicial Work in T'ai-hang* Translation of *Taihang qu sifa gongzuo gaikuang* [General condition of judicial work in Taihang district] in *Chinese Law and Government* Vol. VI No. 3 Fall 1973.

Ma Guishu 'Wuxiang dashengchanzhong lingdao yu qongzhong jiehede jingyan' ['The Experience of Unity between Masses and Leadership in Wuxiang during the Great Production Campaign'] in Wuxiangxian xianzhi bianji weiyuanhui bangongshi (ed) *Wuxiang xianzhi* [The Record of Wuxiang County] Taiyuan, Shanxi renmin chubanshe, 1986, p.870.

Mao Zedong 'Rectify the Party's Style of Work' 1 February 1942, in *Selected Works of Mao Tse-tung* Beijing, Foreign Languages Press, 1967, vol.3, p.45.

Peng Tao 'Zai Zhonggong JiYuJin shengwei huodong fenzi huiyishangde jianghua' ['Speech at Meeting of CCP Hebei-Henan-Shanxi Provincial Committee Activists'] February 1938, in *Jinzhong shizhi ziliao* [Central Shanxi Historical Materials] no.2 1984, p.1.

Peng Tao 'JinJiYu shiqigeyuede qunzhong gongzuo' ['17 Months of Mass Work in Shanxi-Hebei-Henan'] April 1939, in *Jinzhong shizhi ziliao* [Central Shanxi Historical Materials] no.1 1988, p.41.

Peng Tao 'Lun Xingzheng zuzhide gaige' ['On the Reform of Administrative Organization'] March 1940, in Shanxisheng danganguan (ed) *Taihang dangshi ziliao huibian* [Collection of Materials on the History of the Party in the Taihang Base Area] Taiyuan, Shanxi renmin chubanshe, 1994, vol.3: 1940, p.109.

Peng Tao 'Yinian zhuanbian Wuxiang gongzuode jinyan jiaoxun' ['Work Experience Transforms Wuxiang in a Year'] May 1941, in Shanxisheng danganguan (ed) *Taihang dangshi ziliao huibian* [Collection of Materials on the History of the Party in the Taihang Base Area] Taiyuan, Shanxi renmin chubanshe, vol.4: 1941, 1994, p.342.

Peng Tao 'JinJiYu qude xinxingshi yu xinrenwu' ['New circumstances and new tasks in the Shanxi-Hebei-Henan base area'] 27 June 1941, in Shanxisheng danganguan (ed) *Taihang dangshi ziliao huibian* [Collection of Materials on the History of the Party in the Taihang Base Area] Taiyuan, Shanxi renmin chubanshe, 1994, vol.4: 1941, p.479.

Peng Tao 'Sanfenqu qunzhong yundongde yiban gaikuang yu jingyan jiaoxun' ['The circumstances of the masses movement in the Third District and the lessons to be learnt'] 10 March 1942, in Zhonggong Taihang qudangwei *Taihang gefenqu tangde wenjian xuanbian* [Selected Party Documents of Districts in the Taihang] Huabei Xinhuashudian, 1944, vol.3: 1942, p.130.

Peng Tao 'Qunzhong yundong de fazhan yu jieji guanxi de bianhua' ['The development of mass movements and the transformation of class relations'] February 1943, in Taihang geming genjudi shi zongbian weihui (ed) *Tudi wenti* [The Land Question] Taiyuan, Shanxi renmin chubanshe, 1987, p.227.

Peng Teh-huai *Unity and the Defense of North China* New China Information Committee, Chungking, China, 1940.

Peng Zhen 'Zai Zhonggong JiYuJin shengwei huodong fengzi huiyi shangde jianghua' ['Speech at a Meeting of Activitists under the CCP Hebei-Henan-Shanxi Committee'] February 1938, in *Jinzhong shizhi ziliao* [Central Shanxi Historical Materials] no.2 1984, p.1.

Qiu Tan 'Nongminde zuzhi wenti' ['Problems of Peasant Organization'] in *Zhandou* [Combat] 9 November 1937, in Shanxisheng danganguan (ed) *Taihang dangshi ziliao huibian* [Collection of Materials on the History of the Party in the Taihang Base Area] Taiyuan, Shanxi renmin chubanshe, 1989, vol.1, p.29.

Rong Zihe 'Jiajin jinxing heli fudan zoushang tongyi de suode leijinshui' ['Strengthen implementation of the "reasonable burden" so that it becomes a progressive income tax'] 18 September 1940, in Taihang geming genjudishi zongbian weihui (ed) *Caizheng jingji jianshe* [Financial and Economic Development] Taihang geming genjudi shiliao congshu No.6, Taiyuan, Shanxi renmin chubanshe, 1987, vol.2, p.540.

Rong Zihe 'Jiaqiang jingji zhanxian, kaizhan dui di jingji douzheng' ['Strengthen the Economic Battlefront, Develop the Economic Struggle against the Enemy'] 28 April 1941, in Taihang geming genjudishi zongbian weihui (ed) *Caizheng jingji jianshe* [Financial and Economic Development] Taihang geming genjudi shiliao congshu No.6, Taiyuan, Shanxi renmin chubanshe, 1987, vol.1, p.136.

Rong Zihe 'JiTai lianban Rong fuzhuren xiang JinJiLuYu Bianqu linshi canyihuide caizheng jianshe gongzuo baogao' ['Deputy Chair of the Joint Office for the South Hebei, Taihang, and Taiyue Base Areas Rong Zihe's work report on financial administration to the Shanxi-Hebei-Shandong-Henan Border Region Provisional Assembly'] 15 July 1941, in *Xinhua Ribao* [New China News Daily] (North China Edition) 5 August 1941; and in JinJiLuYu Bianqu caizheng jingji shi bianjizu and Shanxi, Hebei, Shandong, Henan sheng danganguan (ed) *KangRi zhanzheng shiqi JinJiLuYu Bianqu caizheng jingjishi ziliao xuanbian* [Collection of Materials on the Economic and Financial History of the Shanxi-Hebei-Shandong-Henan Border Region during the War of Resistance to Japan] Beijing, Caizheng jingji chubanshe, 1990, vol.1, p.260.

Rong Zihe 'Taihang Taiyue yinian laide cailiang gongzuo' ['A Year of Finance and Grain Work in the Taihang and Taiyue Regions'] (Rong Zihe's Report to the Second Session of the Shanxi-Hebei-Shandong-Henan Border Region Provisional Assembly) 20 September 1942, in *Shanxi geming genjudi* [Shanxi Revolutionary Base Areas] no.2 1984, p.3.

Rong Zihe 'Jinyibu jiaqiang caijing jianshe, kaizhan dui di jingji douzheng' ['Advance Financial and Economic Construction, Develop the Economic Struggle against the Enemy'] February 1943, in Taihang geming genjudishi zongbian weihui (ed) *Caizheng jingji jianshe* [Financial and Economic Development] Taihang geming genjudi shiliao congshu No.6, Taiyuan, Shanxi renmin chubanshe, 1987, vol.1, p.152.

Rong Zihe *Taihangqu jingji jianshe wenti* [The Problem of Economic Development in the Taihang Base Area] JinJiLuYu Bianqu zhengfu, 1945.

Rong Zihe 'Taihangqu sannian laide jianshe he fazhan—sanshisinian sanyue bari Rong fuzhuxi zai JinJiLuYu Bianqu diyijie canhuiyi Taihangqu huiyi baogao' ['Reconstruction and Development in the Taihang Base Area during the last three years—Vice Chairman Rong's Report to the Taihang Session of the 1st meeting of the JinJiLuYu Border Region Assembly'] 8 March 1945, in Taihang geming genjudishi zongbian weihui (ed) *Zhengquan jianshe* [Political Development] Taihang geming genjudi shiliao congshu No.4, Taiyuan, Shanxi renmin chubanshe, 1990, p.299.

South Hebei Bank 'Guanyu Jinan yinhang faxing Jinanbi de bugao' ['Bulletin on the issue of Jinan dollars by the Jinan Bank'] Bulletin Number 2 of the Director of the South Hebei Executive Office, September 1939, in JinJiLuYu Bianqu caizheng jingji shi bianjizu, and Shanxi, Hebei, Shandong, Henan sheng danganguan (ed) *KangRi zhanzheng shiqi JinJiLuYu Bianqu caizheng jingji shi ziliao xuanbian* [Collection of Materials on the History of Finance and Economics in the Shanxi-Hebei-Shandong-Henan Border Region during the War of Resistance to Japan] Beijing, Caizheng jingji chubanshe, 1990, vol.2, p.700.

Taihang Fuwei 'Funu gongzuo chubu yanjiu' ['Preliminary Research on Women's Work'] 4 October 1945, in Taihang geming genjudishi zongbian weihui (ed) *Qunzhong yundong* [The Mass Movement] Taihang geming genjudi shiliao congshu No.7, Taiyuan, Shanxi renmin chubanshe, 1989, p.434.

Taihang junqu zhengwei yuanhui 'Taihang junqude zuzhi jiqi gongzuo gangyao' ['Outline of Organisation and Work of the Taihang Military District'] 9 July 1939, in *Shanxi geming genjudi* [Shanxi Revolutionary Base Areas] 1987, no.4, p.3.

Taihang junqu 'Xiaji fan saodang chubu zongjie' ['Preliminary Summary of the Summer's Resistance to "Mop-up" Activities'] 4 July 1942, in *Shanxi geming genjudi* [Shanxi Revolutionary Base Areas] no.2 1990, p.3.

Taihang junqu 'Yijiusisannian shiyue zhi yijiusisinian liuyuede shengchan chubu zongjie' ['Preliminary summary of production, October 1943 to June 1944'] 3 August 1944, in JinJiLuYu genjudi shiliao xuanbianzhe (ed) *JinJiLuYu genjudi shiliaoxuan* [Selected Materials on the History of the Shanxi-Hebei-Shandong-Henan Base Area] Taiyuan, Shanxi shengwei, 1989, vol.3 (1943–45) p.689.

Wang Laoci 'Tainan liangnianlaide zhengzhi gongzuo baogao' ['Report on political work in the South Taihang district during the last two years'] September 1941, in Zhonggong Taihang qudangwei *Taihang gefenqu tangde wenjian xuanbian* [Selected Party Documents of Districts in the Taihang] Huabei Xinhuashudian, 1944, vol.2 (1940–41) p.332.

Wang Laoci 'Dangnian Tainan qingkuang yu dangnian Tainan gongzuo' ['Conditions and work this year in the South Taihang district'] June 1943, in Zhonggong Taihang qudangwei *Taihang gefenqu tangde wenjian xuanbian* [Selected Party Documents of Districts in the Taihang] Huabei Xinhuashudian, 1944, vol.4 (1943) p.10.

Wang Naitang 'JinJiLuYu bianqu linshi yihui erci dahui Taihang, Taiyuequ huiyide zongjie' ['Summary of the Shanxi-Hebei-Shandong-Henan Border Region Provisional Assembly 2nd Conferences of the Taihang and Taiyue Districts'] 30 September 1942, in Taihang geming genjudishi zongbian weihui (ed) *Zhengquan jianshe* [Political Development] Taihang geming genjudi shiliao congshu No.4, Taiyuan, Shanxi renmin chubanshe, 1990, p.223.

Wang Zhuoru 'Guanyu heli fudan yu xiaozu xiaoxide yijian' ['Opinions on the reasonable burden and the reduction of rent and interest'] in Shanxisheng danganguan (ed) *Taihang dangshi ziliao huibian* [Collection of Materials on the History of the Party in the Taihang Base Area] Taiyuan, Shanxi renmin chubanshe, 1989, vol.2: 1939, p.509.

Wei Xiaoquan 'Hanbicun tudi wentide dianxing diaocha – shinian douzheng fanxiushen' ['Investigative Case Study of the Land Question in Hanbi Village – Ten Years of Struggle and Transformation'] April 1947, in Wuxiangxian xianzhi bianji weiyuanhui bangongshi (ed) *Wuxiang xianzhi* [The Record of Wuxiang County] Taiyuan, Shanxi renmin chubanshe, 1986, p.876.

Wen Jianping (Jian Ping) 'Wuxiang shiyanxian shouci huodong fenzi dongyuan dahui zongjie' ['Summary of the Conference of Advanced Activists in Mobilization in Wuxiang Experimental County'] 25 April 1940, in Shanxisheng danganguan (ed) *Taihang dangshi ziliao huibian* [Collection of Materials on the History of the Party in the Taihang Base Area] Taiyuan, Shanxi renmin chubanshe, 1994, vol.3: 1940, p.260.

Wuxiangxian zhengfu 'Zhaokai dizhu funong shengchan zuotanhui de shouhuo' ['The Yield from Calling a Discussion Meeting of Landlords and Rich Peasants'] 1 February 1944, in JinJiLuYu Bianqu caizheng jingji shi bianjizu and Shanxi, Hebei, Shandong, Henan sheng danganguan (ed) *KangRi zhanzheng shiqi JinJiLuYu Bianqu caizheng jingjishi ziliao xuanbian* [Collection of Materials on the Economic and Financial History of the Shanxi-Hebei-Shandong-Henan Border Region during the War of Resistance to Japan] Beijing, Caizheng jingji chubanshe, 1990, vol.2, p.133.

Wuxiangxian zhihuibu 'Weikun Panlong di wo douzheng bageyuede jiandan huigu' ['A Brief Memoir of the Eight-Month Seige of Panlong'] November 1943, in Taihang geming genjudishi zongbian weihui (ed) *Difang wuzhuang douzheng* [Local Armed Struggle] Taihang geming genjudi shiliao congshu No.3, Taiyuan, Shanxi renmin chubanshe, 1990, p.405.

Xin Tian 'Zai yige cun ruhe jinxing zhibu zhengfeng' ['How to advance rectification in a village'] February 1945, in Taihang geming genjudishi zongbian weihui (ed) *Dang de jianshe* [Party Development] Taihang geming genjudi shiliao congshu No.2, Taiyuan, Shanxi renmin chubanshe, 1989, p.329.

Xu Zirong 'Zhengfeng yu jiandang shi muqiande yanzhong renwu' ['Rectification and development of the Party is the immediate most important task'] 15 April 1940, in Taihang geming genjudishi zongbian weihui (ed) *Dang de jianshe* [Party Development] Taihang geming genjudi shiliao congshu No.2, Taiyuan, Shanxi renmin chubanshe, 1989, p.186.

Xu Zirong 'Disanci zulianhui de jiben jingshen' ['The Fundamental Ideas of the 3rd Organizational Conference'] August 1940, in Taihang geming genjudishi zongbian weihui (ed) *Dang de jianshe* [Party Development] Taihang geming genjudi shiliao congshu No.2, Taiyuan, Shanxi renmin chubanshe, 1989, p.199.

Xu Zirong 'Guanyu bage xiande zhibu gongzuo' ['Work on Party Branches in Eight Counties'] 30 August 1942, in Taihang geming genjudishi zongbian weihui (ed) *Dang de jianshe* [Party Development] Taihang geming genjudi shiliao congshu No.2, Taiyuan, Shanxi renmin chubanshe, 1989, p.236.

Xue Xun 'Guanyu gaizao dangyuande yishi wenti' ['Problems in changing the consciousness of Party members'] September 1940, in Taihang geming genjudishi zongbian weihui (ed) *Dang de jianshe* [Party Development] Taihang geming genjudi shiliao congshu No.2, Taiyuan, Shanxi renmin chubanshe, 1989, p.205.

Xue Xun 'Guanyu Shexian gongzuode huibao' ['Report on Work in Shexian'] 31 March 1941, in Shanxisheng danganguan (ed) *Taihang dangshi ziliao huibian* [Collection of Materials on the History of the Party in the Taihang Base Area] Taiyuan, Shanxi renmin chubanshe, 1994, vol.4: 1941, p.203.

Yang Daifu (Dai Fu) 'Liaoxian shiyanxian juti lingdaode jidian jingyan' ['Aspects of Concrete Leadership in Liaoxian Experimental County'] April 1940, in

Shanxisheng danganguan (ed) *Taihang dangshi ziliao huibian* [Collection of Materials on the History of the Party in the Taihang Base Area] Taiyuan, Shanxi renmin chubanshe, 1994, vol.3: 1940, p.274.
Yang Daifu 'Liaoxian shiyanxian gongzuo zongjie' ['Summary of Work in Liaoxian Experimental County'] October 1940, in Shanxisheng danganguan (ed) *Taihang dangshi ziliao huibian* [Collection of Materials on the History of the Party in the Taihang Base Area] Taiyuan, Shanxi renmin chubanshe, 1994, vol.3: 1940, p.711.
Yang Jue 'JinJiYuqude gongren yundong' ['The Worker's Movement in the Shanxi-Hebei-Henan District'] April 1941, in Taihang geming genjudishi zongbian weihui (ed) *Qunzhong yundong* [The Mass Movement] Taihang geming genjudi shiliao congshu No.7, Taiyuan, Shanxi renmin chubanshe, 1989, p.283.
Yang Shangkun 'Gei JinJiYu quweide zhishixin' ['Letter of Instruction to the Shanxi-Hebei-Henan District Committee'] July 1939, in Shanxisheng danganguan (ed) *Taihang dangshi ziliao huibian* [Collection of Materials on the History of the Party in the Taihang Base Area] Taiyuan, Shanxi renmin chubanshe, 1989, vol.2: 1939, p.420.
Yang Shangkun 'Zhonggong JinJiYuqu diyici daibiao dahui shangde zhengzhi baogao' ['Political Report to the 1st Congress of the Shanxi-Hebei-Henan CCP'] in Shanxisheng danganguan (ed) *Taihang dangshi ziliao huibian* [Collection of Materials on the History of the Party in the Taihang Base Area] Taiyuan, Shanxi renmin chubanshe, 1989, vol.2: 1939, p.473.
Yang Shangkun 'Diyici qu daibiaohui shangde zhengzhi baogao' ['Political Report to the 1st District Representative Conference'] 11–13 September 1939, in Taihang geming genjudishi zongbian weihui (ed) *Dang de jianshe* [Party Development] Taihang geming genjudi shiliao congshu No.2, Taiyuan, Shanxi renmin chubanshe, 1989, p.178.
Yang Shangkun 'Zai Zhonggong zhongyang beifangju Licheng huiyishangde baogao' ['Report to the Licheng Conference of the CCP Central Committee Northern Bureau'] 16 April 1940, in Shanxisheng danganguan (ed) *Taihang dangshi ziliao huibian* [Collection of Materials on the History of the Party in the Taihang Base Area] Taiyuan, Shanxi renmin chubanshe, 1994, vol.3: 1940, p.195.
Yang Wei 'Taihangshan beiqude tudi wenti' ['Land Issues in the Northern Part of the Taihang Mountains'] May 1940, in Shanxisheng danganguan (ed) *Taihang dangshi ziliao huibian* [Collection of Materials on the History of the Party in the Taihang Base Area] Taiyuan, Shanxi renmin chubanshe, 1994, vol.3: 1940, p.306.
Yang Xiufeng 'Zai Licheng huiyishangde baogao' ['Report to Licheng Meeting'] 16 April 1940, in JinJiLuYu Bianqu caizheng jingji shi bianjizu and Shanxi, Hebei, Shandong, Henan sheng danganguan (ed) *KangRi zhanzheng shiqi JinJiLuYu Bianqu caizheng jingjishi ziliao xuanbian* [Collection of Materials on the Economic and Financial History of the Shanxi-Hebei-Shandong-Henan Border Region during the War of Resistance to Japan] Beijing, Caizheng jingji chubanshe, 1990, vol.1, p.69.
Yin Feng 'Tudi zhengce zhongde jige juti wenti' ['Several specific issues on land policy'] June 1941, in Shanxisheng danganguan (ed) *Taihang dangshi ziliao*

huibian [Collection of Materials on the History of the Party in the Taihang Base Area] Taiyuan, Shanxi renmin chubanshe, 1994, vol.4: 1941, p.363.

Yu Yichuan 'Yijiusisinian dongli xiaozu yundong jiben jingyan' ['The Basic Experience of the Winter 1944 Interest Reduction Movement' in Taihang geming genjudishi zongbian weihui (ed) *Tudi wenti* [The Land Question] Taihang geming genjudi shiliao congshu No.5, Taiyuan, Shanxi renmin chubanshe, 1987, p.264.

Zhang Baishi 'Guanyu ganbu jiaoyu gongzuo' ['On Cadre Education Work'] February 1945, in Taihang geming genjudishi zongbian weihui (ed) *Dang de jianshe* [Party Development] Taihang geming genjudi shiliao congshu No.2, Taiyuan, Shanxi renmin chubanshe, 1989, p.396.

Zhang Wentian (Luo Fu) and Liu Shaoqi (Hu Fu) 'Guanyu zai fensui diren jiulu jingonghou jindongnan gongzuo wentide zhishi' ['Instruction on Problems of Work in Southeast Shanxi after Smashing the Enemy's Nine Army Attack'] 4 May 1938, in Shanxisheng danganguan (ed) *Taihang dangshi ziliao huibian* [Collection of Materials on the History of the Party in the Taihang Base Area] Taiyuan, Shanxi renmin chubanshe, 1989, vol.1, p.209.

Zhen Yuan 'Tantan heli fudan leijinshuide fenpei dingfen wenti' ['Discussion of Problems in the Distribution and Determination of a Reasonable Burden Progressive Tax'] August 1940, in Shanxisheng danganguan (ed) *Taihang dangshi ziliao huibian* [Collection of Materials on the History of the Party in the Taihang Base Area] Taiyuan, Shanxi renmin chubanshe, 1994, vol.3: 1940, p.589.

Zhonggong JiYuJin shengwei 'Muqian junshi fazhande xingshi ji women dui XX qu zuzhi wenti de tiyi' ['The Current Military Situation and Suggestions Regarding the Organizational Problems in XX Region'] 15 November 1937, in *Zhandou* [Combat] no.2, 26 November 1937, reprinted in Shanxisheng danganguan (ed) *Taihang dangshi ziliao huibian* [Collection of Materials on the History of the Party in the Taihang Base Area] vol.1, Taiyuan, Shanxi renmin chubanshe, 1989, p.35.

Zhonggong JiYuJin shengwei, Minyunbu 'Qunzhong gongzuo zongjie baogao' ['Summary Report on Work with the Masses'] 16 March 1938, in Taihang geming genjudishi zongbian weihui (ed) *Qunzhong yundong* [The Mass Movement] Taihang geming genjudi shiliao congshu No.7, Taiyuan, Shanxi renmin chubanshe, 1989, p.114.

Zhonggong JiYuJin shengwei 'Jianli Taihang genjudi huiyi baogao' ['Report of Meeting of the Establishment of the Taihang Base Area'] 20 March 1938, in Shanxisheng danganguan (ed) *Taihang dangshi ziliao huibian* [Collection of Materials on the History of the Party in the Taihang Base Area] Taiyuan, Shanxi renmin chubanshe, 1989, vol.1, p.133.

Zhonggong JiYuJin shengwei 'Xin xingshixia shengwei gongzuode xinrenwu' ['New Tasks for the Provincial Committee in New Circumstances'] June 1938, in Shanxisheng danganguan (ed) *Taihang dangshi ziliao huibian* [Collection of Materials on the History of the Party in the Taihang Base Area] Taiyuan, Shanxi renmin chubanshe, 1989, vol.1, p.210.

Zhonggong JiYuJin shengwei 'Gei beifangju bing zhongyangde zong baogao' ['General Report to North China Bureau'] 22 June 1938, in Shanxisheng danganguan (ed) *Taihang dangshi ziliao huibian* [Collection of Materials on the History of the Party in the Taihang Base Area] Taiyuan, Shanxi renmin chubanshe, 1989, vol.1, p.239.

Zhonggong JinJi diwei 'Sangeyueneide gongzuo yaoqiu yu gongzuo rili' ['Work Agenda and Requirements for the Next Three Months'] 30 May 1939, in Shanxisheng danganguan (ed) *Taihang dangshi ziliao huibian* [Collection of Materials on the History of the Party in the Taihang Base Area] Taiyuan, Shanxi renmin chubanshe, 1989, vol.2: 1939, p.122.

Zhonggong JinJiYu quwei yuanhui 'Quanqu gongzuo de fazhan yu dangde lingdao renwu' ['The Development of the Region's Work and the Party's Leadership Tasks'] 18 September 1938, in *Jinzhong shizhi ziliao* [Central Shanxi Historical Materials] no.2 1984, p.20.

Zhonggong JinJiYu quwei 'Guanyu muqian gongzuo renwude jueding' ['Decision on current work tasks'] January 1939, in *Jinzhong shizhi ziliao* [Central Shanxi Historical Materials] no.2 1984, p.32.

Zhonggong JinJiYu quwei 'Diyici zulianhui zongjie' ['Summary of First Organizational Meeting'] 17 March 1939, in Taihang geming genjudishi zongbian weihui (ed) *Dang de jianshe* [Party Development] Taihang geming genjudi shiliao congshu No.2, Taiyuan, Shanxi renmin chubanshe, 1989, p.147.

Zhonggong JinJiYu quwei 'Guanyu gonggu zuzhide zhishixin' ['Letter of Instruction on Consolidating Organization'] 2 November 1939, in Shanxisheng danganguan (ed) *Taihang dangshi ziliao huibian* [Collection of Materials on the History of the Party in the Taihang Base Area] Taiyuan, Shanxi renmin chubanshe, 1989, vol.2: 1939, p.685.

Zhonggong JinJiYu quwei 'Dierci minyun ganbu huiyi jilu' ['Summary of the CCP Shanxi-Hebei-Henan district committee 2nd meeting of propaganda cadres'] April 1940, reprinted in *Shanxi geming genjudi* [Shanxi Revolutionary Base Areas] 1988, no.3, p.7.

Zhonggong JinJiYu quwei 'Zhigong weiyuanhui gongyun gongzuo baogao' ['Workers Union Report on Workers Mobilization Work'] 10 May 1940, in Shanxisheng danganguan (ed) *Taihang dangshi ziliao huibian* [Collection of Materials on the History of the Party in the Taihang Base Area] Taiyuan, Shanxi renmin chubanshe, 1994, vol.3: 1940, p.333.

Zhonggong JinJiYu qudangwei 'Guanyu Wuxiang gongzuode yijian' ['Opinions on Wuxiang's Work'] July 1940, in Shanxisheng danganguan (ed) *Taihang dangshi ziliao huibian* [Collection of Materials on the History of the Party in the Taihang Base Area] Taiyuan, Shanxi renmin chubanshe, 1994, vol.3: 1940, p.509.

Zhonggong JinJiYu qudangwei 'Zuzhibu gei Beifangjude gongzuo baogao' ['Organization Department Report to North China Bureau'] August 1940, in *Shanxi geming genjudi* [Shanxi Revolutionary Base Areas] no.1 1989, p.3; and in Shanxisheng danganguan (ed) *Taihang dangshi ziliao huibian* [Collection of Materials on the History of the Party in the Taihang Base Area] Taiyuan, Shanxi renmin chubanshe, 1994, vol.3: 1940, p.536.

Zhonggong JinJiYu qudangwei 'Wuxiang shiyanxian gongzuode jiantao yu zhuanbian fangxiang' ['A Self-criticism of Wuxiang Experimental County's Work and Its Change of Direction'] 7 January 1941, in Shanxisheng danganguan (ed) *Taihang dangshi ziliao huibian* [Collection of Materials on the History of the Party in the Taihang Base Area] Taiyuan, Shanxi renmin chubanshe, 1994, vol.4: 1941, p.9.

Zhonggong JinJiYu qudangwei 'Guanyu chunjing yongdongde zhishi' ['CCP Shanxi-Hebei-Henan regional committee instruction concerning spring ploughing mobilization'] 12 February 1941, in Shanxisheng danganguan (ed) *Taihang dangshi ziliao huibian* [Collection of Materials on the History of the Party in the Taihang Base Area] Taiyuan, Shanxi renmin chubanshe, 1994, vol.4: 1941, p.139.

Zhonggong JinJiYu qudangwei 'Guanyu jiaqiang qunzhong gongzuode jueding' ['CCP Shanxi-Hebei-Henan regional committee decision concerning strengthening mass work' 15 February 1941, in Shanxisheng danganguan (ed) *Taihang dangshi ziliao huibian* [Collection of Materials on the History of the Party in the Taihang Base Area] Taiyuan, Shanxi renmin chubanshe, 1994, vol.4: 1941, p.151.

Zhonggong JinJiYu qudangwei 'Guanyu funu gongzuode zhishi' ['CCP Shanxi-Hebei-Henan regional committee instruction concerning women's work'] February 1941, in Shanxisheng danganguan (ed) *Taihang dangshi ziliao huibian* [Collection of Materials on the History of the Party in the Taihang Base Area] Taiyuan, Shanxi renmin chubanshe, 1994, vol.4: 1941, p.177.

Zhonggong JinJiYu qudangwei 'Guanyu muqian qingnian gongzuode zhishi' ['CCP Shanxi-Hebei-Henan regional committee instruction concerning the current situation in youth work'] March 1941, in Shanxisheng danganguan (ed) *Taihang dangshi ziliao huibian* [Collection of Materials on the History of the Party in the Taihang Base Area] vol.4: 1941, Taiyuan, Shanxi renmin chubanshe, 1994, p.197.

Zhonggong JinJiYu qudangwei 'Guanyu zhigong yundongde zhishi' ['CCP Shanxi-Hebei-Henan regional committee instruction concerning the labor movement'] March 1941, in Shanxisheng danganguan (ed) *Taihang dangshi ziliao huibian* [Collection of Materials on the History of the Party in the Taihang Base Area] Taiyuan, Shanxi renmin chubanshe, 1994, vol.4: 1941, p.189.

Zhonggong JinJiYu quwei *JinJiYu quwei disici zuzhihui jilu* [Minutes of the Fourth Organizational Conference of the Shanxi-Hebei-Henan Regional Committee] June 1941. [FOC]

Zhonggong JinJiYu qudangwei 'Zuzhi gongzuo baogao' ['Report on Organization Work'] 1 August 1941, in Shanxisheng danganguan (ed) *Taihang dangshi ziliao huibian* [Collection of Materials on the History of the Party in the Taihang Base Area] Taiyuan, Shanxi renmin chubanshe, 1994, vol.4: 1941, p.540.

Zhonggong JinJiYu qudangwei 'Yinianlai qunzhong wuzhuang gongzuo baogao' ['Report on the Last Year of Mass Armed Mobilization Work'] September 1941, in Taihang geming genjudishi zongbian weihui (ed) *Difang wuzhuang douzheng* [Local Armed Struggle] Taihang geming genjudi shiliao congshu No.3, Taiyuan, Shanxi renmin chubanshe, 1990, p.184.

Zhonggong JinJiYu qudangwei 'Guanyu gonggu dangde gongzuode zongjie' ['Summary of the Work of Consolidating the Party'] 8 October 1941, in Shanxisheng danganguan (ed) *Taihang dangshi ziliao huibian* [Collection of Materials on the History of the Party in the Taihang Base Area] Taiyuan, Shanxi renmin chubanshe, 1994, vol.4: 1941, p.820.

Zhonggong JinJuYu qudangwei 'Licheng Liguadao bodongde jingguo ji jingyan jiaoxun' ['The Experience and Lessons of the Licheng Sixth Trigram Rebellion'] 12 October 1941, in Taihang geming genjudishi zongbian weihui (ed) *Gongan baowei gongzuo* [Security and Protection] Taihang geming genjudi shiliao congshu No.9, Taiyuan, Shanxi renmin chubanshe, 1989, p.100.

Zhonggong JinJiYu qudang wuweihui (Peng Tao) 'Guanyu fan "saodang" zhong wuweihui gongzuode zongjie' ['Summary of the Work of the Armed Forces Committee against the enemy's "Mopping-up" operations'] December 1941, in Shanxisheng danganguan (ed) *Taihang dangshi ziliao huibian* [Collection of Materials on the History of the Party in the Taihang Base Area] Taiyuan, Shanxi renmin chubanshe, 1994, vol.4: 1941, p.954.

Zhonggong JinJiYu qudangwei 'Qu xian cun "sansanzhi" qingkuang tongjibiao' ['Table of the "Three-thirds system" in Counties, Subdistricts and Villages'] 1941, in Shanxisheng danganguan (ed) *Taihang dangshi ziliao huibian* [Collection of Materials on the History of the Party in the Taihang Base Area] Taiyuan, Shanxi renmin chubanshe, 1994, vol.4: 1941, p.990.

Zhonggong JinJiYu qudangwei 'Guanyu ruhe shixing tudi zhengcede zhishi' ['Instructions in carrying out land policy'] 15 April 1942, in Li Xuefeng *Li Xuefeng huiyilu: Taihang shinian* [The Memoirs of Li Xuefeng: Ten Years in the Taihang Mountains] Beijing, Zhonggong dangshi chubanshe, 1998, p.135.

Zhonggong JinJiYu qudangwei Licheng kaochatuan *Li Gua Dao shijian diaocha baogao* [Report of the Investigation into the Sixth Trigram Movement Incident] April 1942. [LGD]

Zhonggong JinJiYu qudangwei *Liaoxian diaocha baogao* [Report of an Investigation into Liaoxian] May 1942. [LDB]

Zhonggong JinJiYu quwei zuzhibu *Xianjinqu zhibu yanjiuhui jilu* [Minutes of the Conference on Party Branches in Advanced Areas] July 1942. [XZYJ]

Zhonggong JinJiYu quwei zuzhibu *Boruoqu zhibu yanjiuhui jilu* [Minutes of the Conference on Party Branches in Less-Developed Areas] July-August 1942. [BZYJ]

Zhonggong JinJiYu qudangwei 'Guanyu shixing fudan zhengcede zhishi' ['Instruction on Implementing (Tax) Burden Policy'] 10 August 1942, in Taihang geming genjudishi zongbian weihui (ed) *Tudi wenti* [The Land Question] Taihang geming genjudi shiliao congshu No.5, Taiyuan, Shanxi renmin chubanshe, 1987, p.213.

Zhonggong JinJiYu qudangwei 'Guanyu jinhou zhibu jiaoyu gongzuode jueding' ['Decision on Future Party Branch Education Work'] 6 September 1942, in Taihang geming genjudishi zongbian weihui (ed) *Dang de jianshe* [Party Development] Taihang geming genjudi shiliao congshu No.2, Taiyuan, Shanxi renmin chubanshe, 1989, p.262.

Zhonggong JinJiYu qudangwei 'Riwei tongzhi Huabei cailiao huiji' ['Collection of Materials on Japanese Puppet Troops Ruling North China'] 20 September 1942, in *Shanxi geming genjudi* [Shanxi Revolutionary Base Areas] no.4 1988, p.3.

Zhonggong JinJiYu qudangwei 'Guanyu shixing Zhongyang tudi zhengce zhishide baogao' ['Report on Implementing the CCP Central Committee's Directive on Land Policy'] 30 October 1942, in Taihang geming genjudishi zongbian weihui (ed) *Tudi wenti* [The Land Question] Taihang geming genjudi shiliao congshu No.5, Taiyuan, Shanxi renmin chubanshe, 1987, p.217.

Zhonggong JinJiYu qu wu zhuanshu 'Yijiusi'er nian zhengquan jianshe gongzuo zongjie' ['Summary of Work on the Development of Political Power during 1942'] in Zhonggong Henan shengwei dangshi ziliao zhengji bianzuan weiyuanhui (ed) *Taihang kangRi genjudi* [The Taihang Anti-Japanese Base Area] Zhonggong Henan dangshi ziliao congshu, Henan renmin chubanshe, 1986, vol.1, p.223.

Zhonggong JinJiYu qudangwei 'Jiancha Nanweiquan wenti houde jueding' ['Resolution after an Investigation of the Nanweiquan Question'] 25 May 1943, in Taihang geming genjudishi zongbian weihui (ed) *Dang de jianshe* [Party Development] Taihang geming genjudi shiliao congshu No.2, Taiyuan, Shanxi renmin chubanshe, 1989, p.295.

Zhonggong JinJiYu qudangwei *Guanyu zhibu jianshe yanjiu de jige wenti* [Several Questions from Research into Development of Party Branches] 30 September 1943, Minutes of the CCP Shanxi-Hebei-Henan Regional Committee, 5 September 1943. [ZJY]

Zhonggong Taihang qudangwei 'Guanyu jinmingnian liangnian qiedi wancheng quanqu zhengfeng renwu ji muqian jieduande jihua' ['Tasks for the next two years to complete rectification throughout the region and plans for the current stage'] 21 October 1943, in JinJiLuYu genjudi shiliao xuanbianzhe (ed) *JinJiLuYu genjudi shiliaoxuan* [Selected Materials on the History of the Shanxi-Hebei-Shandong-Henan Base Area] Taiyuan, Shanxi shengwei, 1989, vol.3 (1943–45) p.658.

Zhonggong Taihang qudangwei 'Guanyu shiqie xiaozu yundongde zhishi' ['Directive on Implementing the Rent Reduction Movement'] 17 November 1944, in Taihang geming genjudishi zongbian weihui (ed) *Tudi wenti* [The Land Question] Taihang geming genjudi shiliao congshu No.5, Taiyuan, Shanxi renmin chubanshe, 1987, p.257.

Zhonggong Taihang qudangwei *Taihang quwei diliuci zuzhihui jilu* [Minutes of the Sixth Organizational Conference of the Taihang Region Party Committee] February-March 1945. [SOC]

Zhonggong Taihang qudangwei (ed) *Tudi gaige baogao* [Report on Land Reform] Taihang qudangwei, 1947.

Zhonggong Tainan qudangwei 'Muqian Tainan kangRi minzhu zhengquan tongshi qudangde gongzuo fangzhen' ['Current policy on the party committee's work in establishing anti-Japanese democratic political forms in the South Taihang district'] 7 June 1940, in Zhonggong Taihang qudangwei *Taihang gefenqu tangde wenjian xuanbian* [Selected Party Documents of Districts in the Taihang] Huabei Xinhuashudian, 1944, vol.2 (1940–41) p.246.

Zhonggong zhongyang beifangju 'Licheng huiyi guanyu zhengquan jianzheng wentide jielun' ['The Licheng Meeting's Conclusions on Political Development'] April 1940, in Shanxisheng danganguan (ed) *Taihang dangshi ziliao huibian* [Collection of Materials on the History of the Party in the Taihang Base Area] Taiyuan, Shanxi renmin chubanshe, 1989, vol.3: 1940, p.253.

Zhonggong zhongyang beifangju 'Dui JinJiYu bianqu muqian jianshede zhuzhang' ['Proposal to Immediately Develop the Shanxi-Hebei-Henan Border Region'] 5 April 1941, in Taihang geming genjudishi zongbian weihui (ed) *Zhengquan jianshe* [Political Development] Taihang geming genjudi shiliao congshu No.4, Taiyuan, Shanxi renmin chubanshe, 1990, p.109.

Zhonggong zhongyang 'Zhonggong zhongyang guanyu nongmin tudi wenti gei Li Xuefeng de zhishi' ['Instruction to Li Xuefeng on the question of peasants and land from the CCP's Central Committee'] November 1941, in Shanxisheng danganguan (ed) *Taihang dangshi ziliao huibian* [Collection of Materials on the History of the Party in the Taihang Base Area] Taiyuan, Shanxi renmin chubanshe, 1994, vol.4: 1941, p.919.

Zhongguo jiefangqu linshi jiuji weiyuanhui JinJiLuYu Bianqu fenhui Taihang banshichu *Banianlai Riben faxisi cuican Taihangqu renmin de gaishu* [An Outline of the Destruction Wrought by Japanese Fascists in the Taihang Base Area during the Last Eight Years] Zhongguo jiefangqu linshi jiuji weiyuanhui JinJiLuYu Bianqu fenhui Taihang banshichu, 1946.

Zhu Rui 'Lun jianli JinJiYu kangRi genjudi' ['The Establishment of the Shanxi-Hebei-Henan Base Area'] 11 January 1939, in Shanxisheng danganguan (ed) *Taihang dangshi ziliao huibian* [Collection of Materials on the History of the Party in the Taihang Base Area] Taiyuan, Shanxi renmin chubanshe, 1989, vol.1, p.1.

Zhu Rui 'Shiqigeyuelaide JinJiYu quwei gongzuo' ['The Last Seventeen Months' Work under the Shanxi-Hebei-Henan Party Committee'] March 1939, in *Shanxi geming genjudi* [Shanxi Revolutionary Base Areas] no.1 1986, p.3.

Zhu Rui 'Lun Jindongnande qunzhong gongzuo' ['Work with the Masses in Southeast Shanxi'] April 1939, in Shanxisheng danganguan (ed) *Taihang dangshi ziliao huibian* [Collection of Materials on the History of the Party in the Taihang Base Area] Taiyuan, Shanxi renmin chubanshe, 1989, vol.2: 1939, p.242.

Zuoquanxian gongshangke 'Yijiusisinian shangbannian gongye yu shougongye zongjie' ['Summary of Heavy and Handicraft Industry in Zuoquan during the first half of 1944'] 2 July 1944, in JinJiLuYu Bianqu caizheng jingji shi bianjizu and Shanxi, Hebei, Shandong, Henan sheng danganguan (ed) *KangRi zhanzheng shiqi JinJiLuYu Bianqu caizheng jingjishi ziliao xuanbian* [Collection of Materials on the Economic and Financial History of the Shanxi-Hebei-Shandong-Henan Border Region during the War of Resistance to Japan] Beijing, Caizheng jingji chubanshe, 1990, vol.2, p.268.

Unattributed

'Tongyi zhanxian yu mocha wenti' ['The United Front and the Problem of Friction'] 1 May 1939, in Shanxisheng danganguan (ed) *Taihang dangshi ziliao huibian* [Collection of Materials on the History of the Party in the Taihang Base Area] Taiyuan, Shanxi renmin chubanshe, 1989 vol.2: 1939, p.314.

'Liaoxian shiyanxiande dongyuan baogao' ['Report on Mobilization in Liaoxian Experimental County'] October 1939, in Shanxisheng danganguan (ed) *Taihang dangshi ziliao huibian* [Collection of Materials on the History of the Party in the Taihang Base Area] Taiyuan, Shanxi renmin chubanshe, 1989, vol.2: 1939, p.664.

'Yijiusanjiunian gongzuo zongjie yu yijiusilingnian gongzuo jihuade baogao' ['Report on 1939 Work Summary and 1940 Work Plan'] 6 January 1940, in Shanxisheng danganguan (ed) *Taihang dangshi ziliao huibian* [Collection of Materials on the History of the Party in the Taihang Base Area] Taiyuan, Shanxi renmin chubanshe, 1994, vol.3: 1940, p.13.

'Wuxiang shiyanxian shouci huodong fenzi dongyuan dahui zongjie' ['Summary of Wuxiang Experimental County's First Activists' Conference'] April 1940, in Wuxiangxian xianzhi bianji weiyuanhui bangongshi (ed) *Wuxiang xianzhi* [The Record of Wuxiang County] Taiyuan, Shanxi renmin chubanshe, 1986, p.853.

'Chuangzao Liaoxian mofan xiande zhandou renwu ji gongzuo biaozhun' ['Realize the Important Tasks and Standards of Liaoxian Model County'] Summer 1940, in Shanxisheng danganguan (ed) *Taihang dangshi ziliao huibian* [Collection of Materials on the History of the Party in the Taihang Base Area] Taiyuan, Shanxi renmin chubanshe, 1994, vol.3: 1940, p.513.

'Shiba jituanjun zongsilingbu fayanren guanyu Huangyadong baoweizhande tanhua' ['A Spokesman for the 18th Army Group Talks about the Battle to Protect Huangyadong'] in *Xinhua ribao* [New China Daily] North China Edition, 27 November 1941, p.1.

'Tabeiqu tudi zhengcede shixing ji nongmin douzheng celuede cailiao huibian' ['Collection of Materials on the Implementation of Land Policy and the Strategy for Rural Struggle in the (North) Taihang Region'] 1 September 1942, in *Shanxi geming genjudi* [Shanxi Revolutionary Base Areas] no.2 1991, p.17.

'Shisanxian sanshijiuge zhibude chubu yanjiu' ['Preliminary Research on 39 Branches in 13 Counties'] 20 September 1942, in Taihang geming genjudishi zongbian weihui (ed) *Dang de jianshe* [Party Development] Taihang geming genjudi shiliao congshu No.2, Taiyuan, Shanxi renmin chubanshe, 1989, p.266.

'Taihang yifenqu Neiqiuxian lianhe baojia mintuan gongzuo chubu zongjie' ['Preliminary summary on work with the home protection and civil corps in Neiqiu County, Taihang First District'] October 1942, in JinJiLuYu genjudi shiliao xuanbianzhe (ed) *JinJiLuYu genjudi shiliaoxuan* [Selected Materials on the History of the Shanxi-Hebei-Shandong-Henan Base Area] Taiyuan, Shanxi shengwei, 1989, vol.2 (1941–42) p.642.

'Matian shuqian junmin jihui lianhe gongshen panguo hanjian' ['Several Thousand Soldiers and Civilians in Matian Collectively Try the Traitors'] 28 September 1943, in Taihang geming genjudishi zongbian weihui (ed) *Gongan baowei gongzuo* [Security and Protection] Taihang geming genjudi shiliao congshu No.9, Taiyuan, Shanxi renmin chubanshe, 1989, p.151.

'Wuxiang nongmin gejieceng shenghuo tedian jiqi ganbu shengzhangde diaocha' ['Survey of Various Categories of Peasants in Wuxiang and their Characteristics'] July 1943, in JinJiLuYu Bianqu caizheng jingji shi bianjizu and Shanxi, Hebei, Shandong, Henan sheng danganguan (ed) *KangRi zhanzheng shiqi JinJiLuYu Bianqu caizheng jingjishi ziliao xuanbian* [Collection of Materials on the Economic and Financial History of the Shanxi-Hebei-Shandong-Henan Border Region during the War of Resistance to Japan] Beijing, Caizheng jingji chubanshe, 1990, vol.2, p.1395.

'Jianzu jianxi zhongde dianxing nongcun' ['Case Studies of Rent and Interest Reduction'] 1943, in Zhonggong Taihang qudangwei *Taihang dang shiliao biancun* [Collection of Historical Party Materials on Taihang] Huabei Xinhua shudian, 1944, vol.1, p.403.

'Yijiusisinian kaizhan xiaozuxiaoxi douzhengde dianxing ziliao' ['Typical Cases of Rent and Interest Reduction'] 20 December 1944, in Taihang geming genjudishi zongbian weihui (ed) *Tudi wenti* [The Land Question] Taihang geming genjudi shiliao congshu No.5, Taiyuan, Shanxi renmin chubanshe, 1987, p.274.

Xuezhan zai JinJiLuYu Bianqu: Yierjiushi yu JinJiLuYu Bianqu [Bloody Battle in the Shanxi-Hebei-Shandong-Henan Border Region: The 129th Division and the Shanxi-Hebei-Shandong-Henan Border Region] Shandong xinhua shudian chuban, 1944.

Zhanshi xiaoyishu zhiershi *Zhandou zai Taihangshanshang* [The Struggle in the Taihang Mountains] np, 1944.

Taihangqu guomin caifu gaikuang [Outline of national wealth in the Taihang Region] 1944, in JinJiLuYu Bianqu caizheng jingji shi bianjizu and Shanxi, Hebei, Shandong, Henan sheng danganguan (ed) *KangRi zhanzheng shiqi JinJiLuYu Bianqu caizheng jingjishi ziliao xuanbian* [Collection of Materials on the Economic and Financial History of the Shanxi-Hebei-Shandong-Henan Border Region during the War of Resistance to Japan] Beijing, Caizheng jingji chubanshe, 1990, vol.2, p.1334. [TGCG]

Taihangqu renmin shenghuode xiaohao [Everday consumption in the Taihang Region] 1944, in JinJiLuYu Bianqu caizheng jingji shi bianjizu and Shanxi, Hebei, Shandong, Henan sheng danganguan (ed) *KangRi zhanzheng shiqi JinJiLuYu Bianqu caizheng jingjishi ziliao xuanbian* [Collection of Materials on the Economic and Financial History of the Shanxi-Hebei-Shandong-Henan Border Region during the War of Resistance to Japan] Beijing, Caizheng jingji chubanshe, 1990, vol.2, p.1341. [TRSX]

Taihangqu shehui jingji diaocha (diyiji) [Social and Economic Survey of the Taihang Region—First Collection] August 1944, in JinJiLuYu Bianqu caizheng jingji shi bianjizu and Shanxi, Hebei, Shandong, Henan sheng danganguan (ed) *KangRi zhanzheng shiqi JinJiLuYu Bianqu caizheng jingjishi ziliao xuanbian* [Collection of Materials on the Economic and Financial History of the Shanxi-Hebei-Shandong-Henan Border Region during the War of Resistance to Japan] Beijing, Caizheng jingji chubanshe, 1990, vol.2, p.1346. [TSJD1]

Taihangqu shehui jingji diaocha (dierji) [Social and Economic Survey of the Taihang Region—Second Collection] 1945, in JinJiLuYu Bianqu caizheng jingji shi bianjizu and Shanxi, Hebei, Shandong, Henan sheng danganguan (ed) *KangRi zhanzheng shiqi JinJiLuYu Bianqu caizheng jingjishi ziliao xuanbian* [Collection of Materials on the Economic and Financial History of the Shanxi-Hebei-Shandong-Henan Border Region during the War of Resistance to Japan] Beijing, Caizheng jingji chubanshe, 1990, vol.2, p.1406. [TSJD2]

Banianlai Riben faxisi cuihui Taihangqu renminde gaishu [General Description of The People of the Taihang Region after Eight Years of Japan's Fascist Destruction] 1945, in JinJiLuYu Bianqu caizheng jingji shi bianjizu and Shanxi, Hebei, Shandong, Henan sheng danganguan (ed) *KangRi zhanzheng shiqi JinJiLuYu Bianqu caizheng jingjishi ziliao xuanbian* [Collection of Materials on the Economic and Financial History of the Shanxi-Hebei-Shandong-Henan Border Region during the War of Resistance to Japan] Beijing, Caizheng jingji chubanshe, 1990, vol.1 p.534.

Memoirs

Bai Ping 'Fenghuangshan jiande hongqi' ['The Red Flag on Mount Fenghuang'] in *Hongqi piaopiao* [The Red Flag Flutters High] Vol. 8 p.122–140.

Bo Yibo 'Taiyue genjudi shi zenyang jianchi kangzhande' ['How the Taiyue Base Area was Established in the War of Resistance to Japan'] in *Jiefang ribao* [Liberation Daily] 3 July 1943.

Bo Yibo 'Liu Shaoqi tongzhi di yige lishi gongji' ['The Historical Achievement of Comrade Liu Shaoqi'] in *Renmin ribao* [People's Daily] 5 May 1980, p.2.

Bo Yibo and Song Renqiong 'Gongchandangyuande mofan Yang Xiuifeng tongzhi' ['The Model CCP Member Yang Xiufeng'] in *Renmin ribao* [People's Daily] 9 January 1984.

Bo Yibo 'Ximenghui lishi huigu' ['Comments on the History of the Sacrifice League'] 14 October 1986, in *Shanxi dangshi tongxun* [Newsletter of Shanxi Party History] no.4 1986, p.6.

Bo Yibo *Ruogan zhongda jueci yu shijian de huigu: Vol. 1* [Memories of Important Decisions and Events] Beijing, Zhonggong zhongyang dangxiao chubanshe, 1991.

Bo Yibo 'Youguan Shanxi xinjunde jidian huiyi' ['Some reminiscences related to the Shanxi New Army'] in *Zhonggong dangshi yanjiu* [Research on CCP History] no.2 1991, p.3.

Bo Yibo *Lingshen, yuanshi, zhanyou* [Leaders, Generals, Comrades-in-Arm] Zhonggong zhongyang dangxiao chubanshe, Beijing, 1992.

Bo Yibo *Qishinian fendou yu sikao* [Seventy Years of Struggle and Reflections] Vol.1 Zhongong dangshi chubanshe, Beijing, 1996.

Chen Dadong 'Yijiusiyinian zai Heshun Shuangfengchuan jianzu jianxi shidiande huiyi' ['A Memoir of the Rent and Interest Reduction Trial in Shuangfengchuan, Heshun County'] in in Taihang geming genjudi shi zongbian weihui (ed) *Tudi wenti* [The Land Question] Taiyuan, Shanxi renmin chubanshe, 1987, p.201.

Chen Dong 'Deng Xiaoping tongzhi yu JinJiLuYu bianqu jianshe: fang Rong Zihe tongzhi' ['Comrade Deng Xiaoping and the Development of the Shanxi-Hebei-Shandong-Henan Border Region: an interview with Comrade Rong Zihe'] in Yang Guoyu et al (ed) *Ershiba nian jian: xubian* [During Twenty-eight Years: Sequel] Shanghai wenyi chubanshe, 1990, p.19.

Chen Feiqin et al (eds) *Liu-Deng dajun zhengzhan ji xinwen bian* [Reporting the News of the Liu-Deng's Army's Battles] Beijing, Xinhua chubanshe, 1987.

Chen Xilian 'Wo zai Liaoxiande yixie huiyi' ['Some Recollections of My Time in Liaoxian'] in Zhonggong Zuoquan xianweiyuanhui and Zuoquan xian renmin zhengfu (ed) *Balujun zongbu zai Matian* [The Eighth Route Army's HQ in Matian] Taiyuan, Shanxi renmin chubanshe, 1990, p.54.

Chi Biqing 'Tan Taihang qunzhong yundong' ['Mass Mobilization in the

Taihang'] 22 July 1986, in Taihang geming genjudishi zongbian weihui (ed) *Qunzhong yundong* [The Mass Movement] Taihang geming genjudi shiliao congshu No.7, Taiyuan, Shanxi renmin chubanshe, 1989, p.262.

Li Chunfang 'Gaizao jiuzhengquande douzheng' ['The Struggle to Transform the Former System of Political Power'] in Zhonggong Wuxiang xianwei xuanchuanbu and Zhonggong Wuxiang xianwei dangshi bangongshi (ed) *Wuxiang fenghuo* [The Flames of War in Wuxiang] Licheng, Licheng CCP Committee, 1985, vol.1, p.92.

Li Da *KangRi zhanzhengzhongde balujun yierjiushi* [The 129th Division of the Eighth Route Army in the War of Resistance to Japan] Beijing, Renmin chubanshe, 1985.

Li Da 'KangRi zhanzhengzhongde Taihang junqu' ['The Taihang Military District in the War of Resistance to Japan'] January 1986, in Taihang geming genjudishi zongbian weihui (ed) *Difang wuzhuang douzheng* [Local Armed Struggle] Taihang geming genjudi shiliao congshu No.3, Taiyuan, Shanxi renmin chubanshe, 1990, p.76.

Li Daqing and Dong Weifa 'Balujun yierjiushi Licheng gongzuotuan yu Zhanhe youjiduide chuangjian' ['The Licheng Work Team of the Eighth Route Army's 129th Division and the Establishment of the Zhan River Guerilla Unit'] in *Shanxi dangshi tongxun* [Newsletter of Shanxi Party History] no.3 1987, p.33.

Li Guiren *Lai Ruoyu zhuan* [Biography of Lai Ruoyu] Taiyuan, Shanxi renmin chubanshe, 1994.

Li Jiguo 'Gongtongde xinsheng—fang Wuxiang xian sandai gongchandangyuan' ['Common aspirations—three generations of CCP members in Wuxiang County'] in *Renmin ribao* [People's Daily] 18 June 1991, p.1.

Li Xiuren 'Wo liaojiede Liaoxian (Zuoquan) Heshun dangde jianshe he fazhan' ['Comments on the Establishment and Development of the Party in Liaoxian (Zuoquan) and Heshun'] in Taihang geming genjudishi zongbian weihui (ed) *Dang de jianshe* [Party Development] Taihang geming genjudi shiliao congshu No.2, Taiyuan, Shanxi renmin chubanshe, 1989, p.572.

Li Xuefeng *Li Xuefeng huiyilu: Taihang shinian* [The Memoirs of Li Xuefeng: Ten Years in the Taihang Mountains] Beijing, Zhonggong dangshi chubanshe, 1998. [LXH]

Li Yisan 'Dixiadang zuzhi chuangjian jingguo' ['The Experience of Establishing an Underground Party Organization'] in Zhonggong Wuxiang xianwei xuanchuanbu and Zhonggong Wuxiang xianwei dangshi bangongshi (ed) *Wuxiang fenghuo* [The Flames of War in Wuxiang] Licheng, Licheng CCP Committee, 1985, vol.1, p.15.

Li Zeguo 'Fangshi xiangxian sandai gongchandangyuan' ['Three Generations of CCP Members'] in *Renmin ribao* [People's Daily] 18 June 1991 p.4.

Li Zikang 'Taihang lao jiefangqu jiaoyu gongzuo huiyi' ['Remembering Education Work in the Early-Liberated Parts of the Taihang Region'] in Taihang geming genjudishi zongbian weihui (ed) *Wenhua shiye* [Cultural Affairs] Taihang geming genjudi shiliao congshu No.8, Taiyuan, Shanxi renmin chubanshe, 1989, p.475.

Liu Bocheng 'Women zai Taihangshanshang' ['Into the Taihang Mountains'] in *Renmin ribao* [People's Daily] 21 June 1962.

Liu Bocheng et al *Liu Bocheng huiyilu* [Remembering Liu Bocheng] (3 vols) Shanghai wenyi chubanshe, 1981, 1985 and 1987.

Liu Huan 'Licheng jiandang chuqide yidian qingkuang' ['A View of the Early Establishment of the Party in Licheng'] 4 January 1987, in Taihang geming genjudishi zongbian weihui (ed) *Dang de jianshe* [Party Development] Taihang geming genjudi shiliao congshu No.2, Taiyuan, Shanxi renmin chubanshe, 1989, p.643.

Liu Jiang and Lu Qiao (ed) *Taihang xinwen shiliao huibian* [Collection of Historical Materials on the News in Taihang] Taihang xinwen shixuehui, 1994.

Liu Jiuxian 'Liaoxiande gongan baowei gongzuo' ['Liaoxian's Public Security Work'] September 1986, in Taihang geming genjudishi zongbian weihui (ed) *Gongan baowei gongzuo* [Security and Protection] Taihang geming genjudi shiliao congshu No.9, Taiyuan, Shanxi renmin chubanshe, 1989, p.370.

Ma Heshen (ed) *Taiyue fenghuo* [Taiyue at War] Zhongguo renmin jiefangjun dishisi jituan jundangshi ziliao zhengji bangongshi, nd.

Mu Xin (ed) *Chen Kang bingtuan zai Yuxi* [Chen Kang's Troops in West Henan] Henan renmin chubanshe, 1981.

Nie Rongzhen *Nie Rongzhen huiyilu* [Nie Rongzhen's Reminiscences] Hong Kong, Mingbao chubanshe, 1991.

Peng Dehuai *Memoirs of a Chinese Marshal* Beijing, Foreign Languages Press, 1984.

Ren Bishi 'Shanxi kangzhande huiyi' ['A Memoir of the Resistance in Shanxi'] in *Ren Bishi xuanji* [Selecetd Works of Ren Bishi] Beijing, Renmin chubanshe, 1987, p.136. Originally published in *Xinhua ribao* [New China Daily] 13 January 1938.

Rong Zihe 'Dui juesi disan congdui qianyiduan lishi qingkuangde huiyi' ['A Memoir of the Historical Conditions in the period before the Third Column of the Dare-to-Die Troops'] in *Shanxi dangshi tongxun* [Newsletter of Shanxi Party History] no.2 1994, p.25.

Sawa Mashatoshi 'Taihang emeng—yige qin Hua Rijun de riji he huiyi' ['Taihang Nightmare—A Diary and Memoir of the Japanese Army's Invasion of China'] in *Shanxi wenshi ziliao* no.119, May 1998, p.19.

Shanxisheng junqu zhengzhibu (ed) *Shanxi geming douzheng huilu* [Memoirs of the Revolutionary Struggle in Shanxi] (volumes) Taiyuan, Shanxi renmin chubanshe, 1962.

Shanxisheng shehui kexue yanjiusuo (ed) *Shanxi geming huiyilu* [Memoirs of the Revolution in Shanxi] volumes, Taiyuan, Shanxi renmin chubanshe, 1983–.

Song Xingzhong and Liu Yongsheng 'Dui JinJiYuqu chanye gonghui gongzuo de huiyi' ['Memoirs of Industrial Worker's Union Work in the Shanxi-Hebei-Henan District'] in Taihang geming genjudishi zongbian weihui (ed) *Qunzhong yundong* [The Mass Movement] Taihang geming genjudi shiliao congshu No.7, Taiyuan, Shanxi renmin chubanshe, 1989, p.345.

Sun Yuanfa 'Banian chenggang de Jin Cha Ji Bianqu' [Eight Years of the JinChaJi Border Region] in *Jiefang ribao* [Liberation Daily] 10 July 1944.

'Taihang laoqu tugai qianhou nongcun jingji biange kaocha zuotanhui fayan gangyao'' ['Outline of Discussion Meeting on the Investigation of Rural Economic Change in the Taihang Areas of the Revoluton before and after Land Reform'] 7 July 1983, in Taihang geming genjudishi zongbian weihui (ed) *Tudi wenti* [The Land Question] Taihang geming genjudi shiliao congshu No.5, Taiyuan, Shanxi renmin chubanshe, 1987, p.435.

Wang Yutang 'Zhengdun huifu Wuxiang dangzhuzhi jianyi' ['A Concise Recollection of the Resumption and Restoration of the CCP's Organization in Wuxiang'] in Zhonggong Wuxiang xianwei xuanchuanbu and Zhonggong Wuxiang xianwei dangshi bangongshi (ed) *Wuxiang fenghuo* [The Flames of War in Wuxiang] Licheng, Licheng CCP Committee, 1985, vol.1, p.87.

'Weiwei Taihangshan' bianweihui (ed) *Weiwei Taihangshan* [The Towering Taihang Mountains] Taiyuan, Xiwang chubanshe, 1986.

Wu Guangtang bianshen weiyuanhui (ed) *Wu Guangtang wenji* [Collected Works of Wu Guangtang] Taiyuan, Shanxi renmin chubanshe, 1993.

Wu Sanyou 'Huiyi zhongde nongmin kangzhaituan' ['Recalling the Peasants Refusal League'] in Zhonggong Wuxiang xianwei xuanchuanbu and Zhonggong Wuxiang xianwei dangshi bangongshi (ed) *Wuxiang fenghuo* [The Flames of War in Wuxiang] Licheng, Licheng CCP Committee, 1985, vol.1, p.63.

Xin Junshi 'KanRi zhanzhengzhongde Ximenghui he Shanxi xinjun' ['The Sacrifice League and Shanxi's New Army'] in 16 and 20 September 1985 *Renmin ribao* [People's Daily].

Xu Xiangqian *Lishi de huigu* [Remembering History] (3 vols) Beijing, Jiefangchun chubanshe, 1984.

Yang Duangui 'Ji Taihangqu renmin wuzhuangde jianshe' ['A Note on the Development of People's Armed Struggle in the Taihang District'] in *Junshi ziliao* [Materials on Military Affairs] No.3 1986.

Yang Guoyu et al (ed) *Zhanzheng qinliji: Liu-Deng dajun laozhanshi zuopinji* [Records of the War: Articles by Veterans of the The Liu-Deng Army] (vols) Tianjin, Baihua wenyi chubanshe, 1988.

Yang Guoyu et al (ed) *Ershiba nian jian: cong shizhengwei dao zongshuji* [During Twenty-eight Years: From Political Commissar to General-Secretary] Shanghai wenyi chubanshe, 1989.

Yang Guoyu et al (ed) *Ershiba nian jian: xubian* [During Twenty-eight Years: Sequel] Shanghai wenyi chubanshe, 1990.

Yang Guoyu et al (ed) *Ershiba nian jian: sanbian* [During Twenty-eight Years: Volume Three] Shanghai wenyi chubanshe, 1992.

Yang Guoyu and Chen Feiqin *Dieryu zhanjun jishi* [Record of the Second Field Army] Shanghai wenyi chubanshe, 1988.

Yang Jue 'Guanyu Jindongnan gongren yundongde huiyi' ['A Reminiscence of the Worker's Movement in Southeast Shanxi'] July 1983, in Taihang geming genjudishi zongbian weihui (ed) *Qunzhong yundong* [The Mass Movement] Taihang geming genjudi shiliao congshu No.7, Taiyuan, Shanxi renmin chubanshe, 1989, p.336.

Yang Shangkun 'Shanxide tongyi zhanxian jingyan zhide zongjie' ['Summarizing the worth of the experience of the United Front in Shanxi'] in *Zhonggong dangshi yanjiu* [Research on CCP History] no.2 1991, p.1.

Yang Xiufeng 'Guanyu wo zai Jixi minshunchu he Jixi youjiduide gongzuo qingkuang' ['Work Conditions when I was in the West Hebei Training Office and West Hebei Guerilla Troupe'] 1983, in Taihang geming genjudishi zongbian weihui (ed) *Difang wuzhuang douzheng* [Local Armed Struggle] Taihang geming genjudi shiliao congshu No.3, Taiyuan, Shanxi renmin chubanshe, 1990, p.105.

Yang Yikui 'Niuzhuan yanzhong jumian' ['Reversing a serious trend'] in Yang Guoyu et al (ed) *Ershiba nian jian: cong shizhengwei dao zongshuji* [During Twenty-eight Years: From Political Commissar to General-Secretary] Shanghai wenyi chubanshe, 1989, p.25.

Zhai Xiangwei et al (ed) *Shanguang de nianhua—Jinzhong dangshi renwu zhuanlue zhiyi* [Brilliant years—biographies of Jinzhong CCP members] Zhonggong Jinzhong diwei dangshi ziliao zhengji yanjiu bangongshi, 1987.

Zhang Shufan 'Zai Zuoquan gongzuode huiyi' ['Memoir of Work in Zuoquan'] in Taihang geming genjudishi zongbian weihui (ed) *Dang de jianshe* [Party Development] Taihang geming genjudi shiliao congshu No.2, Taiyuan, Shanxi renmin chubanshe, 1989, p.584.

Zhang Yixiang 'Taihang shiniande jici jiechu' ['Several encounters during a decade in the Taihang Mountains'] in Yang Guoyu et al (ed) *Ershiba nian jian: cong shizhengwei dao zongshuji* [During Twenty-eight Years: From Political Commissar to General-Secretary] Shanghai wenyi chubanshe, 1989, p.14.

Zhao Rongsheng *Huiyilu Wei Lihuang* [Remembering Wei Lihuang] Beijing, Wenshiziliao chubanshe, 1985.

Zhao Rongsheng 'Wo shi Wei Lihuang de dixia hei mishu' ['I was Wei Lihuang's black underground secretary'] in *Chuanji wenxue* [Biographical Notes] vol.58, no.6 and vol.59, no.2.

Zhao Rongsheng 'Wei Lihuang xiangyao canjia gongchandang' ['Wei Lihuang wanted to join the CCP'] in *Chuanji wenxue* [Biographical Notes] vol.59, no.3.

Zhonggong Jiaozuo shiwei danshiban (ed) *Jin Yu fenghuo—Balujun Jin Yu bian youji zhidui huiyilu* [The Flames of War in Shanxi-Henan—Memoirs of the Guerilla Troops supporting the Eighth Route Army in the Shanxi-Henan Area] Zhonggong Henan dangshi ziliao congshu, Henan renmin chubanshe, 1989.

Zhonggong Shanxishengwei dangshi yanjiushi and Zhonggong Taiyuan shiwei dangshi yanjiushi (ed) *Zhonggong Shanxi lishi yishi* [Recollections of the History of the Shanxi CCP] (vols) Taiyuan, Shanxi renmin chubanshe, 1991.

Zhonggong Wuxiang xianwei xuanchuanbu and Zhonggong Wuxiang xianwei dangshi bangongshi (ed) *Wuxiang fenghuo* [The Flames of War in Wuxiang] (2 vols) Licheng, Licheng CCP Committee, 1985. [WF]

Zhonggong Wuxiang xianwei xuanchuanbu (ed) *Zai laoqu de woyeshang* [The Fertile Wastes of the Earlier Liberated Areas] Wuxiang, 1987.

Zhonggong Zuoquan xianweiyuanhui and Zuoquan xian renmin zhengfu (ed) *Balujun zongbu zai Matian* [The Eighth Route Army's HQ in Matian] Taiyuan, Shanxi renmin chubanshe, 1990.

Zhongguo renmin jiefangjun lishi ziliao congshu bianshen weiyuanhui (ed) *Balujun huiyi shiliao* [Memoirs of the Eighth Route Army] (3 vols) Beijing, Jiefangjun chubanshe, 1991.

Gazetteers

Li Bu'an (ed) *Licheng zhilue* [Licheng Chronicle] Beijing, Renwen chubanshe, 1993. [LZ]

Licheng xianzhi bianxi weiyuanhui (ed) *Licheng xianzhi* [The Record of Licheng County] Beijing, Zhonghua shuju, 1994. [LX]

Sanjin wenhua yanjiu yeshu bianzhi weiyuanhui (ed) *Shanxi Tongzhi* [Encyclopedia of Shanxi] Beijing, Zhonghua shuju, 1990, 22 volumes.

Shanxisheng difangzhi bianzuan weiyuanhui (ed) *Minguo shiqi Shanxisheng gezhong zuzhi jigou jianlu* [Record of Organizations in Shanxi during the Republican Era] Taiyuan, 1983.

Shanxisheng shizhi yanjiuyuan (ed) *Shanxi tongzhi* [Encyclopedia of Shanxi] vol.7 *Tudi zhi* [Land] Beijing, Zhonghua shuju, 1998.

Shi Fayin, Xu Laiming, Dong Shuimin (ed) *Guomin shiqi Shanxisheng gezhong zuzhi jigou jianbian* [Summary of Organizations in Shanxi Province during the Republican Era] Shanxi difang shizhi ziliao congshu no.1, Shanxisheng difangzhi bianzuan weiyuanhui bangongshi, 1983.

Wuxiangxian xianzhi bianji weiyuanhui bangongshi (ed) *Wuxiang xianzhi* [The Record of Wuxiang County] Taiyuan, Shanxi renmin chubanshe, 1986. [WX]

Zhonggong Shanxisheng Jindong jiwei zuzhibu, Zhonggong Shanxisheng Jinzhong diwei dangshi yanjiushi, Shanxisheng Jinzhong diqu danganju (ed) *Zhongguo gongchandang Shanxisheng Jinzhong diqu zuzhishi ziliao 1925.6–1987.10* [Organizational History of the CCP in the Central Shanxi Region, 1925–1987] Taiyuan, Shanxi renmin chubanshe, 1991.

Zhonggong Shanxisheng Licheng xianwei zuzhibu, Zhonggong Shanxisheng Licheng xianwei dangshi yanjiushi, Shanxisheng Licheng xian danganju (ed) *Zhongguo gongchandang Shanxi sheng Licheng xian zuzhishi ziliao 1937–1987* [Organizational History of Licheng County, Shanxi Province CCP, 1937–1987] Taiyuan, Shanxi renmin chubanshe, 1993. [LOH]

Zhonggong Shanxi shengwei zuzhibu, Zhonggong Shanxi shengwei dangshi yanjiushi, Shanxi sheng danganju (ed) *Zhongguo gongchandang Shanxi sheng zuzhishi ziliao 1924–1949* [Organizational History of the CCP in Shanxi, 1924–1949] Taiyuan, Shanxi renmin chubanshe, 1994. [SOH]

Zhonggong Shanxisheng Wuxiang xianwei zuzhibu, Zhonggong Shanxisheng Wuxiang xianwei dangshi yanjiushi, Shanxisheng Wuxiangxian danganju (ed) *Zhongguo gongchandang Shanxisheng Wuxiangxian zuzhi shi ziliao 1933.8—1993.12* [Organizational History of the CCP in Wuxiang County, Shanxi, 1933–1993] Taiyuan, Shanxi renmin chubanshe, 1994. [WOH]

Zhonggong Shanxisheng Yangquan shiwei zuzhibu, Zhonggong Shanxisheng Yangquan shiwei dangshi yanjiushi, Shanxisheng Yangquanshi danganju (ed) *Zhongguo gongchandang Shanxisheng Yangquanshi zuzhishi ziliao 1922.12–1987.10* [Organizational History of the CCP in Yangquan City, Shanxi, 1922–1987] Taiyuan, Shanxi renmin chubanshe, 1993.

Zhonggong Shanxisheng Zuoquan xianwei zuzhibu, Zhonggong Shanxisheng Zuoquan xianwei dangshi yanjiushi, Shanxisheng Zuoquan xian danganju (ed) *Zhongguo gongchandang Shanxisheng Zuoquan xian zuzhishi ziliao 1937.10–1987.10* [Organizational History of the CCP in Zuoquan County, Shanxi, 1937–1987] Taiyuan, Shanxi renmin chubanshe, 1992. [ZOH]

SECONDARY SOURCES

David E Apter and Tony Saich *Discourse on Power: The Revolutionary Process in Mao's Republic* Cambridge, Massachusetts, Harvard University Press, 1996.

David E Apter 'Discourse as power: Yan'an and the Chinese Revolution' in Tony Saich and Hans van de Ven (ed) *New Perspectives on the Chinese CommunistRevolution* New York, M E Sharpe, 1995, p.189.

Stephen C Averill 'Party, society and local elite in the Jiangxi communist movement' in *Journal of Asian Studies* Vol. 46 no.2, 1987, p.279.

Stephen C Averill 'Social elites and communist revolution in the Jiangxi hill country' in J W Esherick and M B Rankin (ed) *Chinese Local Elites and Patterns of Dominance* Berkeley, University of California, 1990.

Baba Takeshi 'Santo konichi konkyochi ni okeru zaisei mondai' ['Problems in financial administration in the Shandong anti-Japanese base areas'] in *Shikan* no.110, 1984.

Balujun Taihang Jinianguan *Jieshuoci* [Introduction to the Eighth Route Army Museum, Wuxiang] 1979.

Bao Guiyin *Peng Dehuai tongzhi zai Taihang* [Comrade Peng Dehuai in Taihang] Taiyuan, Shanxi renmin chubanshe, 1991.

Jack Belden *China Shakes the World* Harmondsworth, Penguin, 1973.

Gregor Benton *Mountain Fires: The Red Army's Three-Year War in South China, 1934–1938* Berkeley, University of California Press, 1992.

Gregor Benton 'Comparative Perspectives: North and Central China in the Anti-Japanese Resistance' in Feng Chongyi and David S G Goodman *North China at War: the social ecology of revolution, 1937–1945* Lanham, Maryland, Rowman & Littlefield, 2000.

Lucien Bianco *Origins of the Chinese Revolution, 1915–1949* Stanford, Stanford University Press, 1971.

Lucien Bianco 'Peasants and revolution: the case of China' in *Journal of Peasant Studies* Vol. 2 no.3, p.313.

Lucien Bianco 'Peasant Movements' in *The Cambridge History of China* Vol 13, Republican China, 1912–1949, Part II, Cambridge, Cambridge University Press, 1986, Chapter 6, p.270.

Lucien Bianco 'Peasant Responses to CCP Mobilization Policies, 1937–1945' in Tony Saich and Hans van de Ven (ed) *New Perspectives on the Chinese Communist Revolution* New York, M E Sharpe, 1995, p.175.

Bo Shansong 'Shanxi "Shieryue shibian" yu Ximenghui Juesiduide zhuyao jingyan jiaoxun' ['The 12th December Incident in Shanxi and the Important Lessons from the Experience for the Dare-to-Die Troops of the Sacrifice League'] in *Shanxi dangshi tongxun* [Newsletter of Shanxi Party History] no.2 1990, p.8.

Bo Yibo 'Wodang zai Shanxi tongyizhanxian chenggongde yizhao' ['The Success of the Party in the Shanxi United Front'] in *Dangshi wenhui* [Selections from Party History] no.2 1985.

Paul Richard Bohr *Famine in China and the Missionary: Timothy Richard as Relief Administrator and Advocate of National Reform 1876–1884* East Asia Monograph, Cambridge, Massachusetts, Harvard University Press, 1972

John Hunter Boyle *China and Japan at War, 1937–1945: The politics of collaboration* Stanford, Stanford University Press, 1972.

John Lossing Buck *Chinese Farm Economy* Chicago, University of Chicago Press, 1930.

Chen Zhongshi *Bai Luyuan* [Bai Luyuan] Beijing, Renmin wenxue chubanshe, 1993.

Chen Yung-fa 'Rural elections in wartime central China' in *Modern China* Vol. 6 No. 3, 1980, p.267.

Chen Yung-fa *Making Revolution: The Communist Movement in Eastern and Central China, 1937–1945* Berkeley, University of California Press, 1986.

Chen Yung-fa 'The blooming poppy under the red sun: The Yan'an Way and the Opium Trade' in Tony Saich and Hans van de Ven (ed) *New Perspectives on the Chinese Communist Revolution* New York, M E Sharpe, 1995, p.263.

Chen Yung-fa and Gregor Benton *Moral Economy and the Chinese Revolution* Centre for Anthropology and Sociology, University of Amsterdam, 1986.

Chen Zhili (ed) *Zhongguo gongchandang jianshe shi* [History of the Development of the CCP] Shanghai renmin chubanshe, 1991.

Cheng Qingfeng '*Xinhua ribao* (Huabeiban) baoshe zai wuyue fan "saodang" zhong' ['The newspaper office of the *New China Daily* (North China edition) during the May "mop-up"'] in *Weiwei Taihang* [The Towering Taihang Mountains] no.1 1989, p.41.

Cheng Wenhua 'KangRi zhanzheng shiqi Zuoquan xian jiji kaizhan "shuangyong" gongzuo' ['Zuoquan County's lively development of "Two supports" work in the period of the War of Resistance'] in *Shanxi Dangshi Tongxun* [Shanxi Party History Newsletter] 1995, no.4, p.5.

Jean Chesneaux *Peasant Revolts in China 1840–1949* London, Thames and Hudson, 1973.

Boyd Compton *Mao's China: Party Reform Documents, 1942–44* Seattle, University of Washington Press, 1966.

Anthony Coogan 'Northeast China and the Origins of the Anti-Japanese United Front' in *Modern China* Vol.20 no.3 July 1994, p.282.

Isabel and David Crook *Revolution in a Chinese Village: Ten Mile Inn* London, Routledge, 1959.

Dai Jianbing 'KangRi shiqide ZhongRi huabizhan' ['The Sino-Japanese Currency War of the Period of the War of Resistance to Japan'] in *Dangshi wenhui* [Selections from Party History] no.1 1995, p.8.

Dang Dexin and Yang Yuwen (eds) *KangRi zhanzheng Guomindang zhenwang jiangling lu* [Nationalist Party Generals in the War of Resistance to Japan] Beijing, Jiefangjun chubanshe, 1987.

James C Davies 'Towards a Theory of Revolution' in the *American Sociological Review* vol.28, no.1, February 1962, p.5.

Deng Maomao *My Father Deng Xiaoping* Basic Books, HarperCollins, New York, 1995.

Ding Ling *Yierjiushi yu JinJiLuYu Bianqu* [The 129th Division and the Shanxi-Hebei-Shandong-Henan Border Region] Beijing, Xinhuashe, 1950 (originally *Jiefang ribao* [Liberation Daily] 14–19 August 1944).

Dong Kuisheng 'Licheng gaogan huiyi jiankuang' ['An Introduction to the Licheng Senior Cadre's Meeting'] in *Weiwei Taihang* [The Towering Taihang Mountains] no.2 1986, p.56.

Dong Kuisheng 'Licheng tudi gaige yundong jianxi' ['A brief analysis of the land reform campaign in Licheng'] in *Weiwei Taihang* [The Towering Taihang Mountains] no.4 1988, p.21.

Dong Qian *Meiyou renmin de shijie—weikun Qinyuan tongxun* [A world without people—the story of the seige of Qinyuan] Beijing, Renmin chubanshe, 1979.

Carl E Dorris 'Peasant Mobilization in North China and the Origins of Yenan Communism' in *The China Quarterly* No. 68, December 1976, p.697.

Du Zhongde 'Liangtiao kangzhan luxian, liangzhong butong jieguo—cong Jin dongnan kangRi genjudide chuangjian yu fazhan, kan dangde quanmian kangzhan luxiande zhengquexing' ['Two Lines of Resistance, Two Different Results—The Correctness of the Party's Line in the War of Resistance can be seen in the Establishment and Development of the Southeast Shanxi Anti-Japanese Base Area'] in *Weiwei Taihang* [The Towering Taihang Mountains] no.3 1987, p.7.

Duan Yiting 'Gongchandangren lingdaoxiade duodang hezuo zhengquan de yici huishi—JinJiLuYu Bianqu linshi huiyi pingjie' ['A Form of Multiparty Political Power led by Communists—An Introduction to the Provisional Assembly of the Shanxi-Hebei-Shandong-Henan Border Region'] in *Hebei xuekan* [Hebei Academic Journal] no.2 1990.

Prasenjit Duara *Culture, Power and the State: Rural North China, 1900–1942* Stanford, Stanford University Press, 1988.

Prasenjit Duara *Rescuing History from the Nation: Questioning Narratives of Modern China* Chicago, Chicago University Press, 1995.

John Dunn *Modern Revolutions: an introduction to the analysis of a political phenomenon* Cambridge, Cambridge University Press, 1972.

Peter Duus (ed) *The Japanese Informal Empire in China, 1895–1937* Princeton, New Jersey, Princeton University Press, 1989.

Lloyd E Eastman *Seeds of Destruction: Nationalist China in War and Revolution, 1937–1949* Stanford, Stanford University Press, 1984.

Lloyd E Eastman 'Nationalist China during the Sino-Japanese War, 1937–1945' in *The Cambridge History of China* Vol. 13, Republican China, 1912–1949, Part II, Cambridge, Cambridge University Press, 1986, Chapter 11, p.547.

Lloyd E Eastman 'State Building and the Revolutionary Transformation of Rural Society in North China' in *Modern China* Vol.16 no.2, p.226.

Israel Epstein *The People's War* London, Victor Gollancz, 1939.

Joseph W Esherick 'Deconstructing the Construction of the Party-State: Gulin County in the Shaan-Gan-Ning Border Region' in *The China Quarterly* No.140, December 1994, p.1052.

Joseph W Esherick 'Ten Theses on the Chinese Revolution' in *Modern China* Vol.21 no.1 January 1995, p.45.

Joseph W Esherick 'Revolution in a Feudal Fortress: Yangjiagou, Mizhi County, Shaanxi, 1937–1948' in *Modern China* vol.24 no.4, October 1998.

Feng Chongyi 'The Making of the Jin Sui Base Area: Peasants, Intellectuals and Democratization' in Feng Chongyi and David S G Goodman *North China at War: the social ecology of revolution, 1937–1945* Lanham, Maryland, Rowman & Littlefield, 2000.

Feng Chongyi and David S G Goodman 'Explaining Revolution' in Feng Chongyi & David S G Goodman *North China at War: the social ecology of revolution, 1937–1945* Lanham, Maryland, Rowman & Littlefield, 2000.

Feng Chongyi and David S G Goodman *North China at War: the social ecology of revolution, 1937–1945* Lanham, Maryland, Rowman & Littlefield, 2000.

Morton Fried *Fabric of Chinese Society: A Study of the Social Life of a County Seat* London, Atlantic Press, 1956.

Edward Friedman, Paul Pickowicz and Mark Selden *Chinese Village, Socialist State* New Haven, Connecticut, Yale University Press, 1991.

Fu Jianwen *Taihang xiongshi: Balujun yierjiushi zhengzhanji* [The Heroic Division of Taihang: The Campaigns of the 129th Division of the Eighth Route Army] Beijing, Jiefangjun wenyi chubanshe, 1995.

Edmund S K Fung *The Military Dimension of the Chinese Revolution* Vancouver, University of British Columbia Press, 1980.

Gao Muhong *Taihang yin* [The Taihang Spirit] Taiyuan, Shanxi renmin chubanshe, 1956.

Gao Yi '"Shijiu kuai dade jiefangqu" ming'er kao' ['Investigation of the names of the "Nineteen large liberated areas'] in *Dangde wenxian* [Party Documents] no.4 1991, p.64.

James Gardiner *In and Out of China Cities: Hankow-Pingyao-Shanghai* Sydney, Donald F Pettigrew Pty Ltd, 1949.

Ge Lan *Tang Tietong de Gushi* [The Story of Tang Tietong] Beijing, Zuojia chubanshe, 1955.

Stuart Gelder *The Chinese Communists* London, Victor Gollancz, 1946.

Donald G Gillin *Warlord Yen Hsi-shan in Shansi Province, 1911–1949* Princeton, New Jersey, Princeton University Press, 1967.

Donald G Gillin '"Peasant Nationalism" in the History of Chinese Communism' in *Journal of Asian Studies* Vol. 23 No. 2 (1964) p.269.

Jack A Goldstone 'An Analytical Framework' in Jack A Goldstone, Ted Robert Gurr, and Farrokh Moshiri (ed) *Revolutions of the Late Twentieth Century* Boulder, Colorado, Westview Press, 1991, p.37.

Jack A Goldstone, Ted Robert Gurr, and Farrokh Moshiri (ed) *Revolutions of the Late Twentieth Century* Boulder, Colorado, Westview Press, 1991.

Gong Yuzhi 'Guanyu KangRi zhanzheng shi yanjiu' ['Research on the History of the War of Resistance'] in *Zhonggong dangshi yanjiu* [Research on CCP History] No.6 1995, p.7.

David S G Goodman 'Zhongguo gemingde Taihangdaolu: Deng Xiaoping, Mao Zedong yu biande zhengzhi' ['The Taihang Way in China's Revolution: Deng Xiaoping, Mao Zedong and political change'] in Nankai daxue lishixi, Zhongguo jinxiandaishi jiaoyanshi (eds) *Zhongwai xuezhe lun KangRi genjudi* Beijing, Dang'an chubanshe, 1993, pp. 631–641.

David S G Goodman *Deng Xiaoping and the Chinese Revolution: a political biography* London, Routledge, 1994.

David S G Goodman 'JinJiLuYu in the Sino-Japanese War: The Border Region and the Border Region Government' in *The China Quarterly* No.140, December 1994, p.1007.

David S G Goodman 'The Licheng Rebellion of 1941: Class, Gender and Leadership in the Sino-Japanese War' in *Modern China* vol.23 no.2 April 1997 p.216.

Sidney Greenblatt *The People of Taihang* New York, International Arts and Sciences Press, 1976.

Jerome B Grieder *Intellectuals and the State in Modern China* New York, The Free Press, 1981.

Linda Grove 'Creating a Northern Soviet' in *Modern China* Vol.1 No. 3, p.257.

J Guillermaz *A History of the Chinese Communist Party, 1921–1949* London, Methuen, 1972.

Ted Gurr *Why Men Rebel* Princeton, New Jersey, Princeton University Press, 1970.

Ted Gurr and Jack A Goldstone 'Comparisons and Policy Implications' in Jack A Goldstone, Ted Robert Gurr, and Farrokh Moshiri (ed) *Revolutions of the Late Twentieth Century* Boulder, Colorado, Westview Press, 1991, p.324.

Guo Chengbao 'Zuo Quan jiangjun zai Taihangshanshang' ['General Zuo Quan in the Taihang Mountains'] in *Hongqi piaopiao* [The Red Flag Flutters High] Vol. 5 pp.138–148.

Guo Linxiang *Jinglu yizhi chu Taihang* [The Crack Troops from the Taihang] Beijing, Jiefangjun chubanshe, 1987.

Guo Rong 'Yuci zaoqi tangde chuangjian yu gongren yundongde xingqi' ['The early establishment of the CCP in Yuci and the rise of the worker's movement'] in *Shanxi dangshi tongxun* [Newsletter of Shanxi Party History] no.2 1988, p.24.

Hai Hua 'Zhigeng he mengya yu JinJiLuYu kangRi genjudide Deng Xiaoping jingji sixiang' ['The Origins of Deng Xiaoping's Economic Thinking in the Shanxi-Hebei-Shandong-Henan Base Area of the War of Resistance to Japan'] in *Shanxi dangshi tongxun* [Newsletter of Shanxi Party History] no.2 1994, p.1.

Hao Mengbi and Duan Haoran (ed) *Zhongguo gongchandang liushinian* [Sixty Years of the CCP] (2 vols) Beijing, Jiefangjun chubanshe, 1984.

J P Harrison *The Long March to Power: A History of the CCP, 1921–1972* New York, Praeger, 1972.

Kathleen Hartford *Step by Step: Reform, Resistance, and Revolution in Chin-Ch'a-Chi Border Region, 1937–1945* PhD dissertation, Stanford, Stanford University, 1980.

Kathleen Hartford and Steven M Goldstein 'Introduction: Perspectives on the Chinese Communist Revolution' in Kathleen Hartford and Steven M Goldstein (eds) *Single Sparks: China's Rural Revolutions* New York, M E Sharpe, 1989, p.3.

Kathleen Hartford 'Repression and Communist Success: The Case of Jin-Cha-Ji, 1938–1943' in Kathleen Hartford and Steven M Goldstein (eds) *Single Sparks: China's Rural Revolutions* New York, M E Sharpe, 1989, p.92.

Kathleen Hartford and Steven M Goldstein (eds) *Single Sparks: China's Rural Revolutions* New York, M E Sharpe, 1989.

He Dong, Yang Xiancai, and Wang Xunsheng *Zhongguo geming shi renwu cidian* [Biographical Dictionary of the Chinese Revolution] Beijing chubanshe, 1991.

He Gaochao *Dizhu, nongmin, gongchandang: shehui boyilun fenxi* [Landlords, peasants and the Chinese Communist Party: A game theory analysis] Hong Kong, Oxford University Press, 1997.

He Li et al (eds) *Balujun shijian renwu lu* [Record of People and Events in the Eighth Route Army] Shanghai renmin chubanshe, 1988.
William Hinton *Fanshen: A documentary of revolution in a Chinese village* Harmondsworth, Penguin, 1966.
George Hogg *I See a New China* London, Victor Gollancz, 1945.
David Holm *Art and Ideology in Revolutionary China* Oxford, Oxford University Press, 1991.
James C Hsiung and Steven I Levine (ed) *China's Bitter Victory: The War with Japan, 1937–1945* New York, M E Sharpe, 1992.
Hsu Long-hsuen and Chang Ming-kai *History of The Sino-Japanese War (1937–1945)* Taipei, Chung Wu Publishing Co., 1972.
Hu Chiao-mu *Thirty Years of the Communist Party of China: An outline history* London, Lawrence and Wishart, 1951.
Philip C C Huang *The Peasant Economy and Social Change in North China* Stanford, Stanford University Press, 1985.
Philip C C Huang 'Analyzing the Twentieth Century Chinese Countryside' in *Modern China* Vol.1 no.2, 1975, p.132.
Philip C C Huang 'Paradoxes in Social and Economic History' in *Modern China* Vol.17 no.3 July 1991, p.299.
Philip C C Huang 'Rural Class Struggle in the Chinese Revolution: Representational and Objective Realities from the Land Reform to the Cultural Revolution' in *Modern China* Vol.21, no.1, January 1995, p.105.
Huang Xuanwen *Xiaohe fengyun: Henansheng Neihuangxian Qiankoucun* [Storm on the River: Qiankou Village, Neihuang County, Henan Province] Henan renmin chubanshe, 1976.
Huang Yao and Zhang Mingzhe (ed) *Luo Ruiqing zhuan* [Biography of Luo Ruiqing] Beijing, Dangdai zhongguo chubanshe, 1996.
Chang-tai Hung *War and Popular Culture: Resistance in Modern China, 1937–1945* Berkeley, University of California Press, 1994.
Issues and Studies 'Bo Yibo: New Vice Premier of the State Council' in *Issues and Studies* August 1979, p.82.
JiLuYu Bianqu gemingshi gongzuozu *JiLuYu Bianqu gemingshi* [History of the Revolution in the JiLuYu Border Area] Jinan, Shandong daxue chubanshe, 1991.
Jiang Shunxing and Li Liangyu (ed) *Shanxi wang Yan Xishan* [Yan Xishan, King of Shanxi] Henan renmin chubanshe, 1990.
Jiang Xianshan *Zhandou zhede rizi* [Diary of the War] Shanghai, Xinwenyi chubanshe, 1953.
Jinzhong shizhi ziliao (ed) *Yierjiushi yu JinJiYuLu Bianqu* [The 129th Division and the Shanxi-Hebei-Shandong-Henan Border Region] 1983, Special issue of *Jinzhong shizhi ziliao* [Central Shanxi Historical Materials].
Jing Zhankui *Yan Xishan guanliao ziben yanjiu* [A Study of Yan Xishan's Bureaucratic Capitalism] Taiyuan, Shanxi jingji chubanshe, 1993.
Chalmers Johnson *Peasant Nationalism and Communist Power* Stanford, Stanford University Press, 1962.
Chalmers Johnson 'Civilian loyalties and guerrilla conflict' in *World Politics* Vol. 14 No. 4, 1962, p.646.

Chalmers Johnson 'Chinese communist leadership and mass response: The Yenan socialist education campaign period' in Ping-ti Ho and Tang Tsou (ed) *China in Crisis* Vol.1, Chicago, University of Chicago Press, 1968, p.397.

Chalmers Johnson *Revolutionary Change* London, University of London Press, 1968.

Chalmers Johnson 'Peasant Nationalism Revisited: The biography of a book' in *The China Quarterly* No. 72, 1977, p.766.

Ju Wenhui 'Yang Shangkun zai jianli Huabei kangRi genjudizhongde zuoyong' ['Yang Shangkun's activities in establishing anti-Japanese base areas in North China'] in *Shizhi yanjiu* [Historical and Archive Research] no.1 1997, p.40.

Ju Yuxiu, Wang Zhiming and Qi Jinrui 'KangRi zhanzheng shiqi Liaoxi xiande duidi douzheng: 1941 nian 9 yue—1945 nian 10 yue' ['West Liao County's Struggle against the Enemy in the War of Resistance against Japan'] in *Shanxi dangshi tongxun* [Newsletter of Shanxi Party History] no.3 1988, p.26.

Ellen R Judd 'Cultural Articulation in the Chinese Countryside, 1937–1947' in *Modern China* Vol.16 no.3, July 1990, p.269.

Junshi kexueyuan junshi tushuguan bianzhe *Zhongguo renmin jiefangjun zuzhi yange he geji lingdao chengyuan minglu, Vol 2: KangRi zhanzheng shiqi* [Organisation and leadership of China's PLA, Vol.2 Era of the War of Resistance to Japan] Beijing, Junshi kexue chubanshe, 1987.

Tetsuya Kataoka *Resistance and Revolution in China: The Communists and the Second United Front* Berkeley, University of California Press, 1974.

Pauline B Keating 'The Ecological Origins of the Yan'an Way' in *The Australian Journal of Chinese Affairs* no.32, July 1994, p.123.

Pauline B Keating 'The Yan'an Way of Cooperativization' in *The China Quarterly* No.140, December 1994, p.1025.

Pauline B Keating *Two Revolutions: Village Reconstruction and the Cooperative Movement in Northern Shaanxi 1934–1945* Stanford, Stanford University Press, 1997.

Pauline B Keating 'Getting Peasants Organized: Village Organizations and the Party-state in the Shaan Gan Ning Border Region' in Feng Chongyi and David S G Goodman *North China at War: the social ecology of revolution, 1937–1945* Lanham, Maryland, Rowman & Littlefield, 2000.

Ilpyong J Kim 'Mass Mobilization Policies and Techniques Developed in the Period of the Chinese Soviet Republic' in A Doak Barnett (ed) *Chinese Communist Politics in Action* Seattle, University of Washington Press, 1969.

Donald W Klein and Anne B Clark *Biographic Dictionary of Chinese Communism, 1921–1965* (2 vols) Cambridge, Massachusetts, Harvard University Press, 1971.

Philip A Kuhn 'Local self-government under the Republic: Problems of control, autonomy and mobilization' in F Wakeman and C Grant (ed) *Conflict and Control in Late Imperial China* Berkeley, University of California Press, 1975, p.293.

Krishan Kumar (ed) *Revolution: The Theory and Practice of a European Idea* London, Weidenfeld and Nicholson, 1971.

Warren Kuo *Analytical History of the Chinese Communist Party* (4 vols) Taipei, Institute of International Relations, 1970.

Lao Bo 'Guomindang jundui zai Huabei dihou youjizhan de shibai' ['The Defeat of Nationalist Party Troops in the Guerilla War behind the Enemy Lines in North China'] in *Dangshi wenhui* [Selections from Party History] no.9 1995, p.29.

Lee Ngok 'Problems of Mass Mobilisation and Village Administration in Chinese Communist Bases in North China, 1938–1942' in *Journal of Oriental Society of Australia* Vol.11, 1976, p.81.

John W Lewis (ed) *Peasant Rebellion and Communist Revolution in Asia* Stanford, Stanford University Press, 1974.

Li Chengrui 'KangRi zhanzheng shiqi jige geming genjudi nongye shuishou zhidu nongmin fudan' ['Tax systems and peasant burdens in several base areas of the War of Resistance to Japan'] in *Jingji yanjiu* [Economic Research] No. 2 1956, p.108–9.

Li Guiren *Lai Ruoyu zhuan* [Biography of Lai Ruoyu] Taiyuan, Shanxi renmin chubanshe, 1994.

Li Ji *Dongzheng jishu* [Record of the Eastern Expedition] Taiyuan, Shanxi renmin chubanshe, 1986.

Lincoln Li *The Japanese Army in North China, 1937–1941* Oxford, Oxford University Press, 1975.

Li Mancun, Chen Ying and Huang Yuzhang (ed) *Liu Bocheng zhuan* [Biography of Liu Bocheng] Beijing, Dangdai zhongguo chubanshe, 1992.

Li Ming 'Jin dongnan kangRi genjudide zhengquan jianshe' ['The Development of Political Power in the Southeast Shanxi Anti-Japanese Base Area'] in *Weiwei Taihang* [The Towering Taihang Mountains] no.4 1987, p.16.

Li Rongcheng 'Dui Yan Xishan liyong shehui zhuyi sixiangde pingxi' ['An Analysis of Yan Xishan's use of Socialist Ideology'] in *Shanxi dangshi tongxun* [Newsletter of Shanxi Party History] no.4 1993, p.24.

Li Rongcheng, Luo Chenpu and Yang Jianzhong *Yan Xishan quanzhuan* [The Complete Biography of Yan Xishan] (2 vols) Beijing, Dangdai Zhongguo chubanshe, 1997.

Li Xifan *Geming nongcun de bianqian shi* [History of the Transformation of a Revolutionary Village] Beijing, Zuojia chubanshe, 1962.

Li Xiaoming *The sound of rifles on the plains* Beijing, Zuojia chubanshe, 1965.

Li Xingren et al (ed) *Dierci ZhongRi zhanzheng jishi, 1931–1945* [Record of the Second Sino-Japanese War] Beijing, Dangan chubanshe, 1988.

Li Yisan 'Zhonggong Wuxiang dixia tang zuzhide chuangjian jingguo' ['After the Establishment of the CCP's Underground Organization in Wuxiang'] in *Weiwei Taihang* [The Towering Taihang Mountains] no.4 1986, p.60.

Li Yong and Zhang Zhongtian (ed) *KangRi minzu tongyi zhanxian dashiji* [Chronology of the United Front in the War of Resistance to Japan] Beijing, Zhongguo jingji chubanshe, 1988.

Li Zhikuan *Zhu De zongsiling zai Taihang* [Commander-in-chief Zhu De in Taihang] Taiyuan, Shanxi renmin chubanshe, 1979.

Li Zhikuan 'Riren fanzhan tongmeng zai Taihang' ['Members of the Japanese Anti-War League in the Taihang Region'] in *Weiwei Taihang* [The Towering Taihang Mountains] no.1 1987, p.52.

Li Zhikuan 'Wuxiang xian geming jiuzhi' ['Wuxiang County Revolutionary Sites'] in *Weiwei Taihang* [The Towering Taihang Mountains] no.2 1989, p.50.

Liang Zhixiang and Zhang Guoxiang 'Dierci guogong hezuo zai Shanxide chenggong shixian' ['The Achievements of the Second United Front in Shanxi'] in *Shizhi yanjiu* [Historical and Archive Research] no.1 1996, p.4.

Lin Min *Red Flag Canal* Peking, Foreign Languages Press, 1974.

Michael Lindsay 'The taxation system of the Shansi-Chahar-Hopei Border Region, 1938–1945' in *The China Quarterly* No.42, April 1970, p.7.

Michael Lindsay *The Unknown War: North China, 1937–1945* London, Bergstrom and Boyle Books Ltd, 1975.

Daniel Little *Understanding Peasant China: Case Studies in the Philosophy of Social Science* New Haven, Connecticut, Yale University Press, 1989.

Liu Jiansheng *Shanxi jindai jingjishi* [Modern Shanxi's Economic History] Taiyuan, Shanxi jingji chubanshe, 1997.

Liu, Zhang and Wang 'Taihang geming genjudi zhengquan jianshe gaishu' ['Summary of the Political Development of the Taihang Revolutionary Base Area'] in Taihang geming genjudishi zongbian weihui (ed) *Zhengquan jianshe* [Political Development] Taihang geming genjudi shiliao congshu No.4, Taiyuan, Shanxi renmin chubanshe, 1990.

Liu Jiang *Taihang Fengyun* [Storm in the Taihang] Beijing, Zuojia chubanshe, 1962.

Liu Mei and Li Jianguo *Taihang geming genjudi jiaoyu jianshi* [Introductory History of Education in the Taihang Revolutionary Base Area] Shanxi Jiaoyu shi zhibianxie lingdao zu and Shanxi jiaoyu shi zhibianshen weiyuanhui, 1989.

Liu Qi *Zhanzheng jiguan* [War Organization] Beijing, Jiefangjun wenyi chubanshe, 1978.

Liu Qingming and Liu Dacheng 'KangRi minzhu zhengquan yanjiu' ['Research on Democratic Political Power during the Anti-Japanese War'] in *Zhonggong dangshi yanjiu* [Research on CCP History] no.2 1992, p.23.

Liu Shufa '"Licheng xianzhi" chubanhoude huigu' ['Reactions to the publication of Licheng County Gazetteer'] in *Cangsang* [Vicissitudes] no.4 1997, p.18.

Liu Tai *Shanhe huxiao—Balujun Yierjiushi zhengzhan shilu* [The Screech of the Rivers and Mountains: The Campaigns of the 129th Division of the Eighth Route Army] Hunan chubanshe, 1995.

Liu Zhi (ed) *Xu Xiangqian zhuan* [Biography of Xu Xiangqian] Beijing, Dangdai zhongguo chubanshe, 1992.

W C Lowdermilk 'Forest Destruction and Slope Denudation in the Province of Shansi' in *China Journal of Science and Arts* Vol.4 p.127, 1926.

Ma Feng *Nu Yingxiong Liu Hulan* [The Heroine Liu Hulan] Beijing, Renmin chubanshe, 1975.

Ma Feng *Liu Hulan zhuan* [The Story of Liu Hulan] Beijing, Zhongguo qingnian chubanshe, 1978.

Ma Feng *Vendetta* Beijing, Foreign Languages Press, 1989.

Ma Qibin et al (ed) *Zhongguo gongchandang chuangye sanshinian, 1919–1949* [Thirty Years of the CCP's Pioneering Work] Beijing, Zhonggong dangshi chubanshe, 1991.

Walter H Mallory *China: Land of Famine* New York, American Geographical Society, 1926.

Fred R von der Mehden *Comparative Political Violence* Englewood Cliffs, New Jersey, Prentice-Hall, 1973.

Joel S Migdal *Peasants, Politics and Revolution: Pressures toward Political and Social Change in the Third World* Princeton, New Jersey, Princeton University Press, 1974.

Farrokh Moshiri 'Revolutionary Conflict Theory in an Evolutionary Perspective' in Jack A Goldstone, Ted Robert Gurr, and Farrokh Moshiri (ed) *Revolutions of the Late Twentieth Century* Boulder, Colorado, Westview Press, 1991, p.4.

Mu Xiang *Jinyang qiu* [Autumn in Taiyuan] Beijing, Jiefangjun wenyi chubanshe, 1962.

Raymond Myers 'North China villages during the Republican period: socio-economic relationships' in *Modern China* Vol.6 no.3, 1980, p.243.

Raymond Myers *The Chinese Peasant Economy: Agricultural Development in Hopei and Shantung, 1890–1949* Cambridge, Massachusetts, Harvard University Press, 1970.

Jan Myrdal *Report from a Chinese Village* London, Picador, 1975.

Victor Nee 'Towards a social anthropology of the Chinese revolution' in *Bulletin of Concerned Asian Scholars* vol.11 no.3, p.40.

Niu Chonghui and Guo Zuxiang 'Shanxi kangRi genjudide xiaozu xiaoxi yundong' ['The Campaign to Reduce Rents and Interest during the War of Resistance in Shanxi'] in *Cangsang* [Vicissitudes] no.4 1995, p.7.

David Ownby 'The Heaven and Earth Society as Popular Region' in *The Journal of Asian Studies* vol.54 no.4, 1995, p.1023.

David M Paulson *War and Revolution in North China: The Shandong Base Area, 1937–1945* PhD dissertation, Stanford, Stanford University, 1982.

David M Paulson 'Nationalist guerillas in the Sino-Japanese War: The "Diehards" of Shandong Province' in Kathleen Hartford and Steven M Goldstein (eds) *Single Sparks: China's Rural Revolutions* New York, M E Sharpe, 1989, p.128.

David M Paulson 'Leadership and spontaneity: Recent approaches to Communist Base Areas studies' *Chinese Republican Newsletter* No. 1, October 1981, p.7.

Elizabeth J Perry *Rebels and Revolutionaries in North China, 1845–1945* Stanford, Stanford University Press, 1980.

Kenneth Pomeranz *The Making of a Hinterland: State, Society and Economy in Inland North China, 1853–1937* Berkeley, University of California Press, 1993.

Qi Wu *Yige geming genjudi de chengzhang: KangRi zhanzheng he jiefang zhanzheng shiqi de JinJiLuYu Bianqu gaikuang* [The Transformation of a Revolutionary Base Area: An Outline of the Shanxi-Hebei-Shandong-Henan Border Region during the War of Resistance and the War of Liberation] Beijing, Renmin chubanshe, 1957.

Qi Wu 'JinJiLuYu Bianqu gaikuang' ['An Outline of the Shanxi-Hebei-Shandong-Henan Border Region'] in *Shanxi dangshi tongxun* [Newsletter of Shanxi Party History] no.3 1987, p.3.

Qi Wu 'Fazhan jingji, baozhang gonggei' ['Develop the economy, ensure supply'] Introduction to Taihang geming genjudishi zongbian weihui (ed) *Caizheng jingji jianshe* [Financial and Economic Development] Taihang geming genjudi shiliao congshu No.6, Taiyuan, Shanxi renmin chubanshe, 1987, vol.1.

Qi Wu *JinJiLuYu bianqu shi* [A History of the Shanxi-Hebei-Shandong-Henan Border Region] Beijing, Dangdai Zhongguo chubanshe, 1995.

Qiao Zhiqiang (ed) *Shanxi tongshi* [General History of Shanxi] Beijing, Zhonghua shuju, 1997.

Qu Liuxiu, Shi Shaodong et al *Shanxi kangzhan wenxueshi* [History of Literature in Shanxi during the War of Resistance to Japan] Taiyuan, Beiyue chubanshe, 1988.

Rong Zihe 'JinJiLuYu Bianqu shi zenyang duguo kangRi shiqi xiang te jieduan caijing kunnande' ['How the Shanxi-Hebei-Shandong-Henan Border Region Overcame the Difficult Stages of the War of Resistance'] in *Weiwei Taihang* [The Towering Taihang Mountains] no.1 1986, p.4.

Harrison E Salisbury *The Long March: The Untold Story* New York, McGraw-Hill, 1985.

Peter Schran *Guerilla Economy: The Development of the Shensi-Kansu-Ninghsia Border Region, 1937–1945* New York, State University of New York Press, 1976.

Henry G Schwartz *Liu Shao-chi and 'People's War': A Report on the Creation of Base Areas in 1938* Laurence, Kansas University, East Asia Research Publications, 1969.

Mark Selden *The Yenan Way in Revolutionary China* Cambridge, Massachusetts, Harvard University Press, 1971.

Mark Selden *China in Revolution: The Yenan Way Revisited* New York, M E Sharpe, 1995.

Mark Selden 'Yan'an Communism Reconsidered' in *Modern China* Vol.21 no.1, January 1995, p.8.

Shanxisheng difangzhi bianzuan weiyuanhui (ed) *Shanxi dashiji 1840–1985* [Chronology of Shanxi 1840–1985] Taiyuan, Shanxi renmin chubanshe, 1987.

Shanxisheng junqu zhengzhibu *Shanxi minbing yinglie zhuan* [Biographies of the Heroes of the Shanxi Militia] Taiyuan, Shanxi renmin chubanshe, 1986.

Shanxisheng wenhuating wenhuazhi bianzuan bangongshi *geming genjudi wenyi yundongshi jianshu* [Summary of the History of the Culture Movement in Shanxi Revolutionary Base Areas] Shanxisheng wenhuazhi, 1983.

Shao Houding 'Jinan Taihang Taiyue xingzheng lianhe banshichu jianshu' ['An Introduction to the Joint Office of the South Hebei, Taihang and Taiyue Base Areas'] in *Weiwei Taihang* [The Towering Taihang Mountains] no.3 1986, p.6.

Shi Gao 'Shanxi xinjunde youlai' ['Origins of the Shanxi New Army'] in *Zhonggong dangshi yanjiu* [Research on CCP History] no.2 1991, p.5.

Shi Wenhua 'Dangde youlianhe youdouzhengde zhengce zai Shanxi Ximenghuide juti yingyong' ['The Sacrifice League in Shanxi as the Concrete Application of the Party's Policy of Unity and Struggle'] in *Dangshi yanjiu* [Research on Party History] no.4 1984.

Shi Wenhua *Zhongguo gongchandang yu Shanxi kangzhan* [The Chinese Communist Party and the War of Resistance in Shanxi] Taiyuan, Shanxi renmin chubanshe, 1997.

K. K. Shum *The Chinese Communists' Road to Power: The Anti-Japanese United Front (1935–1945)* Hong Kong, Oxford University Press, 1988.

Theda Skocpol 'France, Russia and China: A Structural Analysis of Social Revolutions' in *Comparative Studies in Society and History* Vol.18 no.2, April 1976, p.175.

Theda Skocpol *States and Social Revolutions: A Comparative Analysis of France, Russia and China* Cambridge, Cambridge University Press, 1979.

Lyman Van Slyke 'The Chinese Communist Movement during the Sino-Japanese War, 1937–45' in *The Cambridge History of China* Vol. 13, Republican China, 1912–1949, Part II, Cambridge, Cambridge University Press, 1986 Chapter 12, p.609.

Edgar Snow *Scorched Earth* (2 vols) London, Victor Gollancz, 1941.

Edgar Snow *Random Notes on Red China, 1936–1945* East Asia Research Center, Cambridge, Massachusetts, Harvard University, 1957.

Anna Louise Strong *Tomorrow's China* Committee for a Democratic Far Eastern Policy, New York, 1948.

Su Wenming (ed) *Journey into Revolutionary China* Beijing, Foreign Languages Press, 1984.

Tai Hsuan-chih *The Red Spears, 1916–1949* Translated by Ronald Suleski; Introduction by Elizabeth Perry, Ann Arbor, Center for Chinese Studies, University of Michigan, 1985.

Taihang geming genjudishi zongbian weihui (ed) *Taihang geming genjudi shigao* [Outline History of the Taihang Revolutionary Base Area] Taiyuan, Shanxi renmin chubanshe, 1987.

Taihang geming genjudishi zongbian weihui (ed) *Dashijishu* [Chronology] Taihang geming genjudi shiliao congshu No.1, Taiyuan, Shanxi renmin chubanshe, 1991.

Taihang geming genjudishi zongbian weihui (ed) *Dang de jianshe* [Party Development] Taihang geming genjudi shiliao congshu No.2, Taiyuan, Shanxi renmin chubanshe, 1989.

Taihang geming genjudishi zongbian weihui (ed) *Difang wuzhuang douzheng* [Local Armed Struggle] Taihang geming genjudi shiliao congshu No.3, Taiyuan, Shanxi renmin chubanshe, 1990.

Taihang geming genjudishi zongbian weihui (ed) *Zhengquan jianshe* [Political Development] Taihang geming genjudi shiliao congshu No.4, Taiyuan, Shanxi renmin chubanshe, 1990.

Taihang geming genjudishi zongbian weihui (ed) *Tudi wenti* [The Land Question] Taihang geming genjudi shiliao congshu No.5, Taiyuan, Shanxi renmin chubanshe, 1987.

Taihang geming genjudishi zongbian weihui (ed) *Caizheng jingji jianshe* [Financial and Economic Development] (2 vols) Taihang geming genjudi shiliao congshu No.6, Taiyuan, Shanxi renmin chubanshe, 1987.

Taihang geming genjudishi zongbian weihui (ed) *Qunzhong yundong* [The Mass Movement] Taihang geming genjudi shiliao congshu No.7, Taiyuan, Shanxi renmin chubanshe, 1989.

Taihang geming genjudishi zongbian weihui (ed) *Wenhua shiye* [Cultural Affairs] Taihang geming genjudi shiliao congshu No.8, Taiyuan, Shanxi renmin chubanshe, 1989.

Taihang geming genjudishi zongbian weihui (ed) *Gongan baowei gongzuo* [Security and Protection] Taihang geming genjudi shiliao congshu No.9, Taiyuan, Shanxi renmin chubanshe, 1989.

Taihang geming genjudishi zongbian weihui (ed) *Yubei zhandou* [The Struggle for North Henan] Taihang geming genjudi shiliao congshu No.11, Taiyuan, Shanxi renmin chubanshe, 1988.

Taihang geming genjudishi zongbian weihui (ed) *Jiaotong youzheng* [Communications and Postal Administration] Taihang geming genjudi shiliao congshu No.12, Taiyuan, Shanxi renmin chubanshe, 1995.

Taihang renjia [Taihang People] Beijing, Zhongguo qingnian chubanshe, 1964.

Taiyue xinwen shibianzhi weiyuanhui *Taiyue xinwen shiye shilue* [Chronology of Journalism in Taiyue] Taiyuan, Shuhai chubanshe, 1991.

R H Tawney *Land and Labour in China* Boston, Beacon Press, 1932.

G Taylor *The Struggle for North China* New York, Institute for Pacific Affairs, 1940.

Frederick C Teiwes *Politics and Purges in China* New York, M E Sharpe, 1979.

Frederick C Teiwes *Leadership, Legitimacy and Conflict in China* New York, M E Sharpe, 1984

Ralph Thaxton 'Some Critical Comments on Peasant Revolts and Revolutionary Politics in China' in *Journal of Asian Studies* Vol.33, p.279.

Ralph Thaxton *China Turned Rightside Up: Revolutionary Legitimacy in the Peasant World* New Haven, Connecticut, Yale University Press, 1983.

Ralph Thaxton 'The World Turned Downsideup: three orders of meaning in the peasants' traditional world' in *Modern China* Vol.3 no.2, p.185.

Ralph Thaxton 'Peasants, capitalism, and revolution: on capitalism as a force for liberation in revolutionary China' in *Comparative Political Studies* Vol.12 no.3, 1979, p.289.

Ralph Thaxton 'Tenants in revolution: the tenacity of traditional morality' in *Modern China* Vol.1 no.3, p.323.

Tian Youru 'JiTai lianbande lishi zuoyong' ['The historical function of the Joint Office for the South Hebei, Taihang and Taiyue Base Areas'] in *Shanxi dangshi tongxun* [Newsletter of Shanxi Party History] no.1 1986, p.49.

Tian Youru 'Taihang kangRi genjudi shi yanjiu songshu' ['Research on the History of the Taihang Anti-Japanese Base Area'] in *Dangshi tongxun* [Newsletter on Party History] No. 353 (No.7 1987) p.39.

Tian Youru 'Baituan dazhan de weida yiyi ji bu zu' ['The Significance of the Hundred Regiments Campaign'] in *Dangshi tongxun* [Newsletter on Party History] No. 517 (No.10 1987) p.47.

Tian Youru 'Genjudi shehui xingzhide yanjin yu Zhongguo zuoshang shehui zhuyi daolude biran' ['Evolution of the socialist character of base areas and the inevitability of China's travelling the socialist road'] in *Shanxi dangshi tongxun* [Newsletter of Shanxi Party History] no.2 1991, p.19.

Tian Youru 'Shanxi tudi zhidu gaige lishi gaiyao' ['Outline History of Reform of the Land System in Shanxi'] in *Shanxi dangshi tongxun* [Bulletin of Shanxi Party History] no.2 1993, p.17.

Tian Youru *Liu Bocheng yu Deng Xiaoping* [Liu Bocheng and Deng Xiaoping] Zhonggong zhongyang dangxiao chubanshe, Beijing, 1994.

Tian Youru 'Balujun kaichuang Huabei kangRi zhanlue zhidian jishi' ['A Record of the Eighth Route Army Opening Up North China as the Strategic Fulcrum of the War against Japan'] in *Dangshi wenhui* [Selections from Party History] no.8 1997, p.24; no.9 1997, p.26; no.10 1997, p.42; and no.11 1997, p.33.

Tian Youru 'Social and Political Change in the Villages of the Taihang Anti-Japanese Base Area' in Feng Chongyi and David S G Goodman *North China at*

War: the social ecology of revolution, 1937–1945 Lanham, Maryland, Rowman & Littlefield, 2000.

Charles Tilly *From Mobilization to Revolution* Reading, Massachusetts, Addison-Wesley, 1978.

Frederick Wakeman 'Rebellion and revolution: the study of popular movements in Chinese history' in *Journal of Asian Studies* Vol.36 no.2, 1977, p.213.

Wan Zhida *JinJiLuYude caizheng jingji gongzuo* JinJiYu caizheng bianshichu, 1947.

Wang Dingshen 'Taihang geming genjudi shi zenyang jiejue nongmin de tudi wentide?' ['How Did the Taihang Revolutionary Base Area Solve the Peasants' Land Problem?'] in *Dangshi wenhui* [Selections from Party History] no.3 1985.

Wang Jianfu 'Shishu Shanxi jiantangde lishi jichu' ['The foundations of the CCP's establishment in Shanxi'] in *Shanxi dangshi tongxun* [Newsletter of Shanxi Party History] no.2 1988, p.1.

Wang Jinmei 'Weidade zhanlue xingcheng—ji Balujun zongbu chuanzhan Shanxi' ['The Great Strategic Route—Record of the Movement of the Headquarters of the Eighth Route Army in Shanxi'] in *Dangshi yanjiu* [Research on Party History] no.4 1985.

Wang Jinmei 'Lun Shanxi zhichengwei Huabei dihou kangzhande zhanlue tedian' ['Special Characteristics of Shanxi in the Strategy of Behind-the-lines Anti-Japanese Resistance in North China'] in *Shanxi geming genjudi* [Shanxi's Revolutionary Base Areas] no.4 1987.

Wang Shengbo *Ximenghui shi* [History of the Sacrifice League] Taiyuan, Shanxi renmin chubanshe, 1987.

Wang Shigen *LiuDeng dajun yanjin Dabieshan* [The Army of Liu and Deng enters the Dabie Mountains] Shanghai renmin chubanshe, 1987.

Wang Shuangmei 'Zhongguo gongchandang yu Yan Xishan kangRi tongyi zhanxiande jianli jiqi zai kangzhan chuqi de tedian' ['The Special Characteristics of the United Front between Yan Xishan and the CCP established in the first part of the War against Japan'] in *Dangshi yanjiu* [Research on Party History] no.4 1987.

Wang Tingyue 'JinJiLuYu kangRi genjudi Riren fanzhan yundong xilue' ['A Strategic Analysis of the Movement for Anti-War Japanese in the Shanxi-Hebei-Shandong-Henan Anti-Japanese Base Area'] in *Shanxi geming genjudi* [Shanxi Revolutionary Base Areas] no.1 1990, p.27.

Wang Xiaobai and Liu Yuansheng *Zuo Quan zhuan* [Biography of Zuo Quan] Beijing, Renmin chubanshe, 1990.

Wang Xintai 'Jianshu xinminzhu zhuyi geming shiqi Licheng dang zuzhi de jianshe' ['An Overview of the Development of the Party's Organization in Licheng during the New Democratic Revolution'] in *Shanxi dangshi tongxun* [Newsletter of Shanxi Party History] no.3 1991, p.41.

Wang Xintai and Ge Liping 'Huangyadong baoweizhan jishi' ['Record of the Battle to Protect Huangyadong'] in *Shanxi dangshi tongxun* [Newsletter of Shanxi Party History] no.4 1991, p.28.

Wang Yan (ed) *Peng Dehuai zhuan* [Biography of Peng Dehuai] Beijing, Dangdai zhongguo chubanshe, 1993.

Wang Yongxiang 'Lun KangRi genjudide "san san zhi" zhengquan' ['The "Three-thirds system" regime of the Resistance War base areas'] in *Nankai xuebao* [Nankai University Journal] no.2, 1992, p.70.

Wang Zhongqing (ed) *Zhao Shuli zuopin lunji* [Works of Zhao Shuli] Taiyuan, Beiyue wenyi chubanshe, 1987.

Andrew Watson *Mao Zedong and the Political Economy of the Border Region* Cambridge, Cambridge University Press, 1980.

Wei Aimin 'Deng Xiaoping yu Shanxi kangzhan' ['Deng Xiaoping and the War of Resistance in Shanxi'] in *Shanxi dangshi tongxun* [Newsletter of Shanxi Party History] no.4 1994, p.52.

Wei Hongyun (ed) *Huabei KangRi genjudi jishi* [A Concise History of Base Areas in North China during the War of Resistance to Japan] Tianjin renmin chubanshe, 1986.

Wei Hongyun *KangRi zhanzheng yu Zhongguo shehui* [The War of Resistance to Japan and Chinese Society] Shenyang, Liaoning renmin chubanshe, 1997.

Wei Hongyun 'Taihangshan he Zhongguo gemingde shengli' ['The Taihang Mountains and the Victory of the Chinese Revolution'] in *Guangming ribao* [Guangming Daily] 21 June 1993, p.3.

Wei Hongyun 'Social Reform and Value Change in the Jin Cha Ji Anti-Japanese Border Region' in Feng Chongyi and David S G Goodman *North China at War: the social ecology of revolution, 1937–1945* Lanham, Maryland, Rowman & Littlefield, 2000.

Wei Hongyun and Zuo Zhiyun (eds) *Huabei KangRi genjudi shi* [A History of Base Areas in North China during the War of Resistance to Japan] Beijing, Dangan chubanshe, 1990.

W F Wertheim *Evolution and Revolution* Harmondsworth, Penguin, 1974.

Theodore W White and Annalee Jacoby *Thunder Out of China* New York, Da Capo Press, 1980.

Eric R Wolf *Peasant Wars of the Twentieth Century* New York, Harper & Row, 1969.

John Wong *Land reform in the People's Republic of China: Institutional transformation in agriculture* New York, Praeger, 1973.

Odoric Y K Wou *Mobilizing the Masses: Building Revolution in Henan* Stanford, Stanford University Press, 1994.

Wu Dongcai (ed) *JinJiYu genjudi* [The Shanxi-Hebei-Henan Base Area] Geming genjudi jungong shiliao congshu, Beijing, Bingpin gongye chubanshe, 1990.

Wu Hsiang-hsiang *Dierci ZongRi zhanzheng shi* [History of the Second World War] (2 vols) Taipei, J F Chang, 1973.

Wu Yiji *Zai zhongtang – Qiaojia dayuan* [In the Great Hall: Qiaojia dayuan] Taiyuan, Shanxi renmin chubanshe, 1993.

Wu Yuling 'Taihang geming genjudide fan jia Jichao douzheng' ['The Struggle against Forged South Hebei Ban Banknotes in the Taihang Revolutionary Base Area'] in *Shanxi dangshi tongxun* [Newsletter of Shanxi Party History] no.4 1990, p.39.

Wu Zhimi *Xibei genjudi de lishi diwei* [The Place of the Northwest Base Areas in History] Changsha, Hunan renmin chubanshe, 1991.

Xiyang xian Dazhaishi bianxiezu 'Dazhai zai douzhengzhong chengchang' ['Dazhai's Experience through Struggle'] in *Lishi Yanjiu* [Research on History] No. 1976, p.108.

Xia Hongfei 'Taihang genjudi de yinyue yundong' ['The Music Movement in the Taihang Base Area'] in Wang Yimin and Qi Rongjin *Shanxi geming genjudi wenyi yundong huiyilu* [Memoirs of the Culture Movement in the Shanxi Base Areas] Taiyuan, Beiyue wenyi chubanshe, 1988, p.227.

Xiang Wu 'JinJiLuYu kangRi genjudi de duidi jingji douzheng' ['Economic Warfare against the Enemy in the Shanxi-Hebei-Shandong-Henan Anti-Japanese Base Area'] in *Henan jingji xueyuan xuebao* [Journal of the Henan Economics Institute] no.4 1985.

Xiao Feng and Yao Fei 'Licheng Liguadao Bodong shishiqi jiaoxun' ['The Lesson of the History of the Liguadao Uprising in Licheng'] in *Shanxi geming genjudi* [Shanxi Revolutionary Base Areas] no.2 1991, p.30.

Xie Wushen 'Guanyu Peng Dehuai zhi Deng Xiaoping de xin yijing tan Balujun 129shi de da shengchan yundong' ['A Letter from Peng Dehuai to Deng Xiaoping on the Production Movement in the 129th Division of the Eighth Route Army'] in *Jindaishi yanjiu* [Research on Modern History] no.3 1985.

Xinhua ribao and Qunzhong zhoukan shixuehui (ed) *Jianchi tuanjie kangzhan de haoqiao* [Support and Unity from Overseas Chinese during the War of Resistance] Chongqing chubanshe, 1986.

Xu Guosheng and Chen Ninghua (ed) *Shanxi xian qu jingji fazhan shilue* [Historical outline of the economic development of counties and regions in Shanxi] Taiyuan, Shanxi jingji chubanshe, 1992.

Xu Ruifeng 'Peng Tao' ['Peng Tao'] in *Jinzhong shizhi ziliao* [Central Shanxi Historical Materials] no.1 1989, p.197.

Yan She, Wang Jianzhong and Zhang Zhaojin 'JinJiLuYu Bianqude jingbing jianzheng' ['The Campaign for Better Troops and Simpler Administration in the Shanxi-Hebei-Shandong-Henan Border Region'] in *Weiwei Taihang* [The Towering Taihang Mountains] no.2 1986, p.4.

Benjamin Yang *Deng: A Political Biography* New York, M E Sharpe, 1998.

Yang Song 'Lun Taihang geming genjudi chengfeng yundong' ['On the Rectification Movement in the Taihang Revolutionary Base Area'] in *Shanxi dangshi tongxun* [Newsletter of Shanxi Party History] no.1, 1990, p.35.

Yang Yikui 'Ji Taihangqu renmin wuzhuangde jianshe' ['A Record of the Development of People's Armed Forces in the Taihang Region'] in *Junshi ziliao* [Materials on Military Affairs] no.3, 1986, reprinted in Taihang geming genjudishi zongbian weihui (ed) *Difang wuzhuang douzheng* [Local Armed Struggle] Taihang geming genjudi shiliao congshu No.3, Taiyuan, Shanxi renmin chubanshe, 1990, p.111.

Yao Yinhu and Tian Youru 'Kangzhan shiqi Taihang genjudi renmin fudan zhengcede yanbian' ['The evolution of policy on the burden of the people in the Taihang Base Area during the War of Resistance'] in *Shanxi dangshi tongxun* [Newsletter of Shanxi Party History] no.1 1987, p.51.

Yao Yuan (ed) *Shanxi minbing douzheng shi* [History of the Shanxi Militia's Struggle] Shanxisheng difangzhi bianzuan weiyuanhui bangongshi, 1985.

Yi Ping 'Di bian wo bian, di jin wo jin: ji 1942 nian 5 yue Taihangqu fan "saodang" de waixian zuozhan' ['The Enemy Moves We Move, The Enemy Enters We Enter—External Lines to Oppose the May 1942 "Mop-up" in the Taihang Region' in *Weiwei Taihang* [The Towering Taihang Mountains] no.3 1986, p.22.

Yi Wen and Qi Rongjin *Shanxi geming genjudi wenyi yundong shigao* [Outline History of the Culture Movement in the Shanxi Revolutionary Base Areas] Taiyuan, Shanxi renmin chubanshe, 1989.

Yu Yongbo (ed) *Nie Rongzhen zhuan* [Biography of Nie Rongzhen] Beijing, Dangdai Zhongguo chubanshe, 1994.

Youdianbu Huabei jiaotong youzheng shiliao bianzhizu Taihang zu (ed) *Huabei jiefangqu jiaotong youzheng shiliao huibian—Taihang quan* [Collection of Historical Materials on Communications and Postal Administrations in the North China Liberated Areas—Taihang volume] (2 vols) Beijing, Youdianbu, 1990.

Arthur N Young *China's Wartime Finance and Inflation, 1937–1945* Cambridge, Massachusetts, Harvard University Press, 1965.

Donald S Zagoria 'Asian Tenancy Systems and Communist Mobilization' in John W Lewis (ed) *Peasant Rebellion and Communist Revolution in Asia* Stanford, Stanford University Press, 1974, p.29.

Zeng Changqiu 'Yige jingbing jianzhengde mofan lizi (ji JinJiLuYu Bianqude jingbing jianzheng)' ['A Model Example of "Better Troops, Simpler Administration" (A Record of "Better Troops, Simpler Administration" in the Shanxi-Hebei-Shandong-Henan Border Region'] in *Dangshi wenhui* [Selections from Party History] no.5 1985.

Zeng Fanhua *Ximeng Ximeng . . . Ximenghui ji Xinjun fenqi kangRi* [The Sacrifice League and The New Army rise up to resist Japan] Beijing, Jiefangjun wenyi chubanshe, 1995.

Zhandi zongdongyuan [Battlefield General Mobilization] (2 vols) Taiyuan, Shanxi renmin chubanshe, 1986.

Zhang Bingkun 'Zhu Rui zai Tainan' ['Zhu Rui in the Southern Taihang Region'] in *Weiwei Taihang* [The Towering Taihang Mountains] no.1 1987, p.8.

Zhang Guoxiang 'Weida de zhanlue zhidian jueze' ['The Great Strategic Choice'] in *Dangshi wenhui* [Selections from Party History] no.3 1985.

Zhang Guoxiang et al *Zhangdong zonghui shigao* [An Outline History of the General Mobilization Committees] Taiyuan, Xiwang chubanshe, 1993.

Zhang Guoxiang *Shanxi KangRi zhanzheng shi* [A History of Shanxi in the War of Resistance to Japan] (2 vols) Taiyuan, Shanxi renmin chubanshe, 1992.

Zhang Jizhong *Shanxi Lishi zhengqu dili* [A Political and Administrative Geography of Shanxi] Taiyuan, Shanxi renmin chubanshe, 1992.

Zhang Liyun 'Zhu Rui tongzhi zai Yubei, Tainan' ['Comrade Zhu Rui in North Henan and the Southern Taihang Region'] in *Shanxi dangshi tongxun* [Newsletter of Shanxi Party History] no.1 1986, p.33.

Zhang Yangui 'JinJiLuYu genjudi zai kangRi zhanzheng he jiefang zhanzhengzhong de diwei he zuoyong' ['The status and function of the Shanxi-Hebei-Shandong-Henan Base Area in the War of Resistance to Japan and the Civil War'] in *Dangshi yanjiu* [Research on Party History] no.2 1985.

Zhang Youcheng 'Jianshu Shanxi sanda genjudi chuang jiande tedian' ['Special Characteristics of the Establishment of the Three Most Important Base Areas in Shanxi'] in *Shanxi geming genjudi* [Shanxi's Revolutionary Base Areas] no.1 1988.

Zhang Zhongtian *Zuo Quan jiangjun quan* [Biography of General Zuo Quan] Beijing, Zhongguo qingnian chubanshe, 1986.

Zhao Shuli *Changes in Li Village* Beijing, Foreign Languages Press, 1953.
Zhao Shuli *Xiaxiangji* [Going down to the village] Beijing, Zuojia chubanshe, 1953.
Zhao Wei *Zhao Ziyang quan* [Biography of Zhao Ziyang] Hong Kong, Wenhua jiaoyu chubanshe, 1988.
Zhao Xiushan 'Sanxiang zhongda de mingzhi jueci—Liu Deng dui JinJiLuYu bianqu zhengquan jianshe de gongxian' ['Three important aspects of a wise policy—The achievements of Liu Bocheng and Deng Xiaoping in developing the Shanxi-Hebei-Shandong-Henan Border Region'] in Yang Guoyu et al (ed) *Ershiba nian jian: sanbian* [During Twenty-eight Years: Volume Three] Shanghai wenyi chubanshe, 1992.
Zheng Hui, Zhang Jingru, Liang Zhixiang (ed) *Zhongguo gongchandang tongzhi* [Encyclopedia of the Chinese Communist Party] (3 vols) Beijing, Zhongyang wenxian chubanshe, 1997.
Zhi Xia *The Railway Guerillas* Beijing, Foreign Languages Press, 1966.
Zhonggong Changzhi shiwei dangshi yanjiushi (ed) *Zhongguo gongchandang Shanxisheng Changzhishi lishi dashijishu* [Historical Chronology of the CCP in Changzhi City, Shanxi] Beijing, Zhonggong dangshi chubanshe, 1994.
Zhonggong Hebei Shengwei dangshi ziliao zhengji bianshen weiyuanhui and Taihang (Hebei bufen) shiliao lianhe zhengbian bangongshi (ed) *Jixi minxunchu yu Jixi Youjidui* [The West Hebei Training Regiment and the West Hebei Guerilla Troop] Taihang geming genjudi shiliao congshu No.10, Shijiazhuang, Hebei renmin chubanshe 1989.
Zhonggong JiLuYu Bianqu dangshi bianweihui (ed) *Zhonggong JiLuYu Bianqu dangshi dashiji* [Chronology of CCP History in the JiLuYu Border Area] Jinan, Shandong daxue chubanshe, 1987.
Zhonggong Licheng xianwei dangshi yanjiushi *Zhongguo Gongchandang Licheng xian jianshi 1937–1949* [A Concise History of the CCP in Licheng County 1937–1949] Taihang geming genjudi shiliao congshu, Taiyuan, Xinhua chubanshe, 1991. [CHL]
Zhonggong Shanxisheng Wuxiang xianwei dangshi yanjiushi *Zhonggong Wuxiang jianshi* [An Introductory History to the CCP in Wuxiang] Wuxiang, Zhonggong Shanxisheng Wuxiang xianwei dangshi yanjiushi, 1990. [IHW]
Zhonggong Shanxisheng Zuoquanxian dangshi yanjiushi (ed) *Zhonggong Zuoquanxian lishi dashijishu 1937.7–1949.9* [Historical Chronology of the CCP in Zuoquan County 1937–1949] Taiyuan, Shanxi renmin chubanshe, 1993. [HCZ]
Zhonggong Shanxishengwei dangshi yanjiushi (ed) *Taiyue geming genjudi jishi* [A Chronology of the Taiyue Revolutionary Base Area] Taiyuan, Shanxi renmin chubanshe, 1989.
Zhonggong Shanxishengwei dangshi yanjiushi (ed) *Taiyue geming genjudi jianshi* [A History of the Taiyue Revolutionary Base Area] Beijing, Renmin chubanshe, 1993.
Zhonggong Shanxi shengwei dangshi yanjiushi (ed) *Zhongguo gongchandang Shanxi lishi gangyao* [Outline History of the CCP in Shanxi] Beijing, Zhonggong dangshi chubanshe, 1991.
Zhonggong Shanxi shengwei dangshi yanjiushi (ed) *Zhongguo gongchandang Shanxi lishi dashijishu* [Chronology of the CCP in Shanxi] Beijing, Zhonggong dangshi chubanshe, 1994.

Zhonggong Shanxi shengwei dangshi yanjiushi, Shanxisheng danganguan, Taiyue geming genjudi caizheng shiliao bianweihui (ed) *Taiyue geming genjudi caizheng shiliao xuanbian* [Selected Historical Materials on Financial Management in the Taiyue Revolutionary Base Area] (2 vols) Taiyuan, Shanxi jingji chubanshe, 1991.

Zhonggong Wuxiang xianwei xuanchuanbu and Zhonggong Wuxiang xianwei dangshi yanjiushi (ed) *KangRi zhanzheng zhongde Wuxiang* [Wuxiang in the Anti-Japanese War] Zhonggong Wuxiang, 1995. [KZW]

Zhonggong zhongyang dangxiao dangshi jiaoyanshi (ed) *Zhongguo gongchandang lishi dashiji* [Chronology of the CCP] Beijing, Renmin chubanshe, 1989.

Zhonggong zhongyang dangxiao dangshi jiaoyanshi (ed) *Zhonggong gongchandang lishi Vol 2: 1937–1949* [CCP History: Vol 2:1937–1949] Beijing, Renmin chubanshe, 1990.

Zhonggong zhongyang dangxiao dangshi jiaoyanshi ziliaozu (ed) *Zhongguo gongchandang lici zhongyao huiyi ji: Vol 1* [Record of Important Meetings of the CCP] Shanghai, Renmin chubanshe, 1982.

Zhonggong zhongyang wenxian yanjiushi (ed) *Zhu De nianpu* [Chronology of Zhu De's Life] Beijing, Renmin chubanshe, 1986.

Zhongguo gongchandang lishi dacidian Editorial Group *Zhongguo gongchandang lishi dacidian: Xinminzhuzhuyi geming shiqi* [Dictionary of CCP History: New Democratic Revolutionary Period] Beijing, Zhonggong zhongyang dangxiao chubanshe, 1991.

Zhongguo gongchandang lishi dacidian Editorial Group *Zhongguo gongchandang lishi dacidian: zonglun, renwu* [Dictionary of CCP History: summaries, people] Beijing, Zhonggong zhongyang dangxiao chubanshe, 1991.

Zhongguo gongchandang Zuoquan xianwei dangshi yanjiushi *Zhongguo gongchandang Zuoquan xian jianshi 1937–1949* [A Brief History of the CCP in Zuoquan County 1937–1949] Taihang geming genjudi shiliao congshu, Taiyuan, Shanxi renmin chubanshe, 1995. [HZ]

Zhongguo gongchandang Shanxisheng Qinshui xianwei dangshi yanjiushi (ed) *Zhonggong Qinshui lishi dashijishu 1937.10–1949.9* [Chronology of the CCP in Qinshui 1937–1949] Taiyuan, Xinhua chubanshe, 1991.

Zhongguo gongchandang Shanxisheng Tunliu xianwei dangshi yanjiushi (ed) *Zhonggong Tunliu lishi dashijishu 1926.6–1949.9* [Chronology of the CCP in Tunliu 1926–1949] Taiyuan, Xinhua chubanshe, 1991.

Zhongguo KangRi genjudishi guoji xueshu taolunhui taolunji [Collection of Papers from the International Academic Conference on the History of Base Areas in China's War of Resistance to Japan] Beijing, Dangan chubanshe, 1985.

Zhongguo renmin jiefangjun dieryu zhanjun zhanshi editorial unit *129 Shi yu JinJiLuYu junqu KangRi zhanzheng zhanshi* [Battle History of the 129th Division in the Shanxi-Hebei-Shandong-Henan Military Region during the War of Resistance to Japan] Beijing, Ministry of National Defence, 1962.

Zhongguo renmin jiefangjun Kunming silingbu *Taiyue congdui jian junqu KangRi zhanzheng zhanshi* [A Battle History of the Taiyue Column and its Military District during the War of Resistance to Japan] Kunming Military Region, 1962.

Zhongguo shehui kexueyuan xiandaishi yanjiushi (ed) *Zhongguo gongchandang lici daibiao dahui: Xinminzhuzhuyi geming shiqi* [Congresses of the CCP: Period of the

New Democratic Revolution] Beijing, Zhonggong zhongyang dangxiao chubanshe, 1982.

Zhongguo xiandai shi ziliao congkan *Kangri zhanzheng shiqi jiefangqu gaikuang* [Outline of Liberated Areas during the Period of the War of Resistance to Japan] Beijing, Renmin chubanshe, 1953.

Zhongguo zhengxie wenshi ziliao yanjiu weiyuanhui huaqiaozu (ed) *Zhengrong suiyue: Huaqiao qingnian huiguo canjia Kangzhan jishi* [Years in the Battle: Recollections of Overseas Chinese Youth Returning to China to Participate in the War of Resistance] Beijing, Zhongguo wenshi chubanshe, 1988.

Zhongwai xuezhe lun KangRi genjudi [Chinese and Foreign Academics on the Base Areas of the War of Resistance to Japan] Beijing, Dangan chubanshe, 1993.

Zhu De *On the Battlefronts of the Liberated Areas* Beijing, Foreign Languages Press, 1952.

Zhu De *Zhu De xuanji* [Selected Writings of Zhu De] Beijing, Renmin chubanshe, 1983.

Serials

Cangsang [Vicissitudes]
Dangshi wenhui [Selections from Party History]
Geming lieshi zhuan [Biographies of Revolutionaries]
Geming wenshi ziliao [Revolutionary Literature and History]
Hebei wenshi ziliao xuanbian [Selections from Hebei Literature and History]
Henan wenshi ziliao [Henan Literature and History]
Jiefangjun jiangling zhuan [Biographies of Commanders in the PLA]
Jinan geming douzheng shiliao [Historical Materials on the Revolutionary Struggle in South Hebei]
Jinzhong shizhi ziliao [Central Shanxi Historical Materials]
Nubing liezhuan [Biographies of Women Soldiers]
Shanxi geming genjudi [Shanxi Revolutionary Base Areas]
Shanxi geming yinglie [Shanxi Revolutionary Heroes]
Shanxi dangshi tongxun [Newsletter of Shanxi Party History]
Shanxi difangzhi tongxun [Newsletter of Shanxi Local History]
Shanxi wenshi ziliao [Shanxi Literature and History]
Shizhi yanjiu [Historical and Archive Research]
Weiwei Taihang [The Towering Taihang Mountains]
Wenshi ziliao xuanbian [Selections from Literature and History]
Zhonggong dangshi renwu zhuan [Biographies of People in CCP History]
Zhonggong dangshi ziliao [Materials on CCP History]
Jiangshi minglu [Records of Commanders]

Index

About the Author

David S. G. Goodman is director of the Institute for International Studies, University of Technology, Sydney. He is the editor (with Feng Chongyi) of *North China at War: The Social Ecology of Revolution, 1937–1945* (Rowman & Littlefield) and the author of *Deng Xiaoping and the Chinese Revolution.*